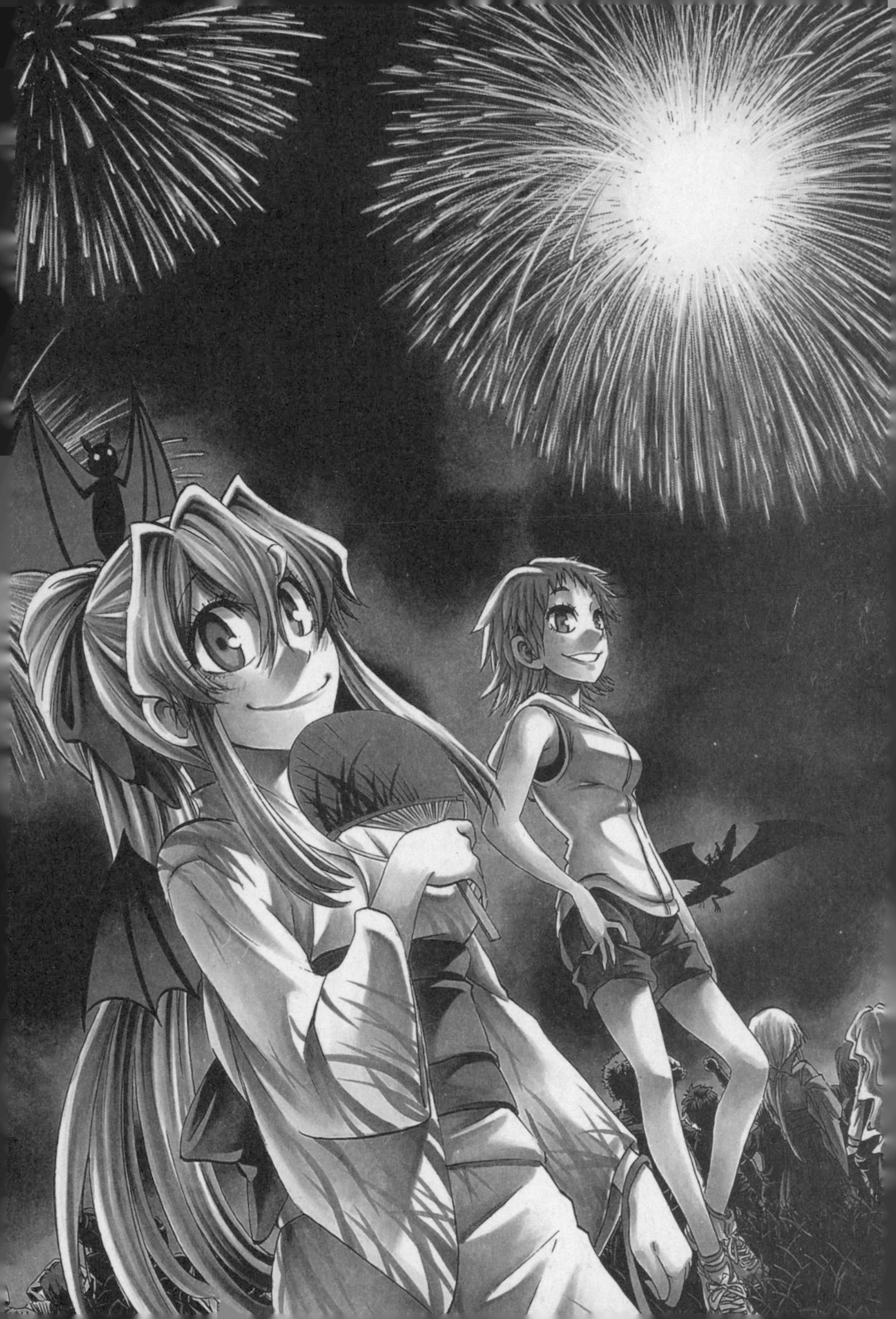

My MONSTER Secret
"Actually, I am..."

Story & Characters

Kuromine Asahi fell in love with Shiragami Youko, a vampire who will have to quit school if anyone finds out what she really is. They've managed to keep her secret safe, and even started dating...but can Asahi keep Youko's secret long enough to graduate?!

THE HOLEY SIEVE

KUROMINE ASAHI

The man with the worst poker face in the world, he's known as *The Sieve with a Hole in it*...because secrets slide right out of him. Now he has to hide the fact that Shiragami-san-- the girl he's in love with--is a vampire.

ACTUALLY A VAMPIRE

SHIRAGAMI YOUKO

She's attending a human high school under the condition that she'll *stop going immediately* if her true identity is discovered. Asahi found out (whoops), but she believes him when he says he'll keep her secret, and the two are now dating.

ACTUALLY AN ALIEN

AIZAWA NAGISA

Currently investigating Earth as a class representative, she once mercilessly tore Asahi to shreds before he could confess his love, but she now harbors an unrequited crush on him. Her true (tiny) form emerges from the screw-shaped cockpit on her head. Her brother Aizawa Ryo is also staying on Earth.

THE QUEEN OF PURE EVIL

AKEMI MIKAN

Editor-in-chief of the school newspaper and a childhood friend of Asahi's. Currently straying from the path of villainy since her favorite pair of glasses became the **Goddess of Fortune, Fuku-chan.**

HORNED DEVIL

KOUMOTO AKANE

The principal of Asahi's high school looks adorable, but she's actually a **millennia-old devil**. The great-great-grandmother of Asahi's homeroom teacher, Koumoto-sensei. Her true weakness is junk food.

FORMER GANGSTER

KOUMOTO AKARI

The teacher in charge of Asahi's class. Although she's a descendant of Principal Akane, she has no demon powers of her own. Formerly a gangster, currently single.

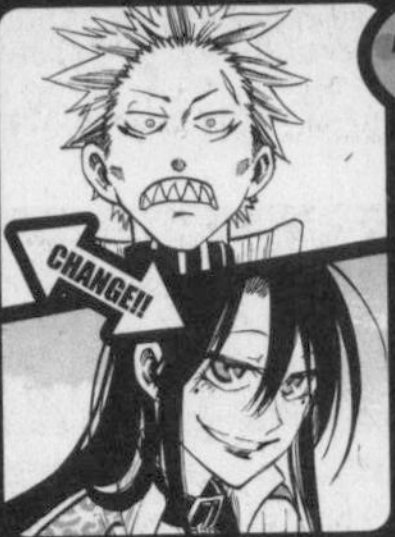
CHANGE!!

ACTUALLY A WOLFMAN

SHISHIDO SHIROU ♂

SHISHIDO SHIHO ♀

This childhood friend of Youko's is a nympho. When she sees the moon, she transforms into the wolfman Shishido Shirou (male body and all), and that dude is in love with Youko. Her mother is a nympho icon.

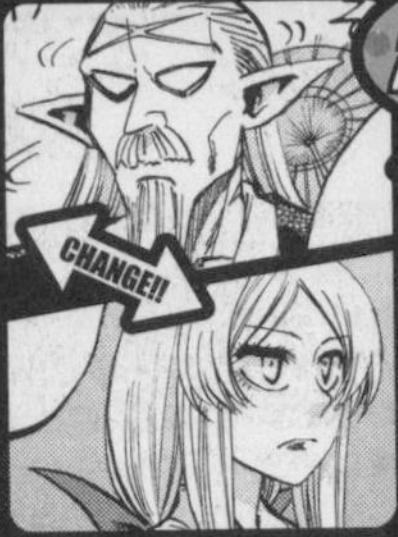
CHANGE!!

ACTUALLY A VAMPIRE

♂ SHIRAGAMI GENJIROU

RYOKUENZAKA YUMI ♀

A full-blooded vampire and Shiragami-san's **father.** Worried about Shiragami-san, he has transformed into Ryokuenzaka-sensei and infiltrated the school as the **assistant teacher** of Asahi's class.

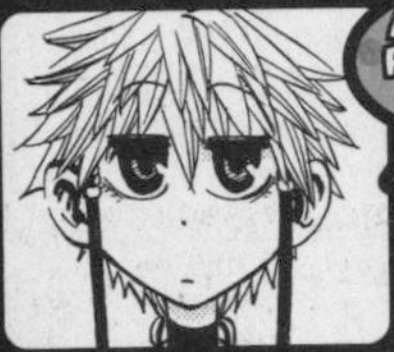

ACTUALLY FROM THE FUTURE

KIRYUIN RIN

Came from fifty years in the future to save the world from the clutches of a nympho tyrant. Now she's a refugee who can't return home because she told Asahi (among others) about the future. Asahi's granddaughter.

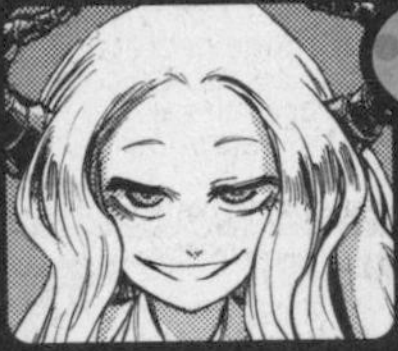

ACTUALLY AN ANGEL

SHIROGANE KAREN

The student council president of Asahi's school. She lost her halo to one of the principal's practical jokes and thus became a (self-proclaimed) **fallen angel.** Was a classmate of Shiragami-san's parents.

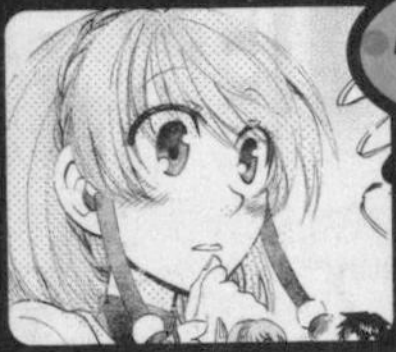

ACTUALLY A NINJA

MOMOCHI YUKA

A first-year at Asahi's school. **Falls in love** ridiculously quickly. She seems to know something about the future.....?!

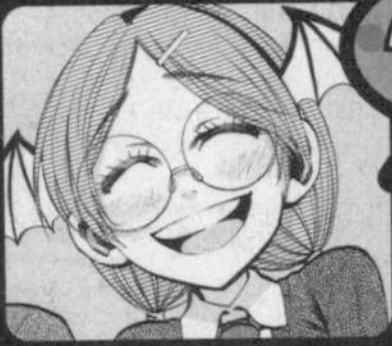

ACTUALLY A SUCCUBUS

MINAGAWA SAKI

A first-year at Asahi's school. Currently fighting to reclaim the honor of the **succubus clan** from the Nympho Icon who stole it.

THEM

ASAHI'S WORTHLESS FRIENDS

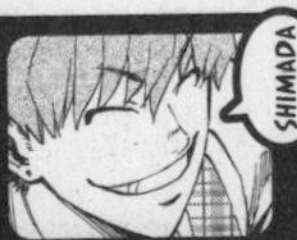

SHIMADA

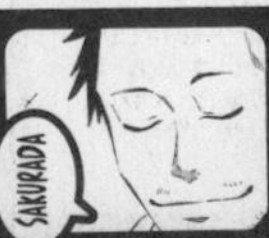

SAKURADA

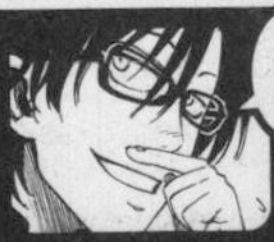

OKADA

SEVEN SEAS ENTERTAINMENT PRESENTS

My Monster Secret

"Actually, I am..."

story and art by Eiji Masuda

VOLUME 15

TRANSLATION
Alethea and Athena Nibley

ADAPTATION
Rebecca Scoble

LETTERING AND RETOUCH
Annaliese Christman

LOGO DESIGN
Karis Page

COVER DESIGN
Nicky Lim

PROOFREADER
Shanti Whitesides
B. Lana Guggenheim

EDITOR
Jenn Grunigen

PRODUCTION ASSISTANT
CK Russell

PRODUCTION MANAGER
Lissa Pattillo

EDITOR IN CHIEF
Adam Arnold

PUBLISHER
Jason DeAngelis

JITSUHA WATASHIHA Volume 15
© EIJI MASUDA 2016
Originally published in Japan in 2016 by Akita Publishing Co., Ltd.
English translation rights arranged with Akita Publishing Co., Ltd.
through TOHAN CORPORATION, Tokyo.

Seven Seas books may be purchased in bulk for promotional, educational, or
business use. Please contact your local bookseller or the Macmillan Corporate
and Premium Sales Department at 1-800-221-7945, extension 5442, or by
e-mail at MacmillanSpecialMarkets@macmillan.com.

Seven Seas and the Seven Seas logo are trademarks of
Seven Seas Entertainment, LLC. All rights reserved.

ISBN: 978-1-64275-013-3

Printed in Canada

First Printing: March 2019

10 9 8 7 6 5 4 3 2 1

FOLLOW US ONLINE: *www.sevenseasentertainment.com*

READING DIRECTIONS

This book reads from *right to left*, Japanese style.
If this is your first time reading manga, you start
reading from the top right panel on each page and
take it from there. If you get lost, just follow the
numbered diagram here. It may seem backwards at
first, but you'll get the hang of it! Have fun!!

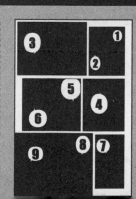

Chapter 125: "Shishido Shiho" ①

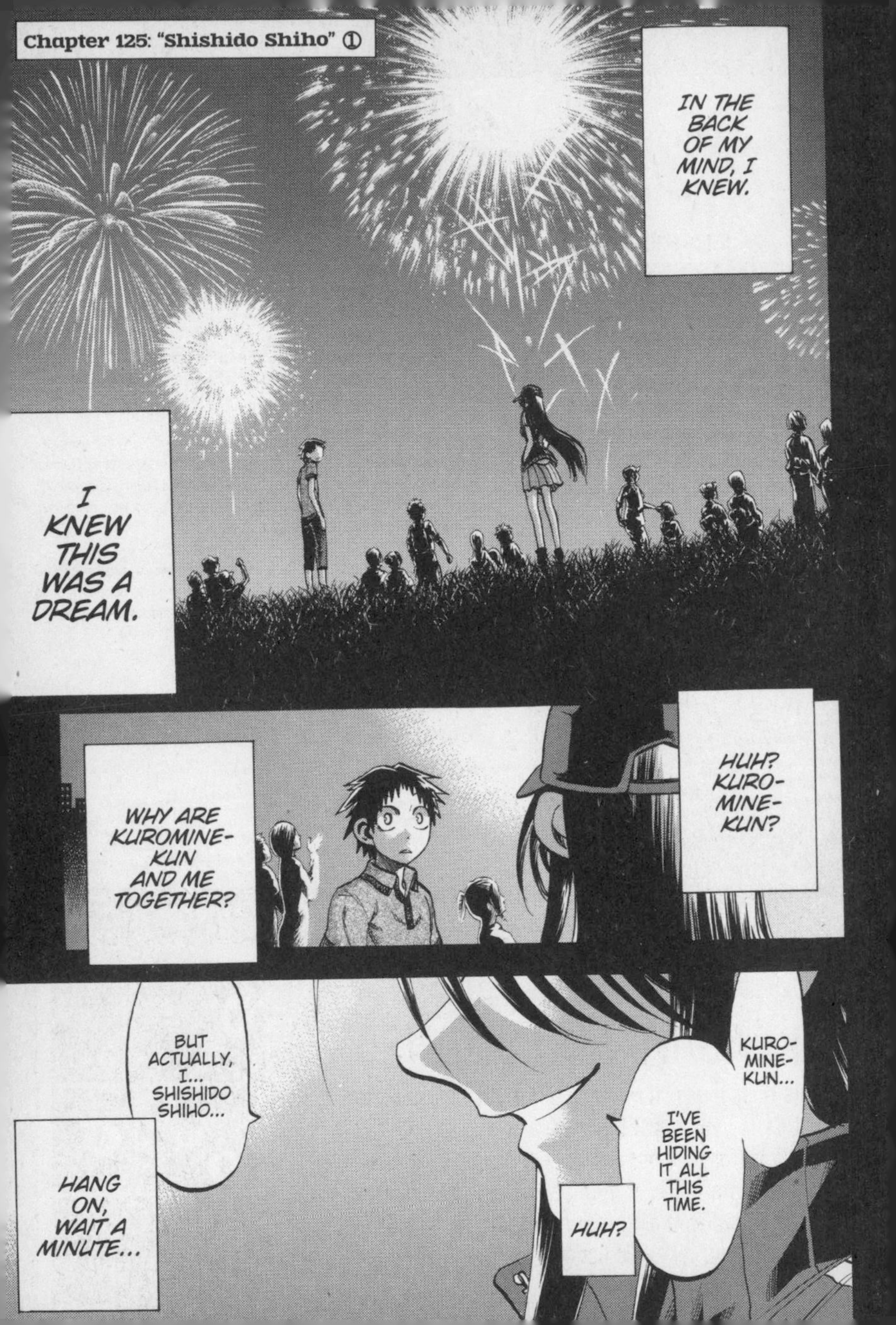
IN THE BACK OF MY MIND, I KNEW.
I KNEW THIS WAS A DREAM.
HUH? KUROMINE-KUN?
WHY ARE KUROMINE-KUN AND ME TOGETHER?
KUROMINE-KUN...
BUT ACTUALLY, I... SHISHIDO SHIHO...
I'VE BEEN HIDING IT ALL THIS TIME.
HUH?
HANG ON, WAIT A MINUTE...

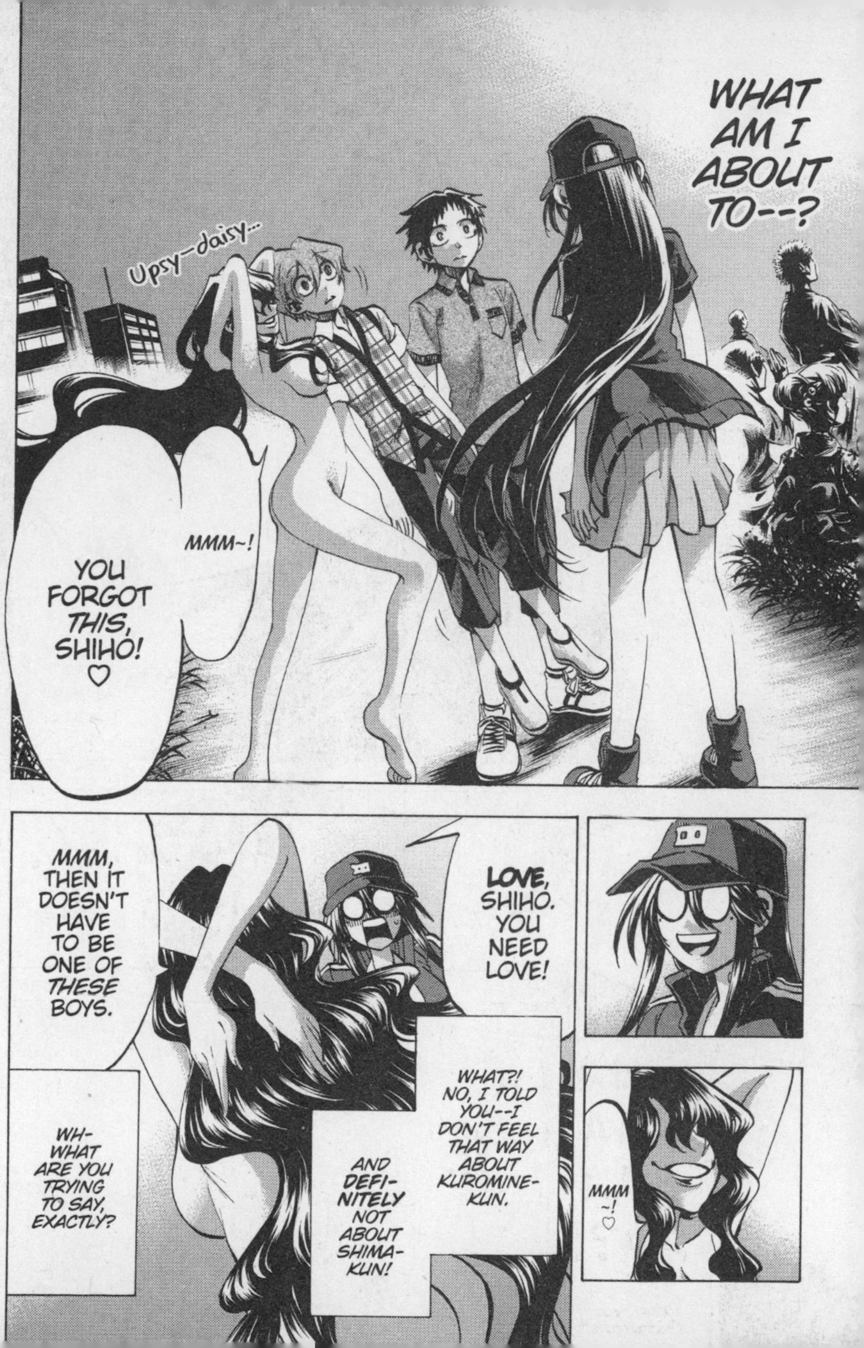
WHAT AM I ABOUT TO--?
Upsy-daisy...
MMM~!
YOU FORGOT THIS, SHIHO! ♡
LOVE, SHIHO. YOU NEED LOVE!
MMM, THEN IT DOESN'T HAVE TO BE ONE OF THESE BOYS.
WHAT?! NO, I TOLD YOU--I DON'T FEEL THAT WAY ABOUT KUROMINE-KUN.
AND DEFINITELY NOT ABOUT SHIMA-KUN!
MMM~! ♡
WH-WHAT ARE YOU TRYING TO SAY, EXACTLY?

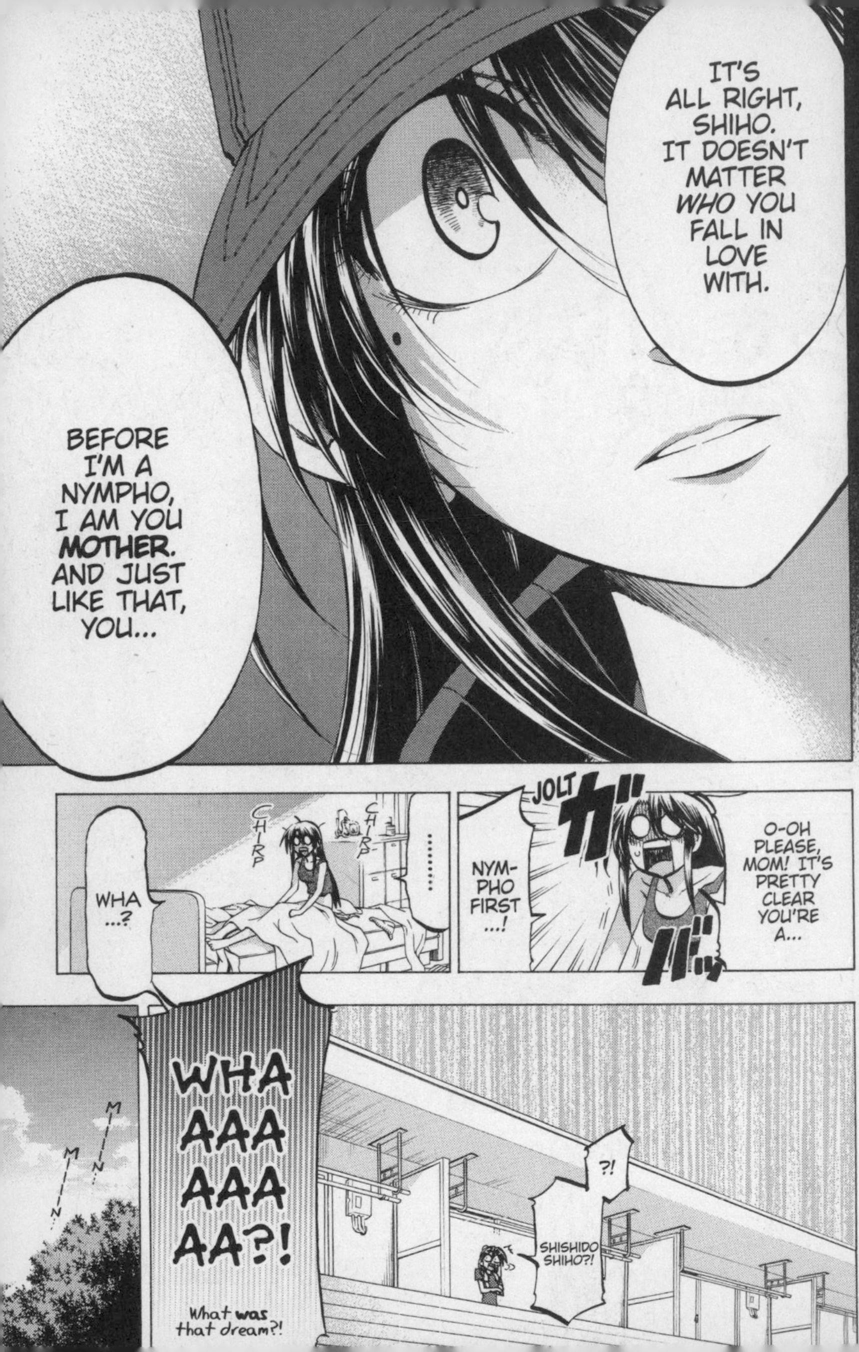
IT'S ALL RIGHT, SHIHO. IT DOESN'T MATTER *WHO* YOU FALL IN LOVE WITH.
BEFORE I'M A NYMPHO, I AM YOU **MOTHER**. AND JUST LIKE THAT, YOU...
JOLT
O-OH PLEASE, MOM! IT'S PRETTY CLEAR YOU'RE A...
NYMPHO FIRST ...!
CHIRP
CHIRP
......
WHA ...?
?!
SHISHIDO SHIHO?!
WHAAAAAAAAAA?!
What **was** that dream?!
MIN
MIN

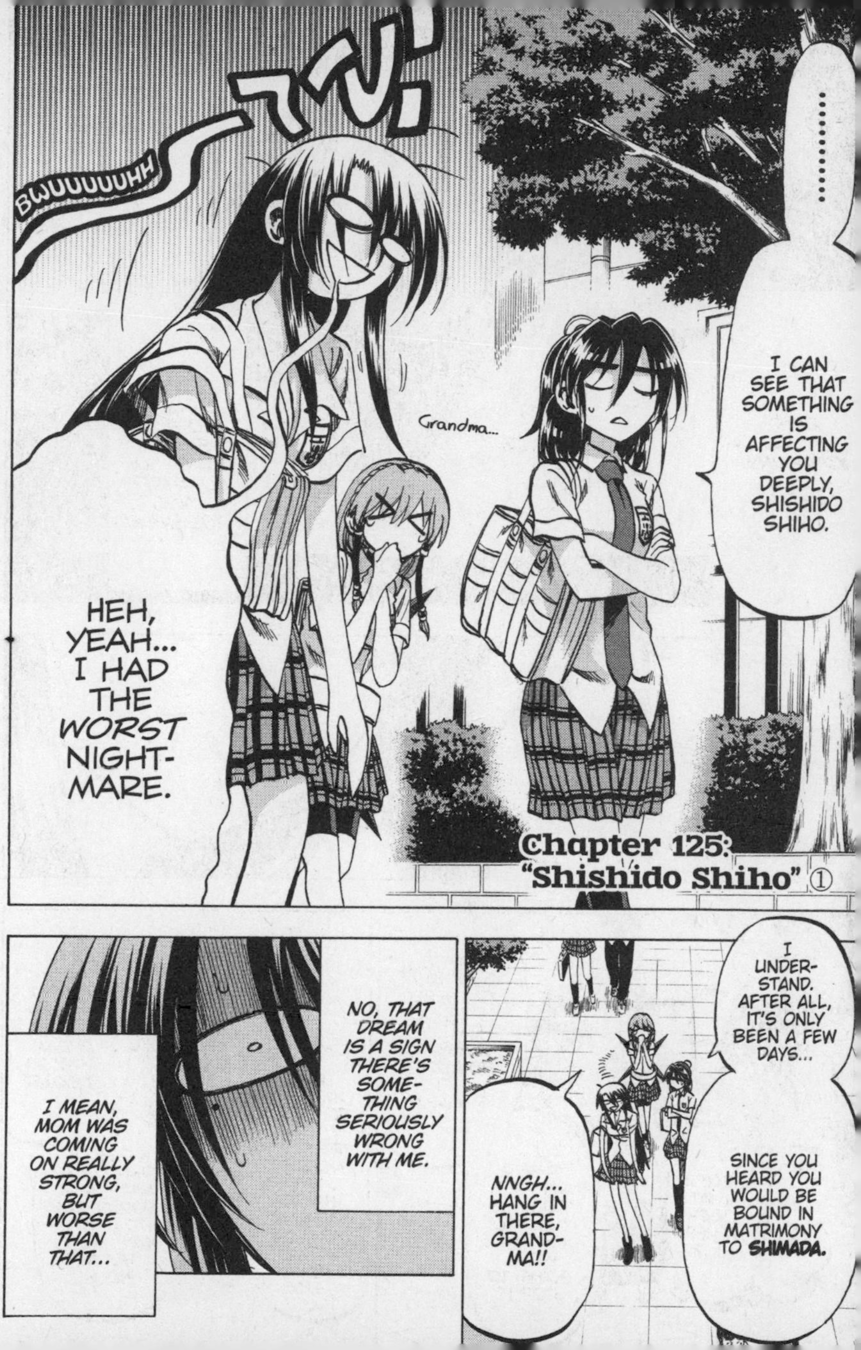
......
I CAN SEE THAT SOMETHING IS AFFECTING YOU DEEPLY, SHISHIDO SHIHO.
Grandma...
BWUUUUUHH
HEH, YEAH... I HAD THE WORST NIGHT-MARE.
Chapter 125: "Shishido Shiho" ①
I UNDER-STAND. AFTER ALL, IT'S ONLY BEEN A FEW DAYS...
SINCE YOU HEARD YOU WOULD BE BOUND IN MATRIMONY TO SHIMADA.
NNGH... HANG IN THERE, GRAND-MA!!
NO, THAT DREAM IS A SIGN THERE'S SOME-THING SERIOUSLY WRONG WITH ME.
I MEAN, MOM WAS COMING ON REALLY STRONG, BUT WORSE THAN THAT...

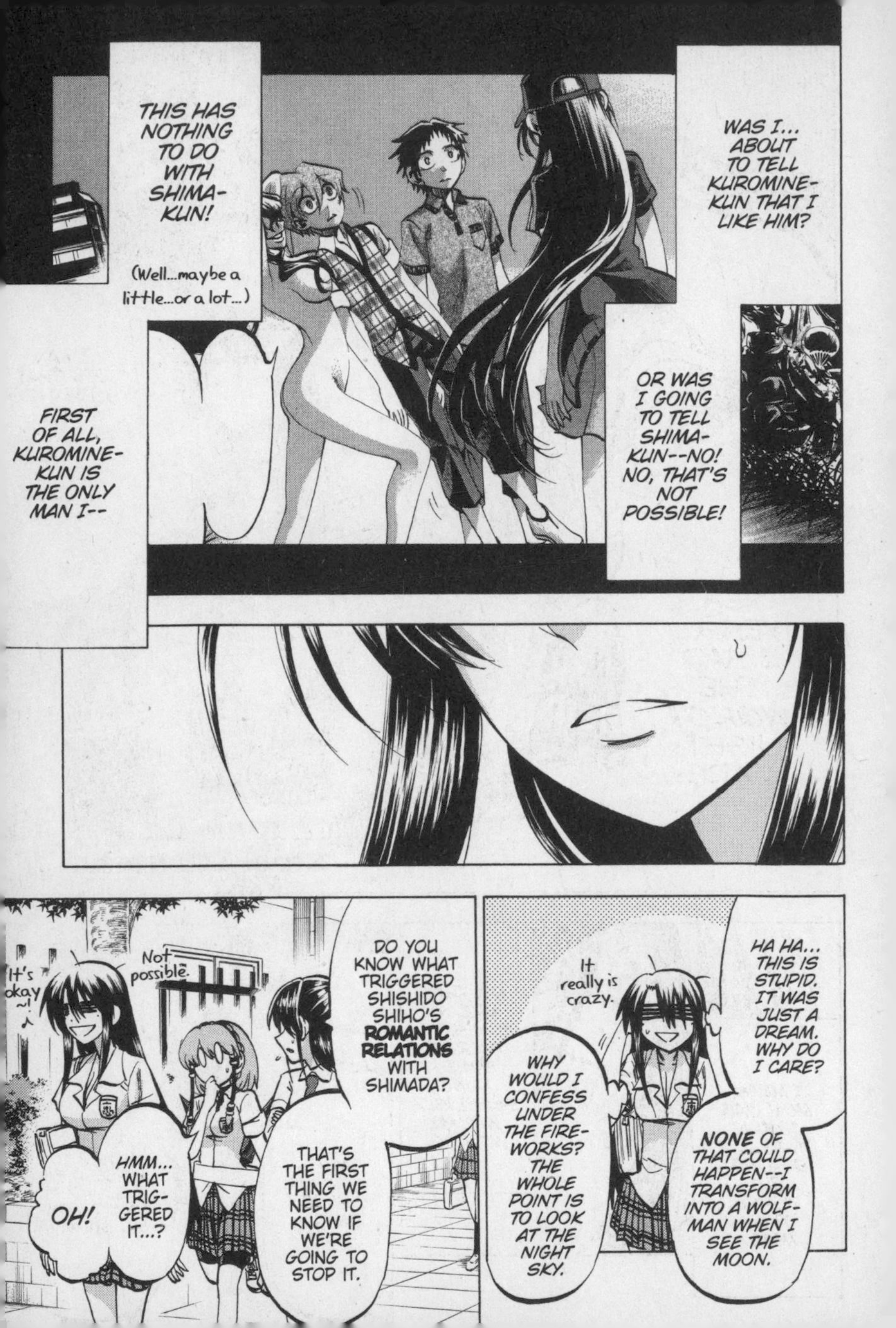

WAS I... ABOUT TO TELL KUROMINE-KUN THAT I LIKE HIM?
OR WAS I GOING TO TELL SHIMA-KUN--NO! NO, THAT'S NOT POSSIBLE!
FIRST OF ALL, KUROMINE-KUN IS THE ONLY MAN I--
THIS HAS NOTHING TO DO WITH SHIMA-KUN!
(Well...maybe a little...or a lot...)
HA HA... THIS IS STUPID. IT WAS JUST A DREAM. WHY DO I CARE?
It really is crazy.
WHY WOULD I CONFESS UNDER THE FIRE-WORKS? THE WHOLE POINT IS TO LOOK AT THE NIGHT SKY.
NONE OF THAT COULD HAPPEN--I TRANSFORM INTO A WOLF-MAN WHEN I SEE THE MOON.
DO YOU KNOW WHAT TRIGGERED SHISHIDO SHIHO'S ROMANTIC RELATIONS WITH SHIMADA?
Not possible.
It's okay~! ♪
THAT'S THE FIRST THING WE NEED TO KNOW IF WE'RE GOING TO STOP IT.
HMM... WHAT TRIG-GERED IT...?
OH!

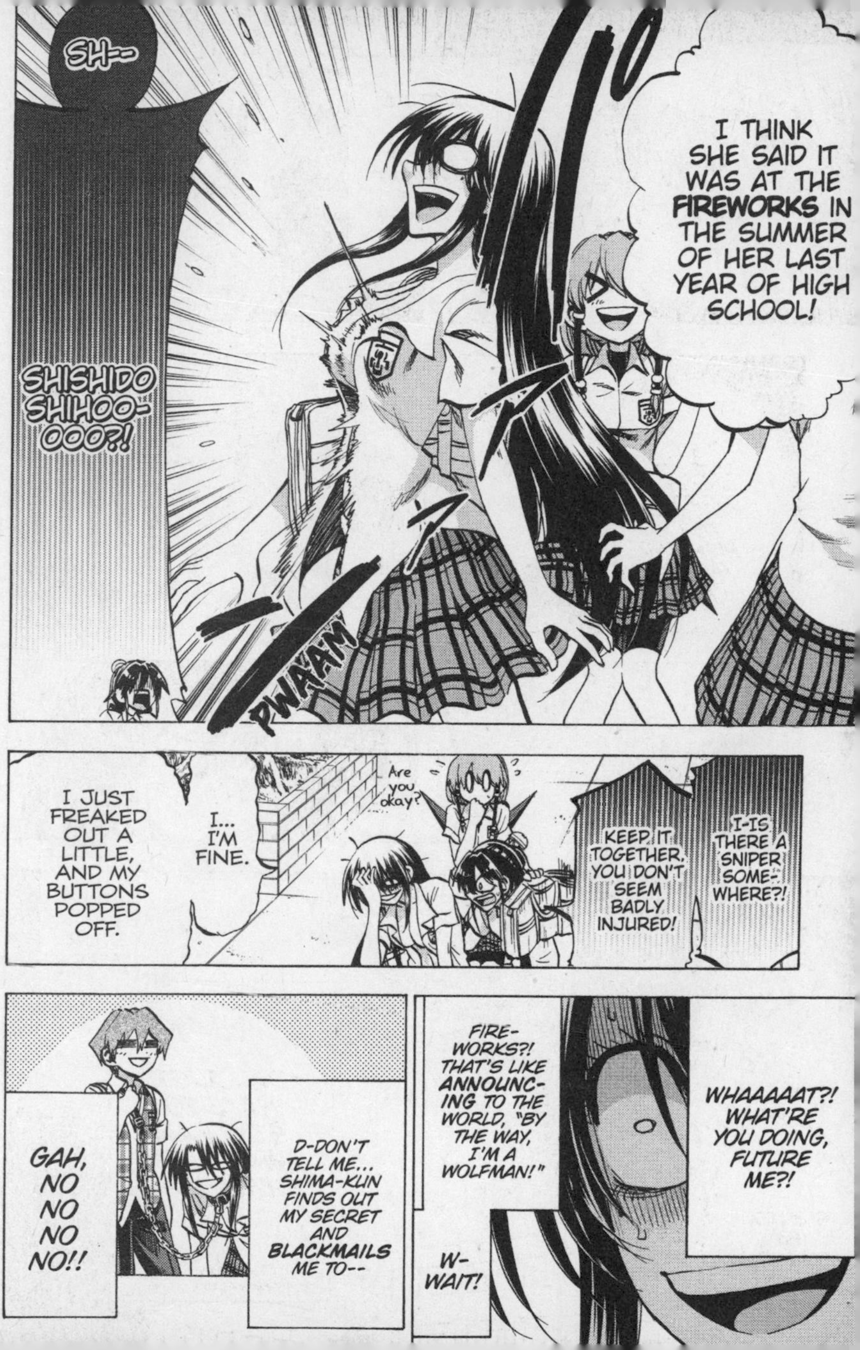
I THINK SHE SAID IT WAS AT THE FIREWORKS IN THE SUMMER OF HER LAST YEAR OF HIGH SCHOOL!
SH--
SHISHIDO SHIHOO-OOO?!
PWAAAM
I-IS THERE A SNIPER SOME-WHERE?!
KEEP IT TOGETHER. YOU DON'T SEEM BADLY INJURED!
Are you okay?
I... I'M FINE.
I JUST FREAKED OUT A LITTLE, AND MY BUTTONS POPPED OFF.
WHAAAAAT?! WHAT'RE YOU DOING, FUTURE ME?!
FIRE-WORKS?! THAT'S LIKE ANNOUNC-ING TO THE WORLD, "BY THE WAY, I'M A WOLFMAN!"
W-WAIT!
D-DON'T TELL ME... SHIMA-KUN FINDS OUT MY SECRET AND BLACKMAILS ME TO--
GAH, NO NO NO NO NO!!

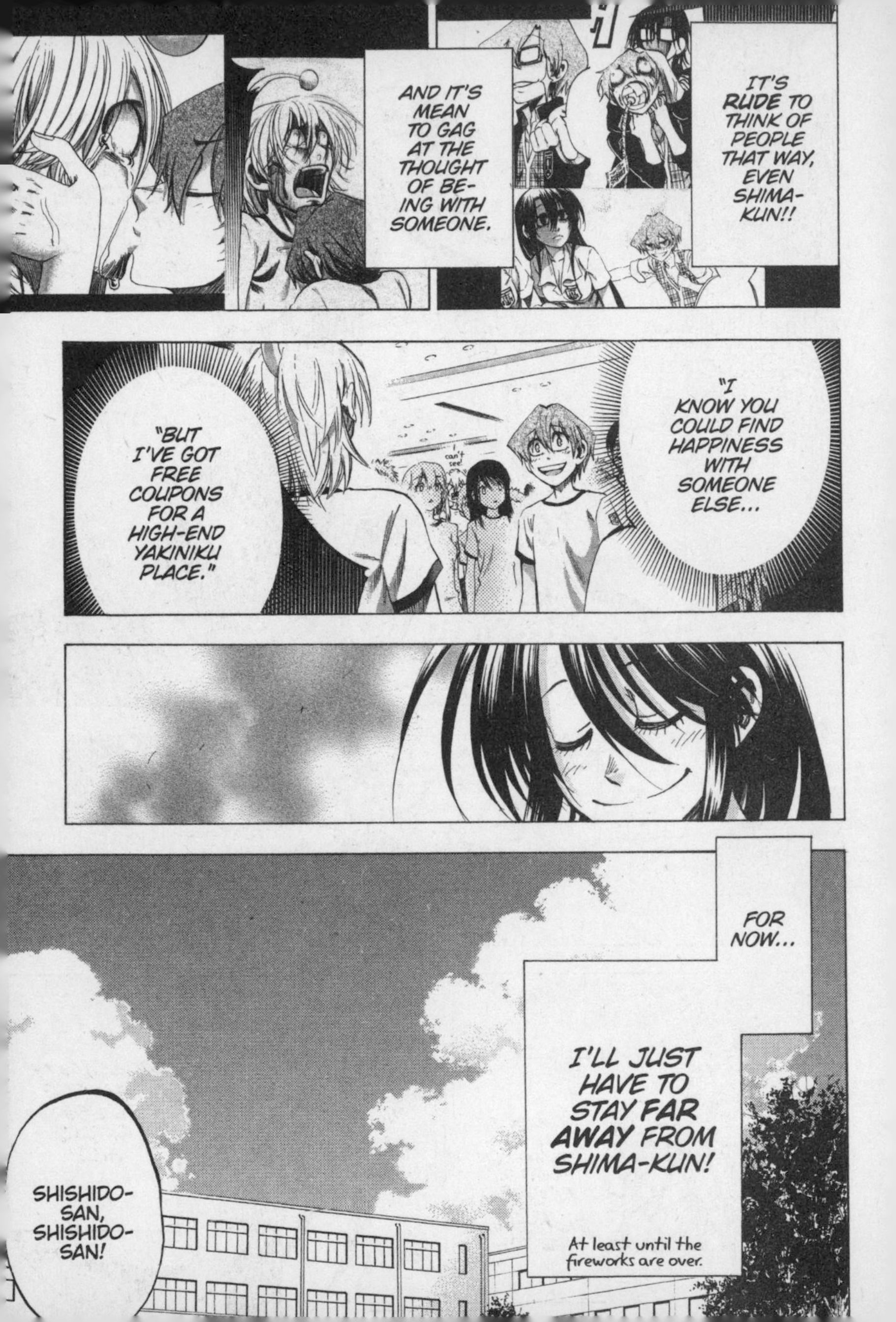
IT'S RUDE TO THINK OF PEOPLE THAT WAY, EVEN SHIMA-KUN!!
AND IT'S MEAN TO GAG AT THE THOUGHT OF BE-ING WITH SOMEONE.
"I KNOW YOU COULD FIND HAPPINESS WITH SOMEONE ELSE...
"BUT I'VE GOT FREE COUPONS FOR A HIGH-END YAKINIKU PLACE."
I can't see!
FOR NOW...
I'LL JUST HAVE TO STAY FAR AWAY FROM SHIMA-KUN!
At least until the fireworks are over.
SHISHIDO-SAN, SHISHIDO-SAN!

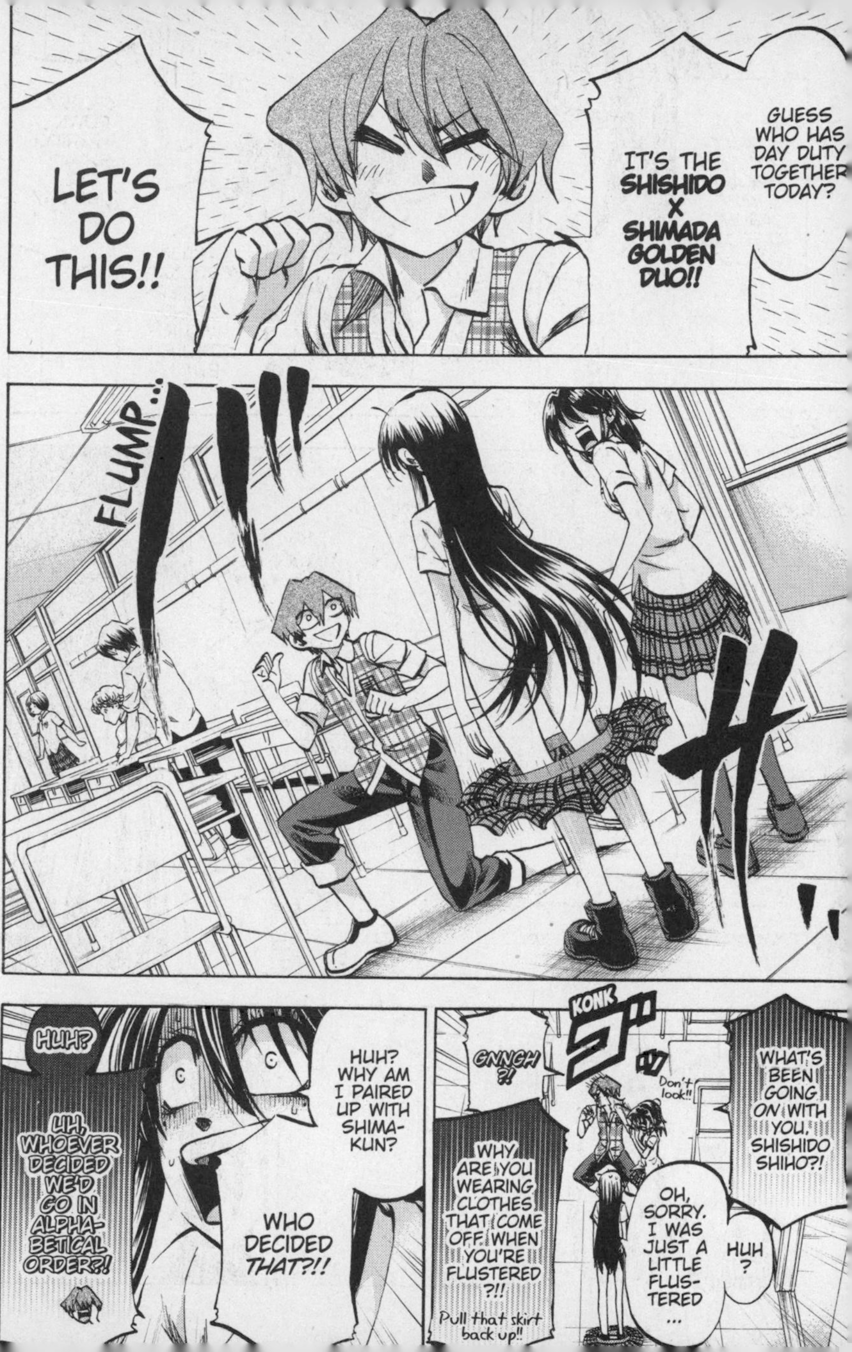
GUESS WHO HAS DAY DUTY TOGETHER TODAY?
IT'S THE SHISHIDO X SHIMADA GOLDEN DUO!!
LET'S DO THIS!!
FLUMP...
WHAT'S BEEN GOING ON WITH YOU, SHISHIDO SHIHO?!
KONK
Don't look!!
GNNGH?!
HUH?
OH, SORRY. I WAS JUST A LITTLE FLUS-TERED ...
WHY ARE YOU WEARING CLOTHES THAT COME OFF WHEN YOU'RE FLUSTERED?!!
Pull that skirt back up!!
HUH? WHY AM I PAIRED UP WITH SHIMA-KUN?
WHO DECIDED THAT?!!
HUH?
UH, WHOEVER DECIDED WE'D GO IN ALPHA-BETICAL ORDER?!

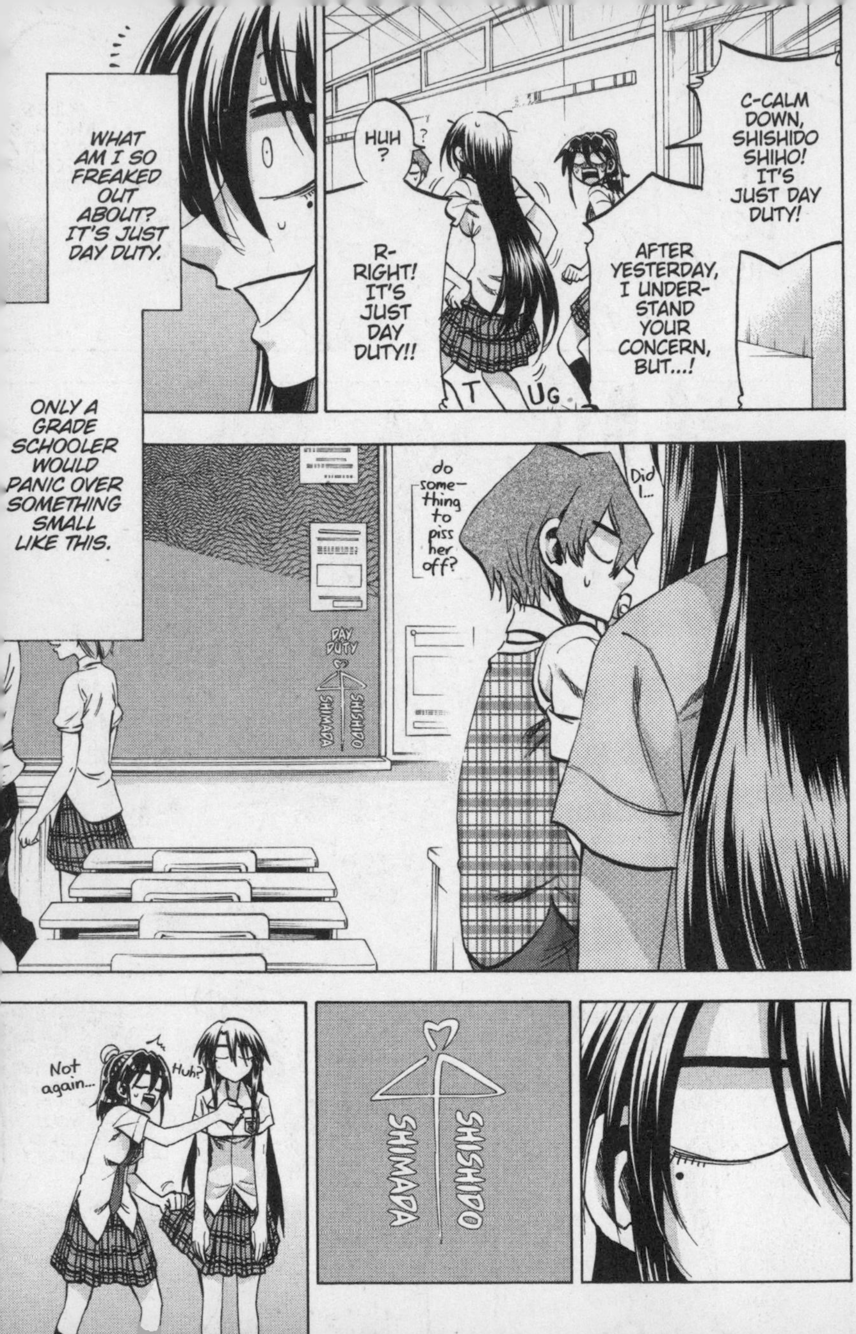
C-CALM DOWN, SHISHIDO SHIHO! IT'S JUST DAY DUTY!
AFTER YESTERDAY, I UNDERSTAND YOUR CONCERN, BUT...!
R-RIGHT! IT'S JUST DAY DUTY!!
HUH?
TUG
WHAT AM I SO FREAKED OUT ABOUT? IT'S JUST DAY DUTY.
ONLY A GRADE SCHOOLER WOULD PANIC OVER SOMETHING SMALL LIKE THIS.
Did I...
do something to piss her off?
DAY DUTY
SHISHIDO
SHIMADA
SHISHIDO
SHIMADA
Huh?
Not again...

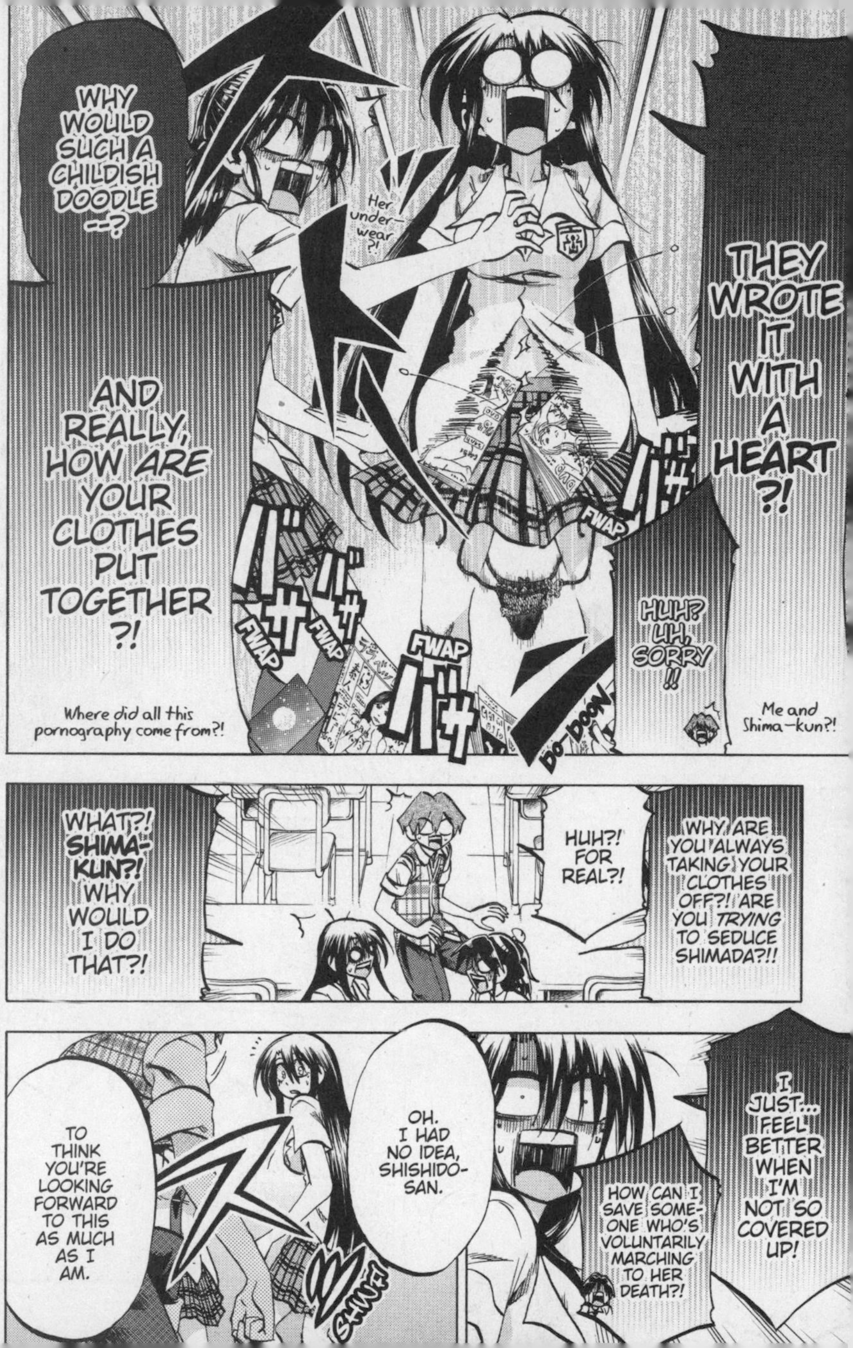
THEY WROTE IT WITH A HEART?!
HUH? UH, SORRY!!
Me and Shima-kun?!
Her under-wear?!
WHY WOULD SUCH A CHILDISH DOODLE--?
AND REALLY, HOW ARE YOUR CLOTHES PUT TOGETHER?!
FWAP
FWAP
FWAP
FWAP
DO-DOON
Where did all this pornography come from?!
WHY ARE YOU ALWAYS TAKING YOUR CLOTHES OFF?! ARE YOU *TRYING* TO SEDUCE SHIMADA?!!
HUH?! FOR REAL?!
WHAT?! **SHIMA-KUN?!** WHY WOULD I DO THAT?!
I JUST... FEEL BETTER WHEN I'M NOT SO COVERED UP!
HOW CAN I SAVE SOME-ONE WHO'S VOLUNTARILY MARCHING TO HER DEATH?!
OH. I HAD NO IDEA, SHISHIDO-SAN.
TO THINK YOU'RE LOOKING FORWARD TO THIS AS MUCH AS I AM.

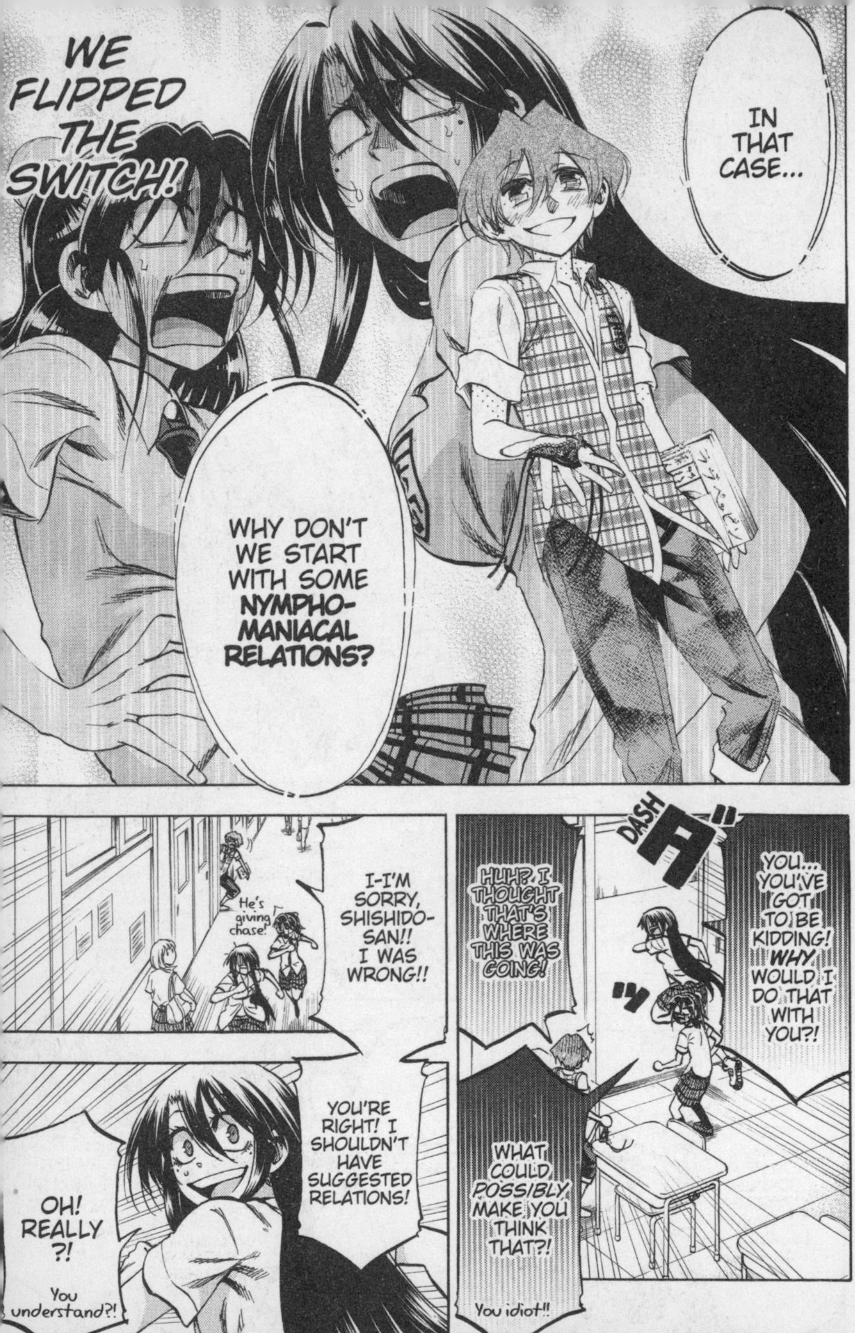
IN THAT CASE...
WE FLIPPED THE SWITCH!
WHY DON'T WE START WITH SOME **NYMPHO-MANIACAL RELATIONS?**
DASH
YOU... YOU'VE GOT TO BE KIDDING! ***WHY*** WOULD I DO THAT WITH YOU?!
HUH? I THOUGHT THAT'S WHERE THIS WAS GOING!
WHAT COULD *POSSIBLY* MAKE YOU THINK THAT?!
You idiot!!
I-I'M SORRY, SHISHIDO-SAN!! I WAS WRONG!!
He's giving chase!
YOU'RE RIGHT! I SHOULDN'T HAVE SUGGESTED RELATIONS!
OH! REALLY?!
You understand?!

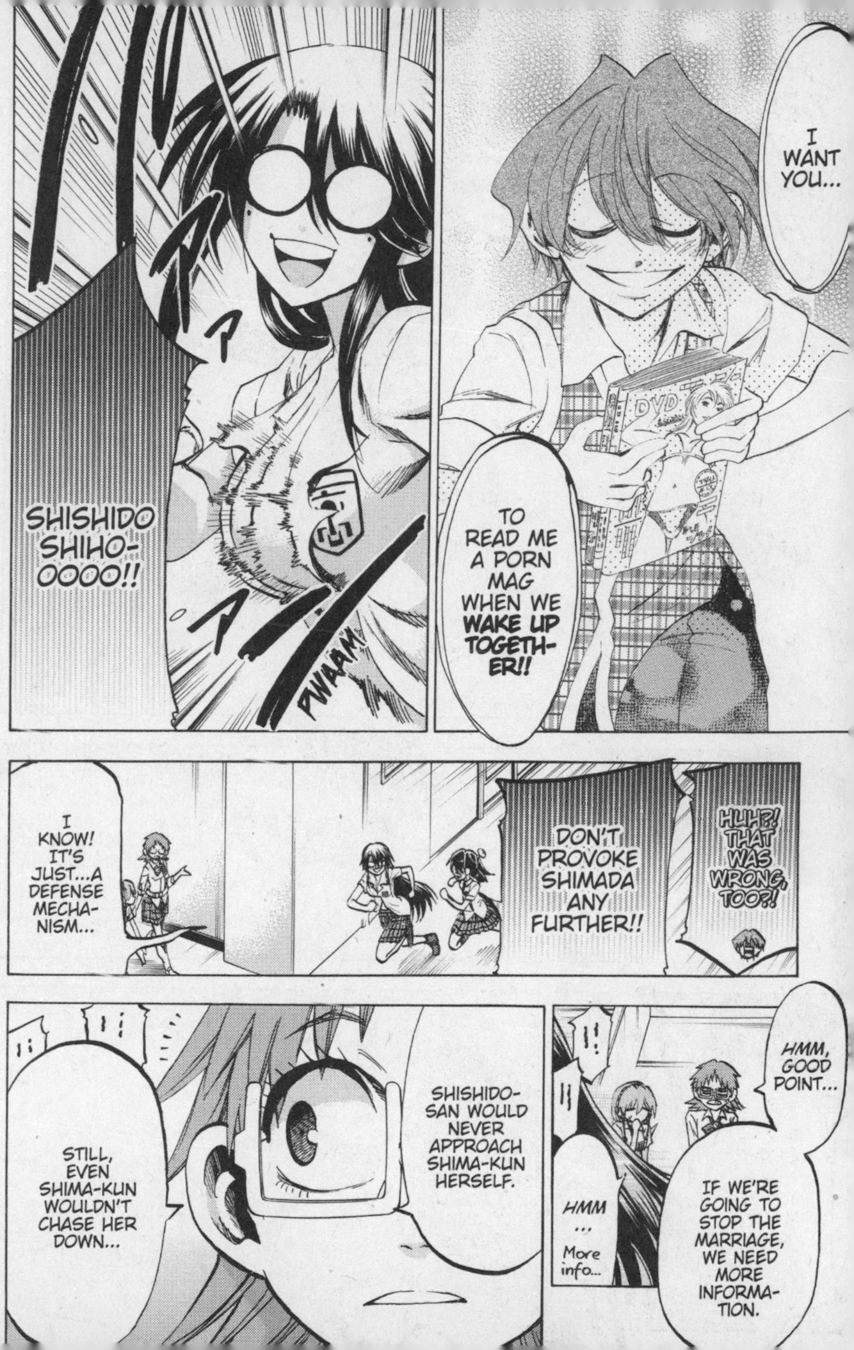
I WANT YOU...
TO READ ME A PORN MAG WHEN WE **WAKE UP TOGETH-ER!!**
SHISHIDO SHIHO-OOOO!!
PWAAM
HUH?! THAT WAS WRONG, TOO?!
DON'T PROVOKE SHIMADA ANY FURTHER!!
I KNOW! IT'S JUST...A DEFENSE MECHA-NISM...
!!
HMM, GOOD POINT...
IF WE'RE GOING TO STOP THE MARRIAGE, WE NEED MORE INFORMA-TION.
HMM ... More info...
SHISHIDO-SAN WOULD NEVER APPROACH SHIMA-KUN HERSELF.
!!
!!
!!
STILL, EVEN SHIMA-KUN WOULDN'T CHASE HER DOWN...

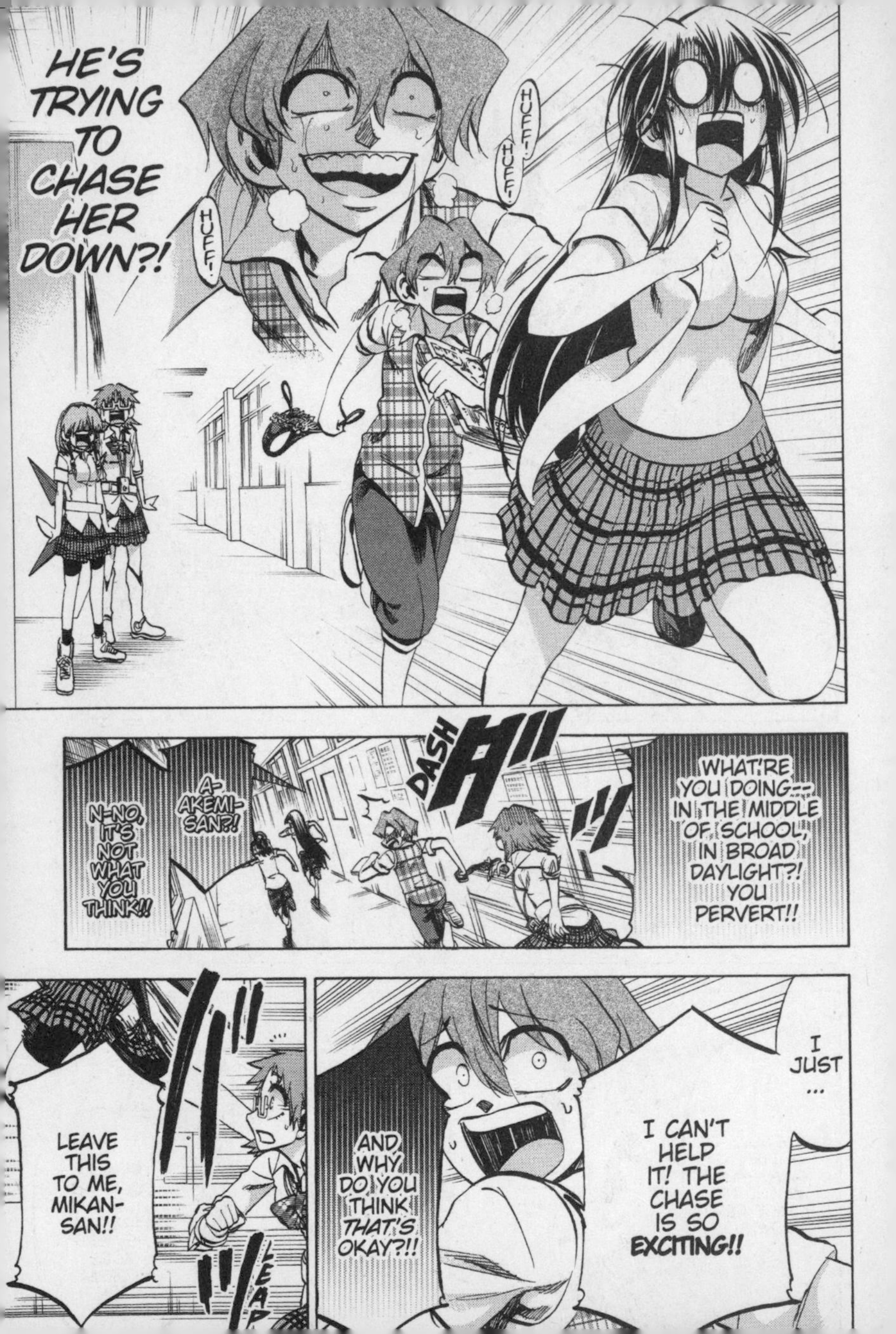
HUFF!
HUFF!
HUFF!
HE'S TRYING TO CHASE HER DOWN?!
WHAT'RE YOU DOING-- IN THE MIDDLE OF SCHOOL, IN BROAD DAYLIGHT?! YOU PERVERT!!
DASH
A-AKEMI-SAN?!
N-NO, IT'S NOT WHAT YOU THINK!!
I JUST ...
I CAN'T HELP IT! THE CHASE IS SO EXCITING!!
AND WHY DO YOU THINK THAT'S OKAY?!!
LEAVE THIS TO ME, MIKAN-SAN!!
LEAP

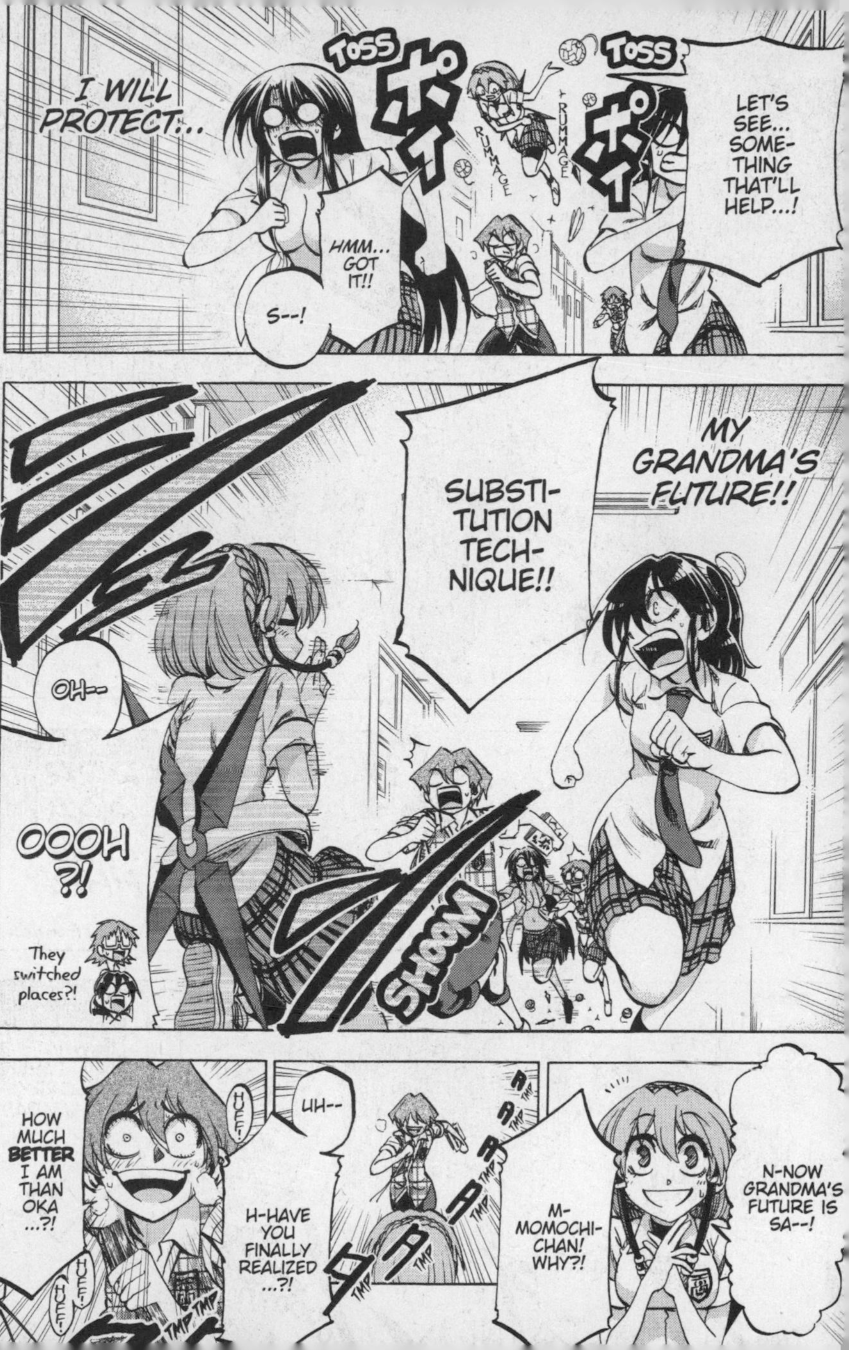
LET'S SEE... SOMETHING THAT'LL HELP...!
TOSS
ポイ
RUMMAGE
RUMMAGE
TOSS
ポイ
I WILL PROTECT...
HMM... GOT IT!!
S--!
MY GRANDMA'S FUTURE!!
SUBSTITUTION TECHNIQUE!!
OH--
OOOH ?!
SHOOM
They switched places?!
N-NOW GRANDMA'S FUTURE IS SA--!
M-MOMOCHI-CHAN! WHY?!
TMP TMP TMP TMP TMP
UH--
H-HAVE YOU FINALLY REALIZED ...?!
HUFF!
HOW MUCH **BETTER** I AM THAN OKA ...?!
HUFF! HUFF!
TMP TMP

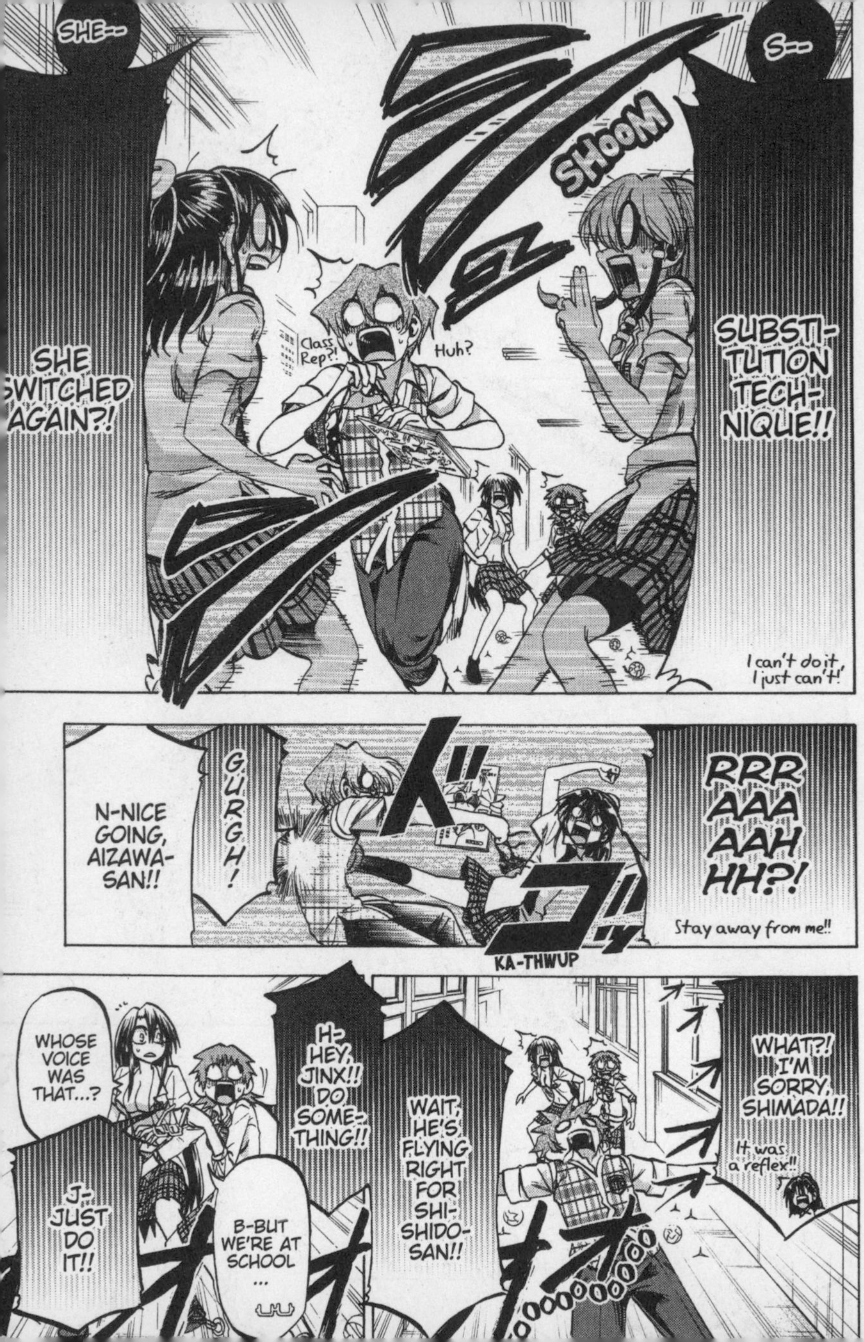
S--
SHE--
SHOOM
SUBSTI-TUTION TECH-NIQUE!!
Huh?
Class Rep?!
SHE SWITCHED AGAIN?!
I can't do it, I just can't!
RRRAAAAAHHH?!
Stay away from me!!
GURGH!
N-NICE GOING, AIZAWA-SAN!!
KA-THWUP
WHAT?! I'M SORRY, SHIMADA!!
It was a reflex!!
WAIT, HE'S FLYING RIGHT FOR SHI-SHIDO-SAN!!
H-HEY, JINX!! DO SOME-THING!!
WHOSE VOICE WAS THAT...?
B-BUT WE'RE AT SCHOOL...
J-JUST DO IT!!

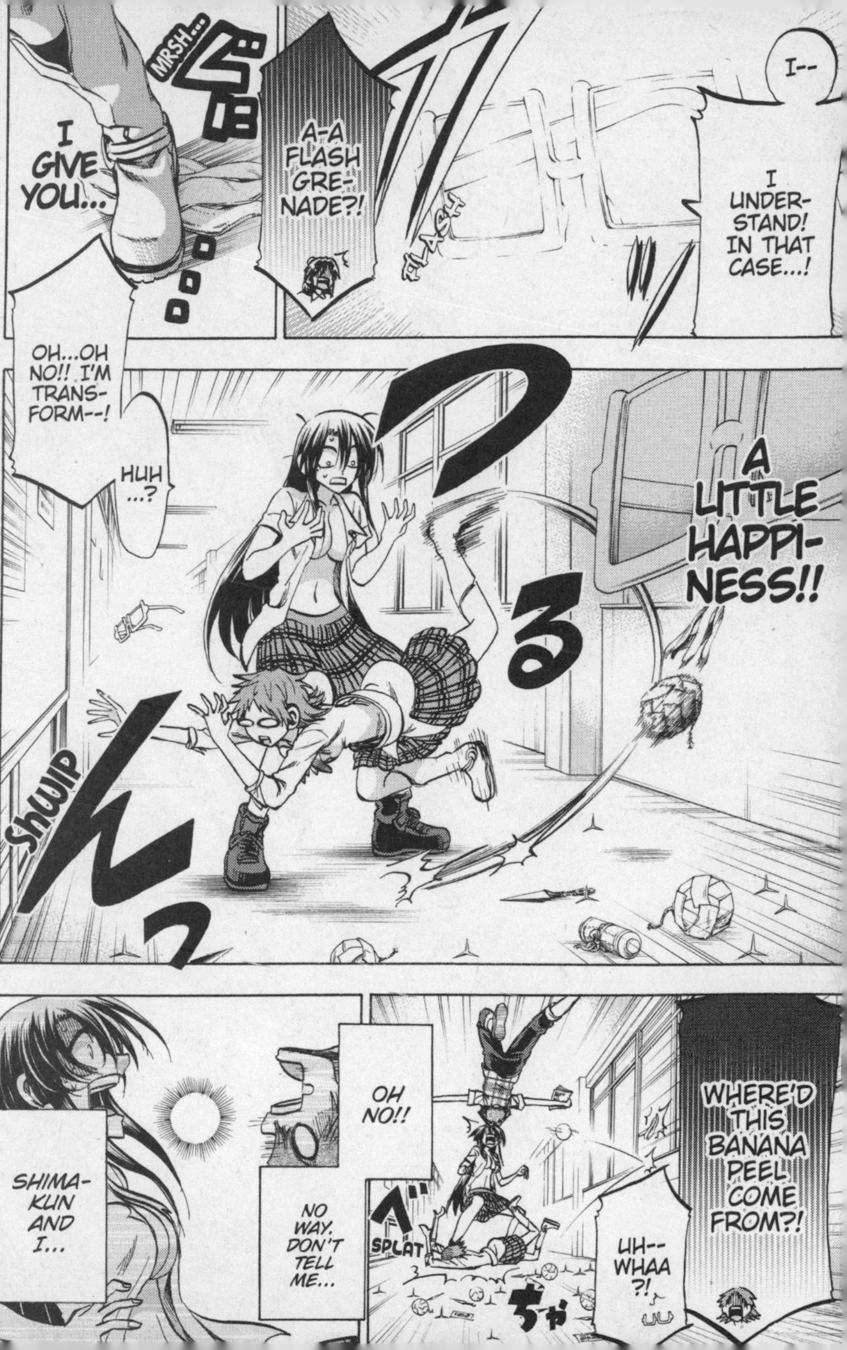
I--
I UNDER-STAND! IN THAT CASE...!
FLASH
A-A FLASH GRE-NADE?!
MRSH...
I GIVE YOU...
OH...OH NO!! I'M TRANS-FORM--!
A LITTLE HAPPI-NESS!!
HUH...?
SHWIP
WHERE'D THIS BANANA PEEL COME FROM?!
UH--WHAA?!
SPLAT
OH NO!!
NO WAY. DON'T TELL ME...
SHIMA-KUN AND I...

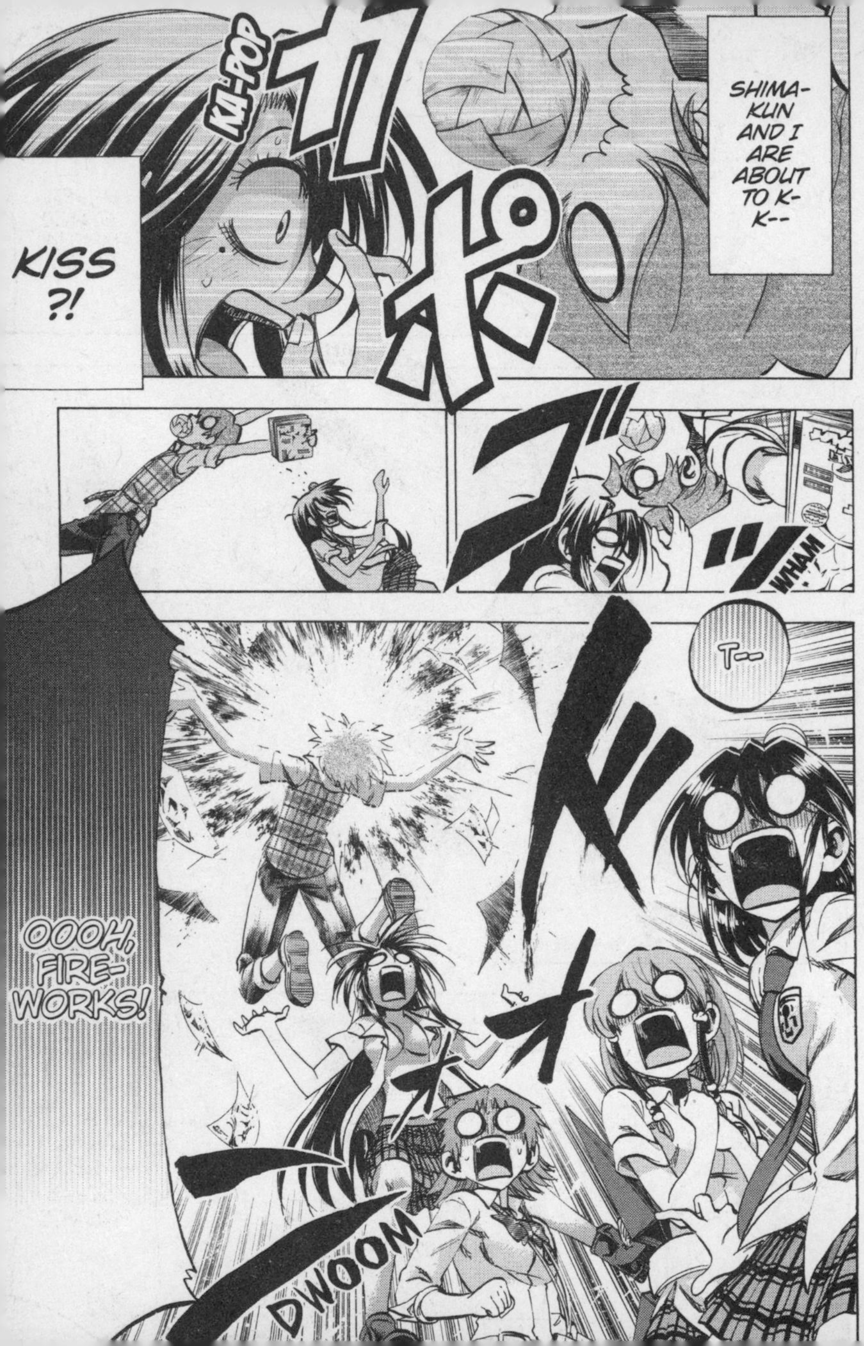
SHIMA-KUN AND I ARE ABOUT TO K-K--
KA-POP
KISS ?!
WHAM
T--
OOOH, FIRE-WORKS!
DWOOM

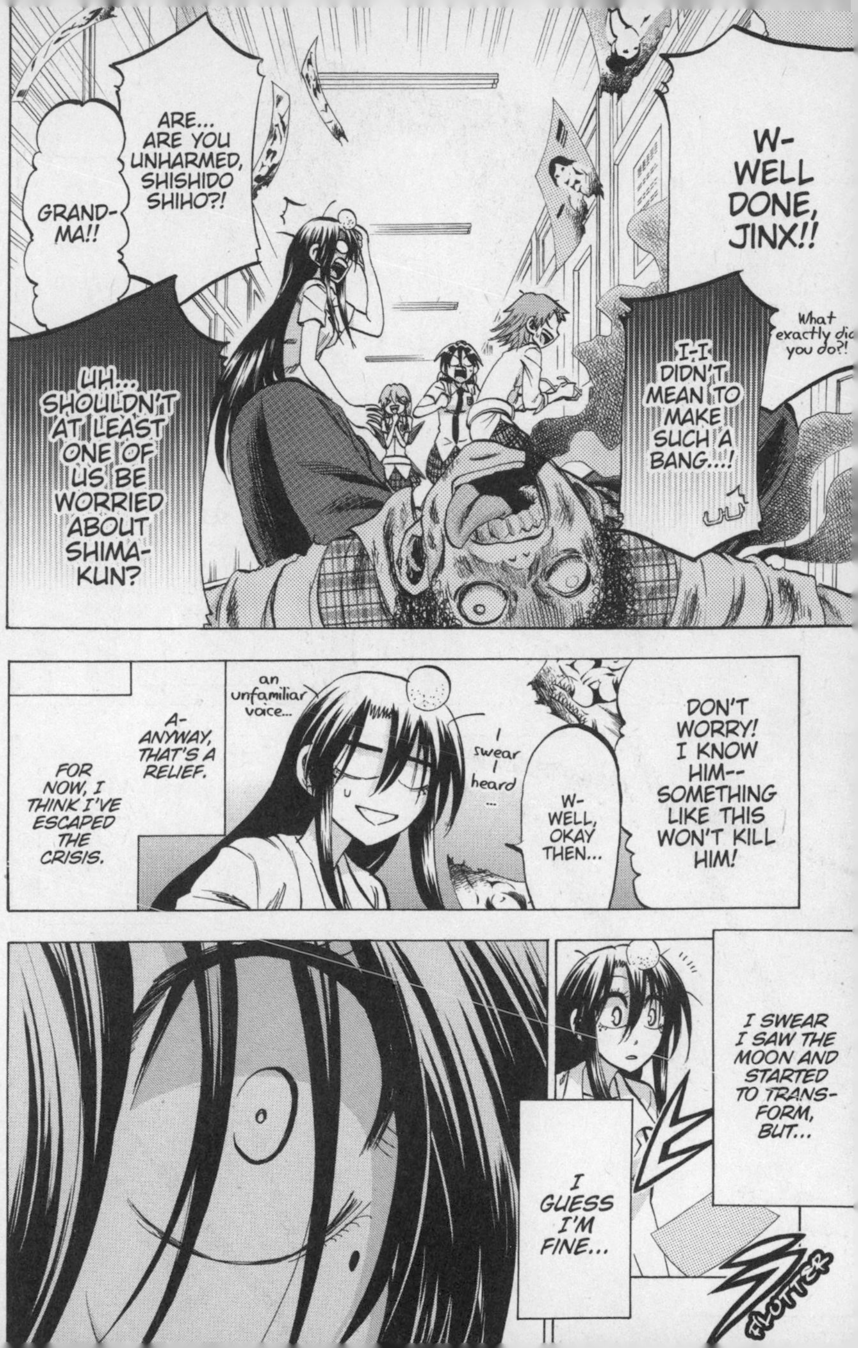
W-WELL DONE, JINX!!
What exactly did you do?!
I-I DIDN'T MEAN TO MAKE SUCH A BANG...!
ARE... ARE YOU UNHARMED, SHISHIDO SHIHO?!
GRAND-MA!!
UH... SHOULDN'T AT LEAST ONE OF US BE WORRIED ABOUT SHIMA-KUN?
DON'T WORRY! I KNOW HIM-- SOMETHING LIKE THIS WON'T KILL HIM!
W-WELL, OKAY THEN...
I swear I heard ...
an unfamiliar voice...
A-ANYWAY, THAT'S A RELIEF.
FOR NOW, I THINK I'VE ESCAPED THE CRISIS.
I SWEAR I SAW THE MOON AND STARTED TO TRANS-FORM, BUT...
I GUESS I'M FINE...
FLUTTER

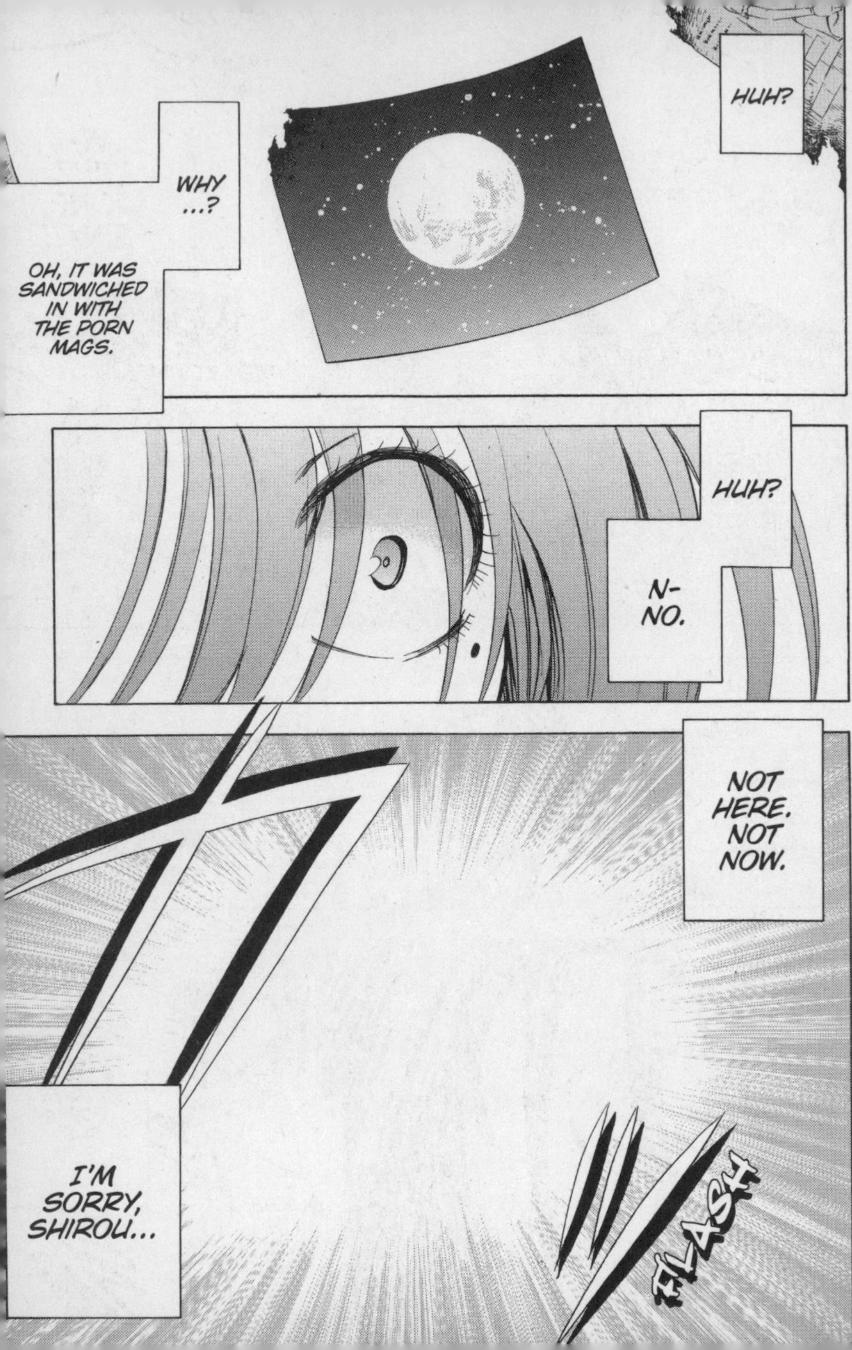
HUH?
WHY ...?
OH, IT WAS SANDWICHED IN WITH THE PORN MAGS.
HUH?
N- NO.
NOT HERE. NOT NOW.
FLASH
I'M SORRY, SHIROU...

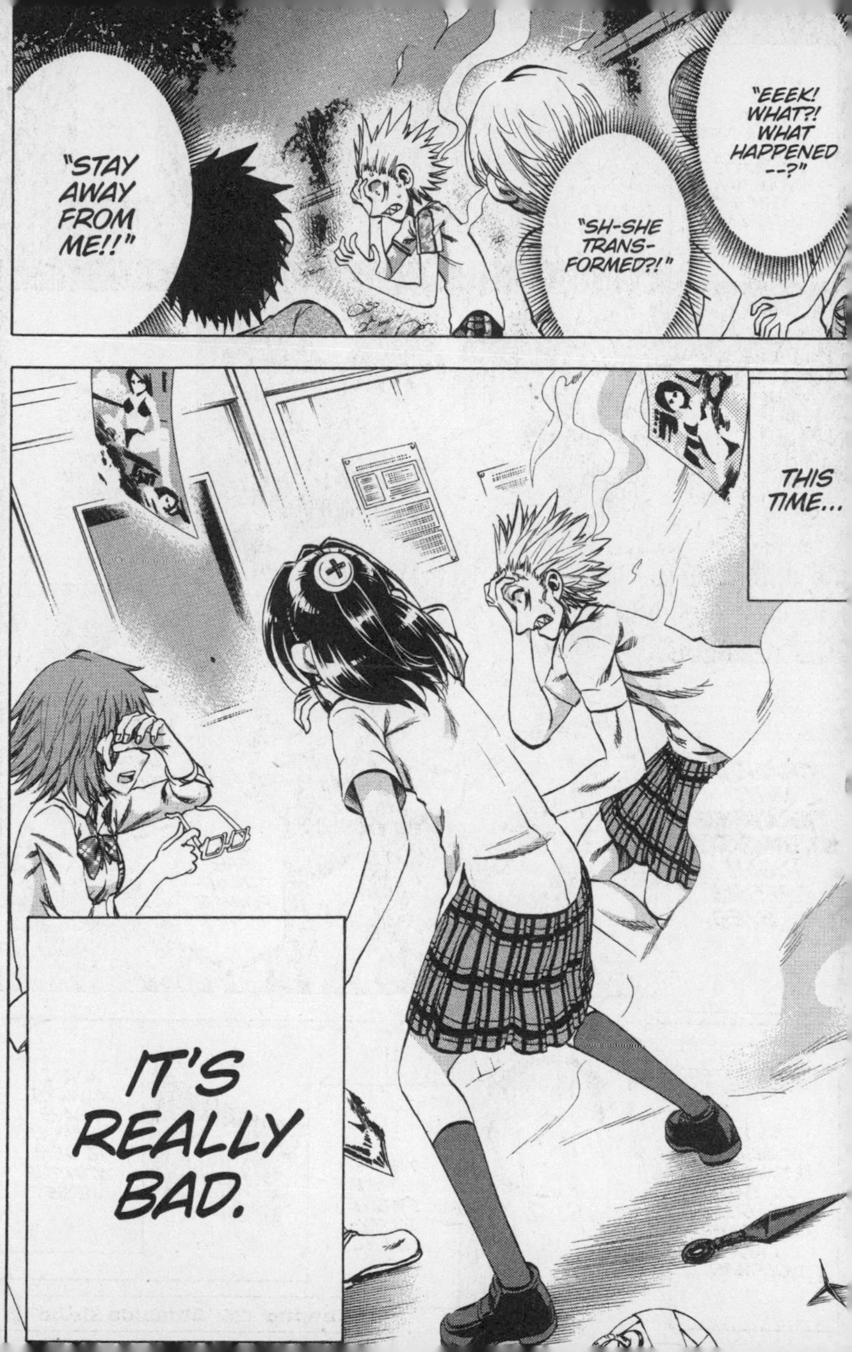
"EEEK! WHAT?! WHAT HAPPENED --?"
"SH-SHE TRANS-FORMED?!"
"STAY AWAY FROM ME!!"
THIS TIME...
IT'S REALLY BAD.

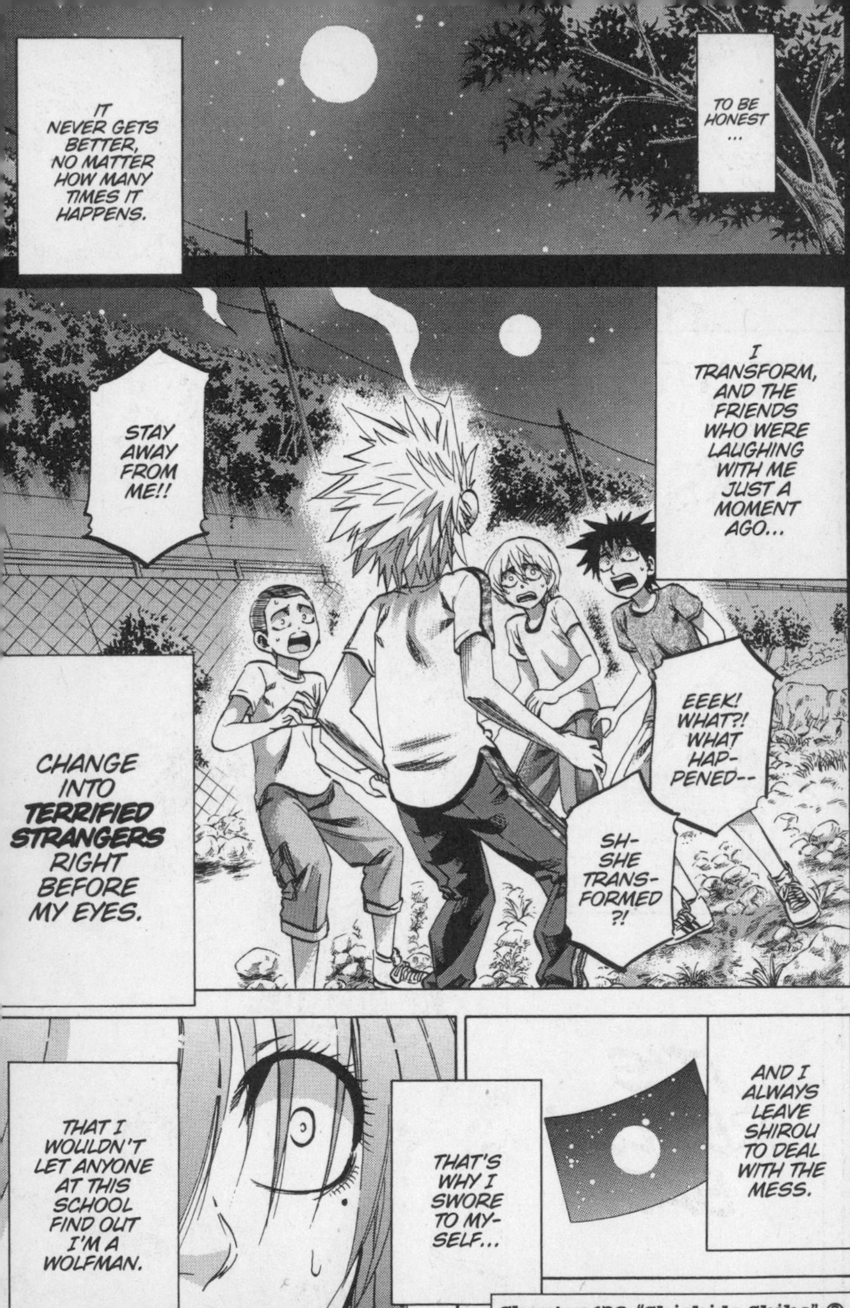
TO BE HONEST ...
IT NEVER GETS BETTER, NO MATTER HOW MANY TIMES IT HAPPENS.
I TRANSFORM, AND THE FRIENDS WHO WERE LAUGHING WITH ME JUST A MOMENT AGO...
STAY AWAY FROM ME!!
EEEK! WHAT?! WHAT HAP-PENED--
SH-SHE TRANS-FORMED?!
CHANGE INTO TERRIFIED STRANGERS RIGHT BEFORE MY EYES.
AND I ALWAYS LEAVE SHIROU TO DEAL WITH THE MESS.
THAT'S WHY I SWORE TO MY-SELF...
THAT I WOULDN'T LET ANYONE AT THIS SCHOOL FIND OUT I'M A WOLFMAN.

Chapter 126: "Shishido Shiho" ②

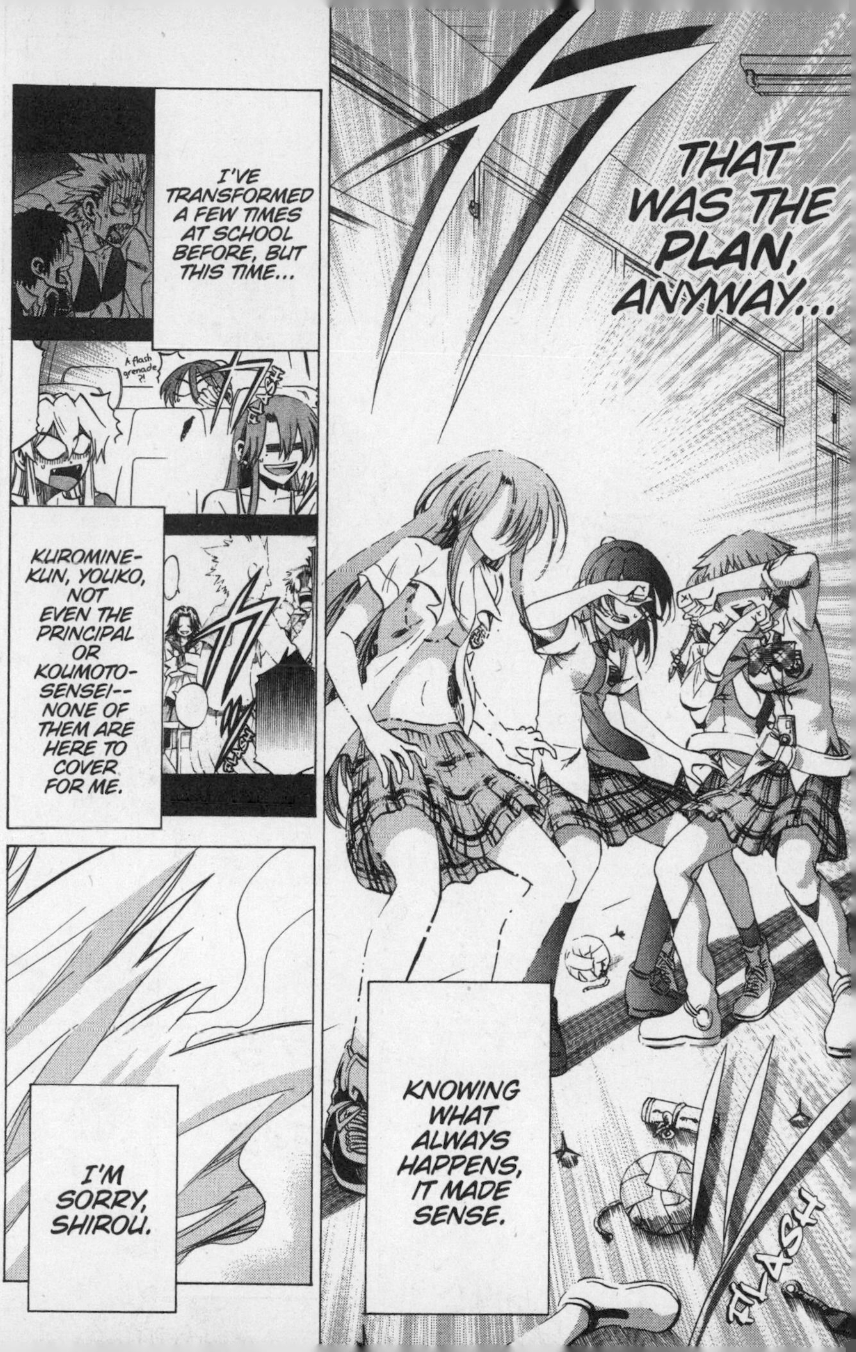
THAT WAS THE PLAN, ANYWAY...
KNOWING WHAT ALWAYS HAPPENS, IT MADE SENSE.
FLASH
I'VE TRANSFORMED A FEW TIMES AT SCHOOL BEFORE, BUT THIS TIME...
A flash grenade?!
FLASH
KUROMINE-KUN, YOUKO, NOT EVEN THE PRINCIPAL OR KOUMOTO-SENSEI-- NONE OF THEM ARE HERE TO COVER FOR ME.
FLASH
I'M SORRY, SHIROU.

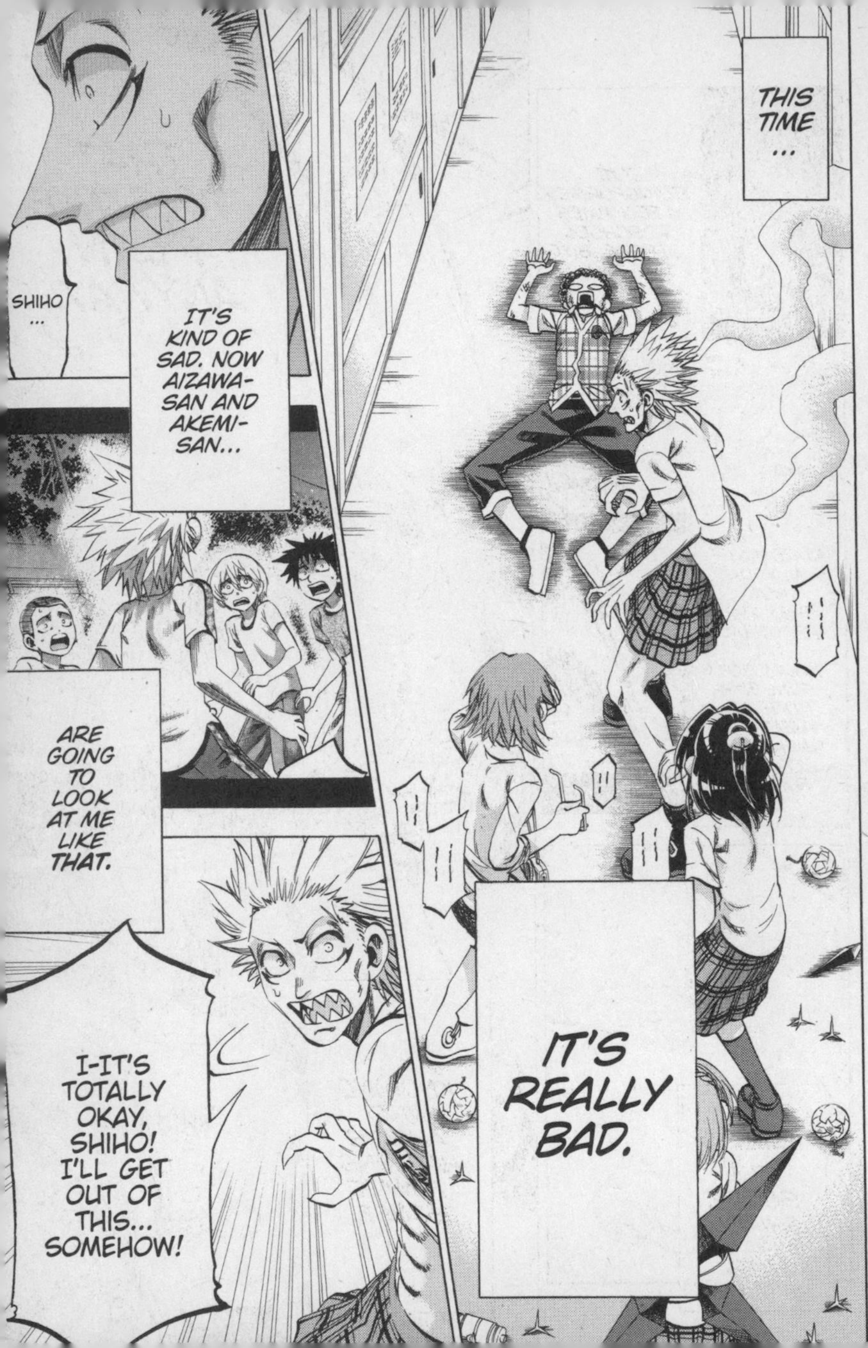
THIS TIME...
IT'S REALLY BAD.
SHIHO...
IT'S KIND OF SAD. NOW AIZAWA-SAN AND AKEMI-SAN...
ARE GOING TO LOOK AT ME LIKE THAT.
I-IT'S TOTALLY OKAY, SHIHO! I'LL GET OUT OF THIS... SOMEHOW!

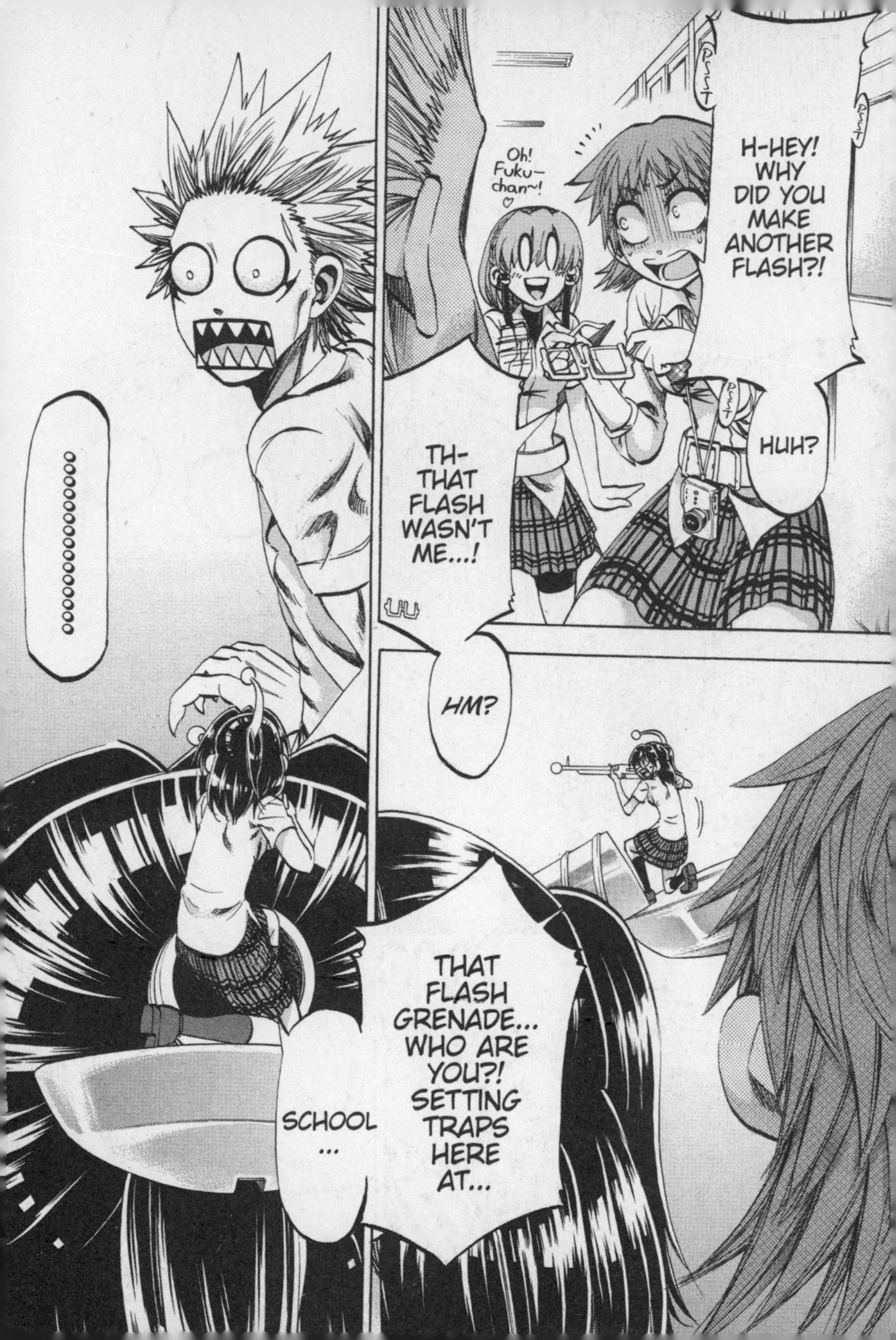
PSST
H-HEY! WHY DID YOU MAKE ANOTHER FLASH?!
Oh! Fuku-chan~!
PSST
PSST
HUH?
TH-THAT FLASH WASN'T ME...!
HM?
THAT FLASH GRENADE... WHO ARE YOU?! SETTING TRAPS HERE AT...
SCHOOL ...
....

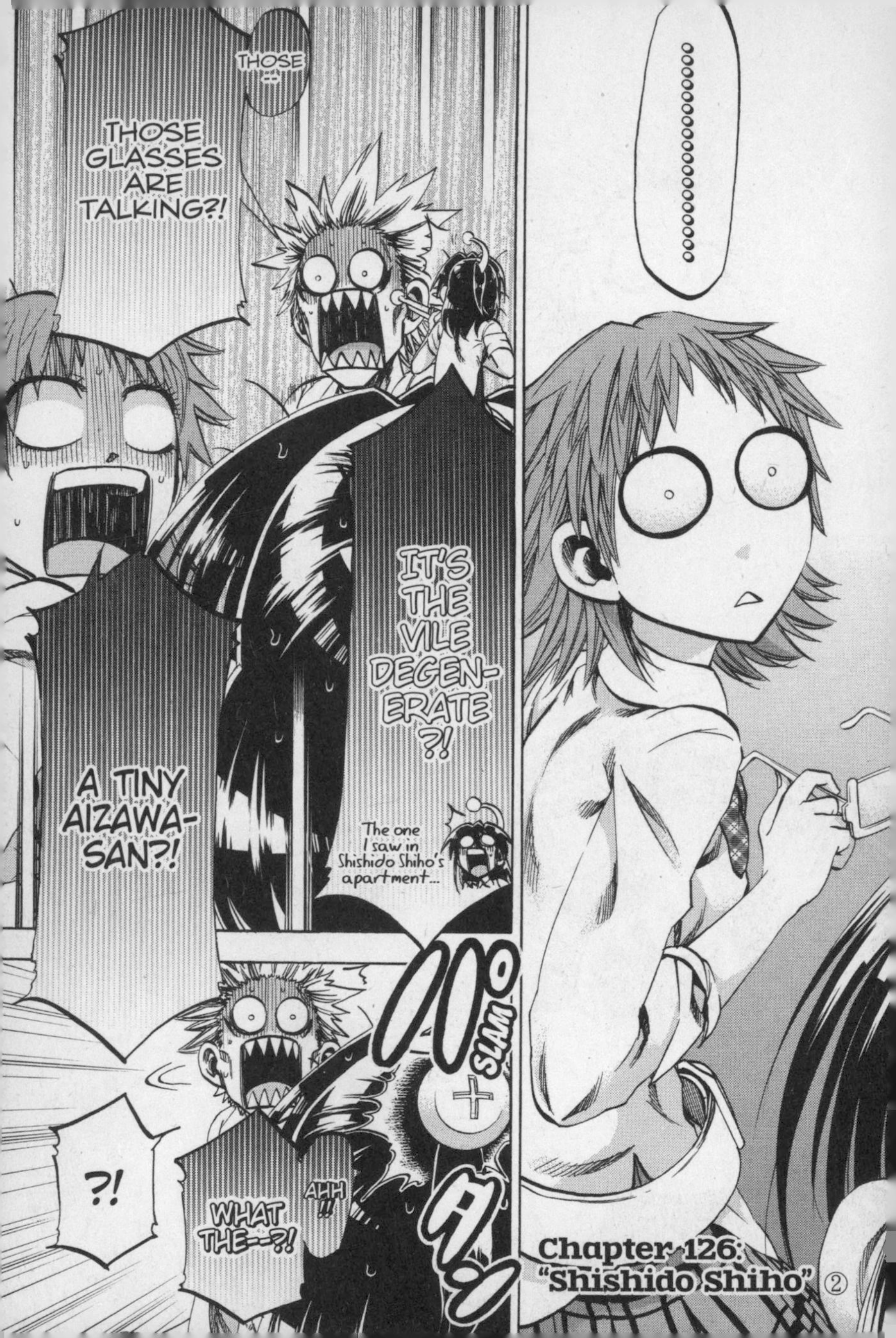
…………………………
Chapter 126: "Shishido Shiho" ②
THOSE--
THOSE GLASSES ARE TALKING?!
IT'S THE VILE DEGEN-ERATE?!
The one I saw in Shishido Shiho's apartment...
A TINY AIZAWA-SAN?!
SLAM
AHH!!
WHAT THE--?!
?!

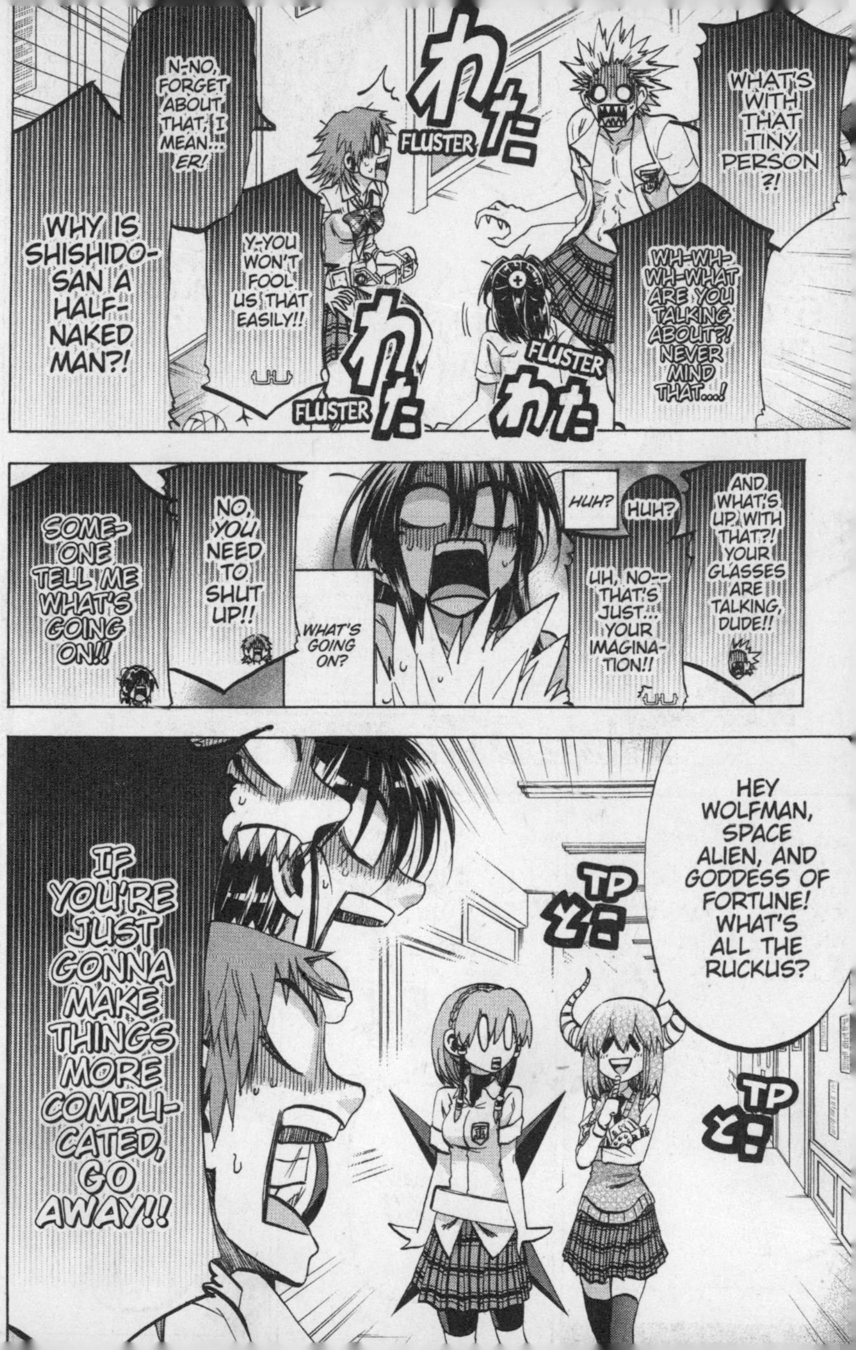
WHAT'S WITH THAT TINY PERSON?!
FLUSTER
WH-WH-WH-WHAT ARE YOU TALKING ABOUT?! NEVER MIND THAT...!
FLUSTER
N-NO, FORGET ABOUT THAT, I MEAN... ER!
FLUSTER
Y-YOU WON'T FOOL US THAT EASILY!!
WHY IS SHISHIDO-SAN A HALF-NAKED MAN?!
AND WHAT'S UP WITH THAT?! YOUR GLASSES ARE TALKING, DUDE!!
HUH?
HUH?
UH, NO-- THAT'S JUST... YOUR IMAGINATION!!
WHAT'S GOING ON?
NO, YOU NEED TO SHUT UP!!
SOMEONE TELL ME WHAT'S GOING ON!!
HEY WOLFMAN, SPACE ALIEN, AND GODDESS OF FORTUNE! WHAT'S ALL THE RUCKUS?
TP
TP
IF YOU'RE JUST GONNA MAKE THINGS MORE COMPLICATED, GO AWAY!!

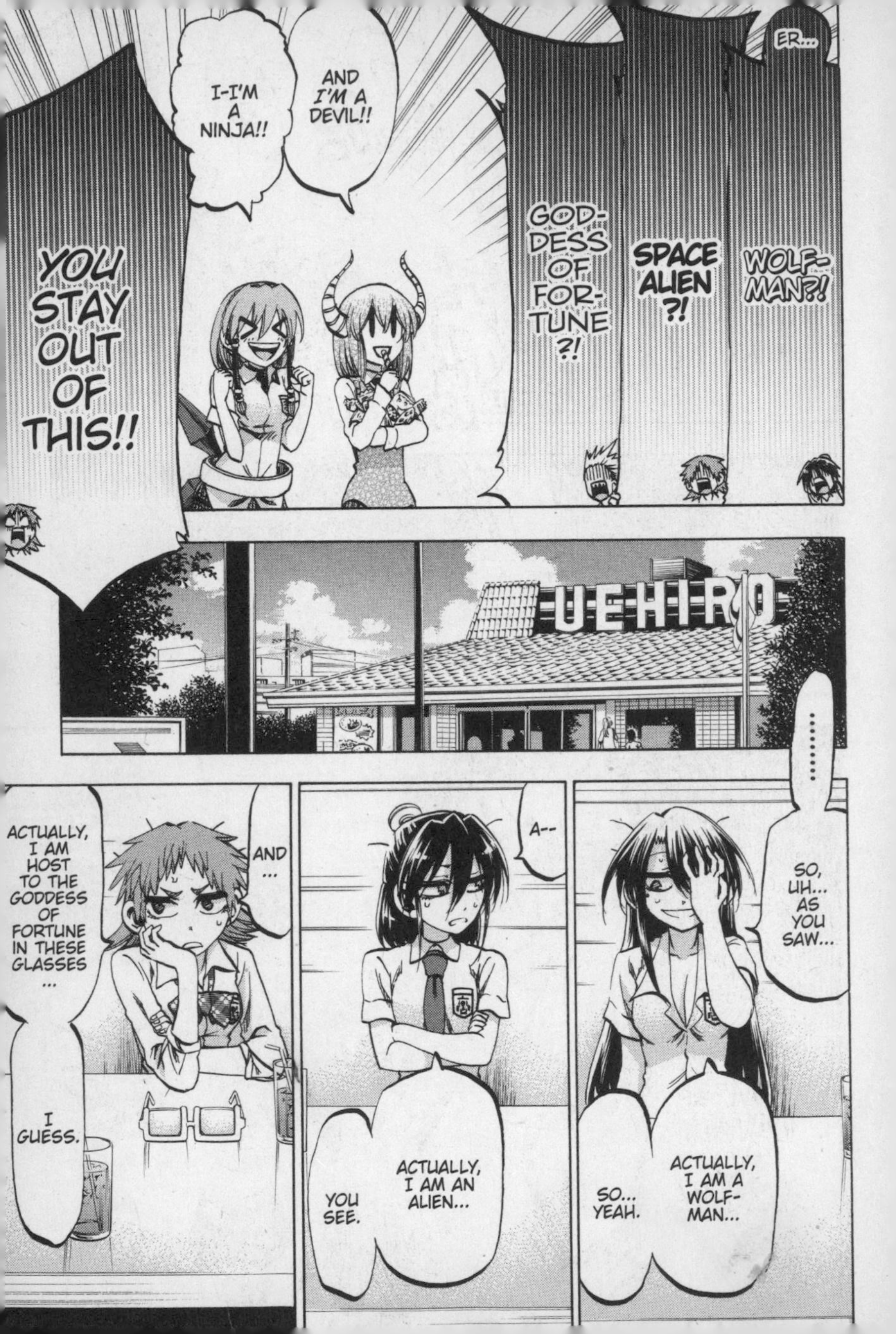
ER...
WOLF-MAN?!
SPACE ALIEN ?!
GOD-DESS OF FOR-TUNE ?!
AND I'M A DEVIL!!
I-I'M A NINJA!!
YOU STAY OUT OF THIS!!
UEHIRO
......
SO, UH... AS YOU SAW...
ACTUALLY, I AM A WOLF-MAN...
SO... YEAH.
A--
ACTUALLY, I AM AN ALIEN...
YOU SEE.
AND ...
ACTUALLY, I AM HOST TO THE GODDESS OF FORTUNE IN THESE GLASSES ...
I GUESS.

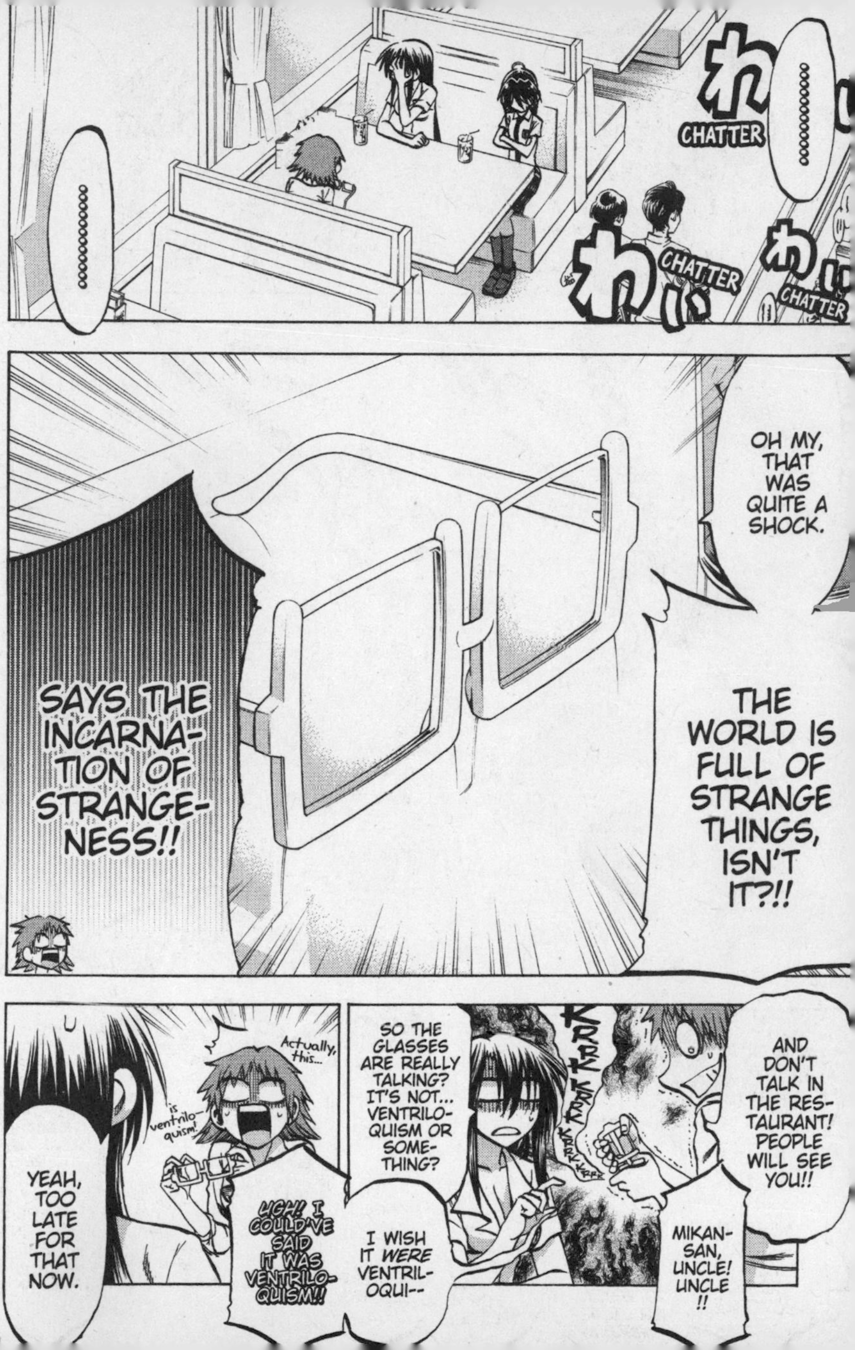
……………
わ
CHATTER
わい
CHATTER
わい
CHATTER
……………
OH MY, THAT WAS QUITE A SHOCK.
THE WORLD IS FULL OF STRANGE THINGS, ISN'T IT?!!
SAYS THE INCARNATION OF STRANGENESS!!
AND DON'T TALK IN THE RESTAURANT! PEOPLE WILL SEE YOU!!
MIKAN-SAN, UNCLE! UNCLE!!
SO THE GLASSES ARE REALLY TALKING? IT'S NOT... VENTRILOQUISM OR SOMETHING?
I WISH IT WERE VENTRILOQUI--
Actually, this...
is ventriloquism!
UGH! I COULD'VE SAID IT WAS VENTRILOQUISM!!
YEAH, TOO LATE FOR THAT NOW.

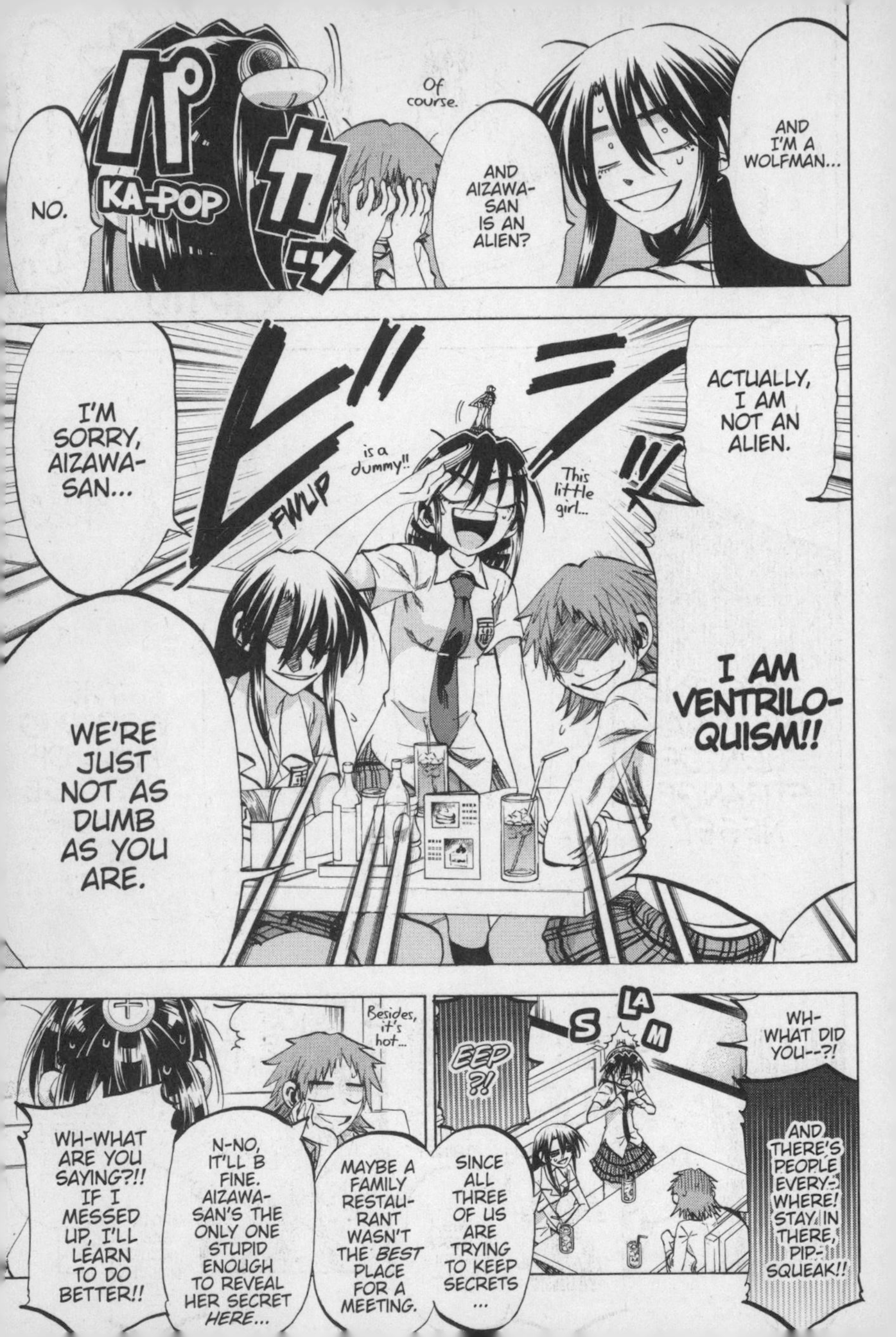
AND I'M A WOLFMAN...
AND AIZAWA-SAN IS AN ALIEN?
Of course.
KA-POP
NO.
ACTUALLY, I AM NOT AN ALIEN.
I AM VENTRILOQUISM!!
This little girl...
is a dummy!!
FWUP
I'M SORRY, AIZAWA-SAN...
WE'RE JUST NOT AS DUMB AS YOU ARE.
WH-WHAT DID YOU--?!
AND THERE'S PEOPLE EVERY-WHERE! STAY IN THERE, PIP-SQUEAK!!
SLAM
EEP ?!
Besides, it's hot...
SINCE ALL THREE OF US ARE TRYING TO KEEP SECRETS ...
MAYBE A FAMILY RESTAURANT WASN'T THE *BEST* PLACE FOR A MEETING.
N-NO, IT'LL B FINE. AIZAWA-SAN'S THE ONLY ONE STUPID ENOUGH TO REVEAL HER SECRET *HERE*...
WH-WHAT ARE YOU SAYING?!! IF I MESSED UP, I'LL LEARN TO DO BETTER!!

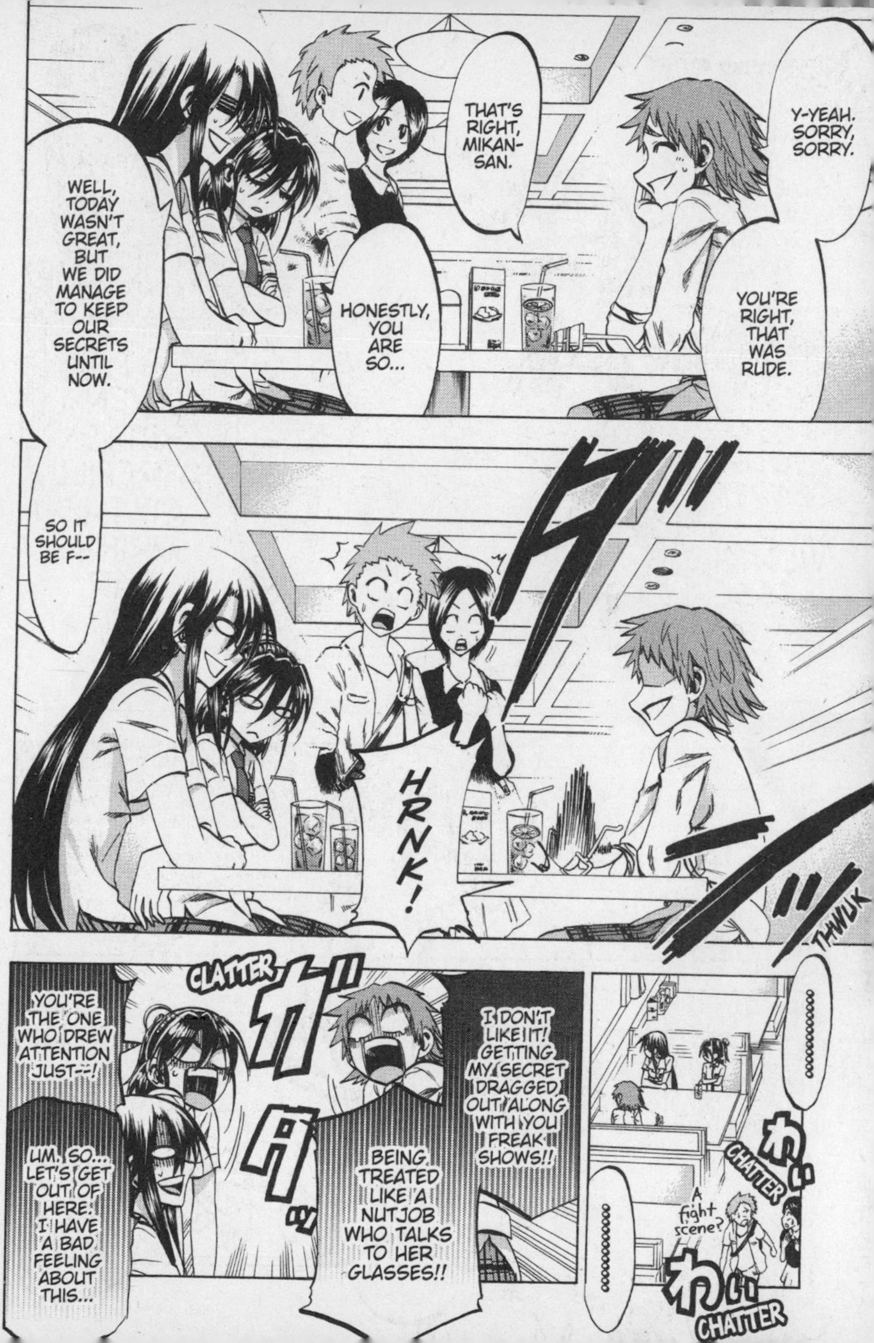
Y-YEAH. SORRY, SORRY.
THAT'S RIGHT, MIKAN-SAN.
YOU'RE RIGHT, THAT WAS RUDE.
HONESTLY, YOU ARE SO...
WELL, TODAY WASN'T GREAT, BUT WE DID MANAGE TO KEEP OUR SECRETS UNTIL NOW.
SO IT SHOULD BE F--
THWUK
HRNK!
......
CHATTER
A fight scene?
......
CHATTER
I DON'T LIKE IT! GETTING MY SECRET DRAGGED OUT ALONG WITH YOU FREAK SHOWS!!
BEING TREATED LIKE A NUTJOB WHO TALKS TO HER GLASSES!!
CLATTER
YOU'RE THE ONE WHO DREW ATTENTION JUST--!
UM. SO... LET'S GET OUT OF HERE. I HAVE A BAD FEELING ABOUT THIS...

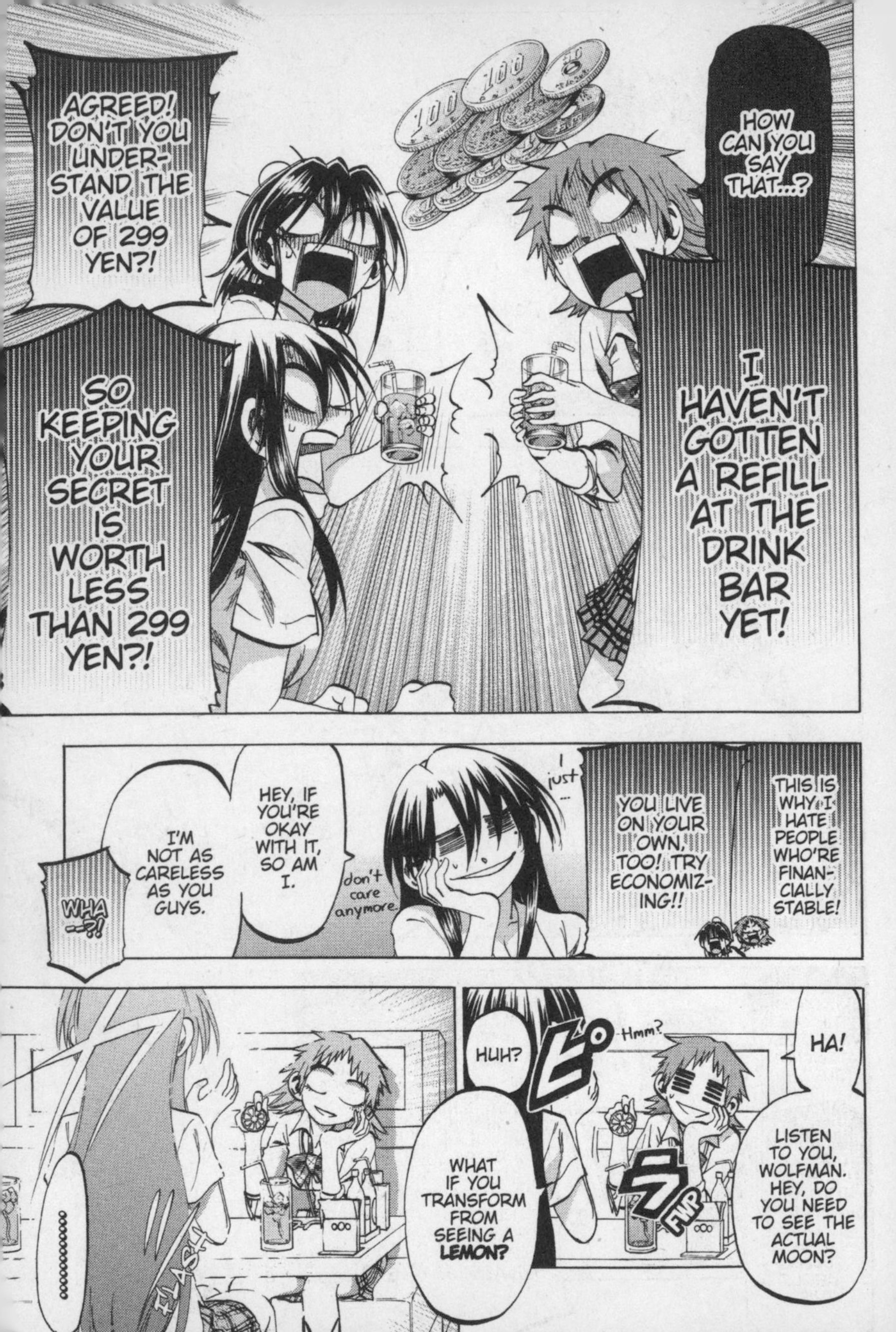

HOW CAN YOU SAY THAT...?
I HAVEN'T GOTTEN A REFILL AT THE DRINK BAR YET!
AGREED! DON'T YOU UNDER-STAND THE VALUE OF 299 YEN?!
SO KEEPING YOUR SECRET IS WORTH LESS THAN 299 YEN?!
THIS IS WHY I HATE PEOPLE WHO'RE FINAN-CIALLY STABLE!
YOU LIVE ON YOUR OWN, TOO! TRY ECONOMIZ-ING!!
I just... don't care anymore.
HEY, IF YOU'RE OKAY WITH IT, SO AM I.
I'M NOT AS CARELESS AS YOU GUYS.
WHA--?!
HA!
Hmm?
LISTEN TO YOU, WOLFMAN. HEY, DO YOU NEED TO SEE THE ACTUAL MOON?
HUH?
WHAT IF YOU TRANSFORM FROM SEEING A **LEMON?**
FWP
FLASH

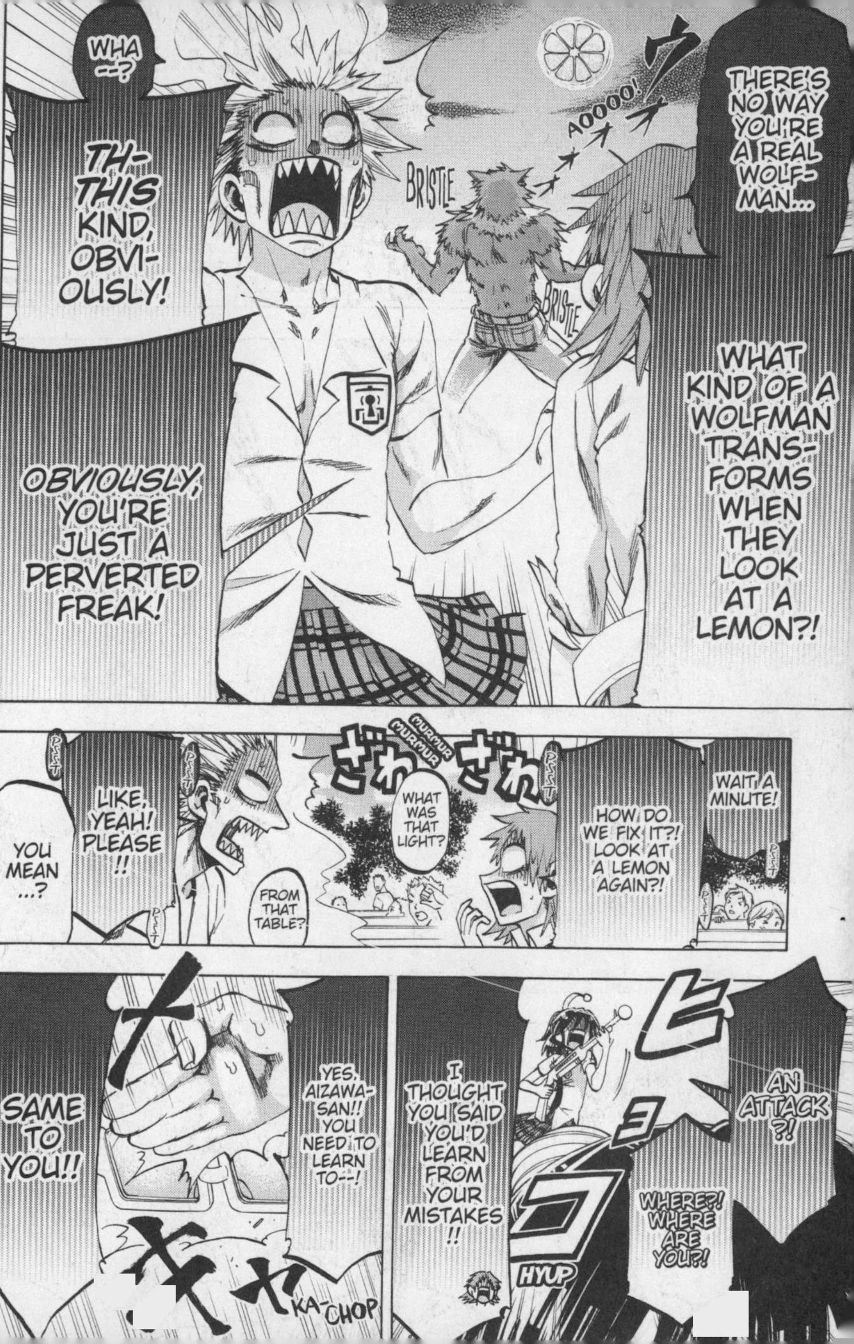
THERE'S NO WAY YOU'RE A REAL WOLF-MAN...
AOOOO!
BRISTLE
BRISTLE
WHAT KIND OF A WOLFMAN TRANS-FORMS WHEN THEY LOOK AT A LEMON?!
WHA--?
TH-THIS KIND, OBVIOUSLY!
OBVIOUSLY, YOU'RE JUST A PERVERTED FREAK!
WAIT A MINUTE!
PSST
HOW DO WE FIX IT?! LOOK AT A LEMON AGAIN?!
PSST
MURMUR MURMUR
WHAT WAS THAT LIGHT?
FROM THAT TABLE?
PSST
LIKE, YEAH! PLEASE!!
PSST
YOU MEAN...?
PSST
AN ATTACK?!
WHERE?! WHERE ARE YOU?!
HYUP
I THOUGHT YOU SAID YOU'D LEARN FROM YOUR MISTAKES!!
YES, AIZAWA-SAN!! YOU NEED TO LEARN TO--!
SAME TO YOU!!
KA-CHOP

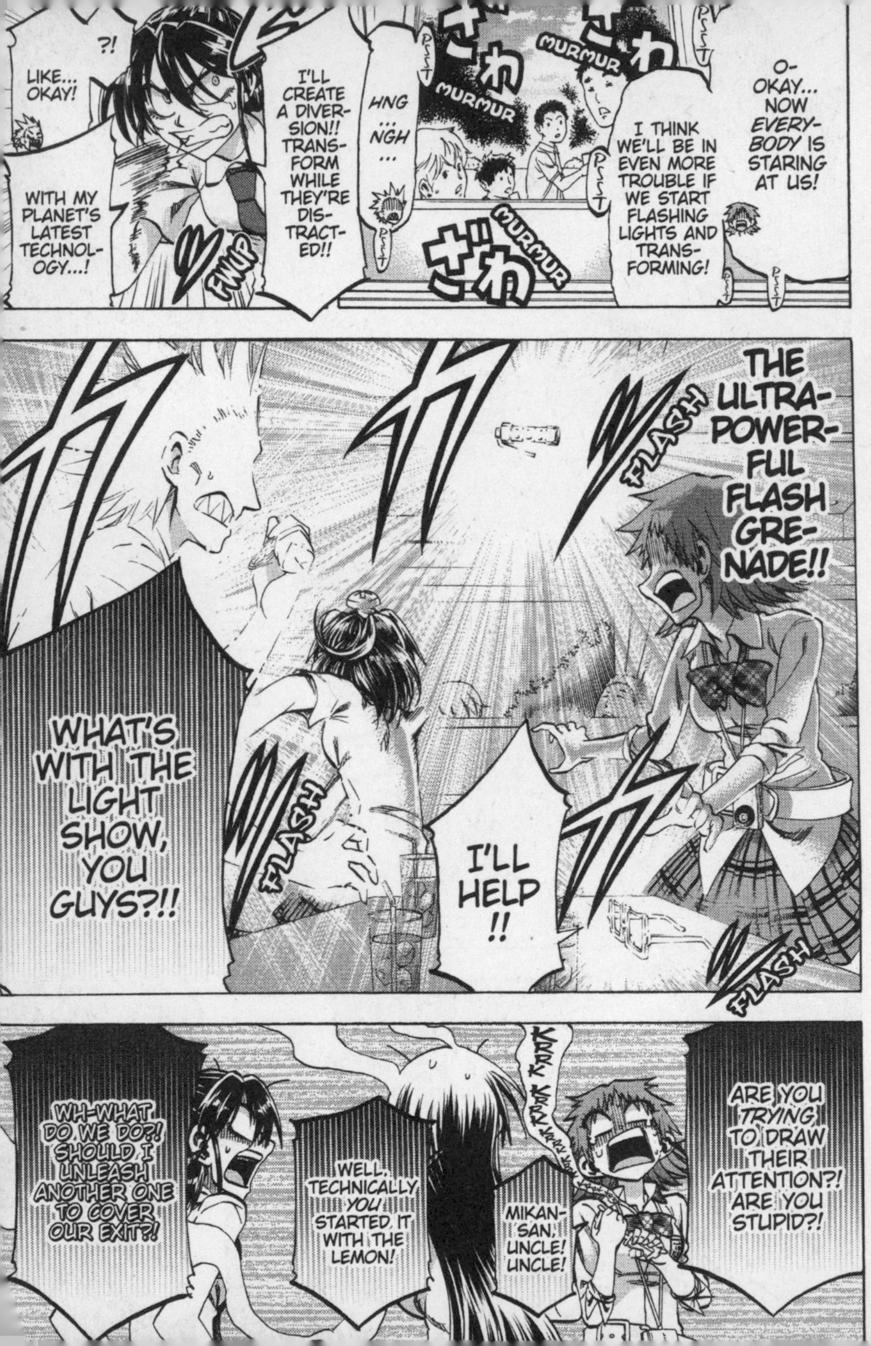
O-OKAY... NOW EVERYBODY IS STARING AT US!
PSST
I THINK WE'LL BE IN EVEN MORE TROUBLE IF WE START FLASHING LIGHTS AND TRANSFORMING!
MURMUR
MURMUR
MURMUR
HNG ...NGH ...
I'LL CREATE A DIVERSION!! TRANSFORM WHILE THEY'RE DISTRACTED!!
?!
LIKE... OKAY!
WITH MY PLANET'S LATEST TECHNOLOGY...!
FWUP
THE ULTRA-POWERFUL FLASH GRENADE!!
FLASH
FLASH
I'LL HELP!!
FLASH
WHAT'S WITH THE LIGHT SHOW, YOU GUYS?!!
ARE YOU TRYING TO DRAW THEIR ATTENTION?! ARE YOU STUPID?!
KRRK KRRK
MIKAN-SAN, UNCLE! UNCLE!
WELL, TECHNICALLY YOU STARTED IT WITH THE LEMON!
WH-WHAT DO WE DO?! SHOULD I UNLEASH ANOTHER ONE TO COVER OUR EXIT?!

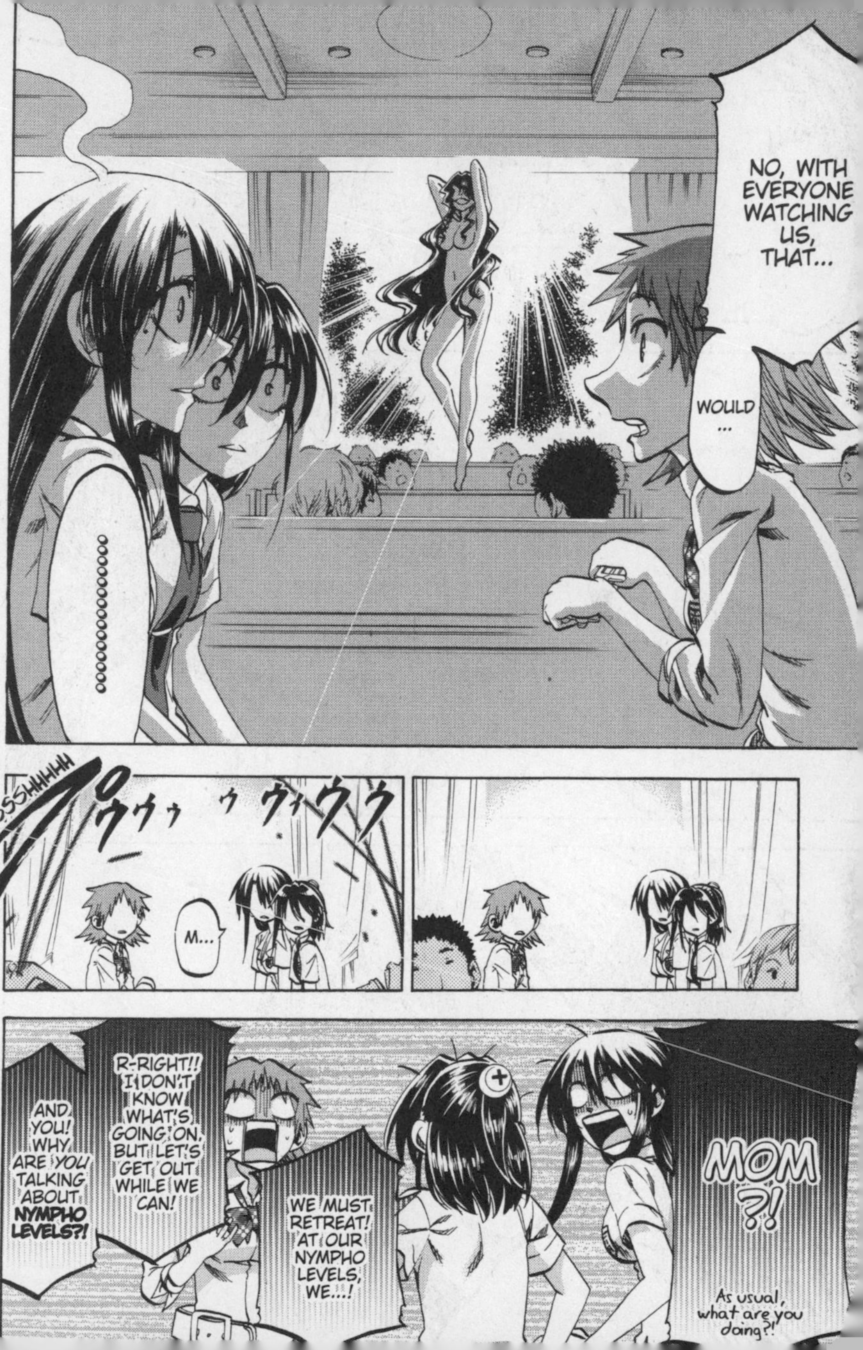
NO, WITH EVERYONE WATCHING US, THAT...
WOULD ...
OOOOOOOOOOOOOOOO
PSSSHHHH
M...
MOM ?!
As usual, what are you doing?!
WE MUST RETREAT! AT OUR NYMPHO LEVELS, WE...!
R-RIGHT!! I DON'T KNOW WHAT'S GOING ON, BUT LET'S GET OUT WHILE WE CAN!
AND YOU! WHY ARE YOU TALKING ABOUT NYMPHO LEVELS?!

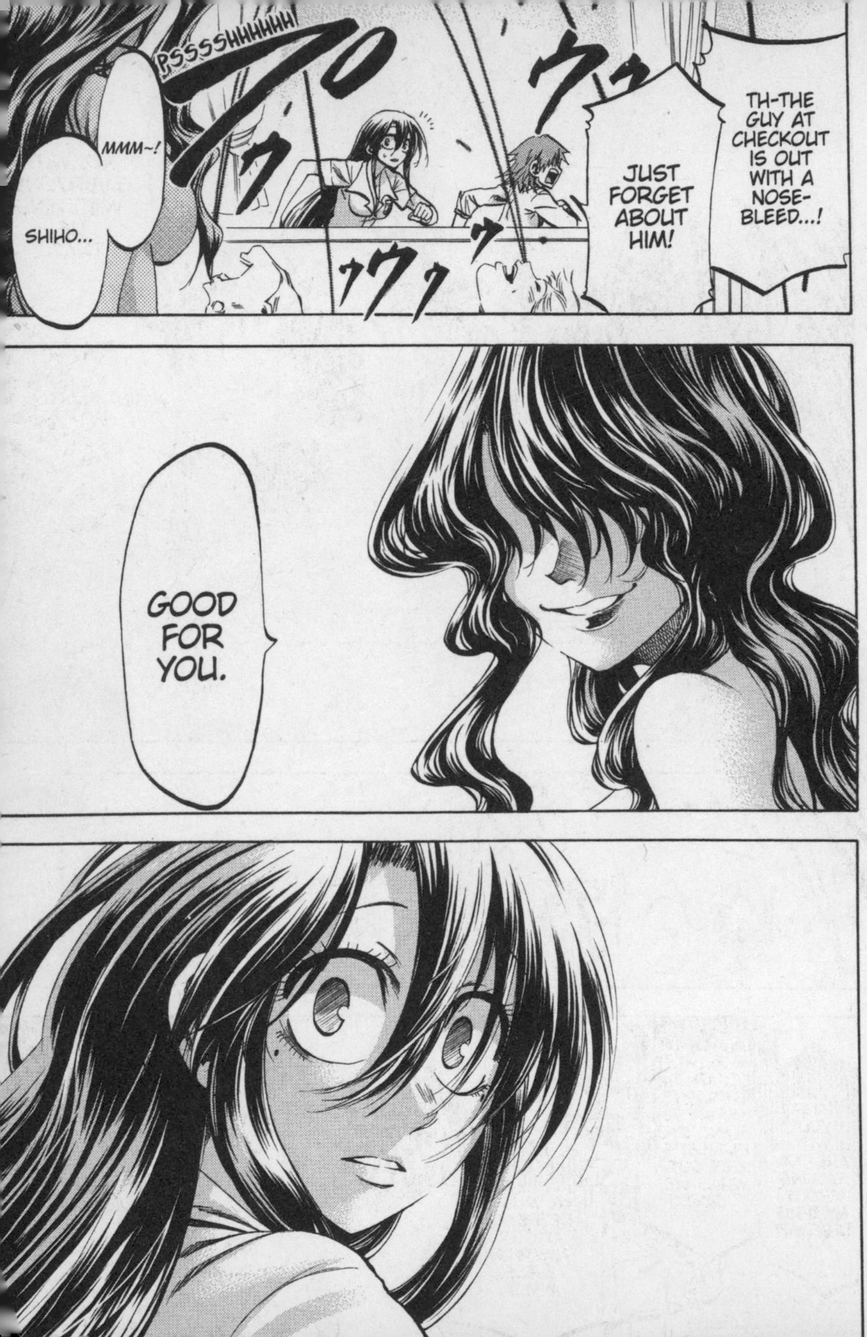
TH-THE GUY AT CHECKOUT IS OUT WITH A NOSE-BLEED...!
JUST FORGET ABOUT HIM!
PSSSSHHHHHH
MMM~!
SHIHO...
GOOD FOR YOU.

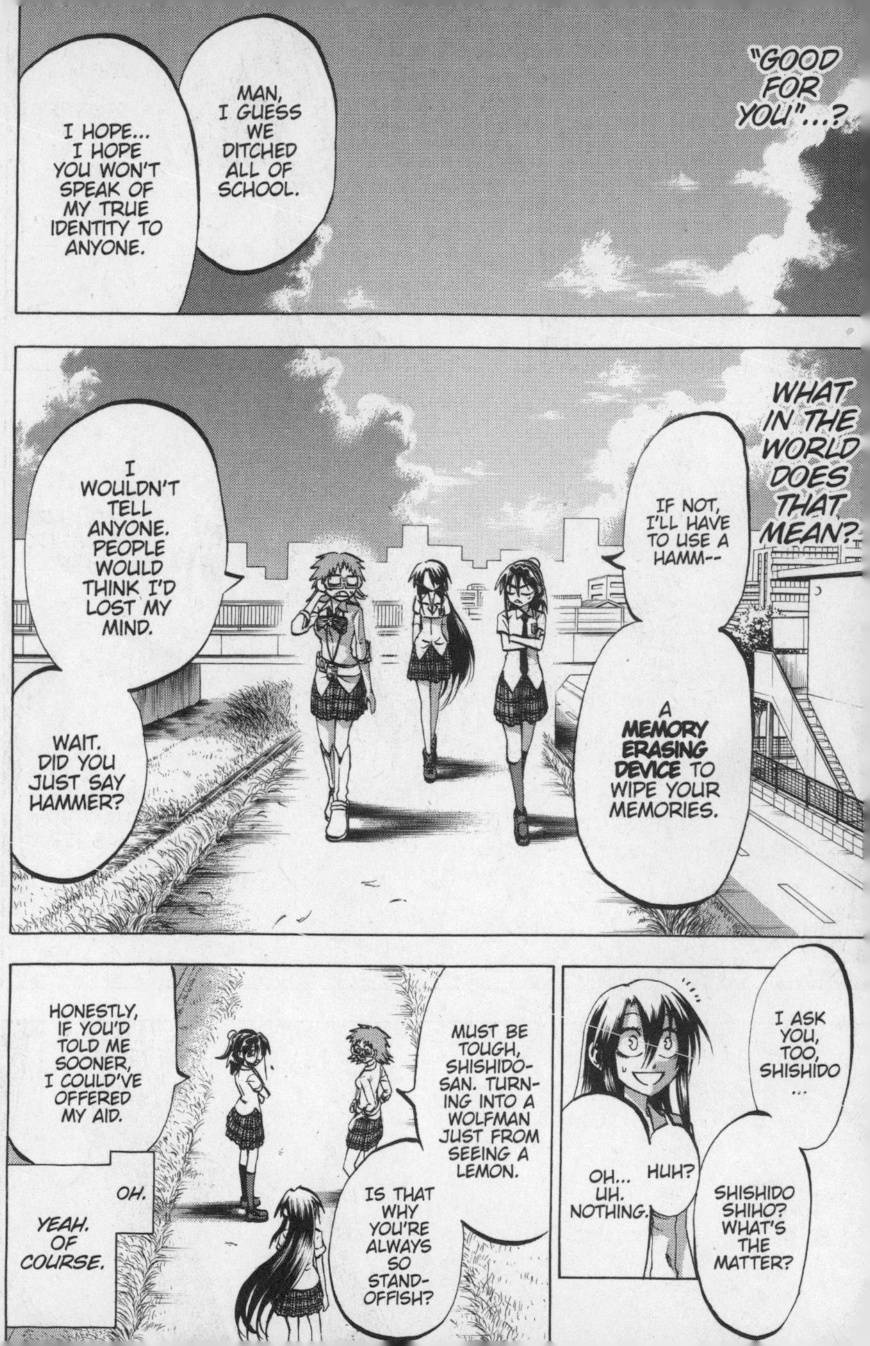

"GOOD FOR YOU"...?
MAN, I GUESS WE DITCHED ALL OF SCHOOL.
I HOPE... I HOPE YOU WON'T SPEAK OF MY TRUE IDENTITY TO ANYONE.
WHAT IN THE WORLD DOES THAT MEAN?
IF NOT, I'LL HAVE TO USE A HAMM--
A **MEMORY ERASING DEVICE** TO WIPE YOUR MEMORIES.
I WOULDN'T TELL ANYONE. PEOPLE WOULD THINK I'D LOST MY MIND.
WAIT. DID YOU JUST SAY HAMMER?
I ASK YOU, TOO, SHISHIDO ...
SHISHIDO SHIHO? WHAT'S THE MATTER?
HUH?
OH... UH. NOTHING.
MUST BE TOUGH, SHISHIDO-SAN. TURNING INTO A WOLFMAN JUST FROM SEEING A LEMON.
HONESTLY, IF YOU'D TOLD ME SOONER, I COULD'VE OFFERED MY AID.
IS THAT WHY YOU'RE ALWAYS SO STAND-OFFISH?
OH.
YEAH. OF COURSE.

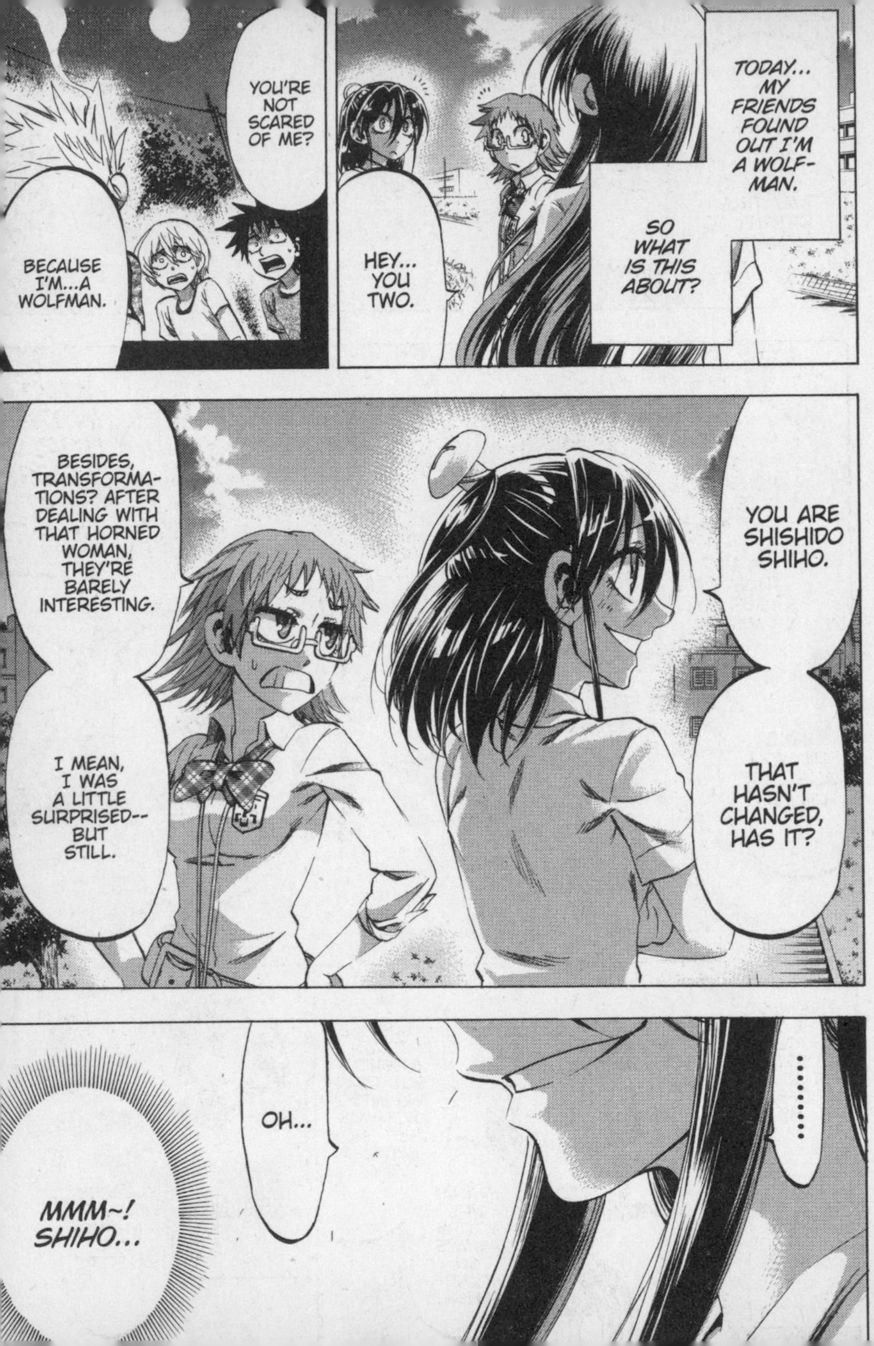
TODAY... MY FRIENDS FOUND OUT I'M A WOLF-MAN.
SO WHAT IS THIS ABOUT?
HEY... YOU TWO.
YOU'RE NOT SCARED OF ME?
BECAUSE I'M...A WOLFMAN.
YOU ARE SHISHIDO SHIHO.
THAT HASN'T CHANGED, HAS IT?
BESIDES, TRANSFORMATIONS? AFTER DEALING WITH THAT HORNED WOMAN, THEY'RE BARELY INTERESTING.
I MEAN, I WAS A LITTLE SURPRISED--BUT STILL.
......
OH...
MMM~! SHIHO...

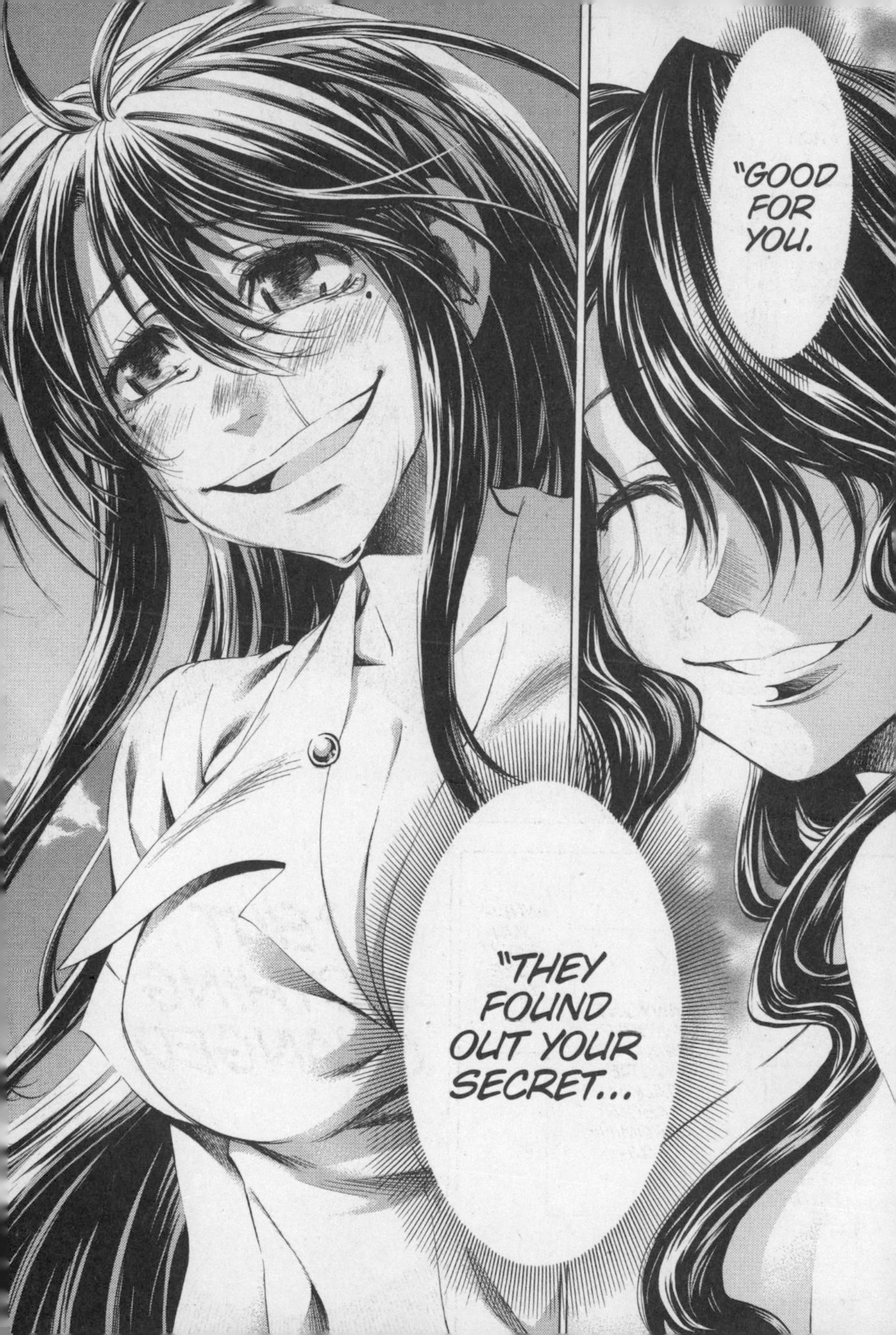
"GOOD FOR YOU.
"THEY FOUND OUT YOUR SECRET...

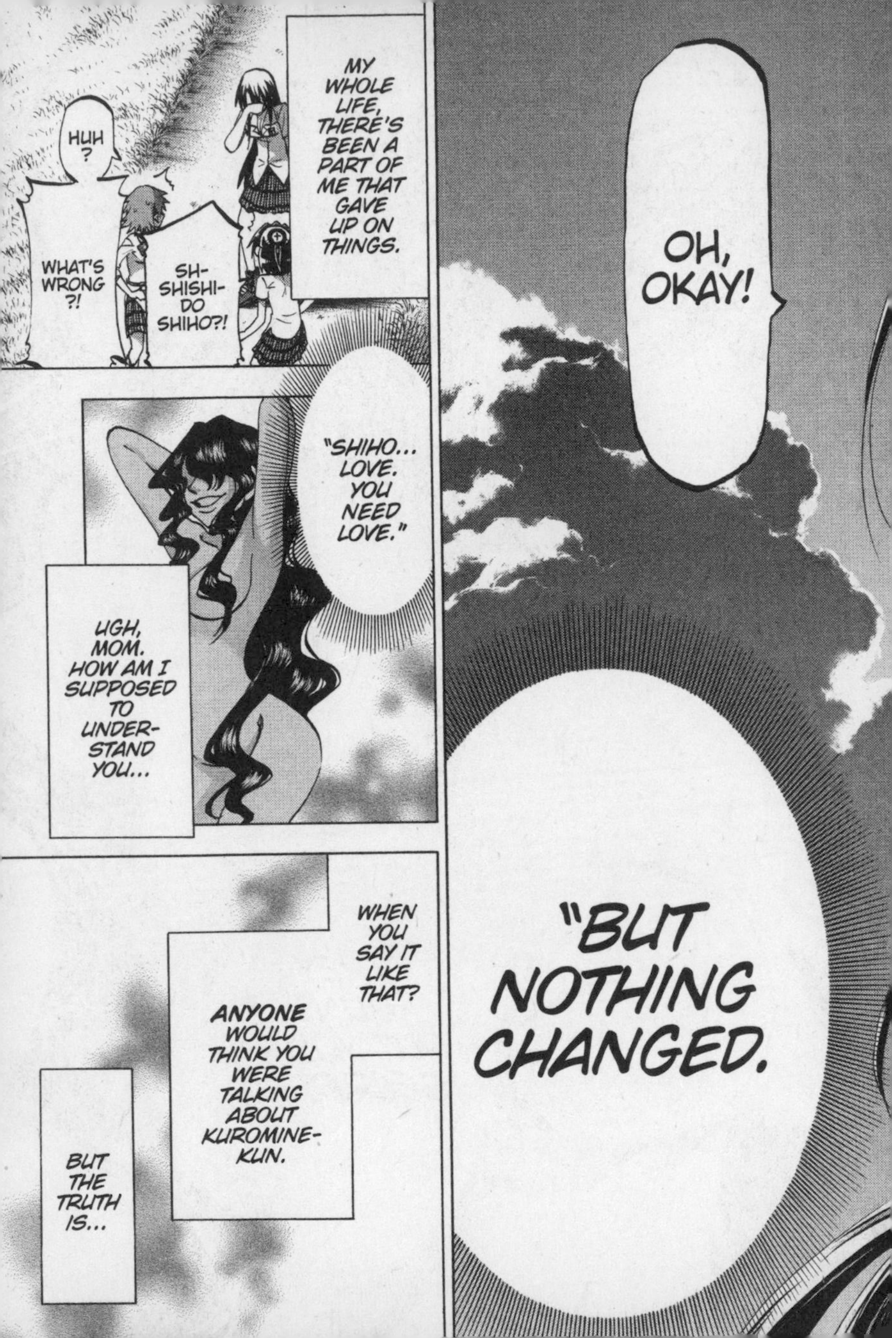
OH, OKAY!
"BUT NOTHING CHANGED.
MY WHOLE LIFE, THERE'S BEEN A PART OF ME THAT GAVE UP ON THINGS.
HUH?
SH-SHISHIDO SHIHO?!
WHAT'S WRONG?!
"SHIHO... LOVE. YOU NEED LOVE."
UGH, MOM. HOW AM I SUPPOSED TO UNDER-STAND YOU...
WHEN YOU SAY IT LIKE THAT?
ANYONE WOULD THINK YOU WERE TALKING ABOUT KUROMINE-KUN.
BUT THE TRUTH IS...

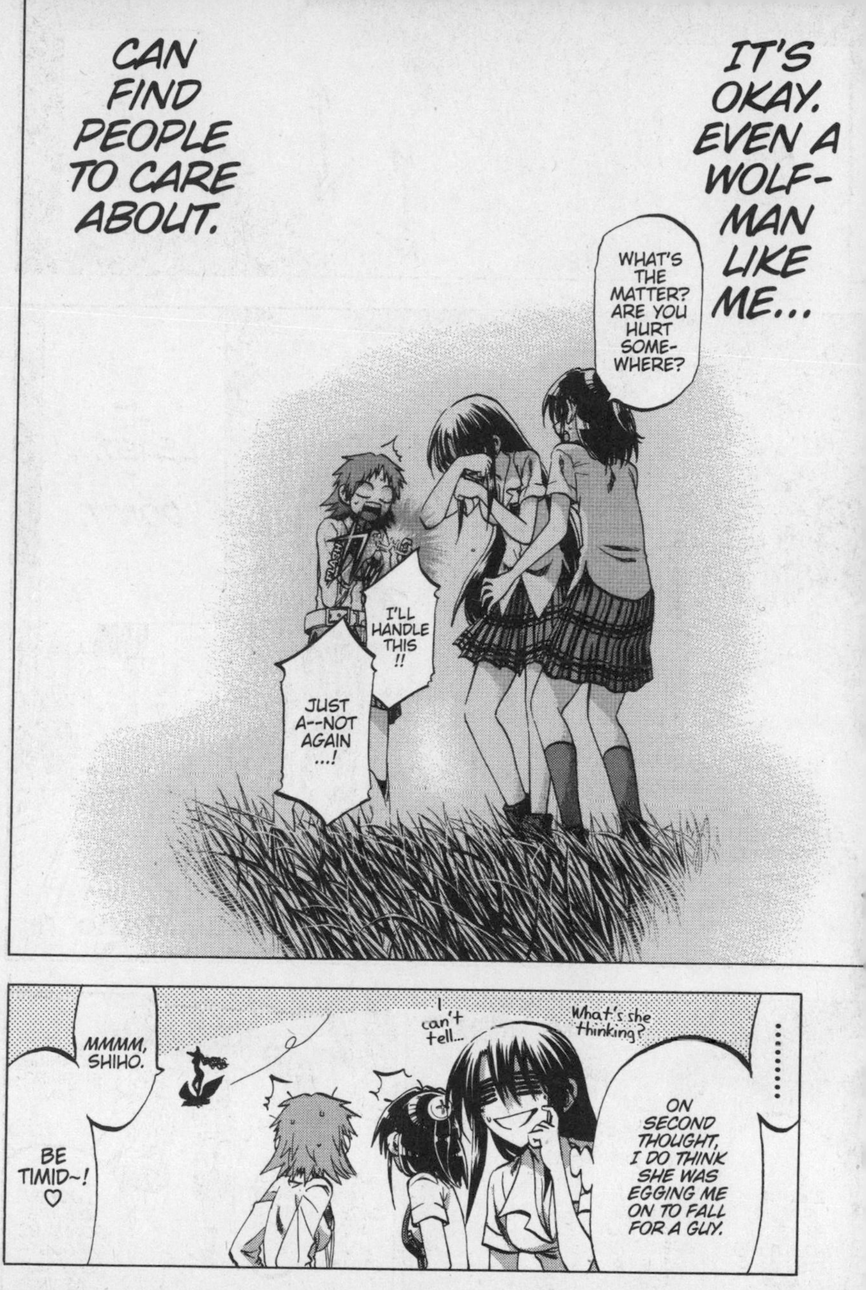
IT'S OKAY. EVEN A WOLF-MAN LIKE ME...
WHAT'S THE MATTER? ARE YOU HURT SOME-WHERE?
CAN FIND PEOPLE TO CARE ABOUT.
I'LL HANDLE THIS !!
JUST A--NOT AGAIN ...!
....
ON SECOND THOUGHT, I DO THINK SHE WAS EGGING ME ON TO FALL FOR A GUY.
What's she thinking?
I can't tell...
MMMM, SHIHO.
BE TIMID~! ♡

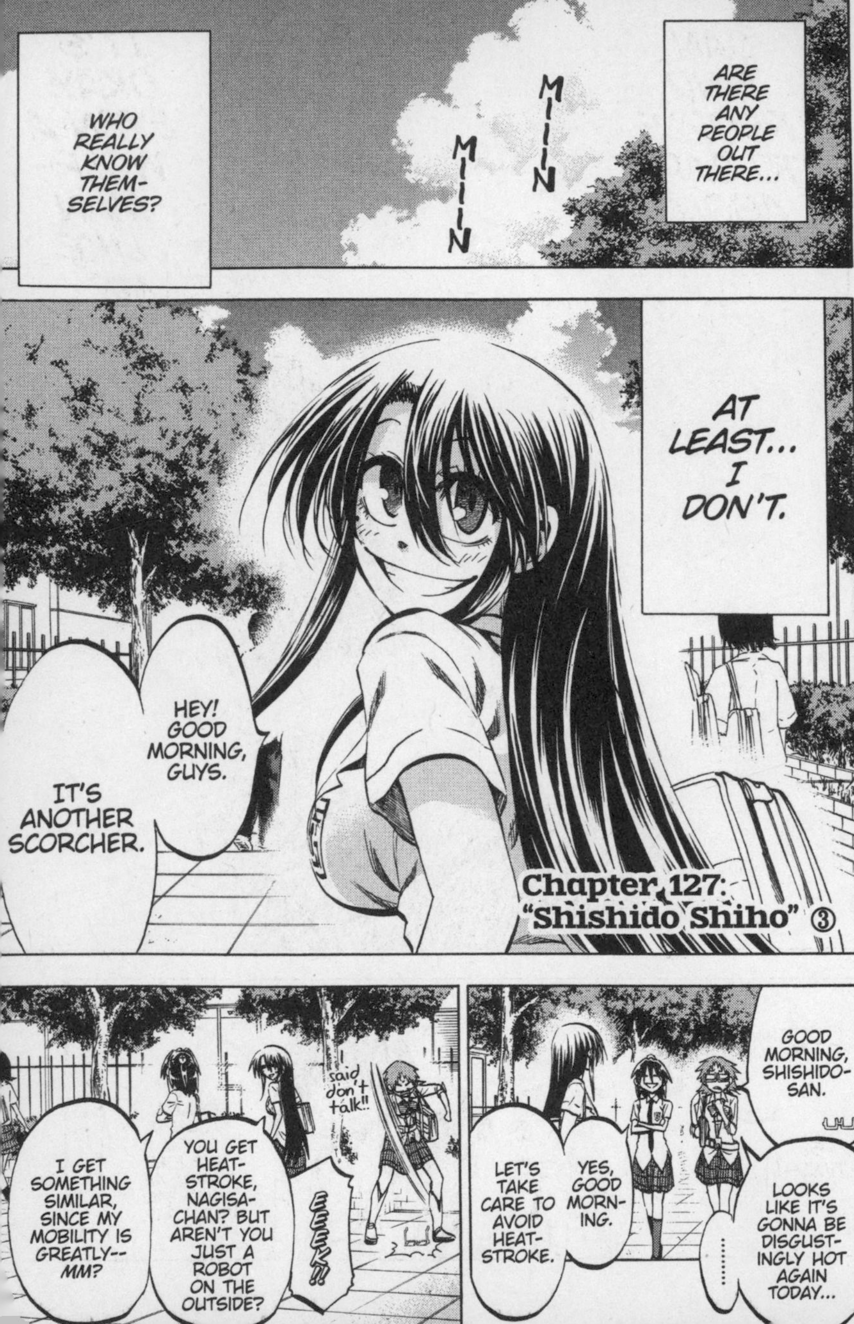
ARE THERE ANY PEOPLE OUT THERE...
MIIIN
MIIIN
WHO REALLY KNOW THEM-SELVES?
AT LEAST... I DON'T.
HEY! GOOD MORNING, GUYS.
IT'S ANOTHER SCORCHER.
Chapter 127: "Shishido Shiho" ③
GOOD MORNING, SHISHIDO-SAN.
LOOKS LIKE IT'S GONNA BE DISGUST-INGLY HOT AGAIN TODAY...
......
YES, GOOD MORN-ING.
LET'S TAKE CARE TO AVOID HEAT-STROKE.
said don't talk!!
EEEK!!
YOU GET HEAT-STROKE, NAGISA-CHAN? BUT AREN'T YOU JUST A ROBOT ON THE OUTSIDE?
I GET SOMETHING SIMILAR, SINCE MY MOBILITY IS GREATLY-- MM?

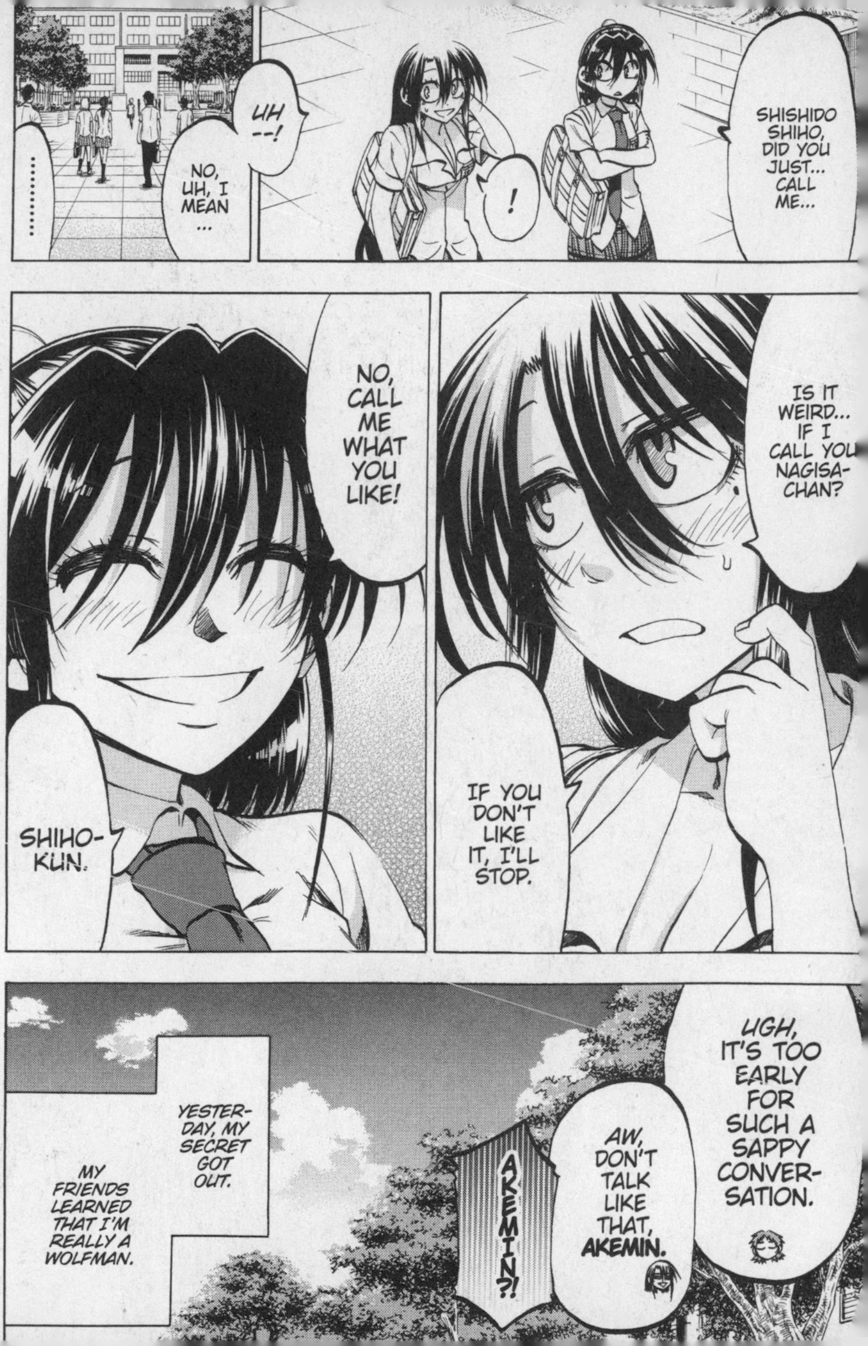
SHISHIDO SHIHO, DID YOU JUST... CALL ME...
!
UH --!
NO, UH, I MEAN ...
......
IS IT WEIRD... IF I CALL YOU NAGISA-CHAN?
IF YOU DON'T LIKE IT, I'LL STOP.
NO, CALL ME WHAT YOU LIKE!
SHIHO-KUN.
UGH, IT'S TOO EARLY FOR SUCH A SAPPY CONVERSATION.
AW, DON'T TALK LIKE THAT, AKEMIN.
AKEMIN?!
YESTER-DAY, MY SECRET GOT OUT.
MY FRIENDS LEARNED THAT I'M REALLY A WOLFMAN.

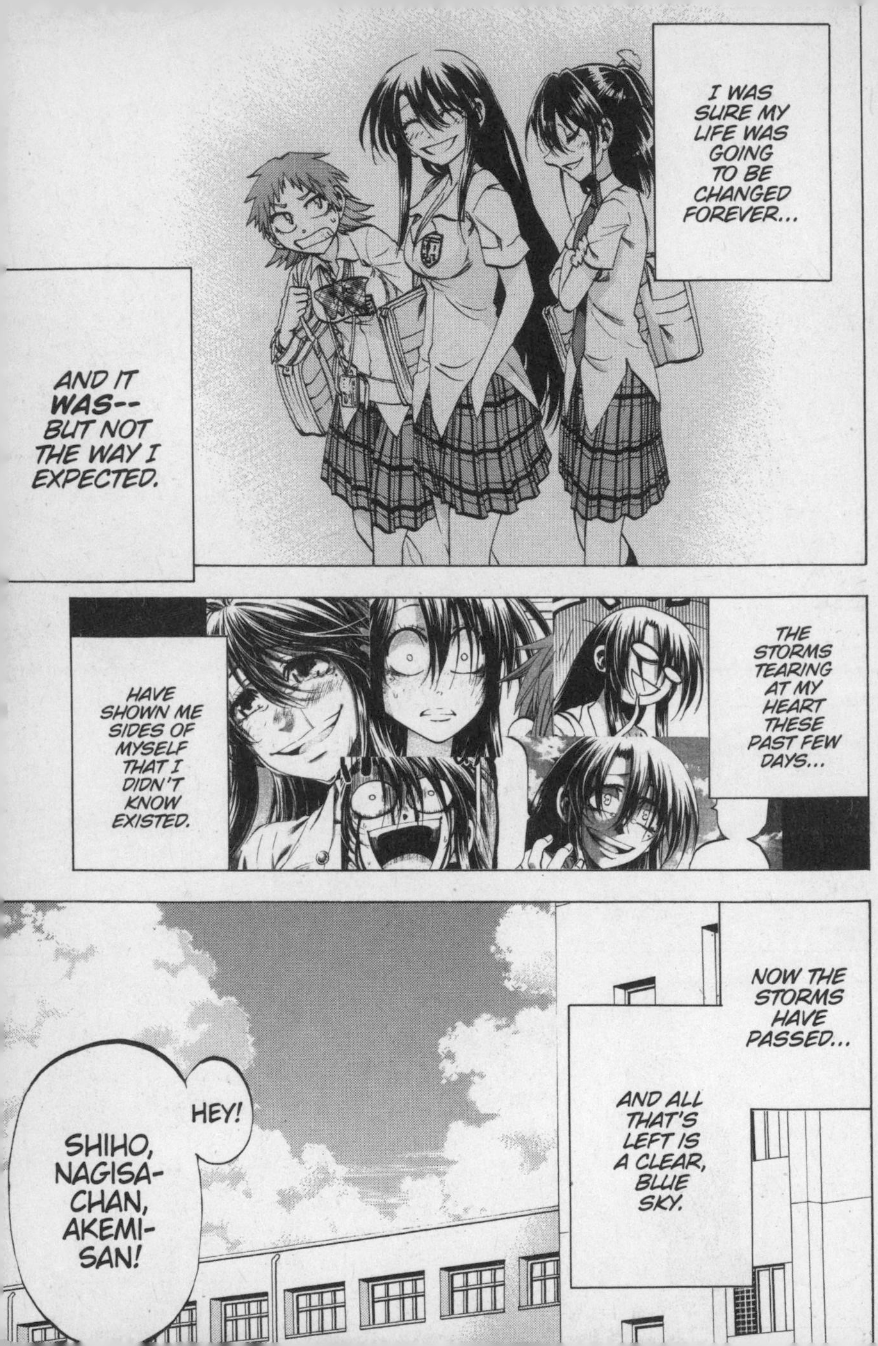
I WAS SURE MY LIFE WAS GOING TO BE CHANGED FOREVER...
AND IT WAS-- BUT NOT THE WAY I EXPECTED.
THE STORMS TEARING AT MY HEART THESE PAST FEW DAYS...
HAVE SHOWN ME SIDES OF MYSELF THAT I DIDN'T KNOW EXISTED.
NOW THE STORMS HAVE PASSED...
AND ALL THAT'S LEFT IS A CLEAR, BLUE SKY.
HEY! SHIHO, NAGISA-CHAN, AKEMI-SAN!

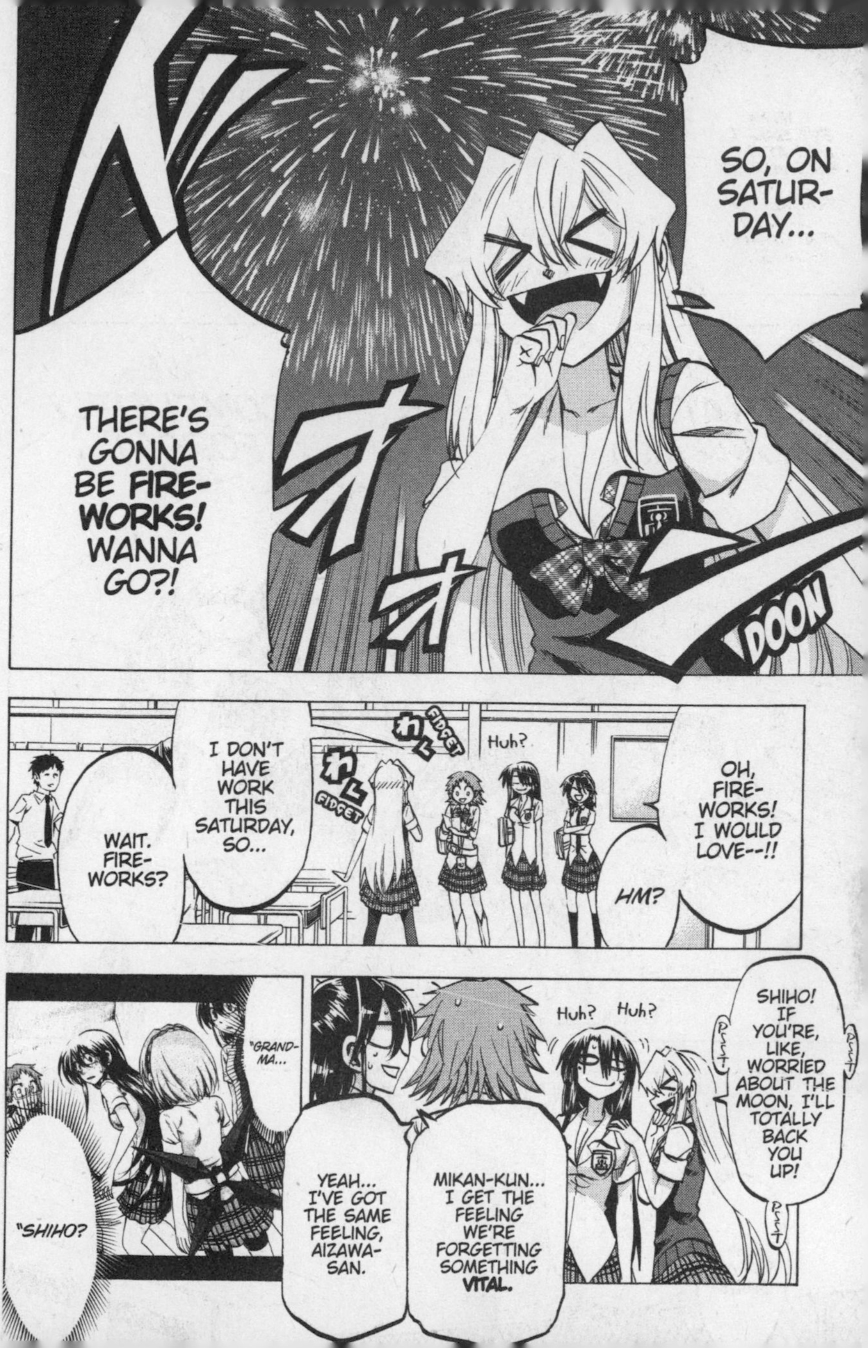
SO, ON SATURDAY...
THERE'S GONNA BE FIREWORKS! WANNA GO?!
DOON
OH, FIREWORKS! I WOULD LOVE--!!
HM?
Huh?
FIDGET
FIDGET
I DON'T HAVE WORK THIS SATURDAY, SO...
WAIT. FIREWORKS?
SHIHO! IF YOU'RE, LIKE, WORRIED ABOUT THE MOON, I'LL TOTALLY BACK YOU UP!
PSST
PSST
PSST
Huh? Huh?
MIKAN-KUN... I GET THE FEELING WE'RE FORGETTING SOMETHING VITAL.
YEAH... I'VE GOT THE SAME FEELING, AIZAWA-SAN.
"GRANDMA...
"SHIHO?

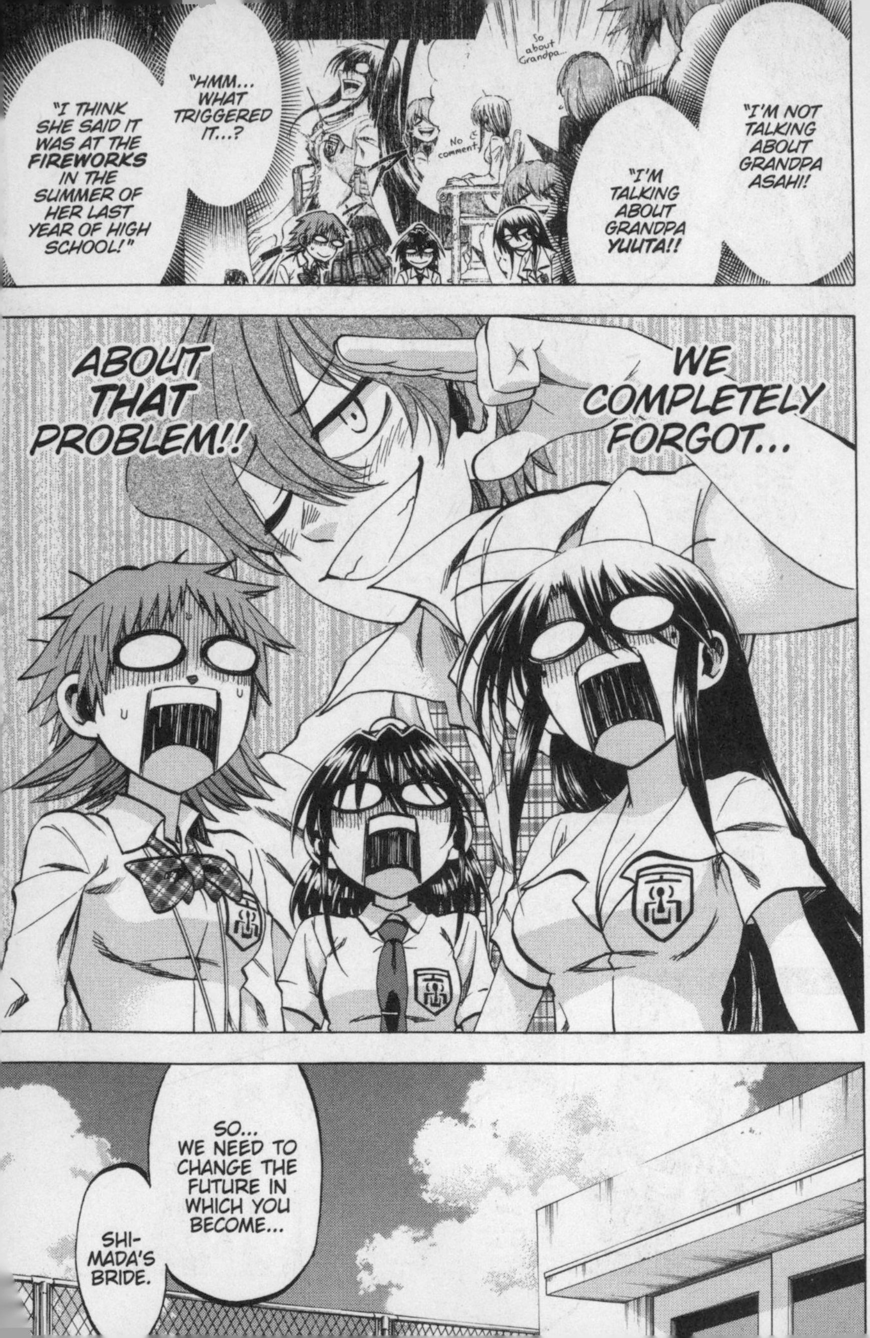
"I'M NOT TALKING ABOUT GRANDPA ASAHI!!
"I'M TALKING ABOUT GRANDPA YUUTA!!
So about Grandpa...
No comment
"HMM... WHAT TRIGGERED IT...?
"I THINK SHE SAID IT WAS AT THE FIREWORKS IN THE SUMMER OF HER LAST YEAR OF HIGH SCHOOL!"
WE COMPLETELY FORGOT...
ABOUT THAT PROBLEM!!
SO... WE NEED TO CHANGE THE FUTURE IN WHICH YOU BECOME...
SHI-MADA'S BRIDE.

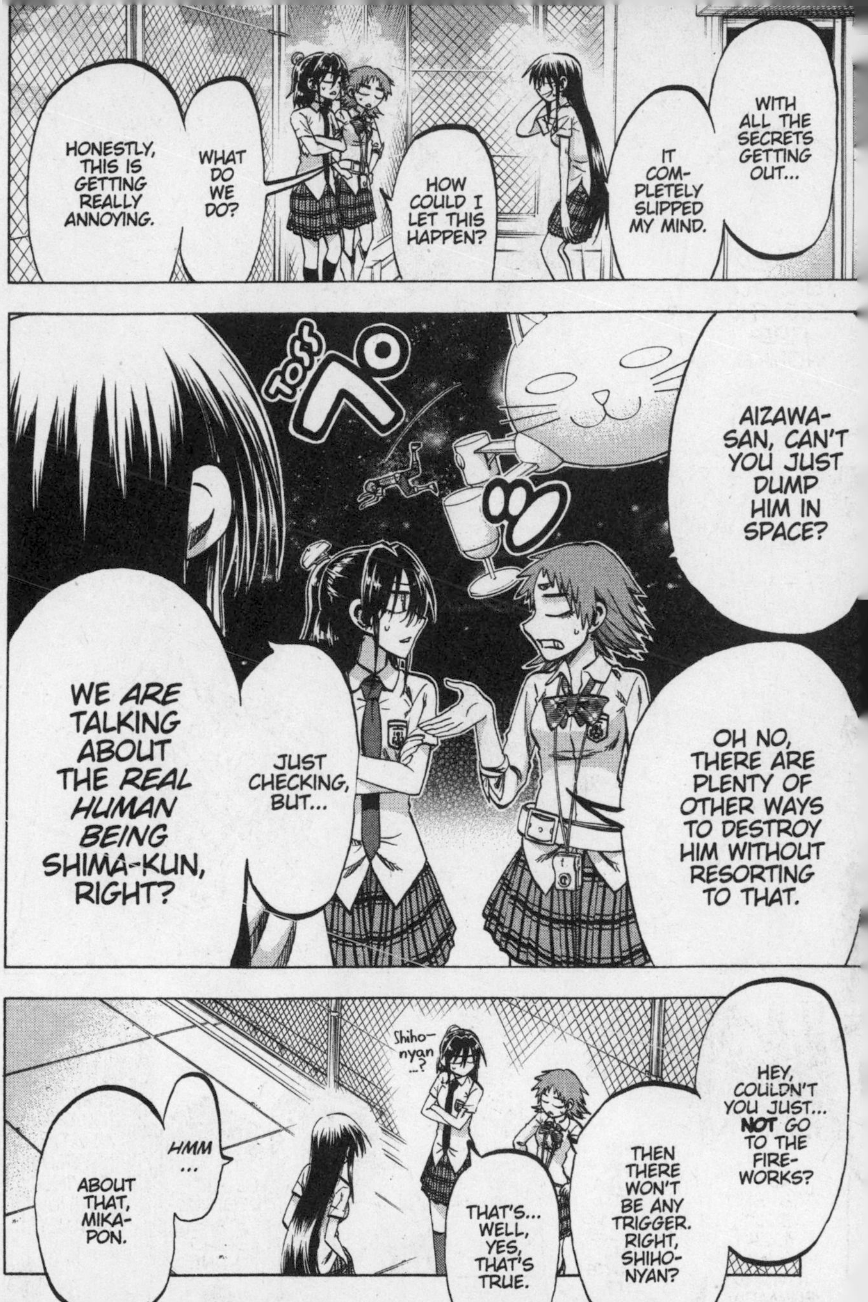

WITH ALL THE SECRETS GETTING OUT...
IT COMPLETELY SLIPPED MY MIND.
HOW COULD I LET THIS HAPPEN?
WHAT DO WE DO?
HONESTLY, THIS IS GETTING REALLY ANNOYING.
AIZAWA-SAN, CAN'T YOU JUST DUMP HIM IN SPACE?
TOSS
ペ
OH NO, THERE ARE PLENTY OF OTHER WAYS TO DESTROY HIM WITHOUT RESORTING TO THAT.
JUST CHECKING, BUT...
WE *ARE* TALKING ABOUT THE *REAL HUMAN BEING* SHIMA-KUN, RIGHT?
HEY, COULDN'T YOU JUST... **NOT** GO TO THE FIRE-WORKS?
THEN THERE WON'T BE ANY TRIGGER. RIGHT, SHIHO-NYAN?
Shiho-nyan...?
THAT'S... WELL, YES, THAT'S TRUE.
HMM...
ABOUT THAT, MIKA-PON.

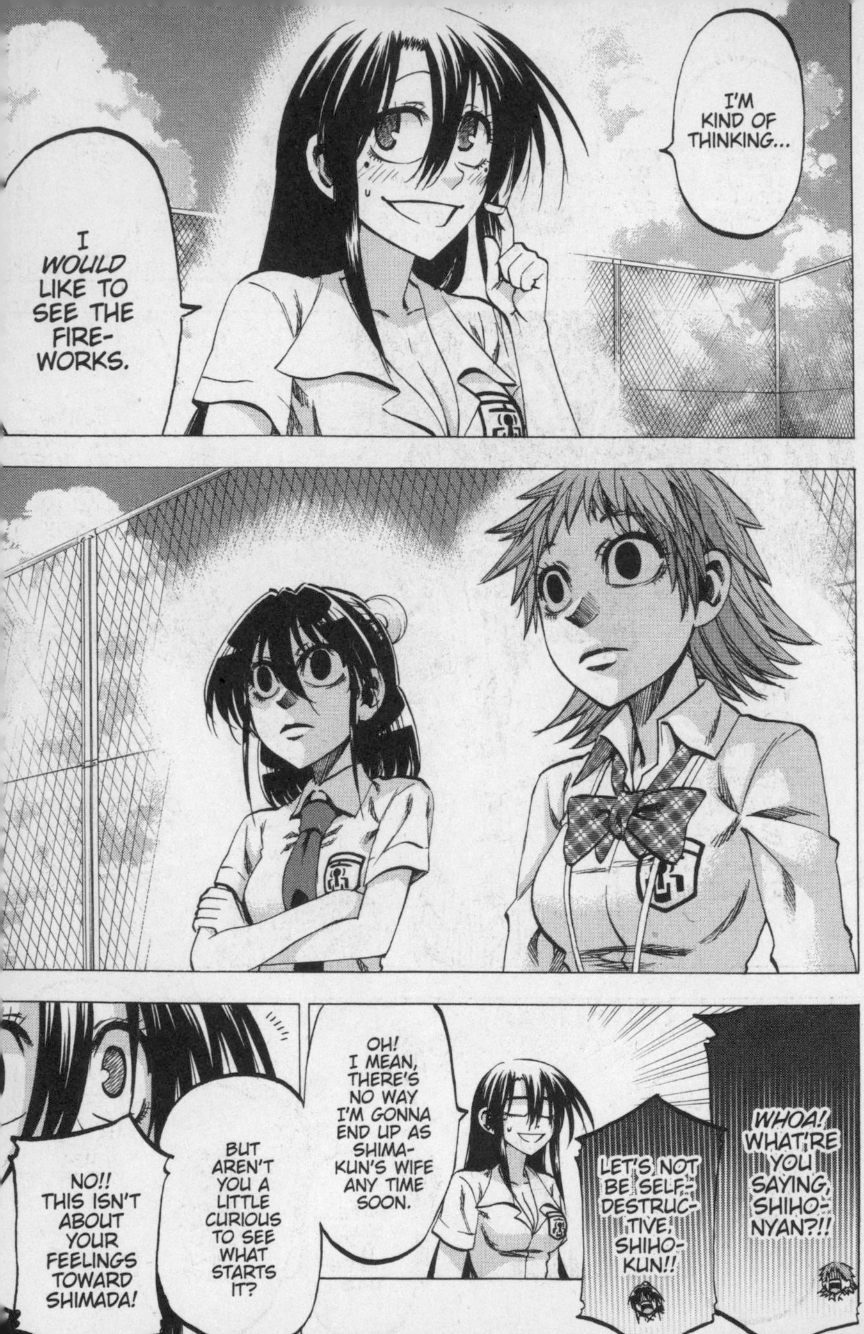
I'M KIND OF THINKING...
I *WOULD* LIKE TO SEE THE FIRE-WORKS.
WHOA! WHAT'RE YOU SAYING, SHIHO-NYAN?!!
LET'S NOT BE SELF-DESTRUCTIVE, SHIHO-KUN!!
OH! I MEAN, THERE'S NO WAY I'M GONNA END UP AS SHIMA-KUN'S WIFE ANY TIME SOON.
BUT AREN'T YOU A LITTLE CURIOUS TO SEE WHAT STARTS IT?
NO!! THIS ISN'T ABOUT YOUR FEELINGS TOWARD SHIMADA!

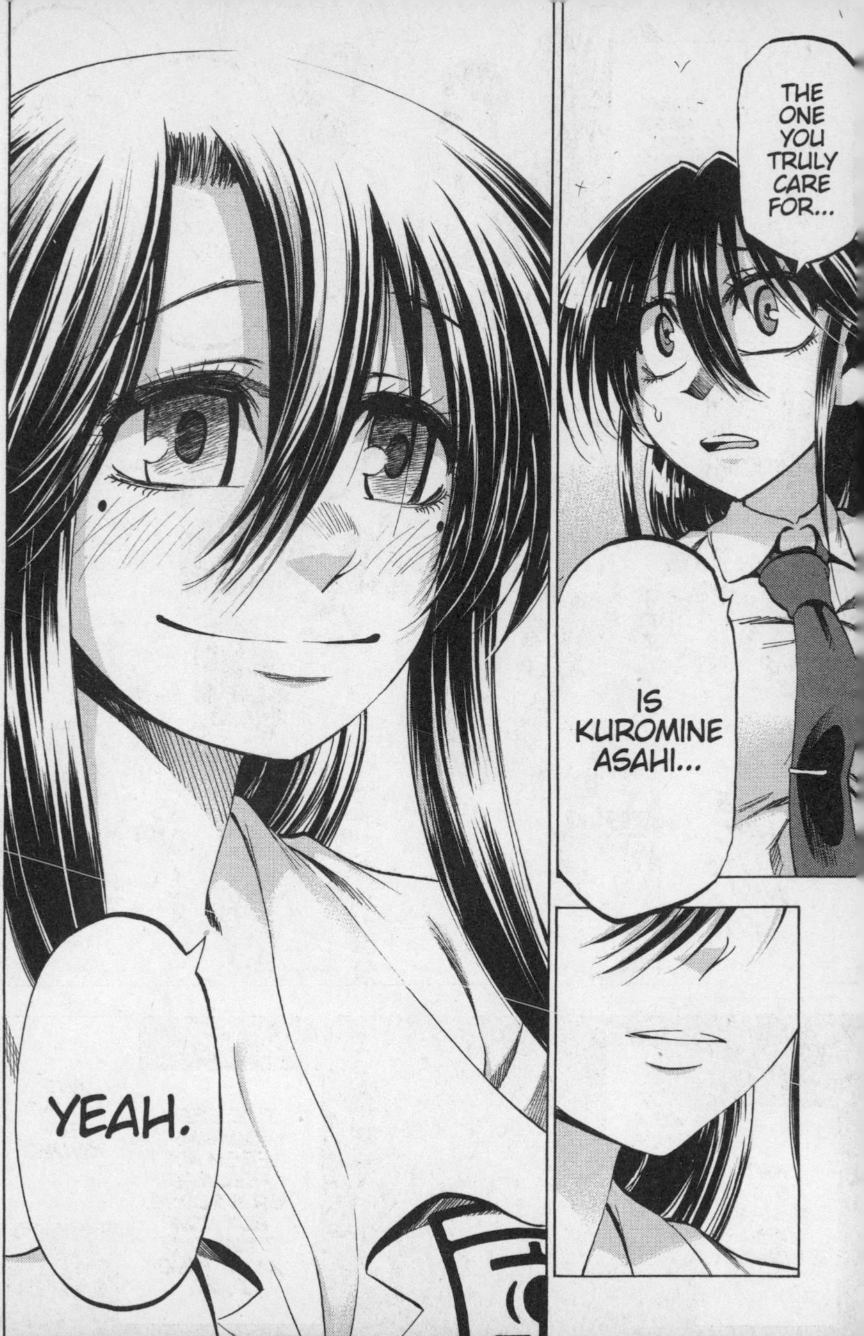
THE ONE YOU TRULY CARE FOR...
IS KUROMINE ASAHI...
YEAH.

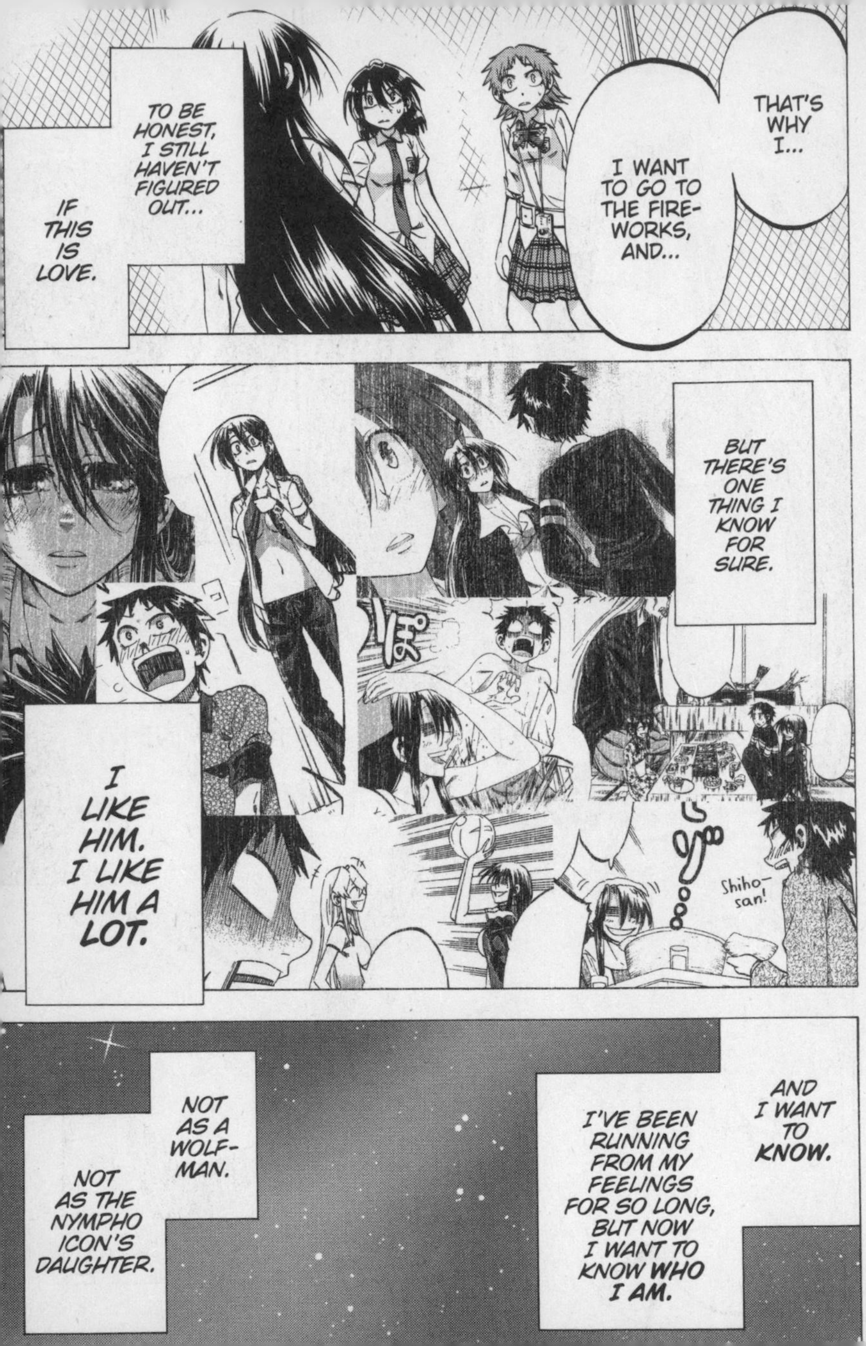
THAT'S WHY I...
I WANT TO GO TO THE FIRE-WORKS, AND...
TO BE HONEST, I STILL HAVEN'T FIGURED OUT...
IF THIS IS LOVE.
BUT THERE'S ONE THING I KNOW FOR SURE.
Shiho-san!
I LIKE HIM. I LIKE HIM A LOT.
AND I WANT TO KNOW.
I'VE BEEN RUNNING FROM MY FEELINGS FOR SO LONG, BUT NOW I WANT TO KNOW WHO I AM.
NOT AS A WOLF-MAN.
NOT AS THE NYMPHO ICON'S DAUGHTER.

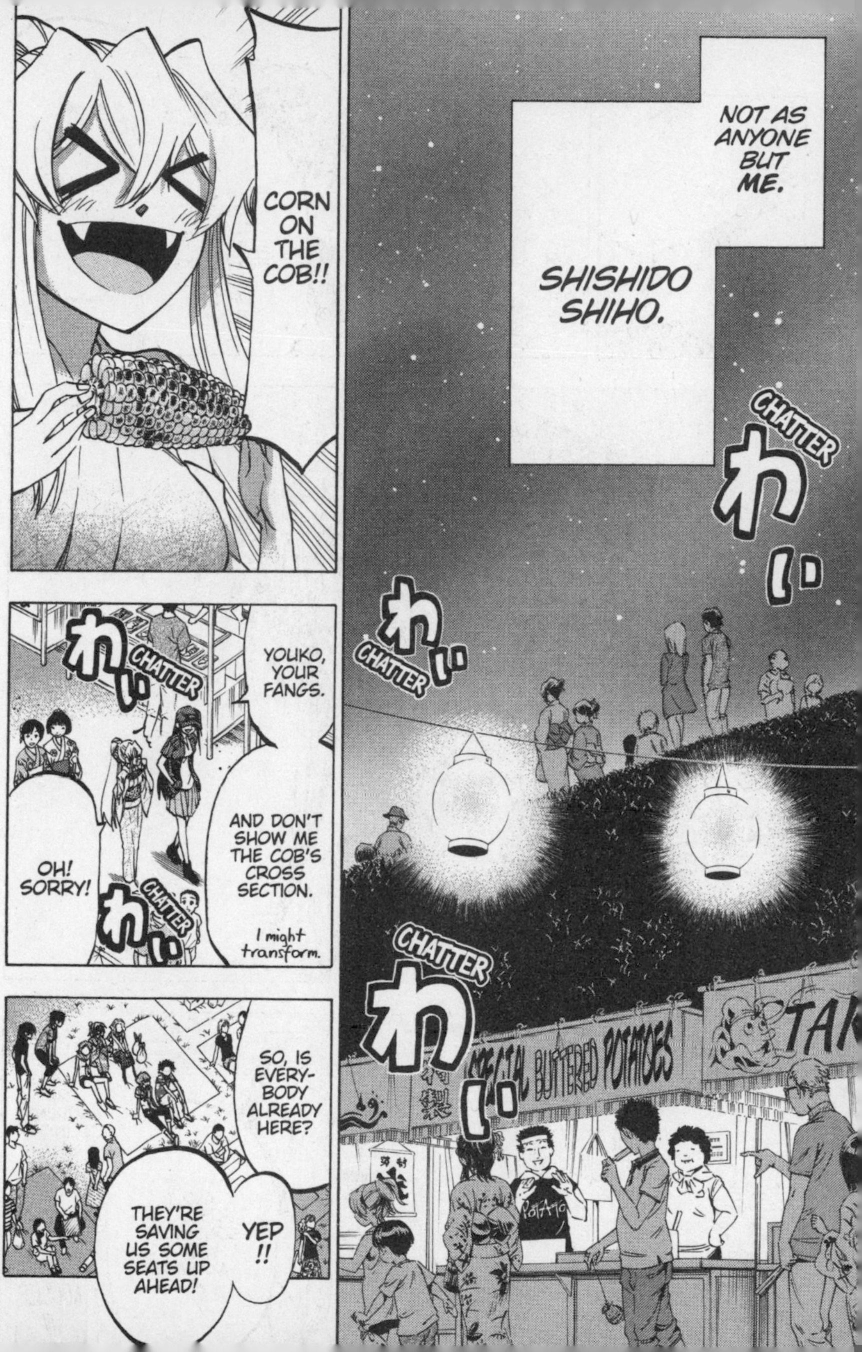
NOT AS ANYONE BUT ME.
SHISHIDO SHIHO.
わい CHATTER
わい CHATTER
わい CHATTER
BUTTERED POTATOES
CORN ON THE COB!!
わい CHATTER
YOUKO, YOUR FANGS.
AND DON'T SHOW ME THE COB'S CROSS SECTION.
I might transform.
OH! SORRY!
わい CHATTER
SO, IS EVERY-BODY ALREADY HERE?
YEP!!
THEY'RE SAVING US SOME SEATS UP AHEAD!

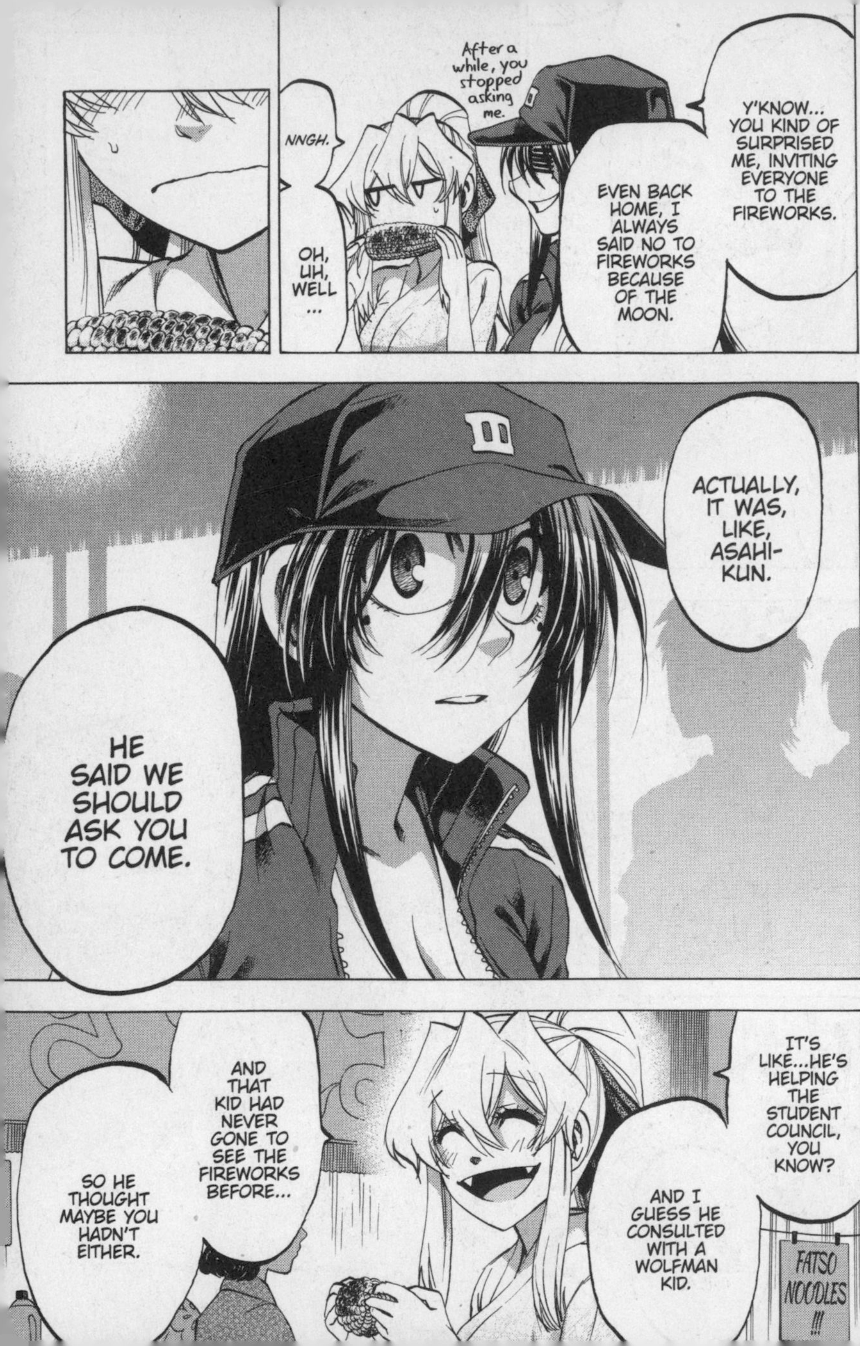
Y'KNOW... YOU KIND OF SURPRISED ME, INVITING EVERYONE TO THE FIREWORKS.
EVEN BACK HOME, I ALWAYS SAID NO TO FIREWORKS BECAUSE OF THE MOON.
After a while, you stopped asking me.
NNGH.
OH, UH, WELL ...
ACTUALLY, IT WAS, LIKE, ASAHI-KUN.
HE SAID WE SHOULD ASK YOU TO COME.
IT'S LIKE...HE'S HELPING THE STUDENT COUNCIL, YOU KNOW?
AND I GUESS HE CONSULTED WITH A WOLFMAN KID.
FATSO NOODLES !!!
AND THAT KID HAD NEVER GONE TO SEE THE FIREWORKS BEFORE...
SO HE THOUGHT MAYBE YOU HADN'T EITHER.

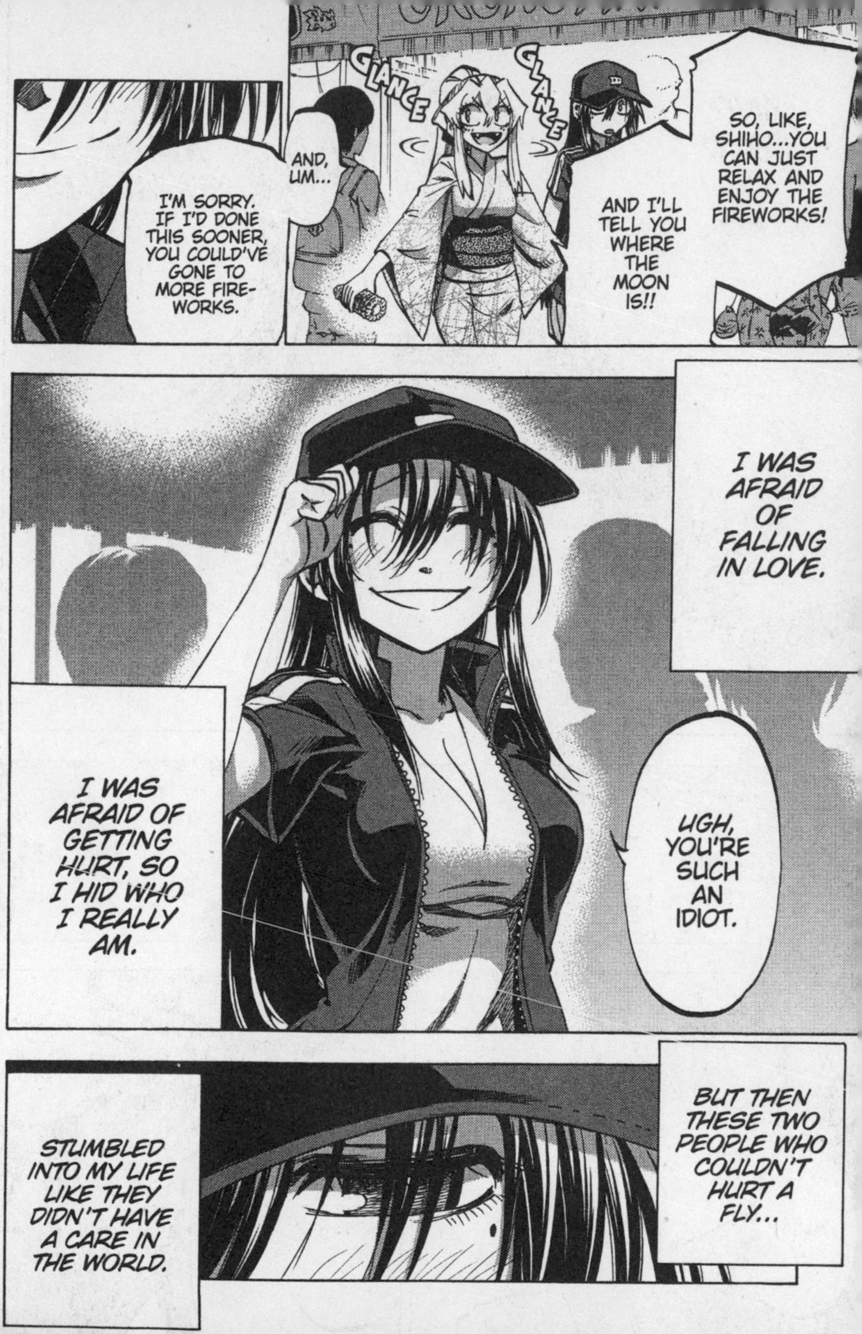
GLANCE
GLANCE
SO, LIKE, SHIHO...YOU CAN JUST RELAX AND ENJOY THE FIREWORKS!
AND I'LL TELL YOU WHERE THE MOON IS!!
AND, UM...
I'M SORRY. IF I'D DONE THIS SOONER, YOU COULD'VE GONE TO MORE FIRE-WORKS.
I WAS AFRAID OF FALLING IN LOVE.
UGH, YOU'RE SUCH AN IDIOT.
I WAS AFRAID OF GETTING HURT, SO I HID WHO I REALLY AM.
BUT THEN THESE TWO PEOPLE WHO COULDN'T HURT A FLY...
STUMBLED INTO MY LIFE LIKE THEY DIDN'T HAVE A CARE IN THE WORLD.

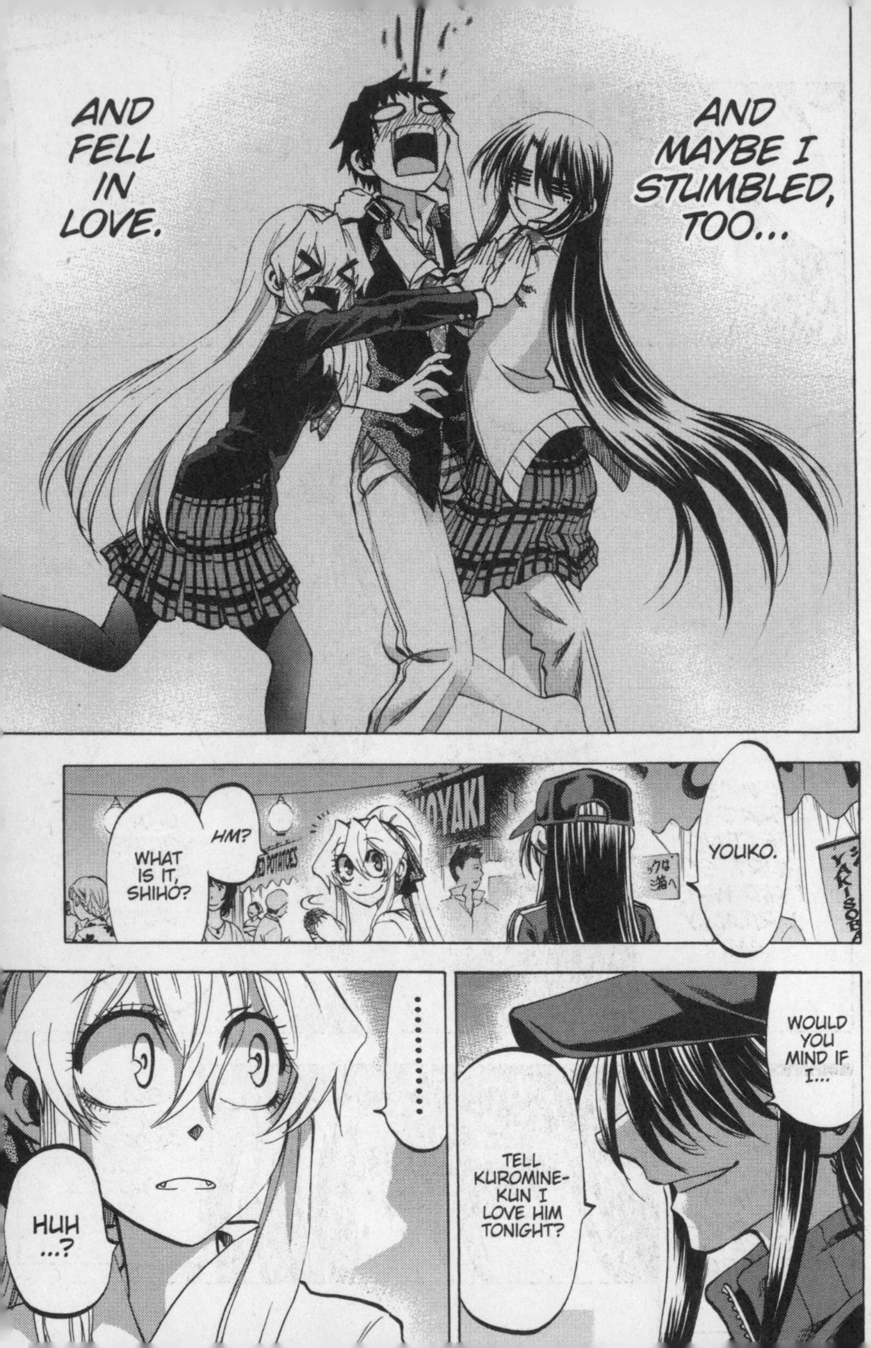
AND MAYBE I STUMBLED, TOO...
AND FELL IN LOVE.
YOUKO.
HM? WHAT IS IT, SHIHO?
WOULD YOU MIND IF I...
TELL KUROMINE-KUN I LOVE HIM TONIGHT?
....
HUH ...?

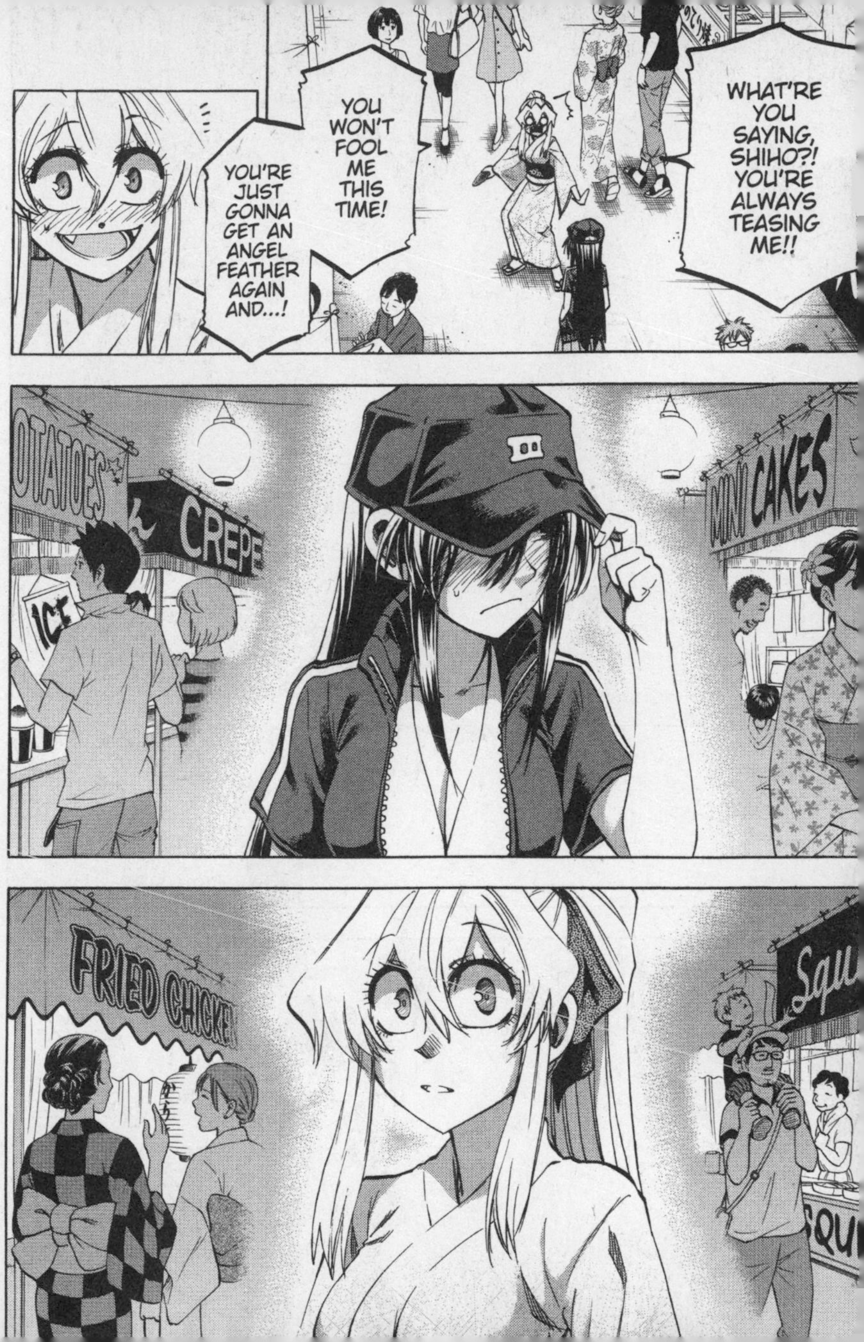
WHAT'RE YOU SAYING, SHIHO?! YOU'RE ALWAYS TEASING ME!!
YOU WON'T FOOL ME THIS TIME!
YOU'RE JUST GONNA GET AN ANGEL FEATHER AGAIN AND...!
MINI CAKES
CREPE
OTATOES
ICE
Squ
FRIED CHICKE
SQU

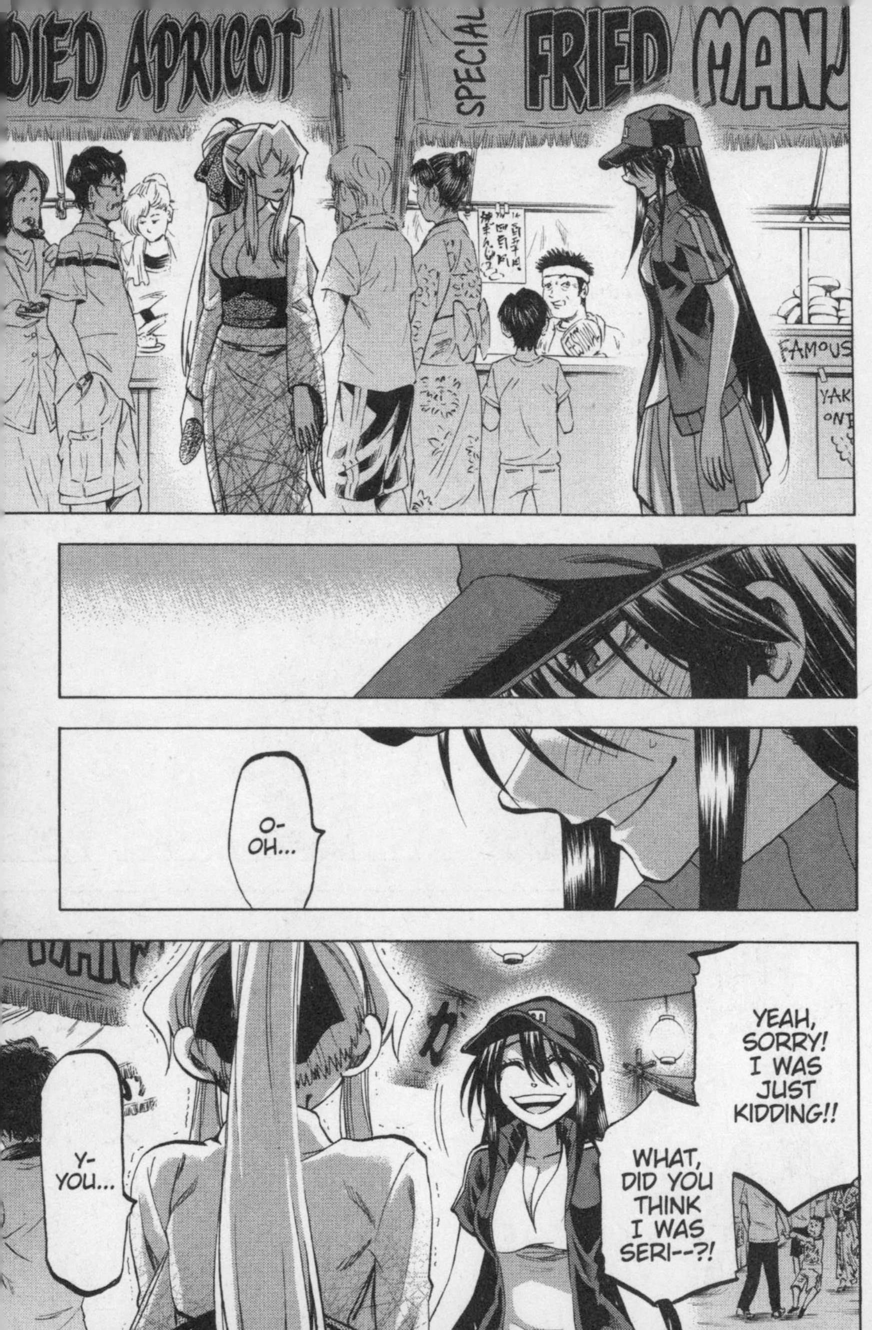
FRIED MAN
SPECIAL
DIED APRICOT
FAMOUS
O-
OH...
YEAH, SORRY! I WAS JUST KIDDING!!
WHAT, DID YOU THINK I WAS SERI--?!
Y-
YOU...

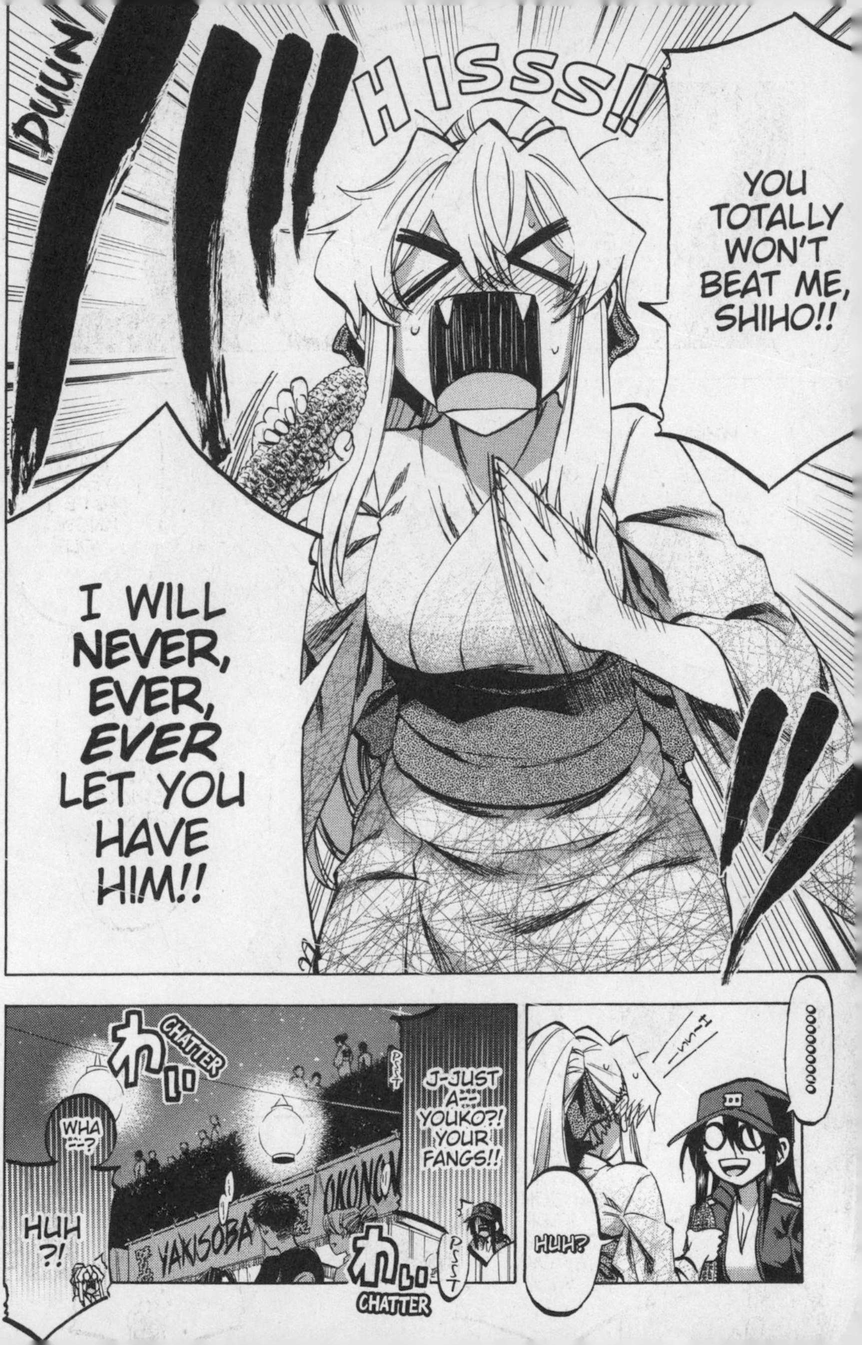
YOU TOTALLY WON'T BEAT ME, SHIHO!!
HISSSS!!
DUUN
I WILL NEVER, EVER, EVER LET YOU HAVE HIM!!
OOOOOOOOO...
HUH?
J-JUST A... YOUKO?! YOUR FANGS!!
PSST
PSST
CHATTER
CHATTER
WHA...?
OKONO
YAKISOBA
HUH?!

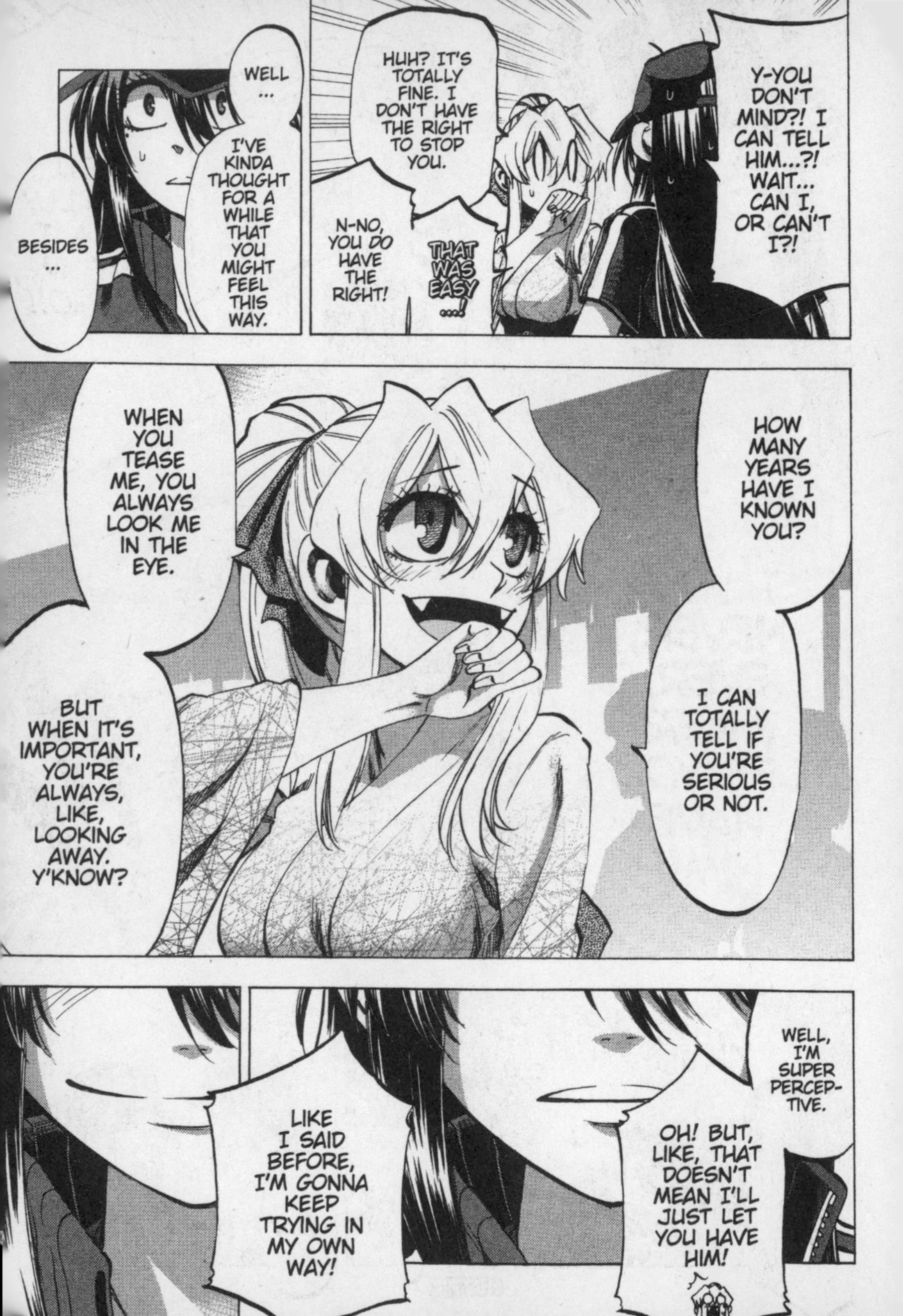
Y-YOU DON'T MIND?! I CAN TELL HIM...?! WAIT... CAN I, OR CAN'T I?!
HUH? IT'S TOTALLY FINE. I DON'T HAVE THE RIGHT TO STOP YOU.
THAT WAS EASY ...!
N-NO, YOU DO HAVE THE RIGHT!
WELL ...
I'VE KINDA THOUGHT FOR A WHILE THAT YOU MIGHT FEEL THIS WAY.
BESIDES ...
HOW MANY YEARS HAVE I KNOWN YOU?
I CAN TOTALLY TELL IF YOU'RE SERIOUS OR NOT.
WHEN YOU TEASE ME, YOU ALWAYS LOOK ME IN THE EYE.
BUT WHEN IT'S IMPORTANT, YOU'RE ALWAYS, LIKE, LOOKING AWAY. Y'KNOW?
WELL, I'M SUPER PERCEPTIVE.
OH! BUT, LIKE, THAT DOESN'T MEAN I'LL JUST LET YOU HAVE HIM!
LIKE I SAID BEFORE, I'M GONNA KEEP TRYING IN MY OWN WAY!

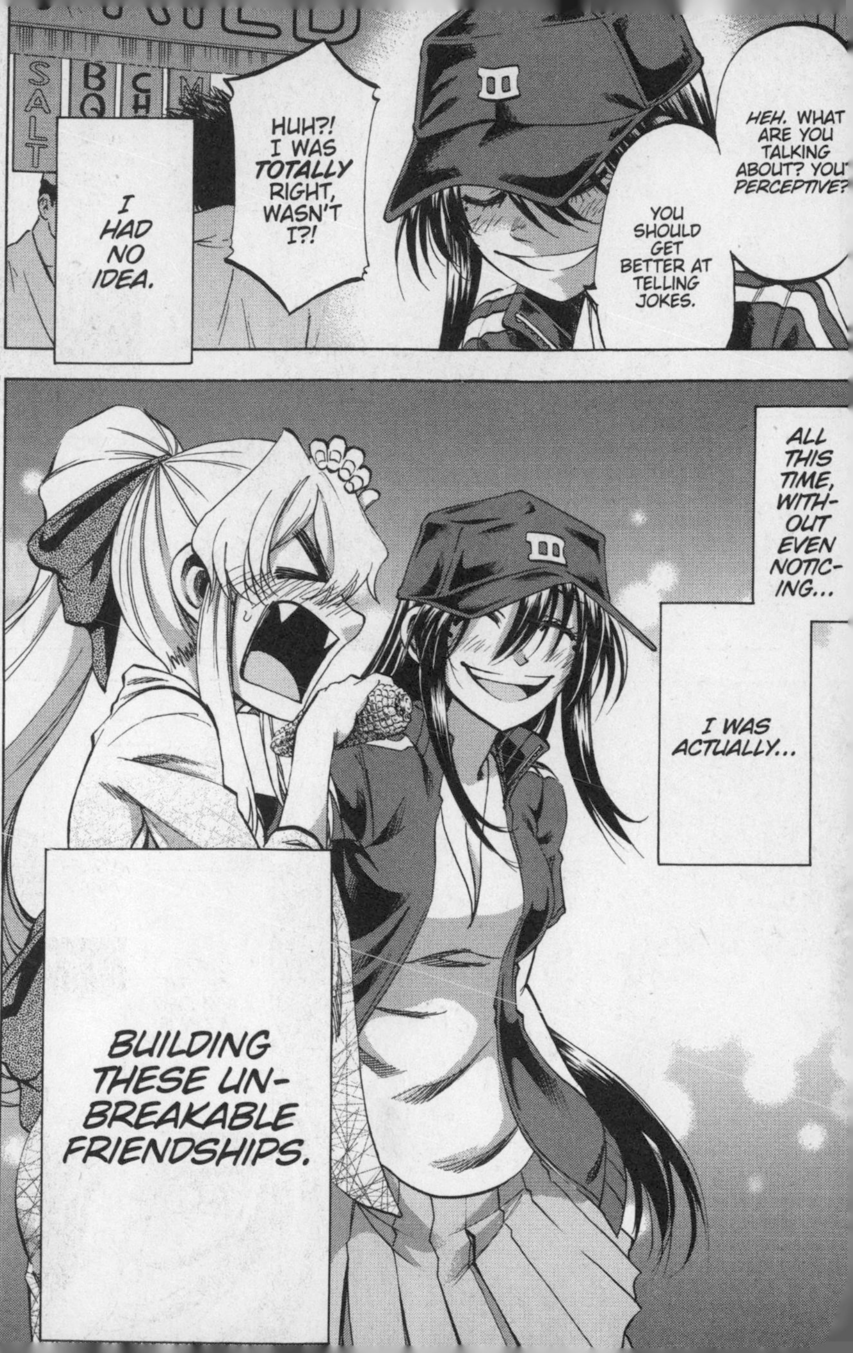
HEH. WHAT ARE YOU TALKING ABOUT? YOU PERCEPTIVE?
YOU SHOULD GET BETTER AT TELLING JOKES.
HUH?! I WAS TOTALLY RIGHT, WASN'T I?!
I HAD NO IDEA.
ALL THIS TIME, WITH-OUT EVEN NOTIC-ING...
I WAS ACTUALLY...
BUILDING THESE UN-BREAKABLE FRIENDSHIPS.

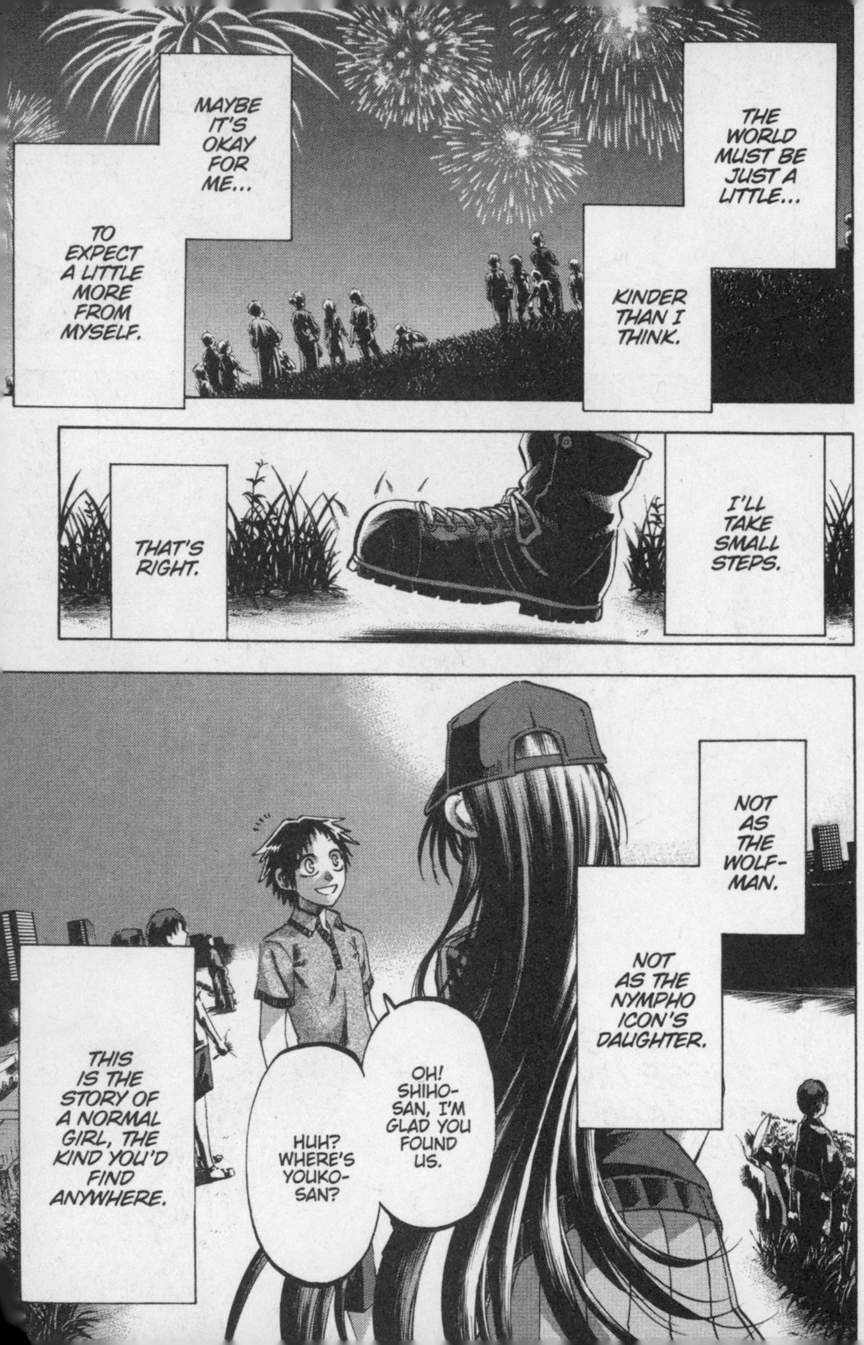
THE WORLD MUST BE JUST A LITTLE...
KINDER THAN I THINK.
MAYBE IT'S OKAY FOR ME...
TO EXPECT A LITTLE MORE FROM MYSELF.
I'LL TAKE SMALL STEPS.
THAT'S RIGHT.
NOT AS THE WOLF-MAN.
NOT AS THE NYMPHO ICON'S DAUGHTER.
OH! SHIHO-SAN, I'M GLAD YOU FOUND US.
HUH? WHERE'S YOUKO-SAN?
THIS IS THE STORY OF A NORMAL GIRL, THE KIND YOU'D FIND ANYWHERE.

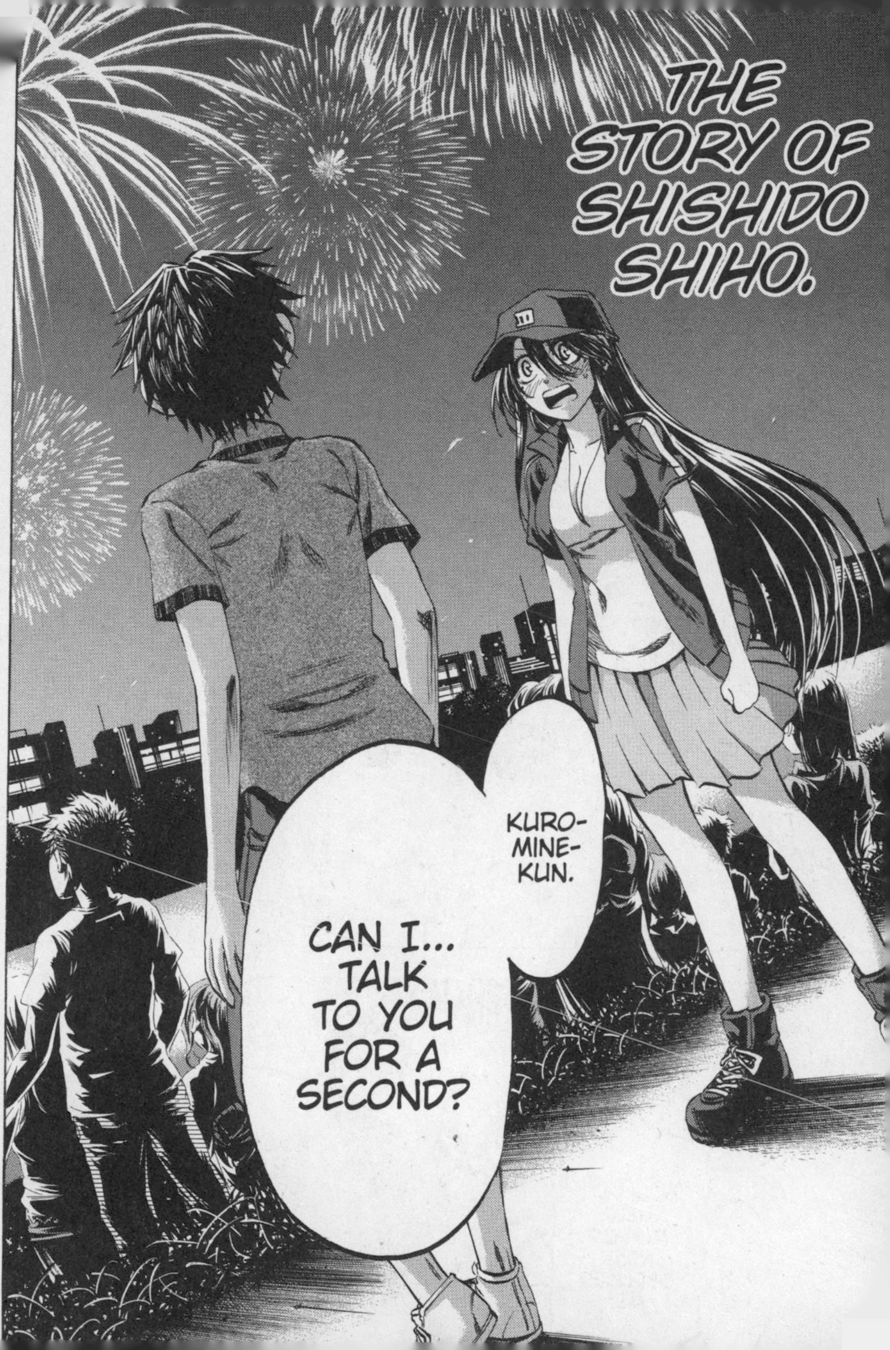
THE STORY OF SHISHIDO SHIHO.
KURO-MINE-KUN.
CAN I... TALK TO YOU FOR A SECOND?

Chapter 128: "Shishido Shiho" ④

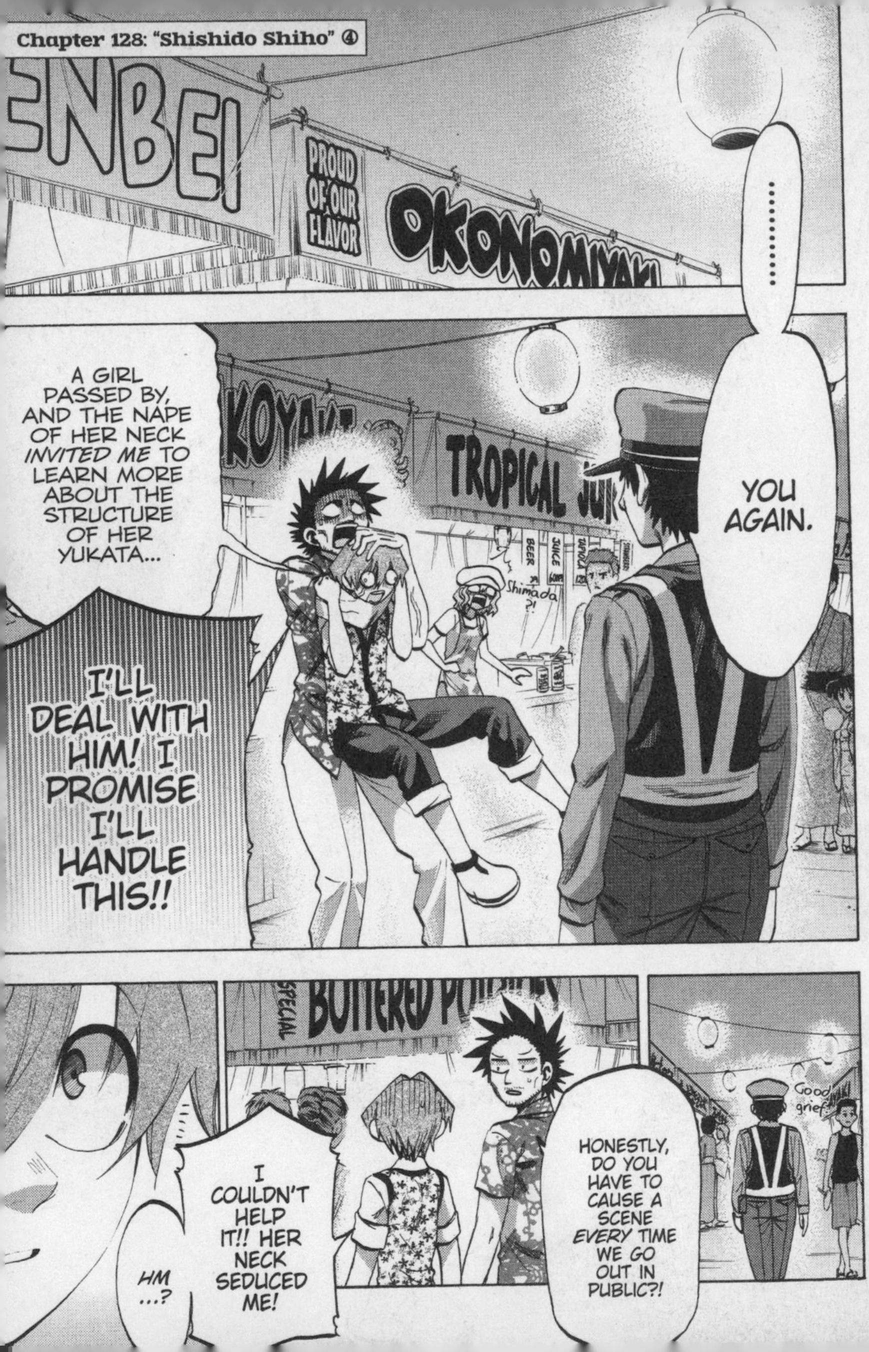
ENBEI
PROUD OF OUR FLAVOR
OKONOMIYAKI
……
YOU AGAIN.
A GIRL PASSED BY, AND THE NAPE OF HER NECK *INVITED ME* TO LEARN MORE ABOUT THE STRUCTURE OF HER YUKATA...
TROPICAL
BEER
JUICE
Shimada?!
I'LL DEAL WITH HIM! I PROMISE I'LL HANDLE THIS!!
Good grief.
SPECIAL
HONESTLY, DO YOU HAVE TO CAUSE A SCENE *EVERY* TIME WE GO OUT IN PUBLIC?!
I COULDN'T HELP IT!! HER NECK SEDUCED ME!
HM ...?

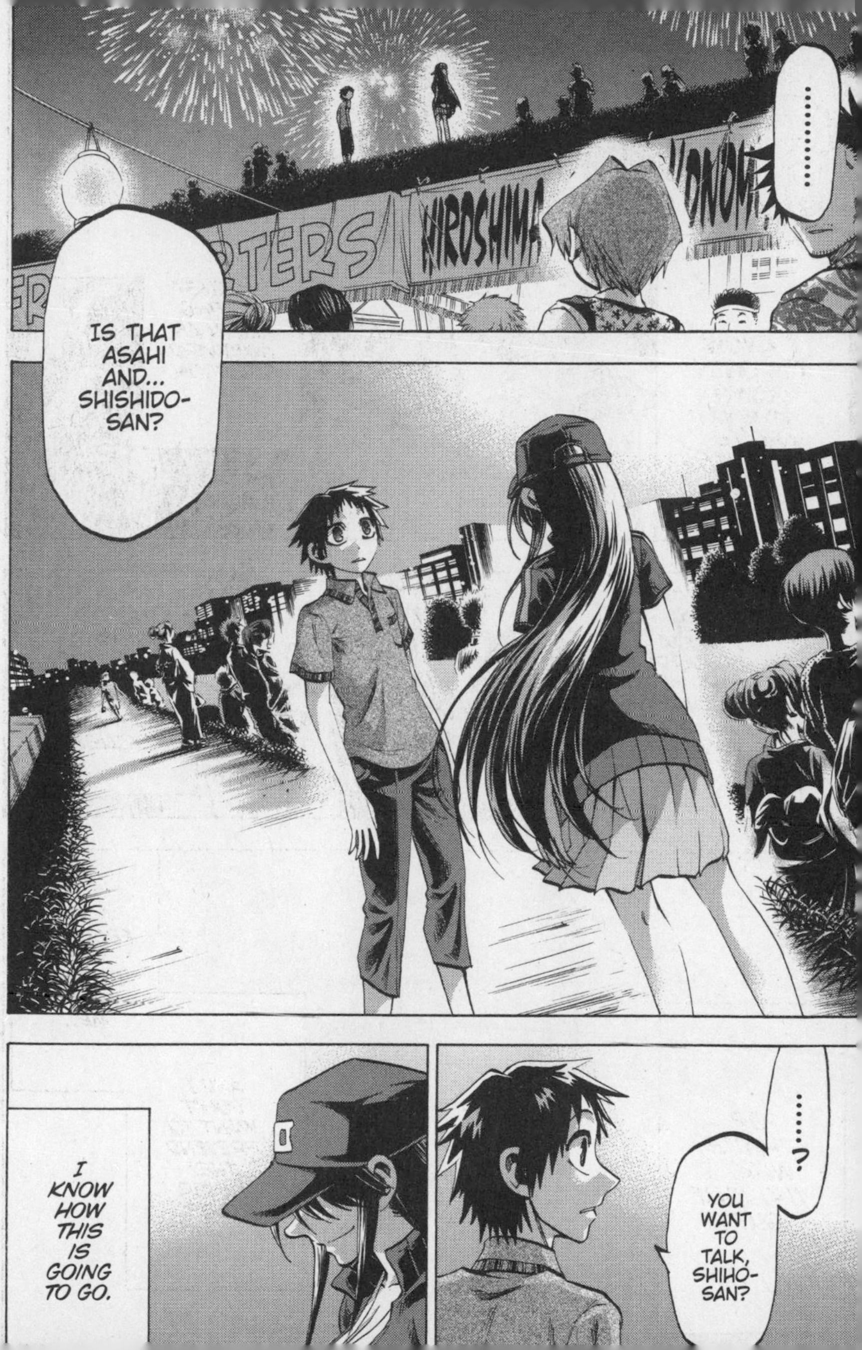
......
IS THAT ASAHI AND... SHISHIDO-SAN?
HIROSHIMA
......?
YOU WANT TO TALK, SHIHO-SAN?
I KNOW HOW THIS IS GOING TO GO.

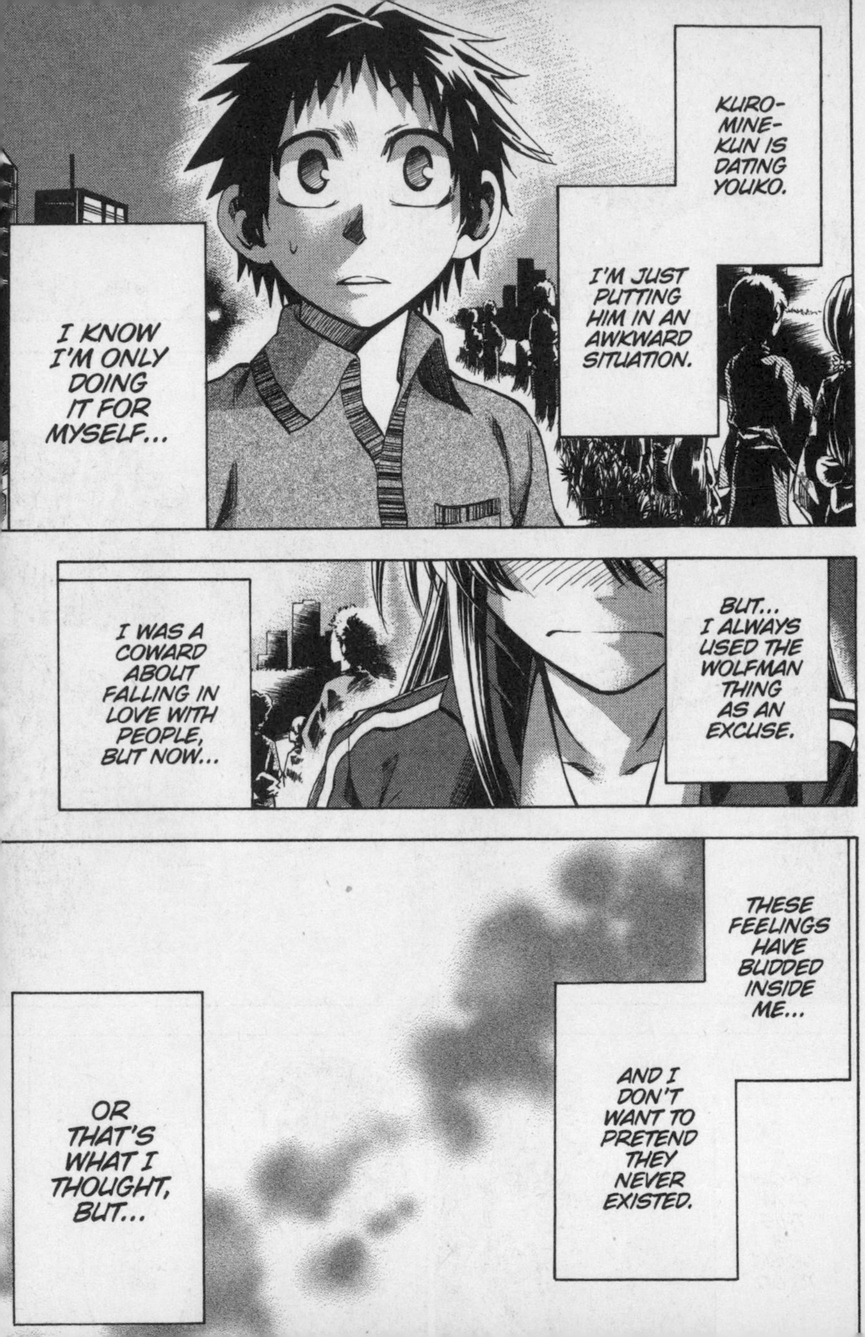
KURO-MINE-KUN IS DATING YOUKO.
I'M JUST PUTTING HIM IN AN AWKWARD SITUATION.
I KNOW I'M ONLY DOING IT FOR MYSELF...
BUT... I ALWAYS USED THE WOLFMAN THING AS AN EXCUSE.
I WAS A COWARD ABOUT FALLING IN LOVE WITH PEOPLE, BUT NOW...
THESE FEELINGS HAVE BUDDED INSIDE ME...
AND I DON'T WANT TO PRETEND THEY NEVER EXISTED.
OR THAT'S WHAT I THOUGHT, BUT...

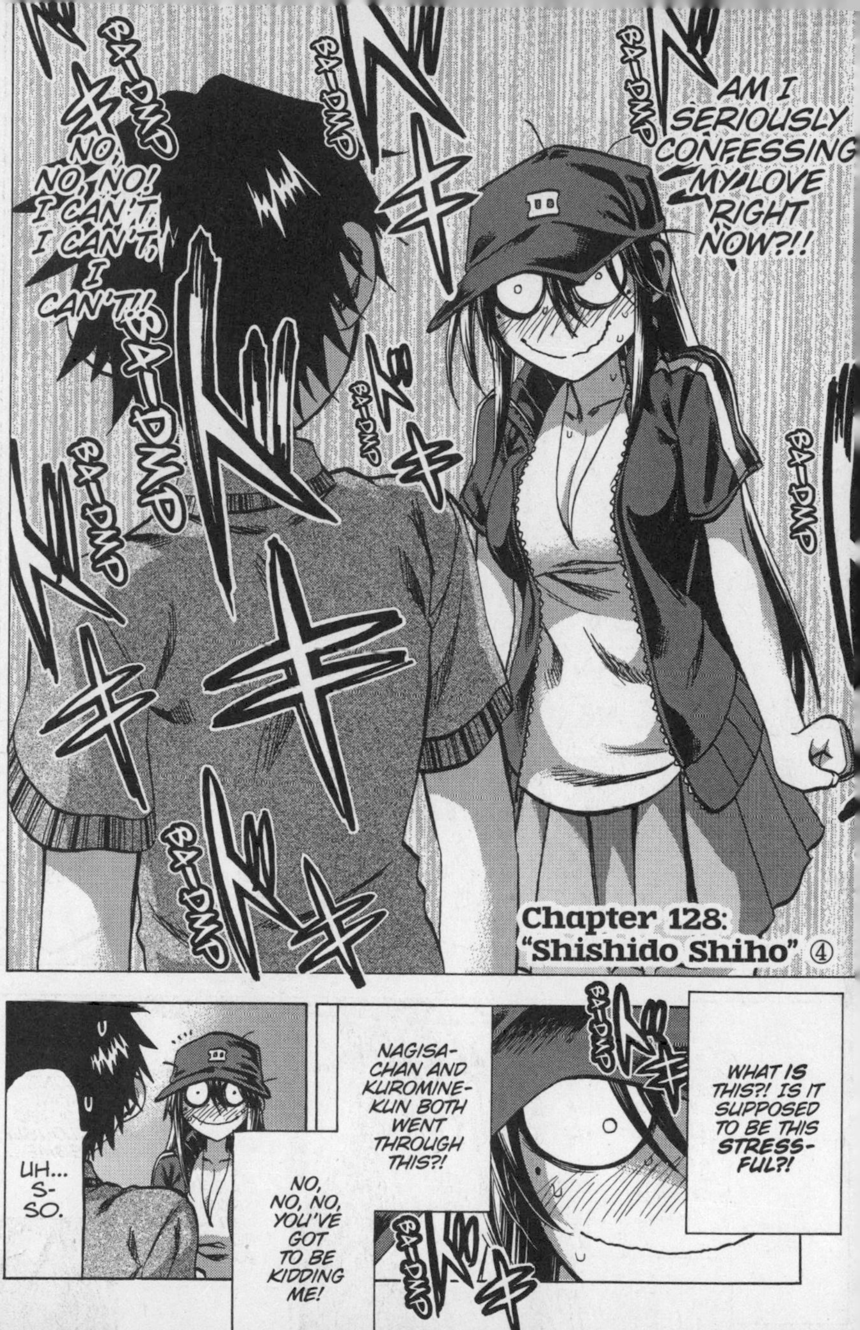

BA-DMP
AM I SERIOUSLY CONFESSING MY LOVE RIGHT NOW?!!
BA-DMP
BA-DMP
NO, NO, NO! I CAN'T, I CAN'T, I CAN'T!!
BA-DMP
BA-DMP
BA-DMP
BA-DMP
BA-DMP
Chapter 128: "Shishido Shiho" ④
BA-DMP
WHAT IS THIS?! IS IT SUPPOSED TO BE THIS STRESS-FUL?!
BA-DMP
NAGISA-CHAN AND KUROMINE-KUN BOTH WENT THROUGH THIS?!
NO, NO, NO, YOU'VE GOT TO BE KIDDING ME!
UH... S-SO.

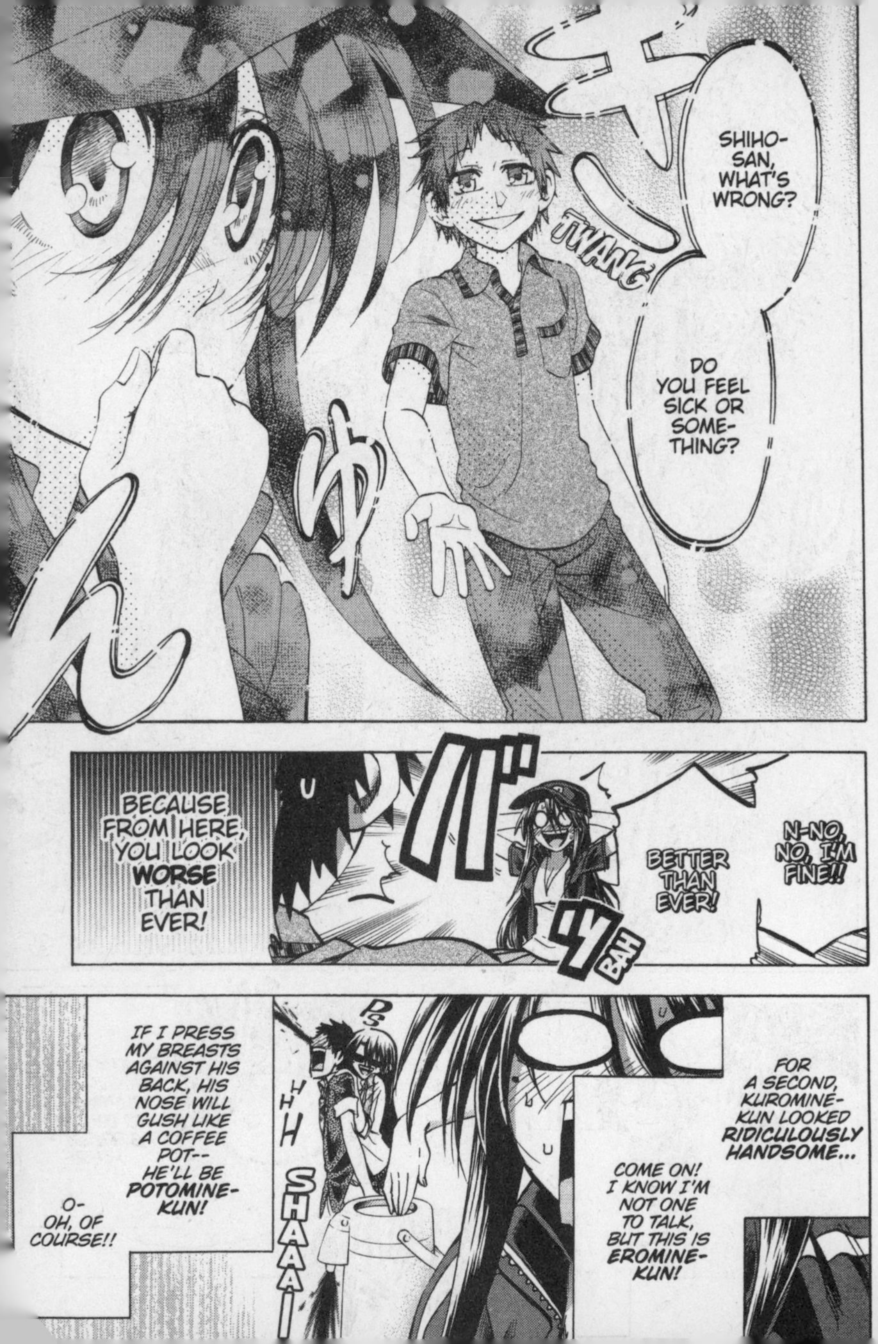
SHIHO-SAN, WHAT'S WRONG?
DO YOU FEEL SICK OR SOMETHING?
TWANG
N-NO, NO, I'M FINE!!
BETTER THAN EVER!
BAH
BECAUSE FROM HERE, YOU LOOK WORSE THAN EVER!
FOR A SECOND, KUROMINE-KUN LOOKED RIDICULOUSLY HANDSOME...
COME ON! I KNOW I'M NOT ONE TO TALK, BUT THIS IS EROMINE-KUN!
DS
HHH
SHAAAAI
IF I PRESS MY BREASTS AGAINST HIS BACK, HIS NOSE WILL GUSH LIKE A COFFEE POT-- HE'LL BE POTOMINE-KUN!
O-OH, OF COURSE!!

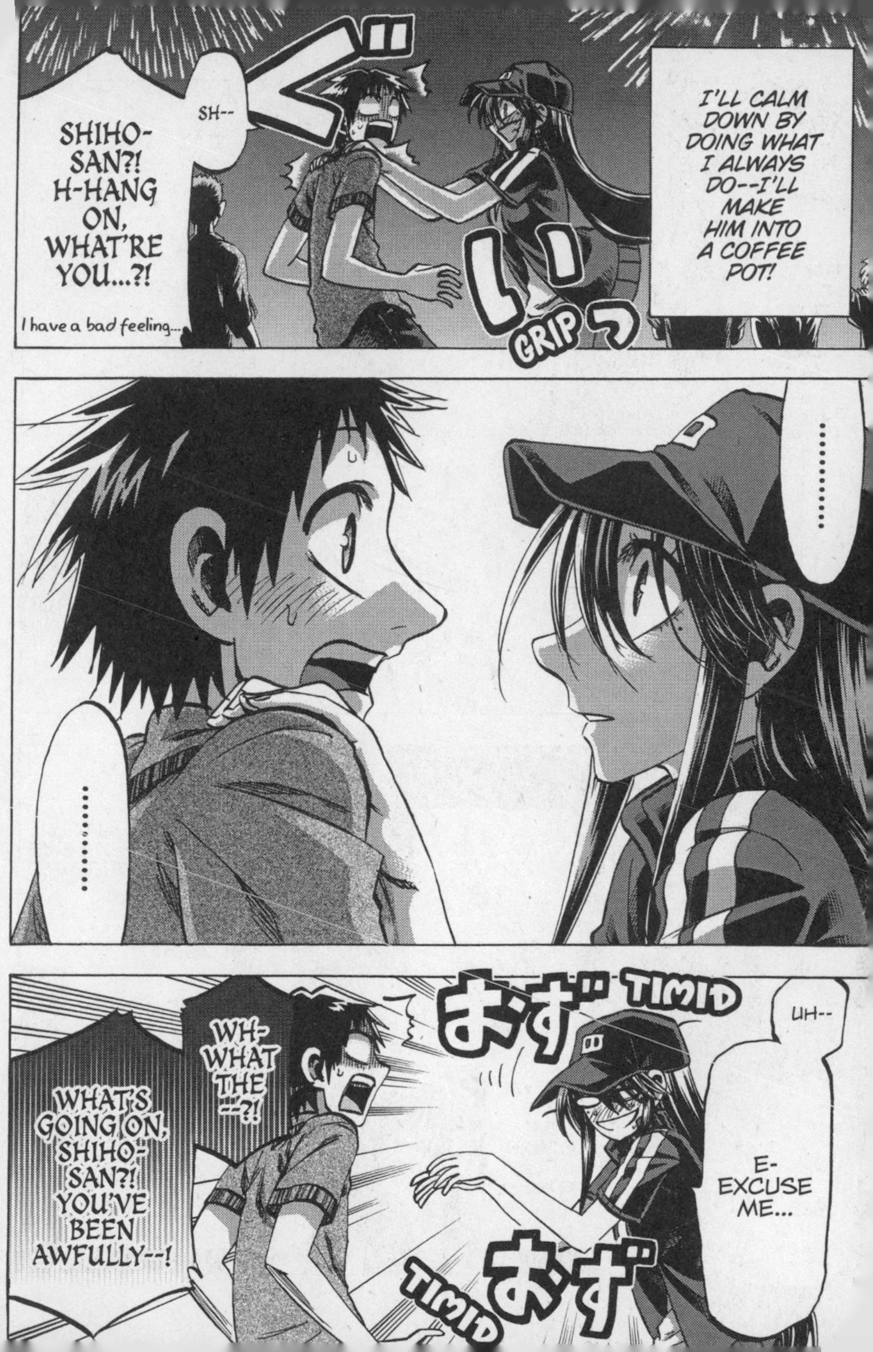

I'LL CALM DOWN BY DOING WHAT I ALWAYS DO--I'LL MAKE HIM INTO A COFFEE POT!
GRIP
SH--
SHIHO-SAN?! H-HANG ON, WHAT'RE YOU...?!
I have a bad feeling...
......
......
UH--
おず TIMID
E-EXCUSE ME...
おず TIMID
WH-WHAT THE--?!
WHAT'S GOING ON, SHIHO-SAN?! YOU'VE BEEN AWFULLY--!

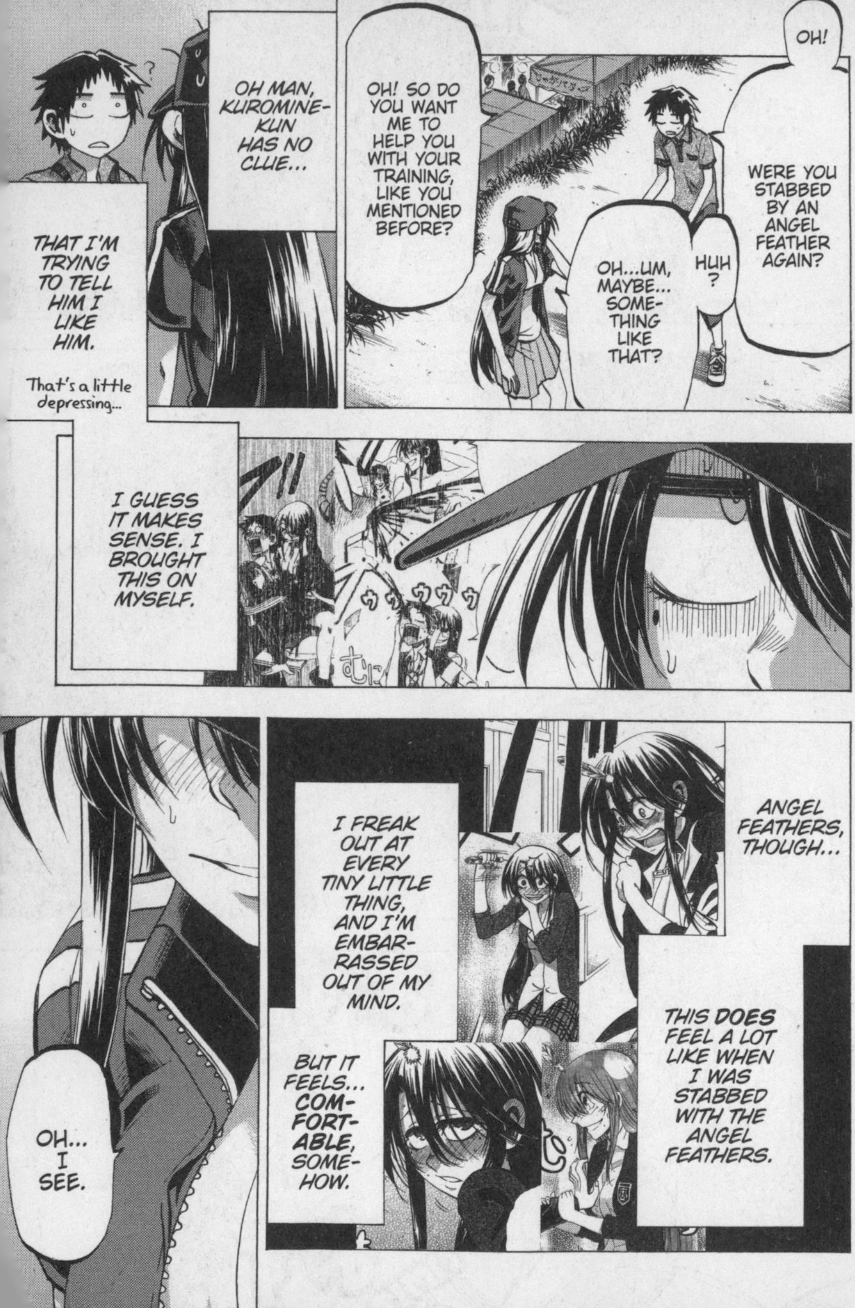
OH!
WERE YOU STABBED BY AN ANGEL FEATHER AGAIN?
HUH?
OH...UM, MAYBE... SOMETHING LIKE THAT?
OH! SO DO YOU WANT ME TO HELP YOU WITH YOUR TRAINING, LIKE YOU MENTIONED BEFORE?
OH MAN, KUROMINE-KUN HAS NO CLUE...
THAT I'M TRYING TO TELL HIM I LIKE HIM.
That's a little depressing...
むに
I GUESS IT MAKES SENSE. I BROUGHT THIS ON MYSELF.
ANGEL FEATHERS, THOUGH...
THIS DOES FEEL A LOT LIKE WHEN I WAS STABBED WITH THE ANGEL FEATHERS.
I FREAK OUT AT EVERY TINY LITTLE THING, AND I'M EMBARRASSED OUT OF MY MIND.
BUT IT FEELS... COMFORTABLE, SOMEHOW.
OH... I SEE.

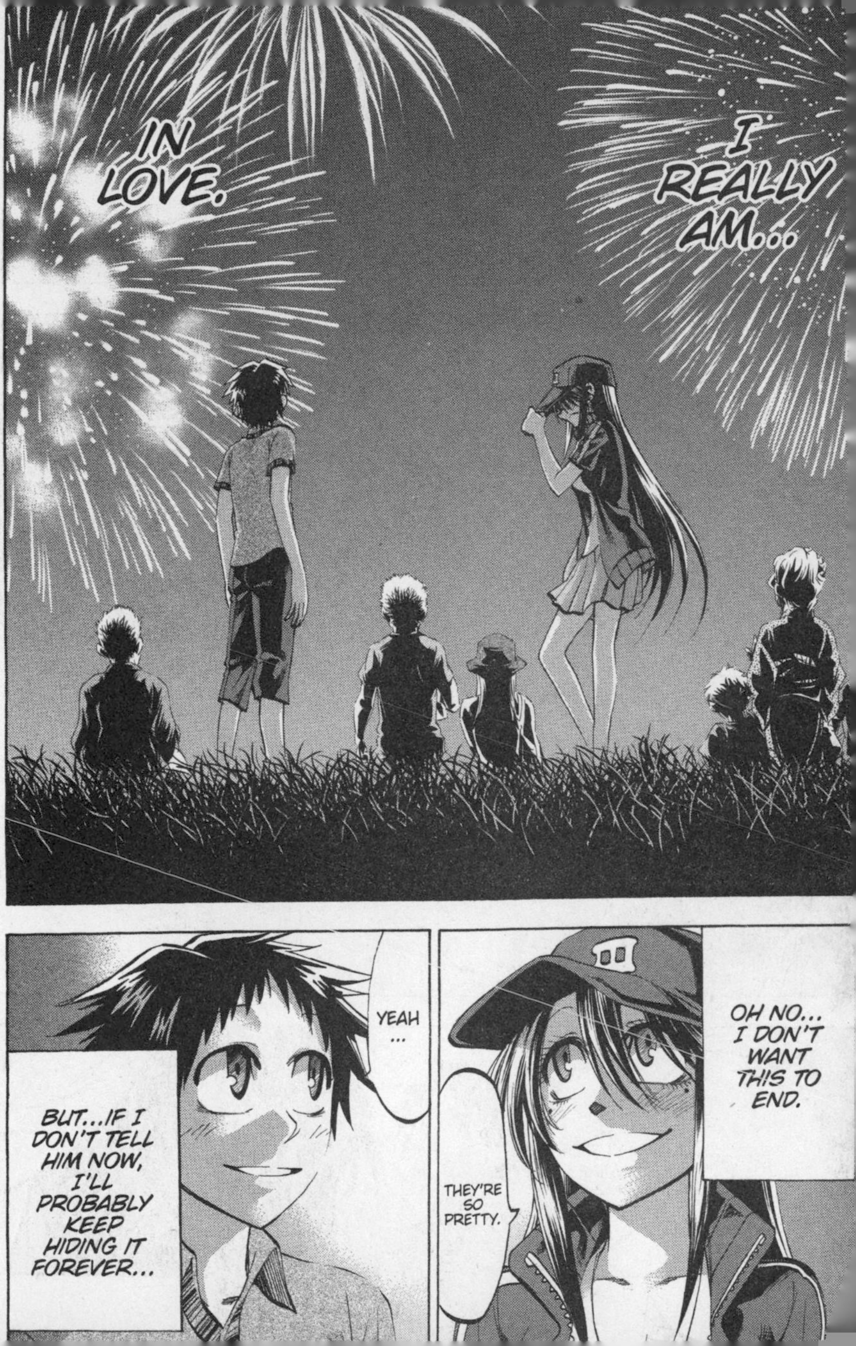
I REALLY AM...
IN LOVE.
OH NO... I DON'T WANT THIS TO END.
THEY'RE SO PRETTY.
YEAH...
BUT...IF I DON'T TELL HIM NOW, I'LL PROBABLY KEEP HIDING IT FOREVER...

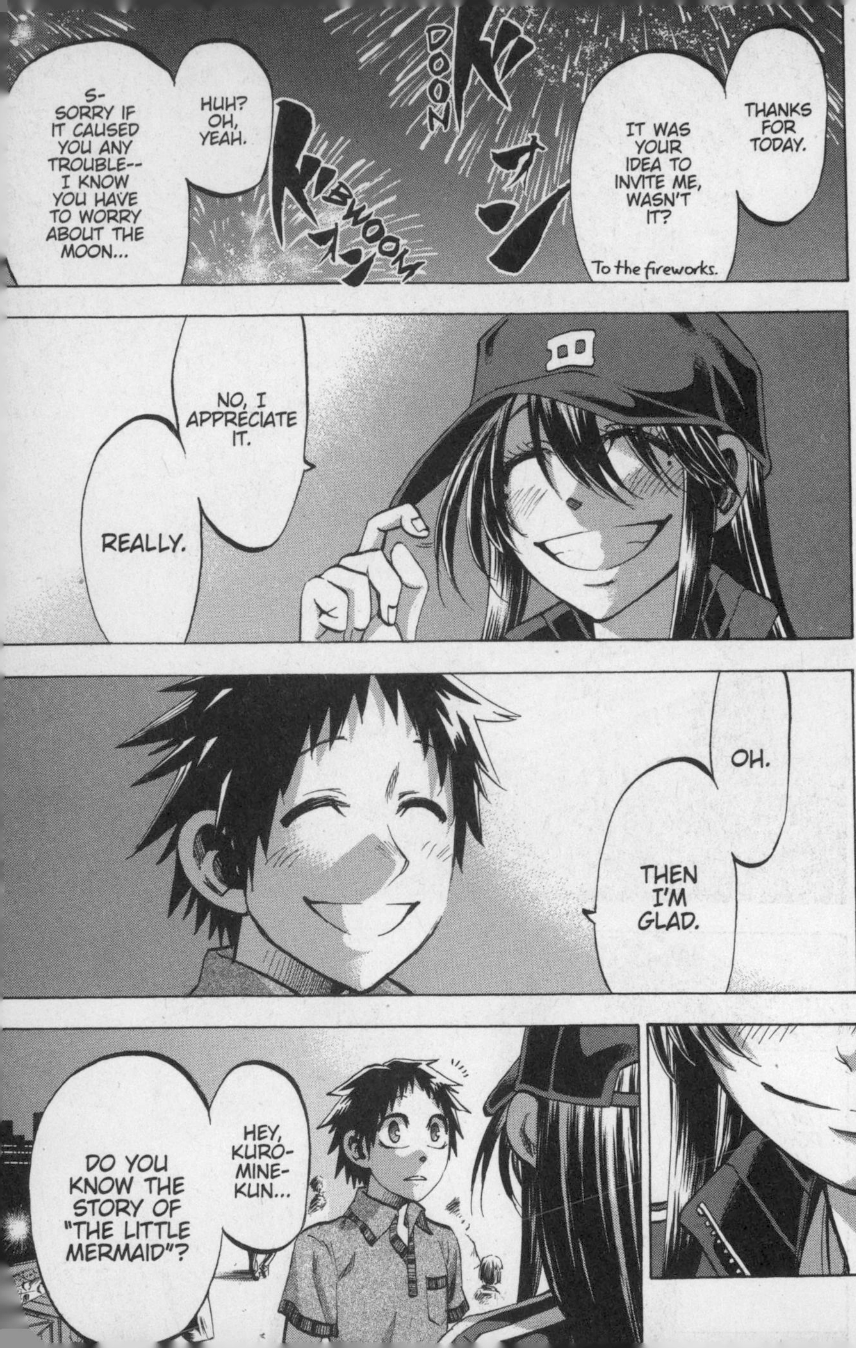
THANKS FOR TODAY.
IT WAS YOUR IDEA TO INVITE ME, WASN'T IT?
To the fireworks.
DOON
BWOOM
HUH? OH, YEAH.
S-SORRY IF IT CAUSED YOU ANY TROUBLE--I KNOW YOU HAVE TO WORRY ABOUT THE MOON...
NO, I APPRECIATE IT.
REALLY.
OH.
THEN I'M GLAD.
HEY, KUROMINE-KUN...
DO YOU KNOW THE STORY OF "THE LITTLE MERMAID"?

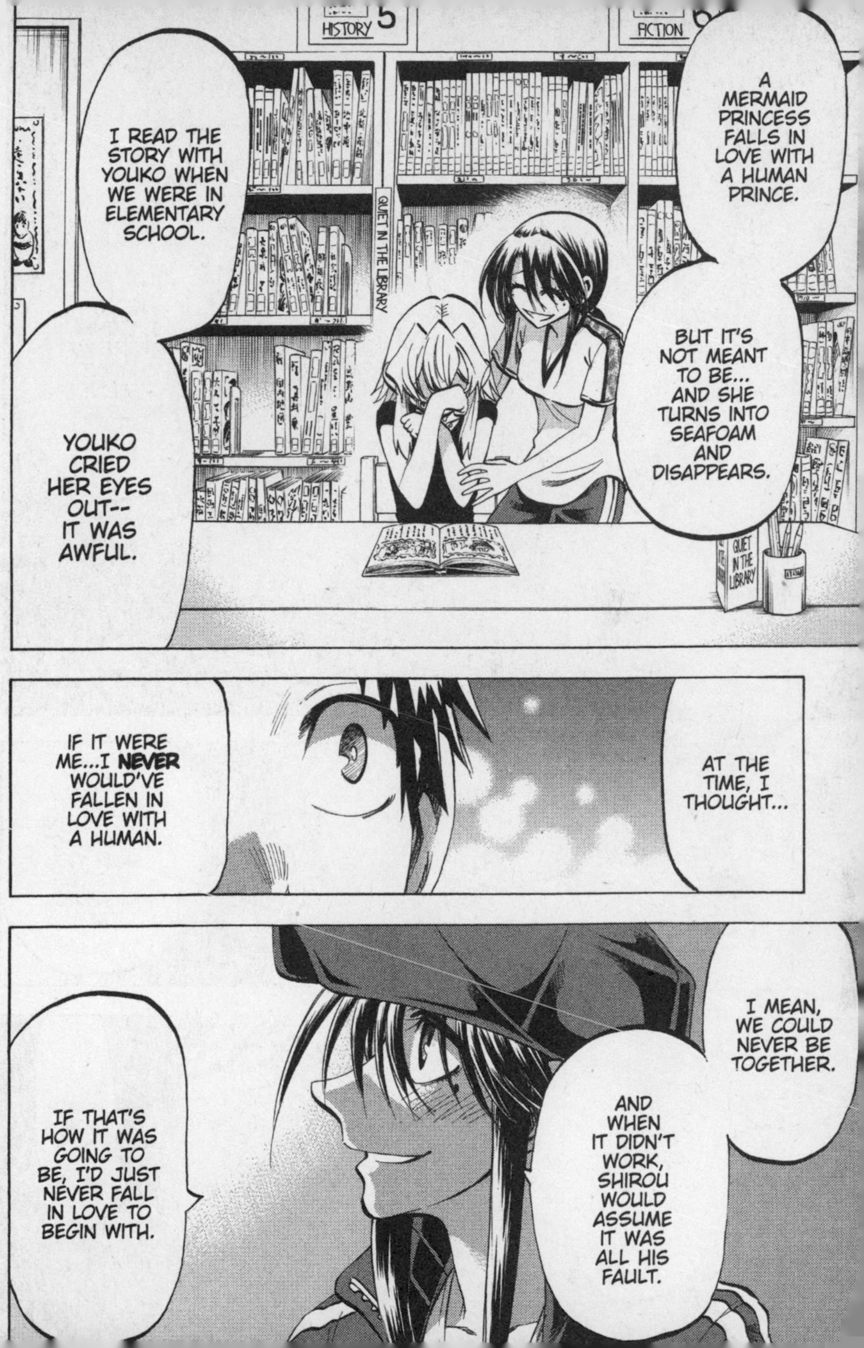
FICTION
HISTORY 5
A MERMAID PRINCESS FALLS IN LOVE WITH A HUMAN PRINCE.
BUT IT'S NOT MEANT TO BE... AND SHE TURNS INTO SEAFOAM AND DISAPPEARS.
QUIET IN THE LIBRARY
I READ THE STORY WITH YOUKO WHEN WE WERE IN ELEMENTARY SCHOOL.
QUIET IN THE LIBRARY
YOUKO CRIED HER EYES OUT-- IT WAS AWFUL.
AT THE TIME, I THOUGHT...
IF IT WERE ME...I **NEVER** WOULD'VE FALLEN IN LOVE WITH A HUMAN.
I MEAN, WE COULD NEVER BE TOGETHER.
AND WHEN IT DIDN'T WORK, SHIROU WOULD ASSUME IT WAS ALL HIS FAULT.
IF THAT'S HOW IT WAS GOING TO BE, I'D JUST NEVER FALL IN LOVE TO BEGIN WITH.

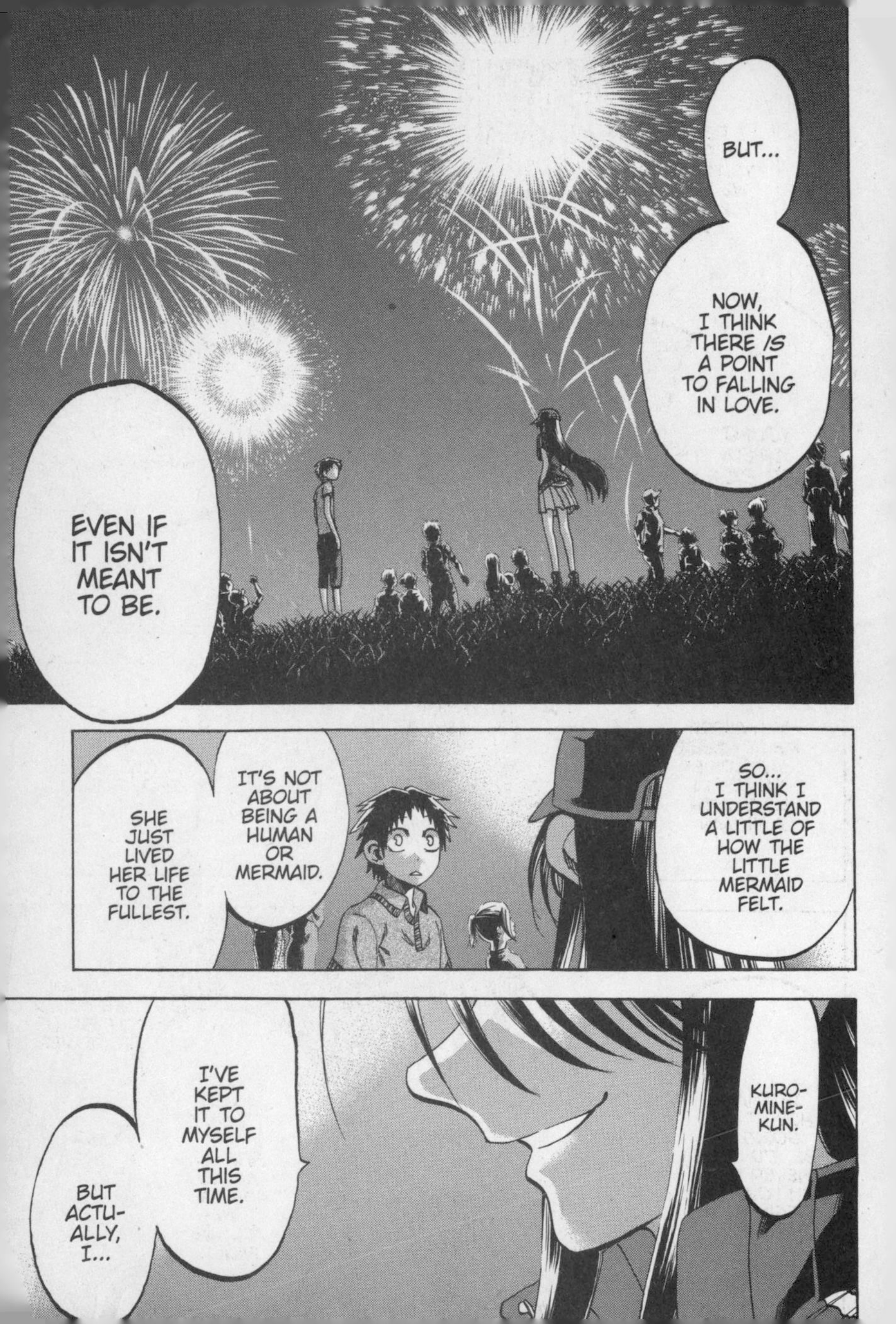
BUT...
NOW, I THINK THERE IS A POINT TO FALLING IN LOVE.
EVEN IF IT ISN'T MEANT TO BE.
SO... I THINK I UNDERSTAND A LITTLE OF HOW THE LITTLE MERMAID FELT.
IT'S NOT ABOUT BEING A HUMAN OR MERMAID.
SHE JUST LIVED HER LIFE TO THE FULLEST.
KURO-MINE-KUN.
I'VE KEPT IT TO MYSELF ALL THIS TIME.
BUT ACTU-ALLY, I...

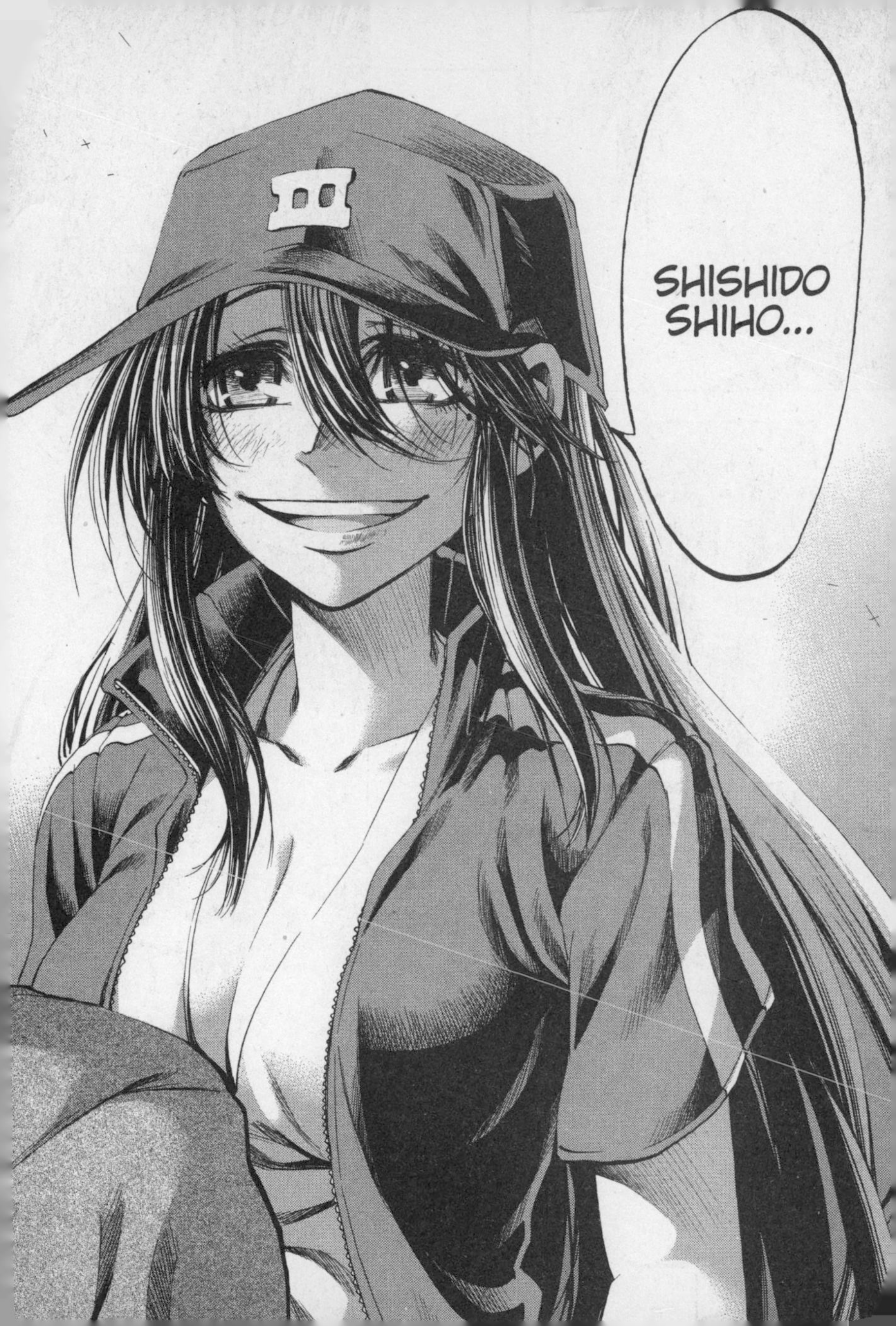
SHISHIDO SHIHO...

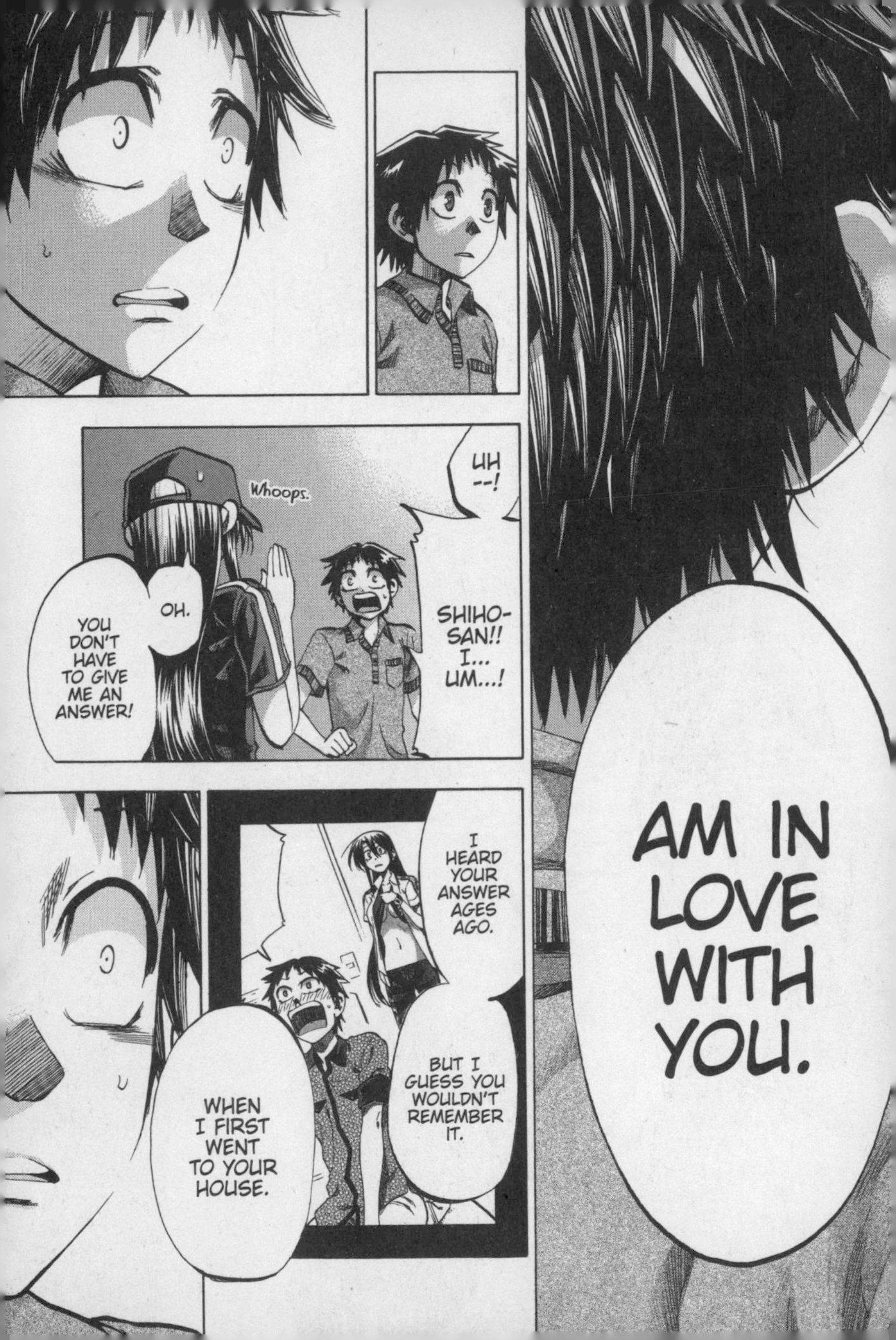
AM IN LOVE WITH YOU.
UH --!
Whoops.
SHIHO-SAN!! I... UM...!
OH.
YOU DON'T HAVE TO GIVE ME AN ANSWER!
I HEARD YOUR ANSWER AGES AGO.
BUT I GUESS YOU WOULDN'T REMEMBER IT.
WHEN I FIRST WENT TO YOUR HOUSE.

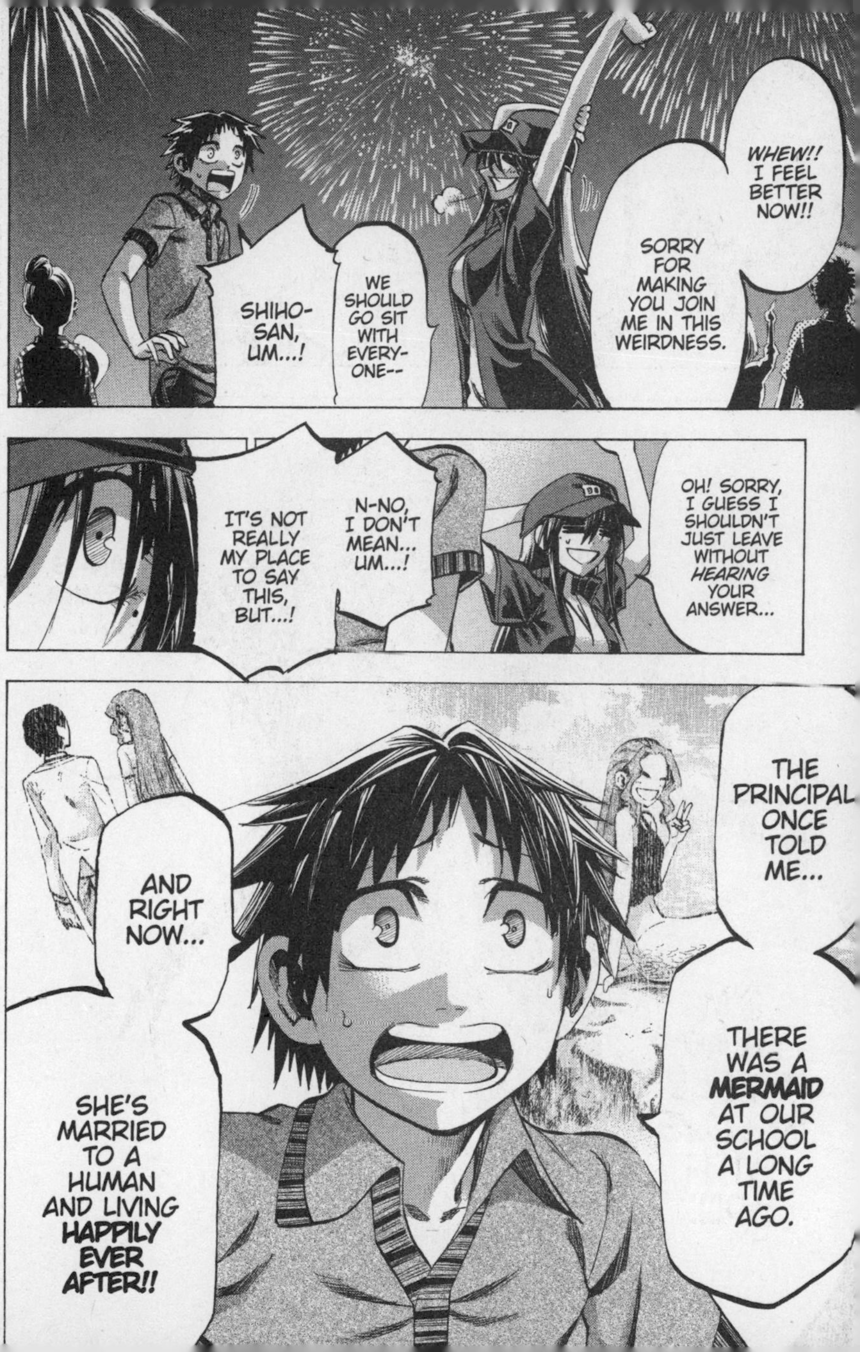
WHEW!! I FEEL BETTER NOW!!
SORRY FOR MAKING YOU JOIN ME IN THIS WEIRDNESS.
WE SHOULD GO SIT WITH EVERY-ONE--
SHIHO-SAN, UM...!
OH! SORRY, I GUESS I SHOULDN'T JUST LEAVE WITHOUT HEARING YOUR ANSWER...
N-NO, I DON'T MEAN... UM...!
IT'S NOT REALLY MY PLACE TO SAY THIS, BUT...!
THE PRINCIPAL ONCE TOLD ME...
THERE WAS A MERMAID AT OUR SCHOOL A LONG TIME AGO.
AND RIGHT NOW...
SHE'S MARRIED TO A HUMAN AND LIVING HAPPILY EVER AFTER!!

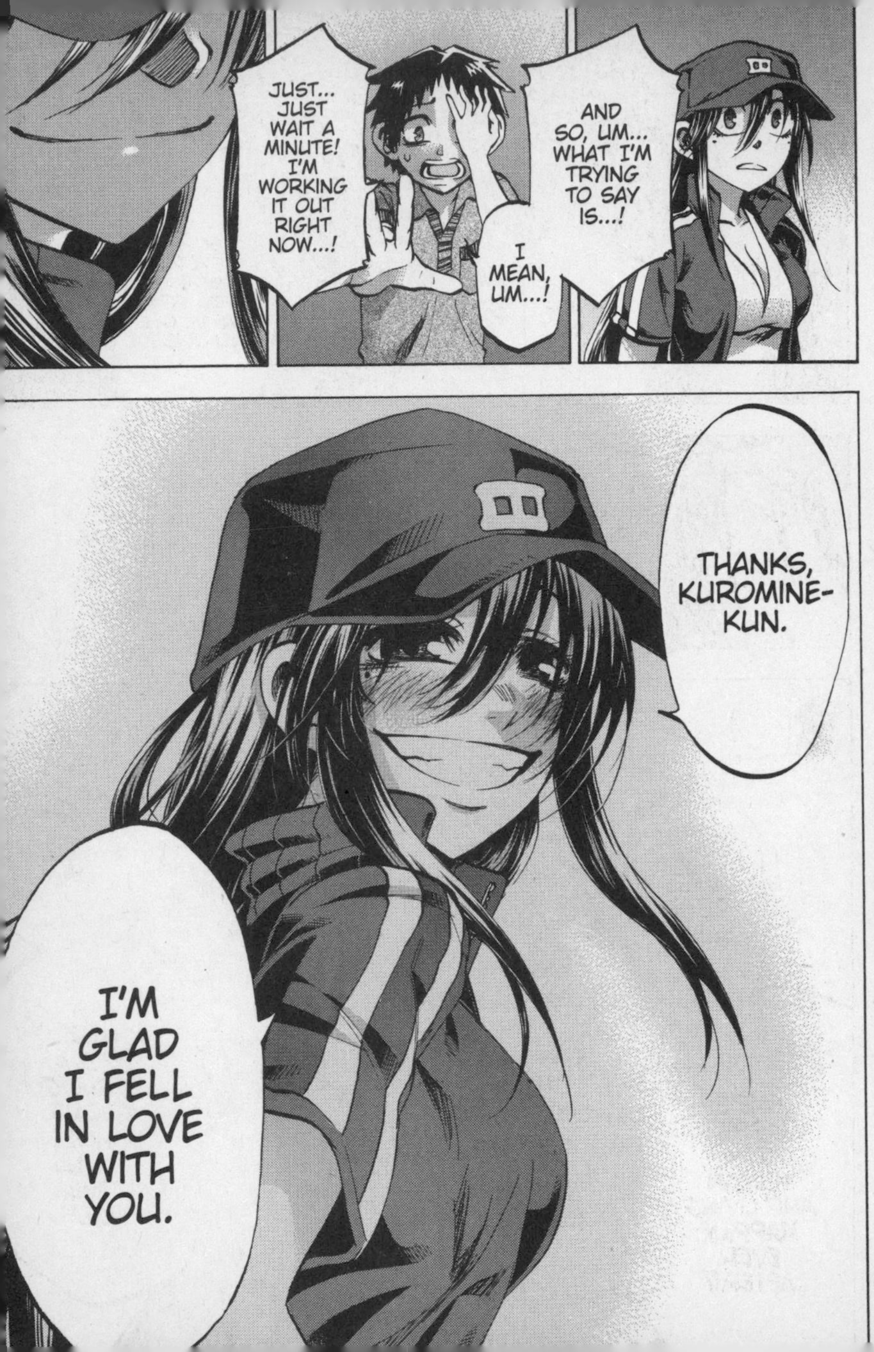
AND SO, UM... WHAT I'M TRYING TO SAY IS...!
I MEAN, UM...!
JUST... JUST WAIT A MINUTE! I'M WORKING IT OUT RIGHT NOW...!
THANKS, KUROMINE-KUN.
I'M GLAD I FELL IN LOVE WITH YOU.

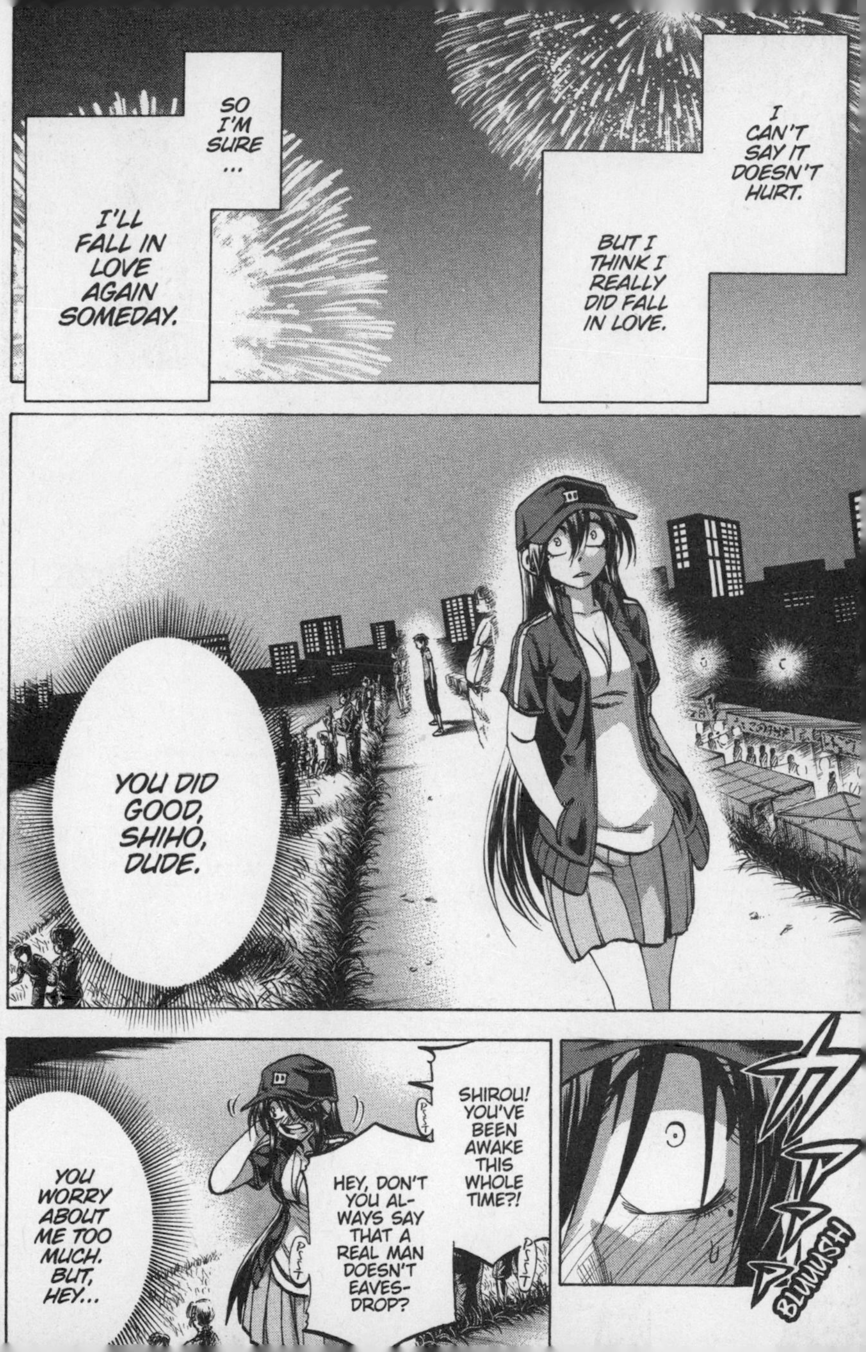
I CAN'T SAY IT DOESN'T HURT.
BUT I THINK I REALLY DID FALL IN LOVE.
SO I'M SURE...
I'LL FALL IN LOVE AGAIN SOMEDAY.
YOU DID GOOD, SHIHO, DUDE.
BLUUUSH
SHIROU! YOU'VE BEEN AWAKE THIS WHOLE TIME?!
HEY, DON'T YOU AL-WAYS SAY THAT A REAL MAN DOESN'T EAVES-DROP?
YOU WORRY ABOUT ME TOO MUCH. BUT, HEY...

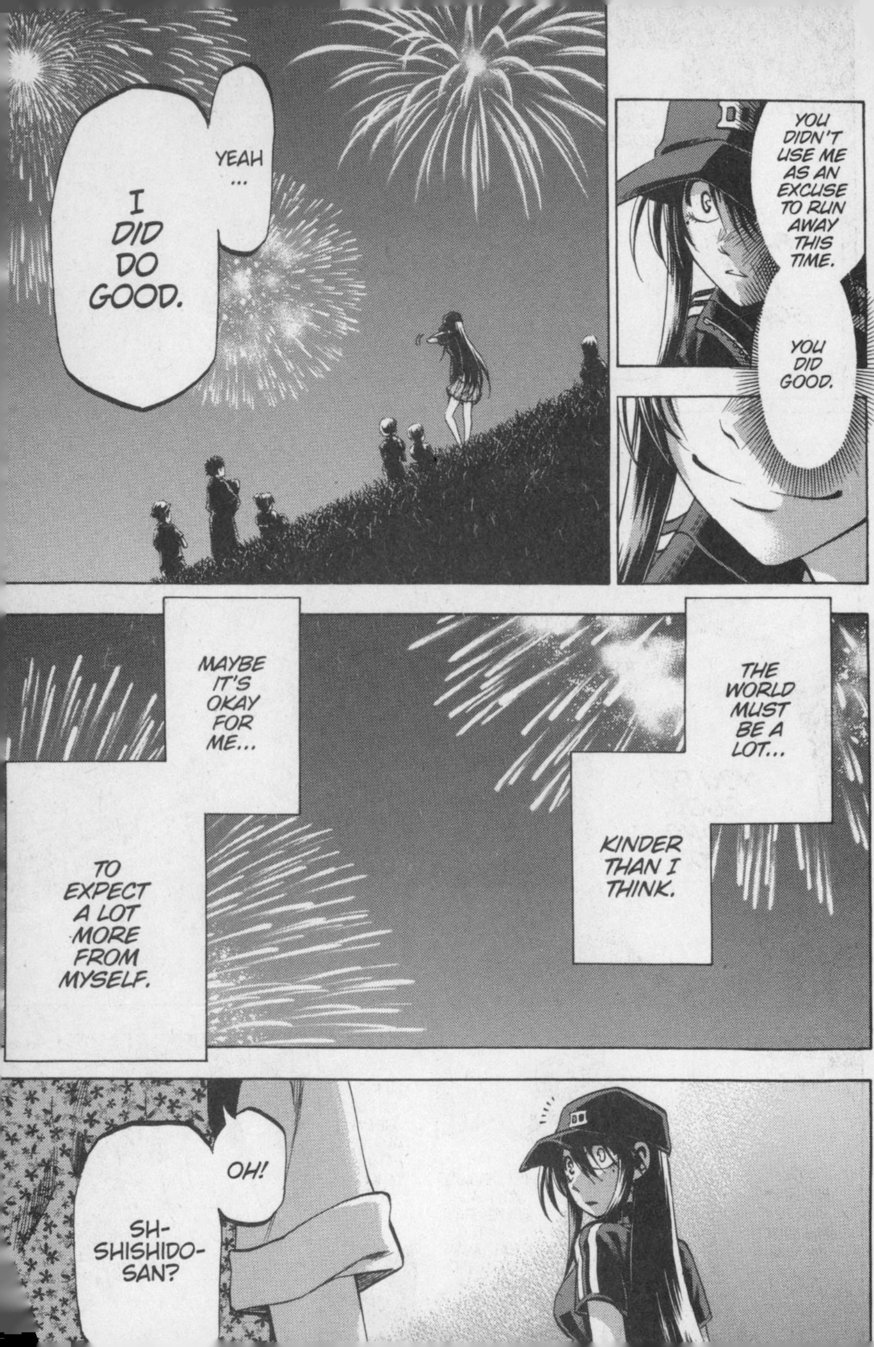
YOU DIDN'T USE ME AS AN EXCUSE TO RUN AWAY THIS TIME.
YOU DID GOOD.
YEAH...
I DID DO GOOD.
THE WORLD MUST BE A LOT...
KINDER THAN I THINK.
MAYBE IT'S OKAY FOR ME...
TO EXPECT A LOT MORE FROM MYSELF.
OH!
SH-SHISHIDO-SAN?

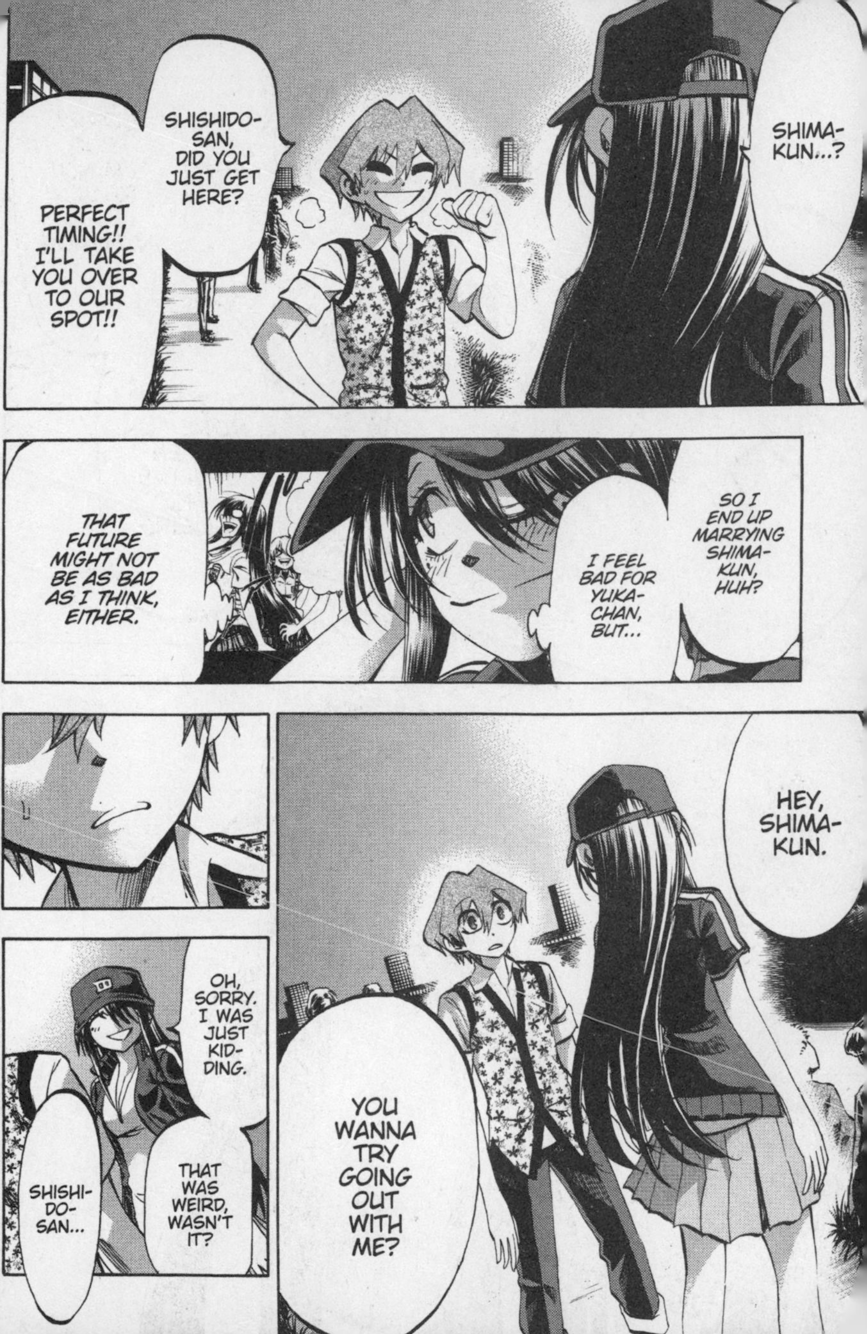
SHIMA-KUN...?
SHISHIDO-SAN, DID YOU JUST GET HERE?
PERFECT TIMING!! I'LL TAKE YOU OVER TO OUR SPOT!!
SO I END UP MARRYING SHIMA-KUN, HUH?
I FEEL BAD FOR YUKA-CHAN, BUT...
THAT FUTURE MIGHT NOT BE AS BAD AS I THINK, EITHER.
HEY, SHIMA-KUN.
YOU WANNA TRY GOING OUT WITH ME?
OH, SORRY. I WAS JUST KIDDING.
THAT WAS WEIRD, WASN'T IT?
SHISHIDO-SAN...

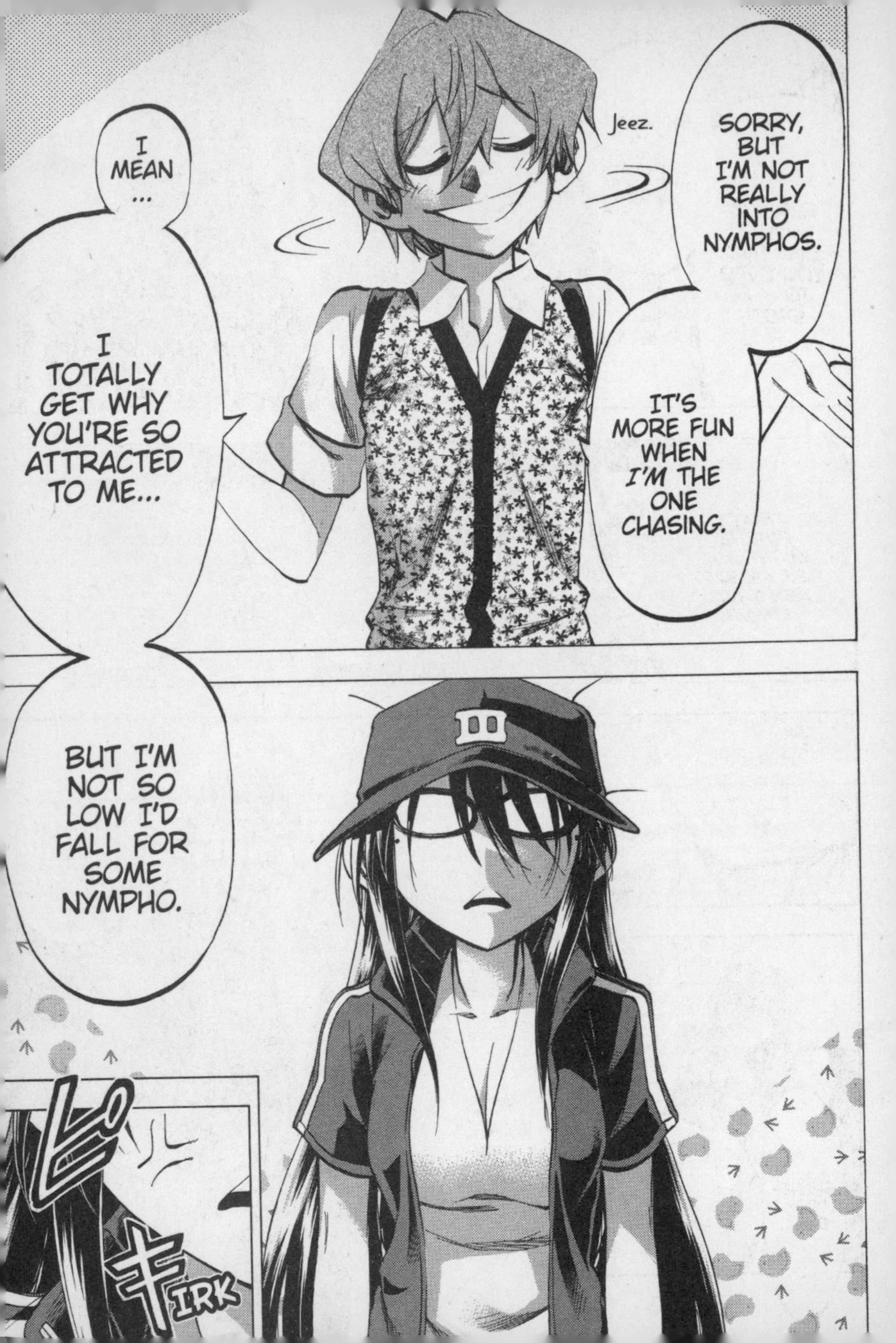
SORRY, BUT I'M NOT REALLY INTO NYMPHOS.
Jeez.
IT'S MORE FUN WHEN *I'M* THE ONE CHASING.
I MEAN ...
I TOTALLY GET WHY YOU'RE SO ATTRACTED TO ME...
BUT I'M NOT SO LOW I'D FALL FOR SOME NYMPHO.
IRK

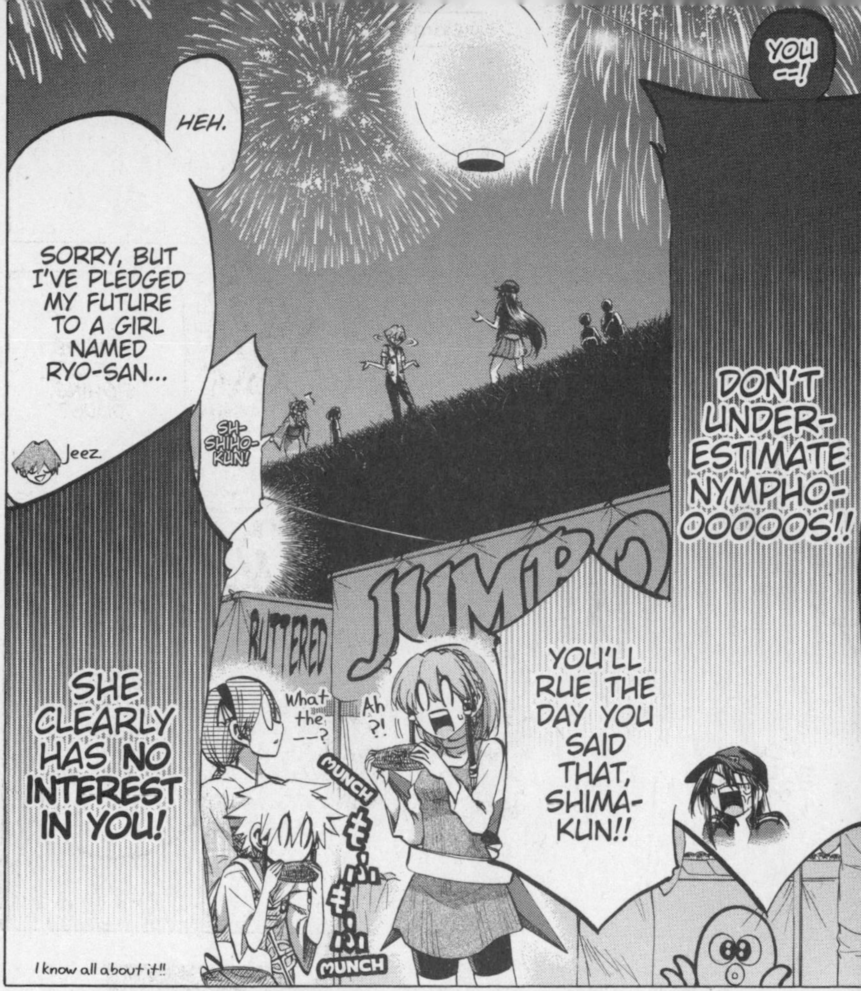
YOU--!
DON'T UNDER-ESTIMATE NYMPHO-OOOOOS!!
HEH.
SORRY, BUT I'VE PLEDGED MY FUTURE TO A GIRL NAMED RYO-SAN...
SH-SHIHO-KUN!
Jeez.
YOU'LL RUE THE DAY YOU SAID THAT, SHIMA-KUN!!
Ah ?!
What the --?
MUNCH
MUNCH
SHE CLEARLY HAS NO INTEREST IN YOU!
I know all about it!!
BUTTERED

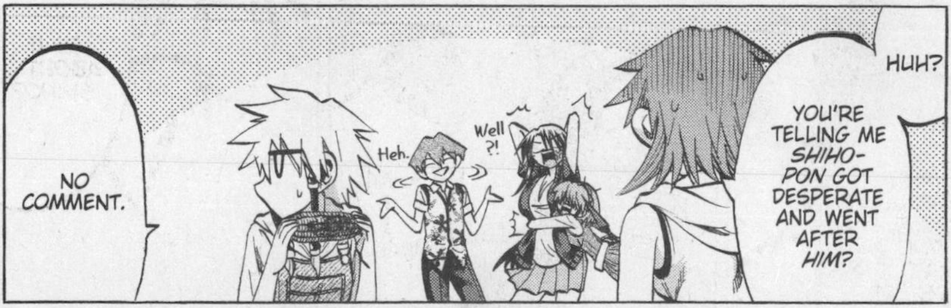
HUH?
YOU'RE TELLING ME SHIHO-PON GOT DESPERATE AND WENT AFTER HIM?
Well ?!
Heh.
NO COMMENT.

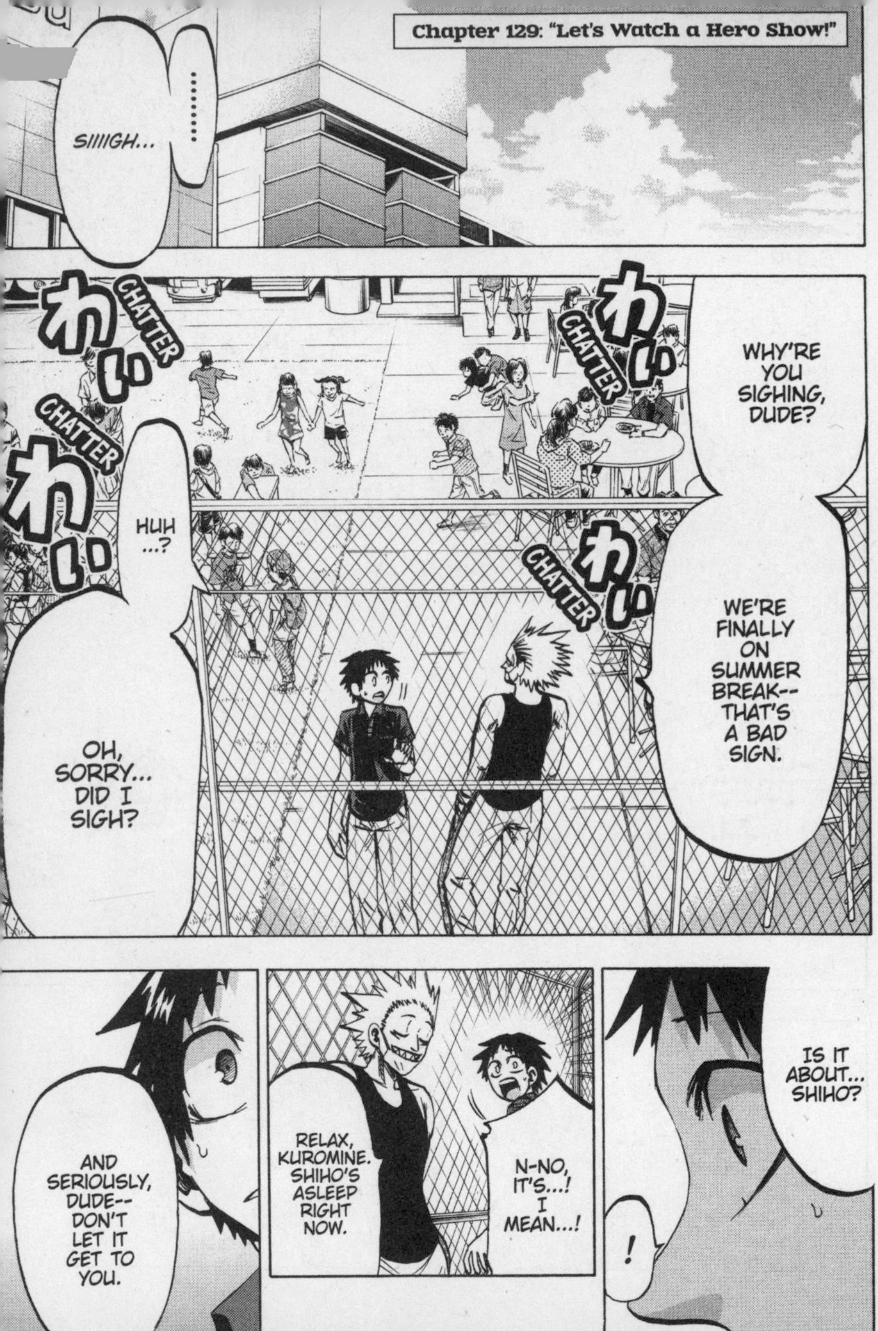
Chapter 129: "Let's Watch a Hero Show!"
......
SIIIGH...
わい CHATTER
WHY'RE YOU SIGHING, DUDE?
わい CHATTER
WE'RE FINALLY ON SUMMER BREAK-- THAT'S A BAD SIGN.
わい CHATTER
わい CHATTER
HUH ...?
OH, SORRY... DID I SIGH?
IS IT ABOUT... SHIHO?
!
N-NO, IT'S...! I MEAN...!
RELAX, KUROMINE. SHIHO'S ASLEEP RIGHT NOW.
AND SERIOUSLY, DUDE-- DON'T LET IT GET TO YOU.

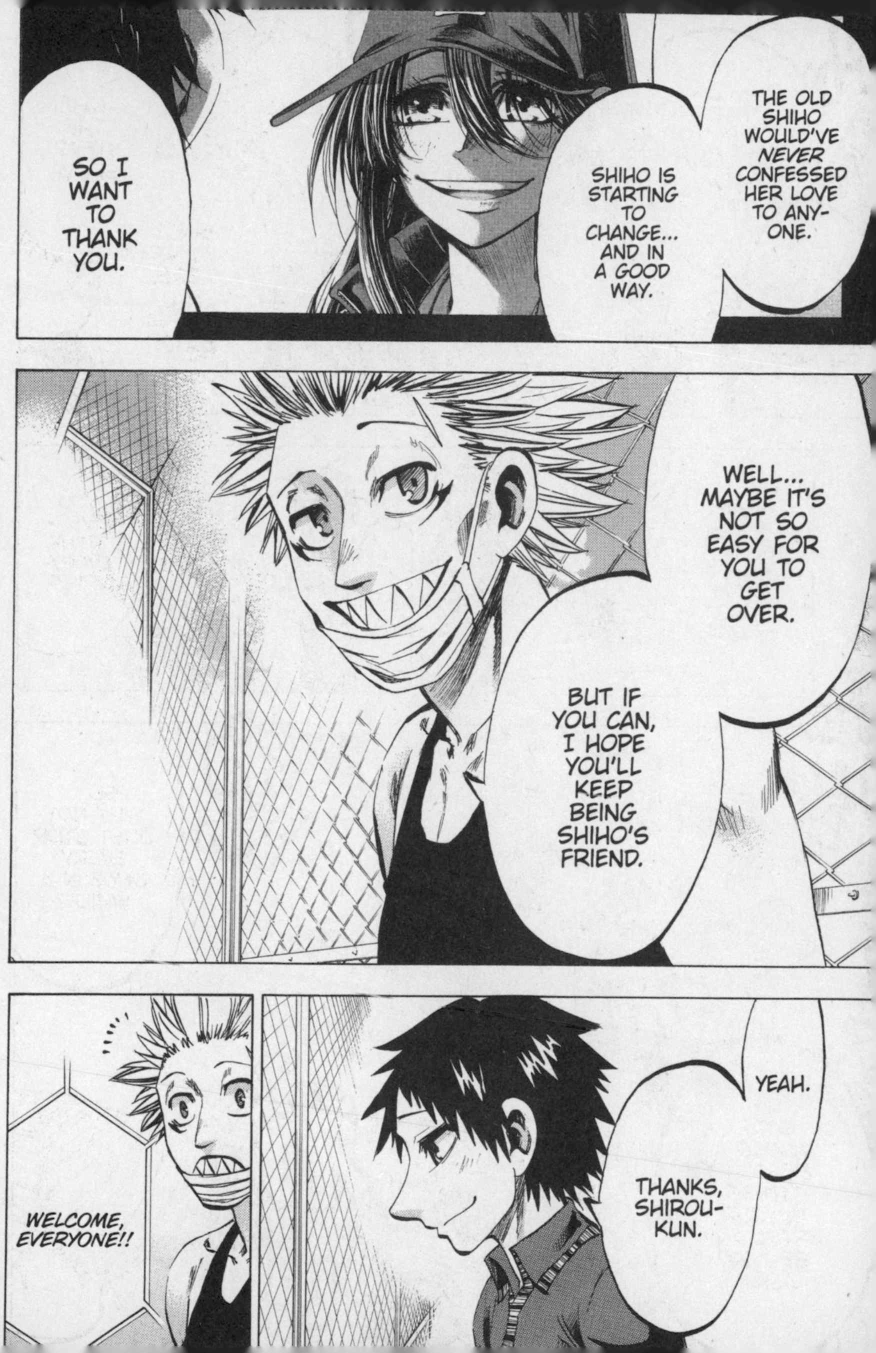
THE OLD SHIHO WOULD'VE *NEVER* CONFESSED HER LOVE TO ANY-ONE.
SHIHO IS STARTING TO CHANGE... AND IN A GOOD WAY.
SO I WANT TO THANK YOU.
WELL... MAYBE IT'S NOT SO EASY FOR YOU TO GET OVER.
BUT IF YOU CAN, I HOPE YOU'LL KEEP BEING SHIHO'S FRIEND.
YEAH.
THANKS, SHIROU-KUN.
WELCOME, EVERYONE!!

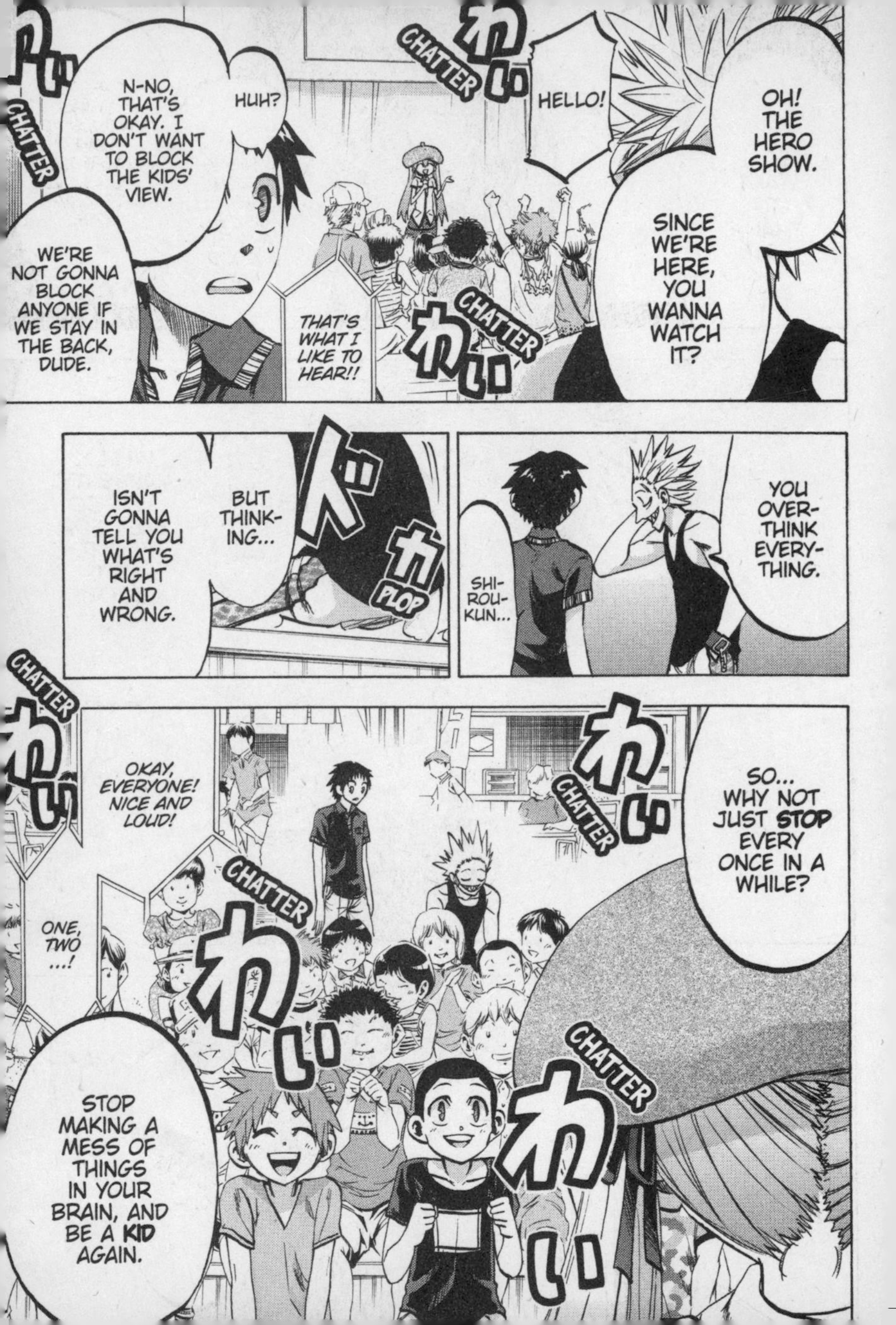
CHATTER
OH! THE HERO SHOW.
SINCE WE'RE HERE, YOU WANNA WATCH IT?
HELLO!
CHATTER
HUH?
N-NO, THAT'S OKAY. I DON'T WANT TO BLOCK THE KIDS' VIEW.
CHATTER
WE'RE NOT GONNA BLOCK ANYONE IF WE STAY IN THE BACK, DUDE.
THAT'S WHAT I LIKE TO HEAR!!
YOU OVER-THINK EVERY-THING.
SHI-ROU-KUN...
BUT THINKING...
PLOP
ISN'T GONNA TELL YOU WHAT'S RIGHT AND WRONG.
CHATTER
SO... WHY NOT JUST **STOP** EVERY ONCE IN A WHILE?
CHATTER
OKAY, EVERYONE! NICE AND LOUD!
CHATTER
CHATTER
ONE, TWO ...!
CHATTER
STOP MAKING A MESS OF THINGS IN YOUR BRAIN, AND BE A **KID** AGAIN.

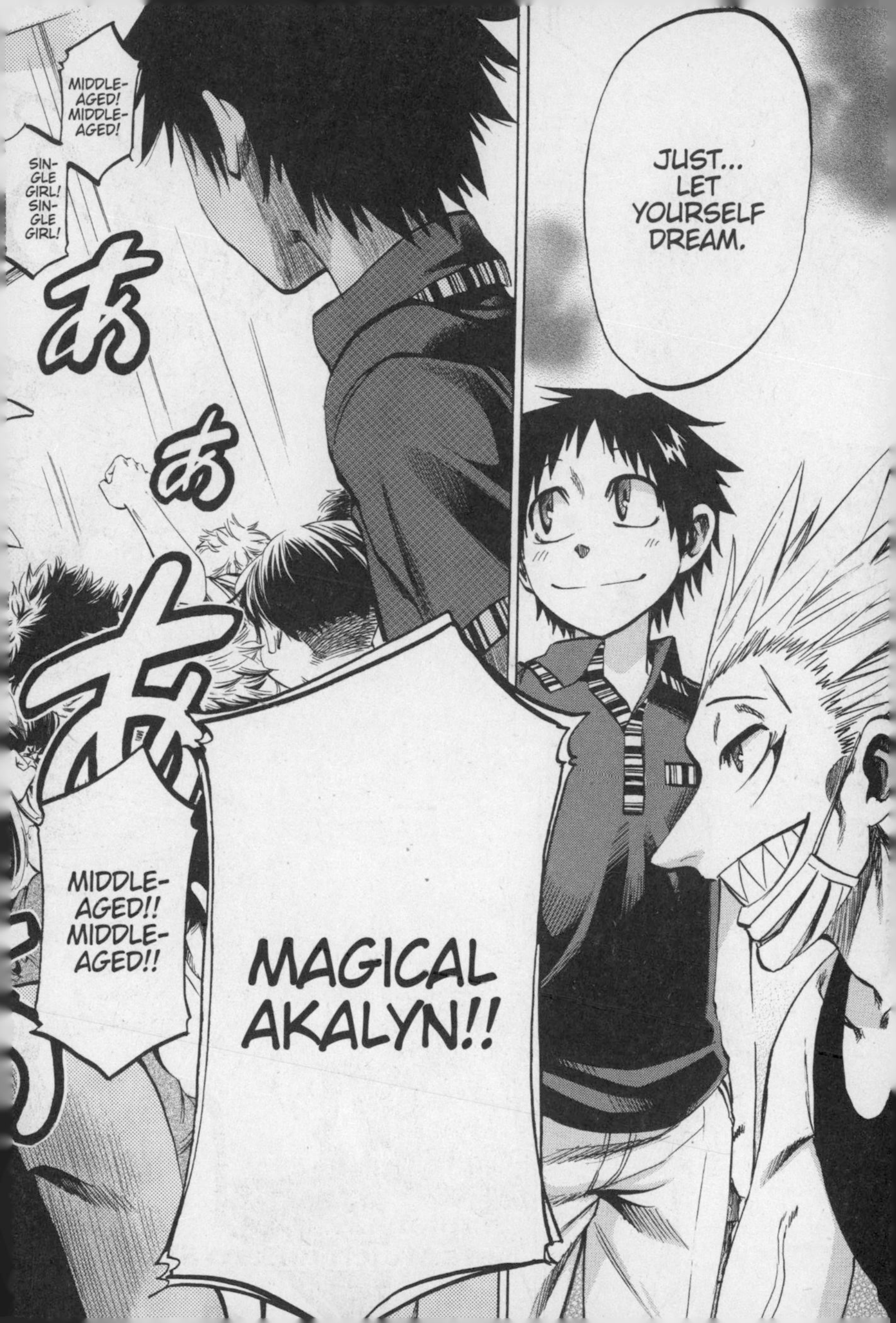
JUST... LET YOURSELF DREAM.
MIDDLE-AGED! MIDDLE-AGED!
SIN-GLE GIRL! SIN-GLE GIRL!
あああ
MIDDLE-AGED!! MIDDLE-AGED!!
MAGICAL AKALYN!!

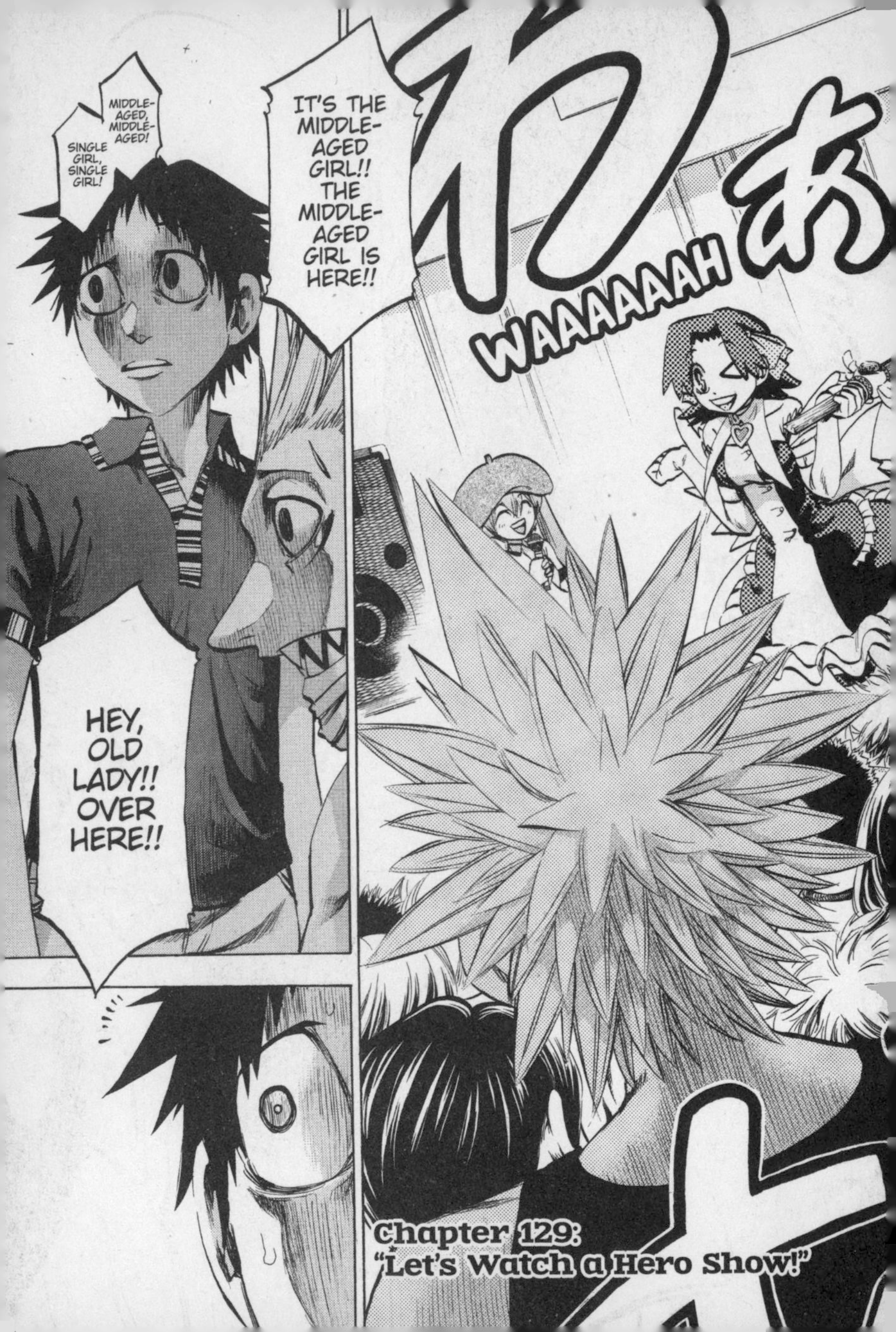
わあ
WAAAAAAAH
Chapter 129:
"Let's Watch a Hero Show!"
IT'S THE MIDDLE-AGED GIRL!! THE MIDDLE-AGED GIRL IS HERE!!
MIDDLE-AGED, MIDDLE-AGED!
SINGLE GIRL, SINGLE GIRL!
HEY, OLD LADY!! OVER HERE!!

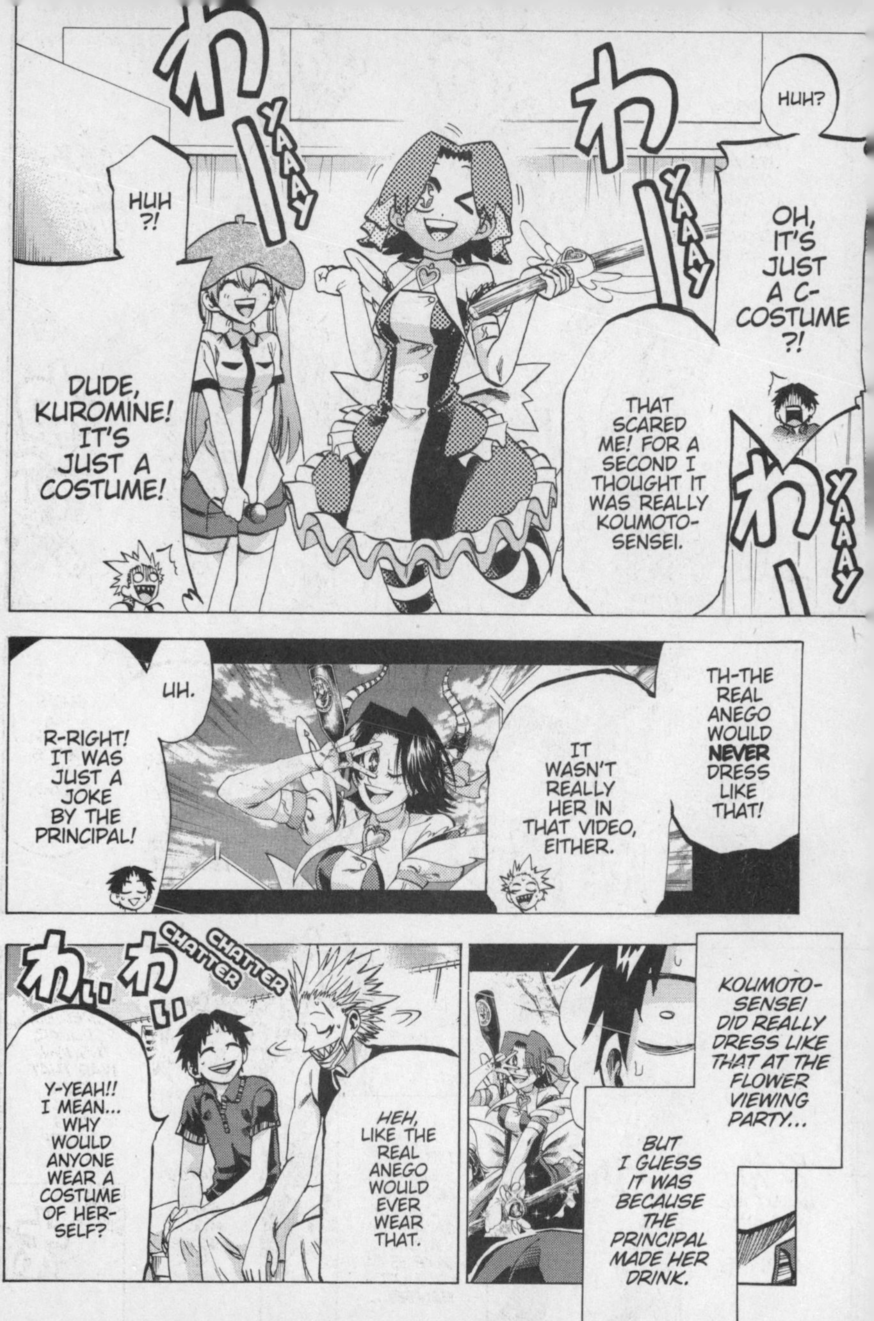
HUH?
OH, IT'S JUST A C-COSTUME ?!
YAAAY
YAAAY
YAAAY
THAT SCARED ME! FOR A SECOND I THOUGHT IT WAS REALLY KOUMOTO-SENSEI.
HUH ?!
DUDE, KUROMINE! IT'S JUST A COSTUME!
TH-THE REAL ANEGO WOULD **NEVER** DRESS LIKE THAT!
IT WASN'T REALLY HER IN THAT VIDEO, EITHER.
UH.
R-RIGHT! IT WAS JUST A JOKE BY THE PRINCIPAL!
KOUMOTO-SENSEI DID REALLY DRESS LIKE THAT AT THE FLOWER VIEWING PARTY...
BUT I GUESS IT WAS BECAUSE THE PRINCIPAL MADE HER DRINK.
CHATTER CHATTER
HEH, LIKE THE REAL ANEGO WOULD EVER WEAR THAT.
Y-YEAH!! I MEAN... WHY WOULD ANYONE WEAR A COSTUME OF HER-SELF?

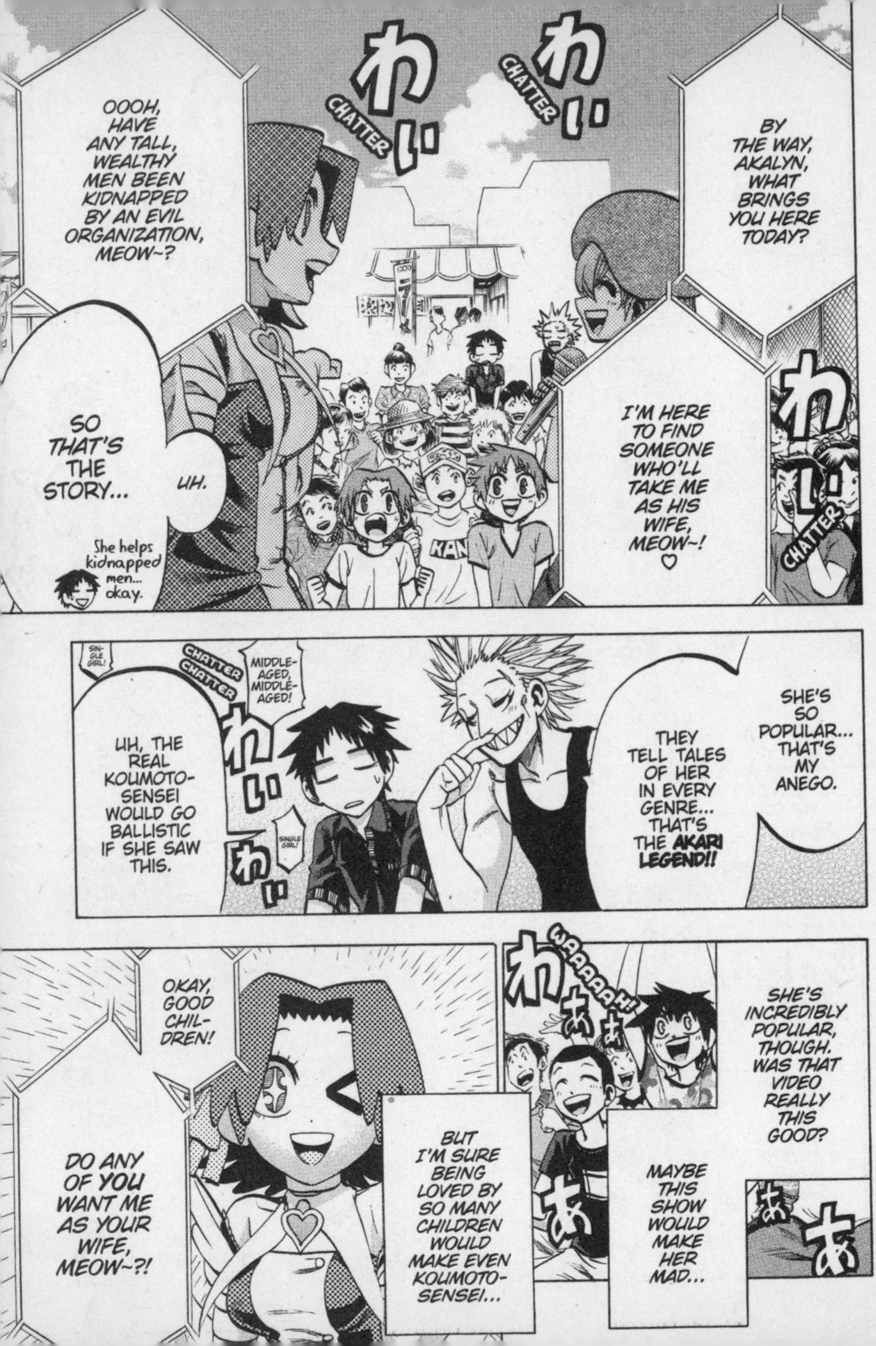
わい
CHATTER
わい
CHATTER
BY THE WAY, AKALYN, WHAT BRINGS YOU HERE TODAY?
わい
CHATTER
I'M HERE TO FIND SOMEONE WHO'LL TAKE ME AS HIS WIFE, MEOW~! ♡
OOOH, HAVE ANY TALL, WEALTHY MEN BEEN KIDNAPPED BY AN EVIL ORGANIZATION, MEOW~?
UH.
SO THAT'S THE STORY...
She helps kidnapped men... okay.
SHE'S SO POPULAR... THAT'S MY ANEGO.
THEY TELL TALES OF HER IN EVERY GENRE... THAT'S THE AKARI LEGEND!!
SINGLE GIRL!
わい
わい
MIDDLE-AGED, MIDDLE-AGED!
CHATTER CHATTER
SINGLE GIRL!
UH, THE REAL KOUMOTO-SENSEI WOULD GO BALLISTIC IF SHE SAW THIS.
SHE'S INCREDIBLY POPULAR, THOUGH. WAS THAT VIDEO REALLY THIS GOOD?
わあぁ
WAAAAAH!
あぁ
MAYBE THIS SHOW WOULD MAKE HER MAD...
BUT I'M SURE BEING LOVED BY SO MANY CHILDREN WOULD MAKE EVEN KOUMOTO-SENSEI...
OKAY, GOOD CHILDREN!
DO ANY OF YOU WANT ME AS YOUR WIFE, MEOW~?!

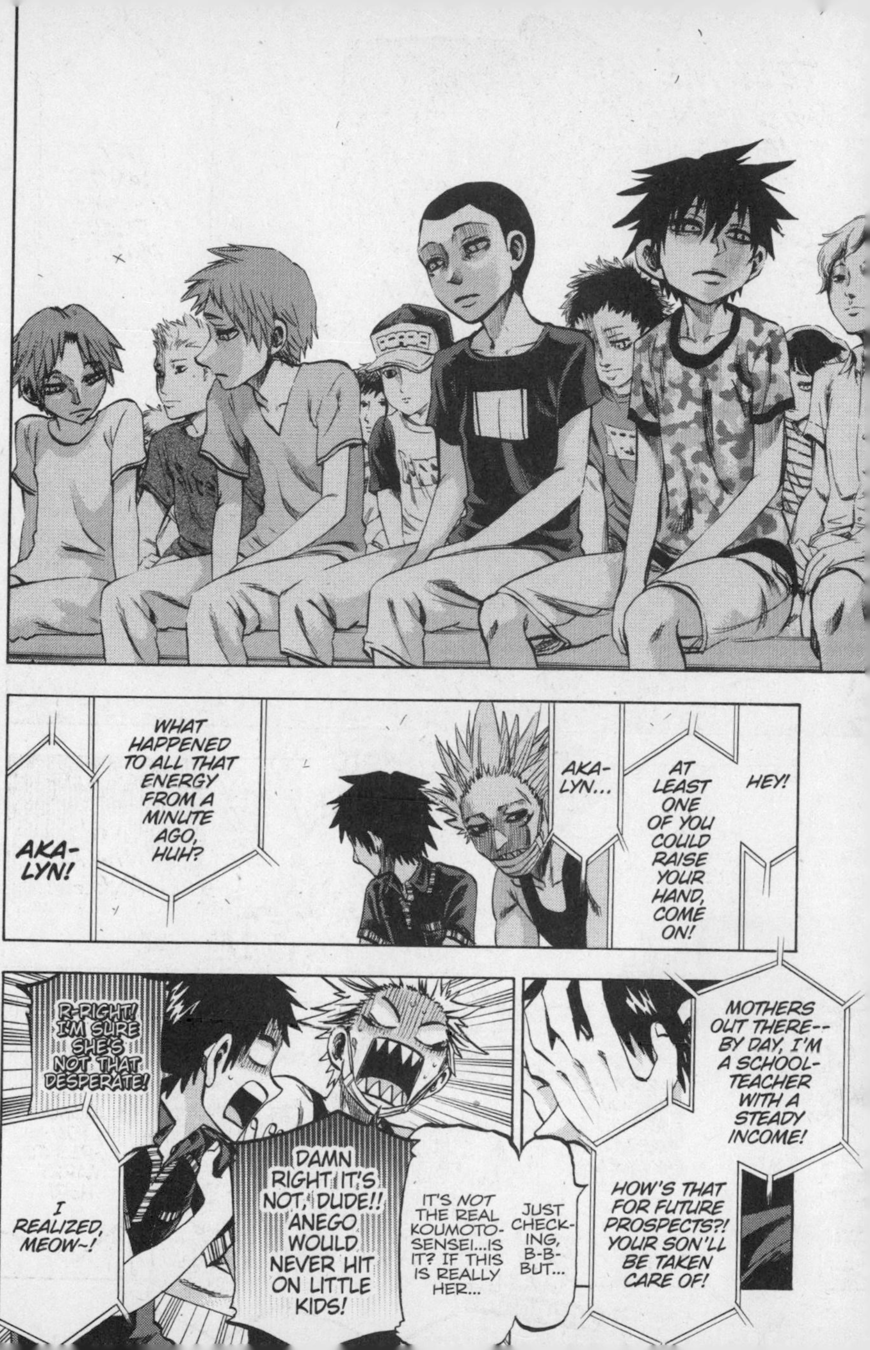
HEY!
AT LEAST ONE OF YOU COULD RAISE YOUR HAND, COME ON!
AKA-LYN...
WHAT HAPPENED TO ALL THAT ENERGY FROM A MINUTE AGO, HUH?
AKA-LYN!
MOTHERS OUT THERE-- BY DAY, I'M A SCHOOL-TEACHER WITH A STEADY INCOME!
HOW'S THAT FOR FUTURE PROSPECTS?! YOUR SON'LL BE TAKEN CARE OF!
JUST CHECKING, B-B-BUT...
IT'S *NOT* THE REAL KOUMOTO-SENSEI...IS IT? IF THIS IS REALLY HER...
R-RIGHT! I'M SURE SHE'S NOT THAT DESPERATE!
DAMN RIGHT IT'S NOT, DUDE!! ANEGO WOULD NEVER HIT ON LITTLE KIDS!
I REALIZED, MEOW~!

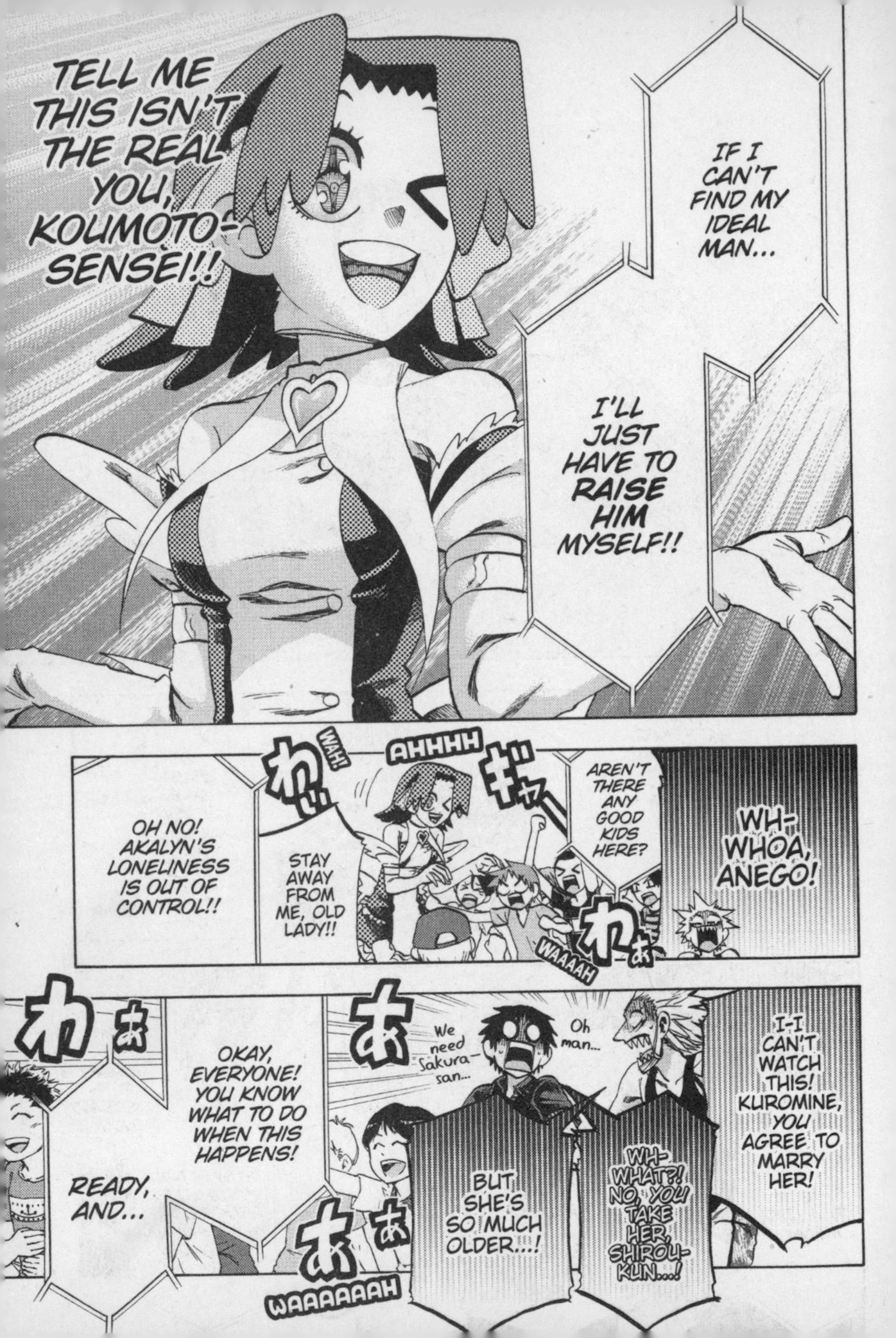

IF I CAN'T FIND MY IDEAL MAN...
I'LL JUST HAVE TO RAISE HIM MYSELF!!
TELL ME THIS ISN'T THE REAL YOU, KOUMOTO-SENSEI!!
WH-WHOA, ANEGO!
AREN'T THERE ANY GOOD KIDS HERE?
AHHHH
WAH!
STAY AWAY FROM ME, OLD LADY!!
WAAAAH
OH NO! AKALYN'S LONELINESS IS OUT OF CONTROL!!
I-I CAN'T WATCH THIS! KUROMINE, YOU AGREE TO MARRY HER!
WH-WHAT?! NO, YOU TAKE HER, SHIROU-KUN...!
Oh man...
BUT SHE'S SO MUCH OLDER...!
We need Sakura-san...
OKAY, EVERYONE! YOU KNOW WHAT TO DO WHEN THIS HAPPENS!
READY, AND...
WAAAAAAH

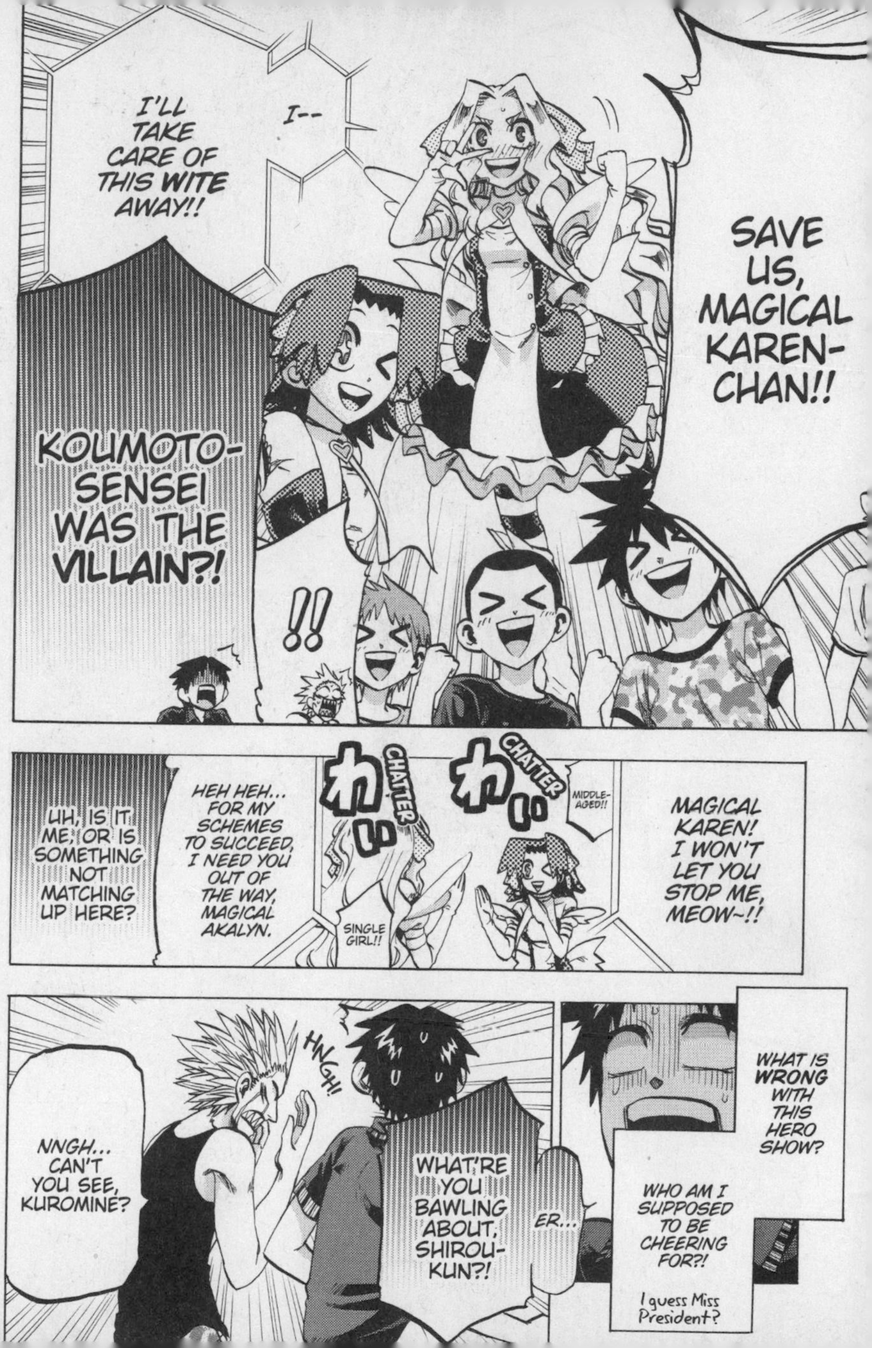
SAVE US, MAGICAL KAREN-CHAN!!
I--
I'LL TAKE CARE OF THIS WITE AWAY!!
KOUMOTO-SENSEI WAS THE VILLAIN?!
!!
MAGICAL KAREN! I WON'T LET YOU STOP ME, MEOW~!!
MIDDLE-AGED!!
わい CHATTER
わい CHATTER
SINGLE GIRL!!
HEH HEH... FOR MY SCHEMES TO SUCCEED, I NEED YOU OUT OF THE WAY, MAGICAL AKALYN.
UH, IS IT ME, OR IS SOMETHING NOT MATCHING UP HERE?
WHAT IS WRONG WITH THIS HERO SHOW?
WHO AM I SUPPOSED TO BE CHEERING FOR?!
I guess Miss President?
HNGH!
ER...
WHAT'RE YOU BAWLING ABOUT, SHIROU-KUN?!
NNGH... CAN'T YOU SEE, KUROMINE?

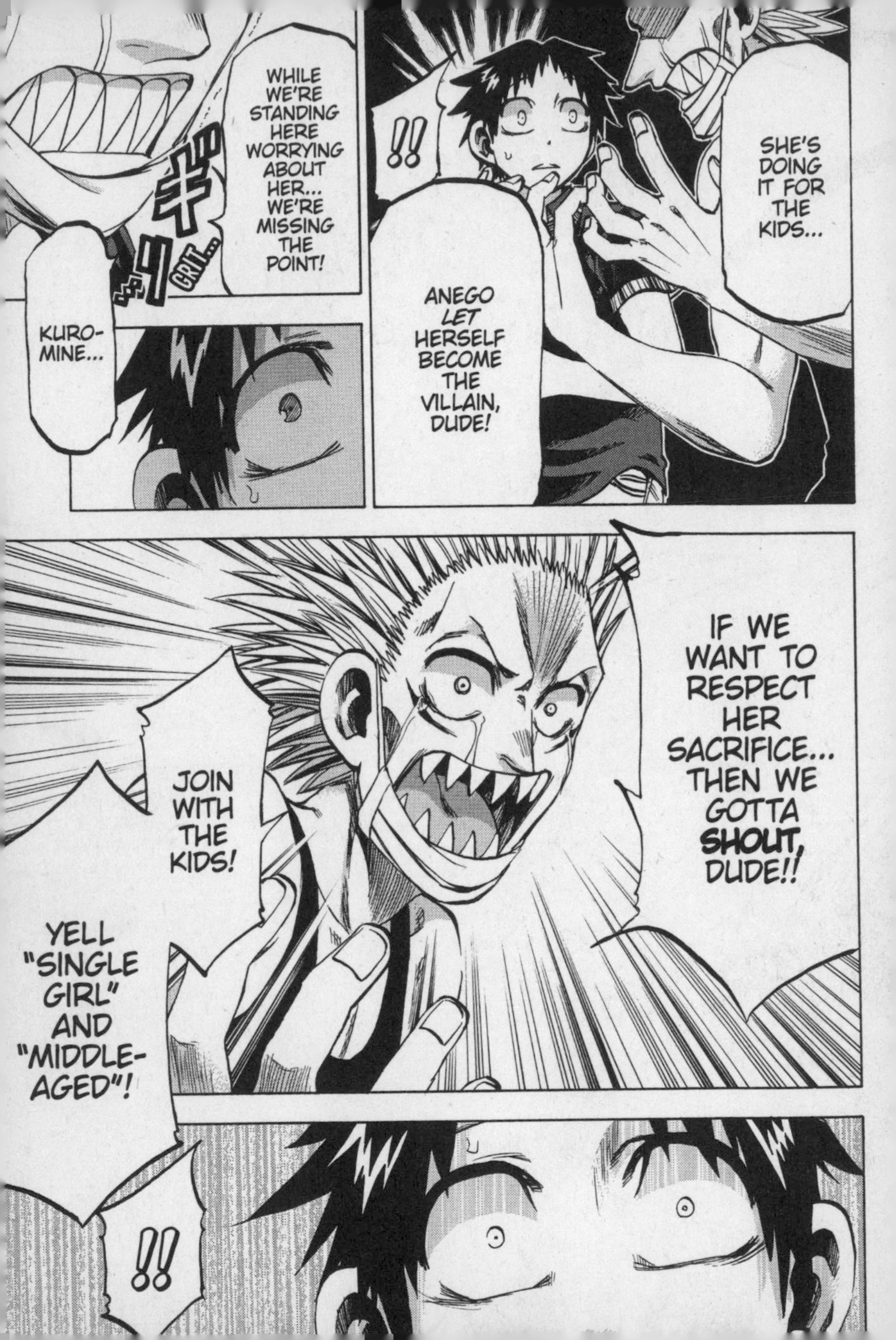
SHE'S DOING IT FOR THE KIDS...
!!
ANEGO LET HERSELF BECOME THE VILLAIN, DUDE!
WHILE WE'RE STANDING HERE WORRYING ABOUT HER... WE'RE MISSING THE POINT!
GRIT...
KURO-MINE...
IF WE WANT TO RESPECT HER SACRIFICE... THEN WE GOTTA **SHOUT**, DUDE!!
JOIN WITH THE KIDS!
YELL "SINGLE GIRL" AND "MIDDLE-AGED"!
!!

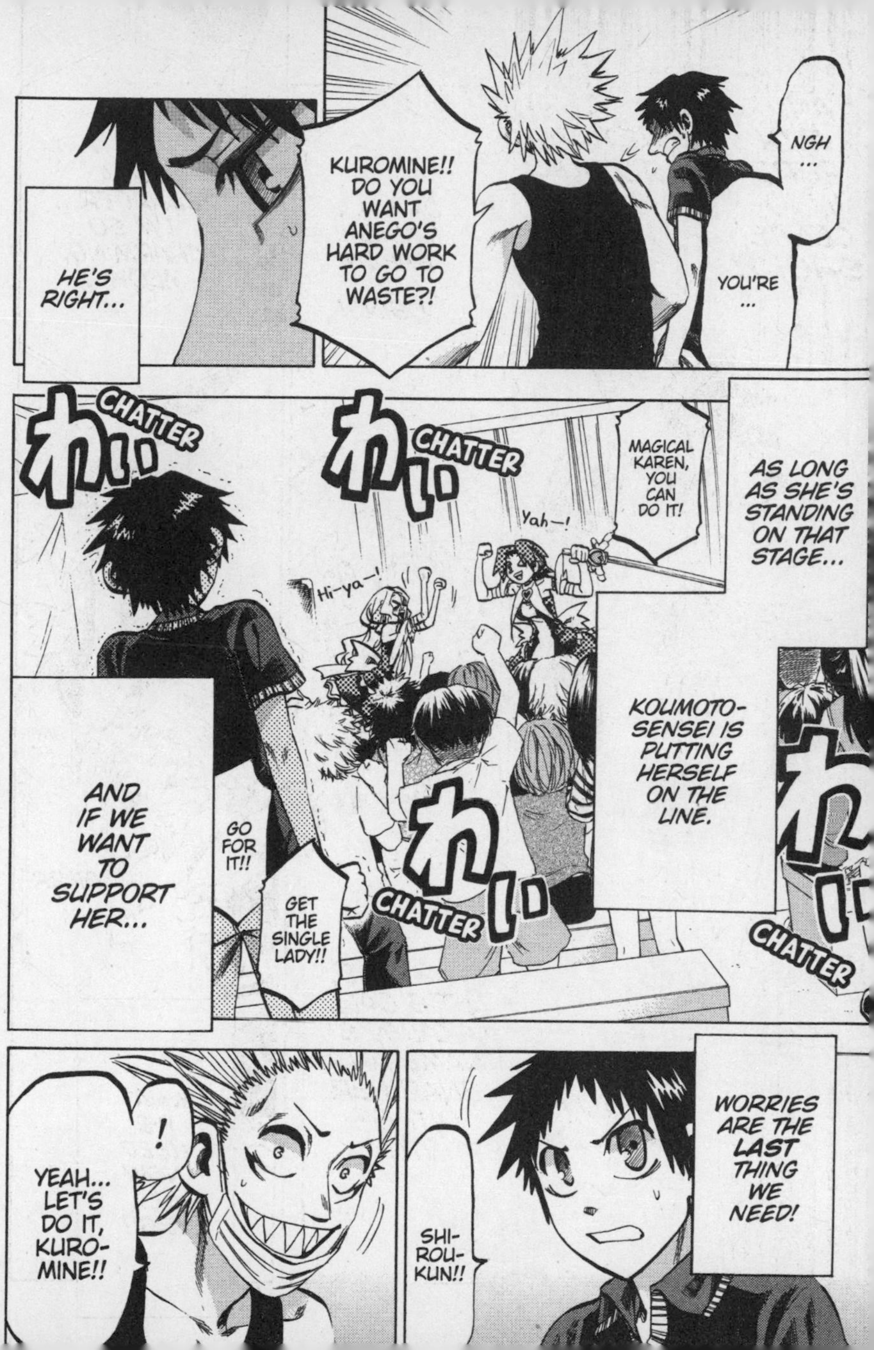
NGH ...
KUROMINE!! DO YOU WANT ANEGO'S HARD WORK TO GO TO WASTE?!
YOU'RE ...
HE'S RIGHT...
AS LONG AS SHE'S STANDING ON THAT STAGE...
KOUMOTO-SENSEI IS PUTTING HERSELF ON THE LINE.
わい CHATTER
MAGICAL KAREN, YOU CAN DO IT!
Yah—!
わい CHATTER
Hi-ya—!
わい CHATTER
わい CHATTER
GO FOR IT!!
GET THE SINGLE LADY!!
AND IF WE WANT TO SUPPORT HER...
WORRIES ARE THE LAST THING WE NEED!
SHI-ROU-KUN!!
!
YEAH... LET'S DO IT, KURO-MINE!!

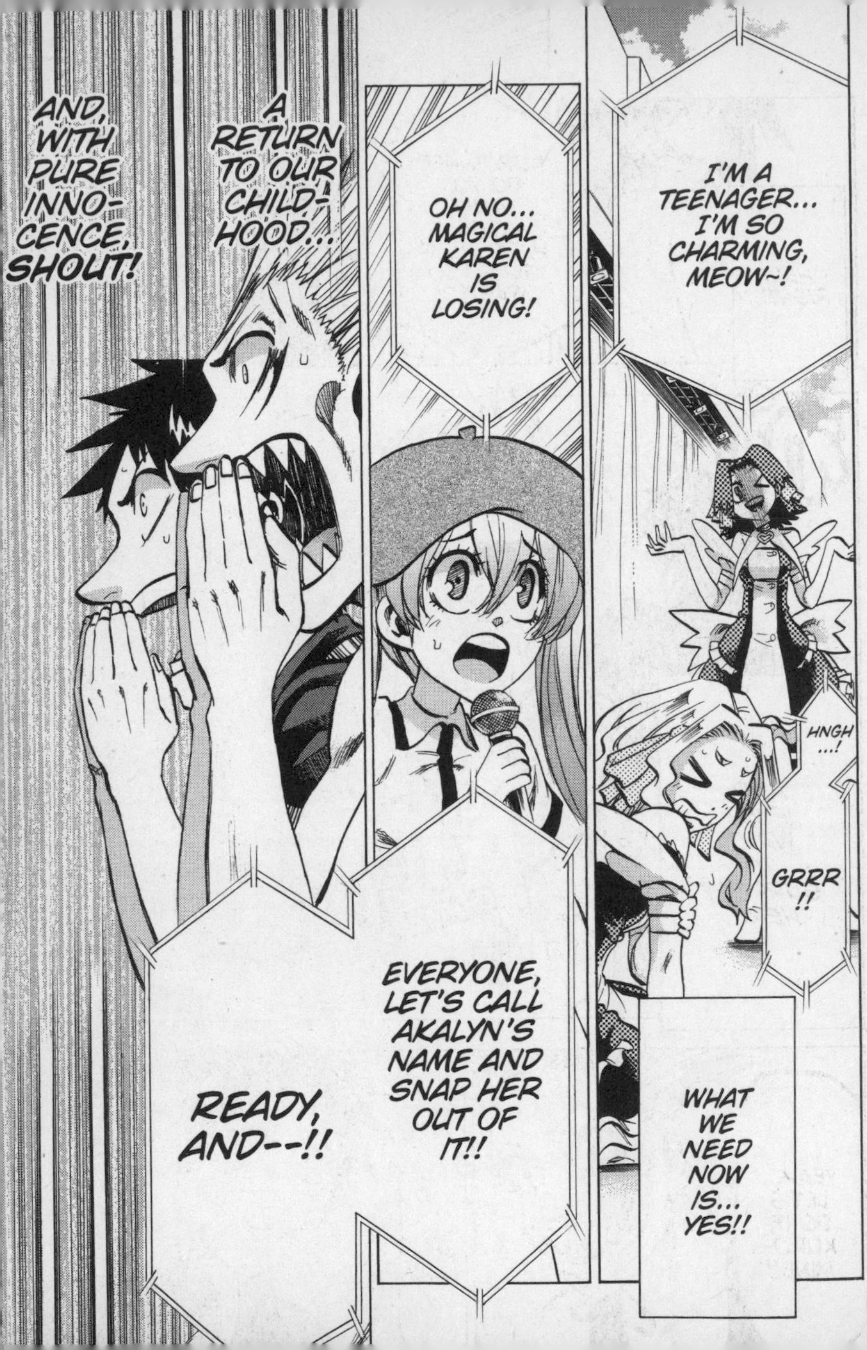
I'M A TEENAGER... I'M SO CHARMING, MEOW~!
HNGH...!
GRRR!!
WHAT WE NEED NOW IS... YES!!
OH NO... MAGICAL KAREN IS LOSING!
EVERYONE, LET'S CALL AKALYN'S NAME AND SNAP HER OUT OF IT!!
READY, AND--!!
A RETURN TO OUR CHILD-HOOD...
AND, WITH PURE INNO-CENCE, SHOUT!

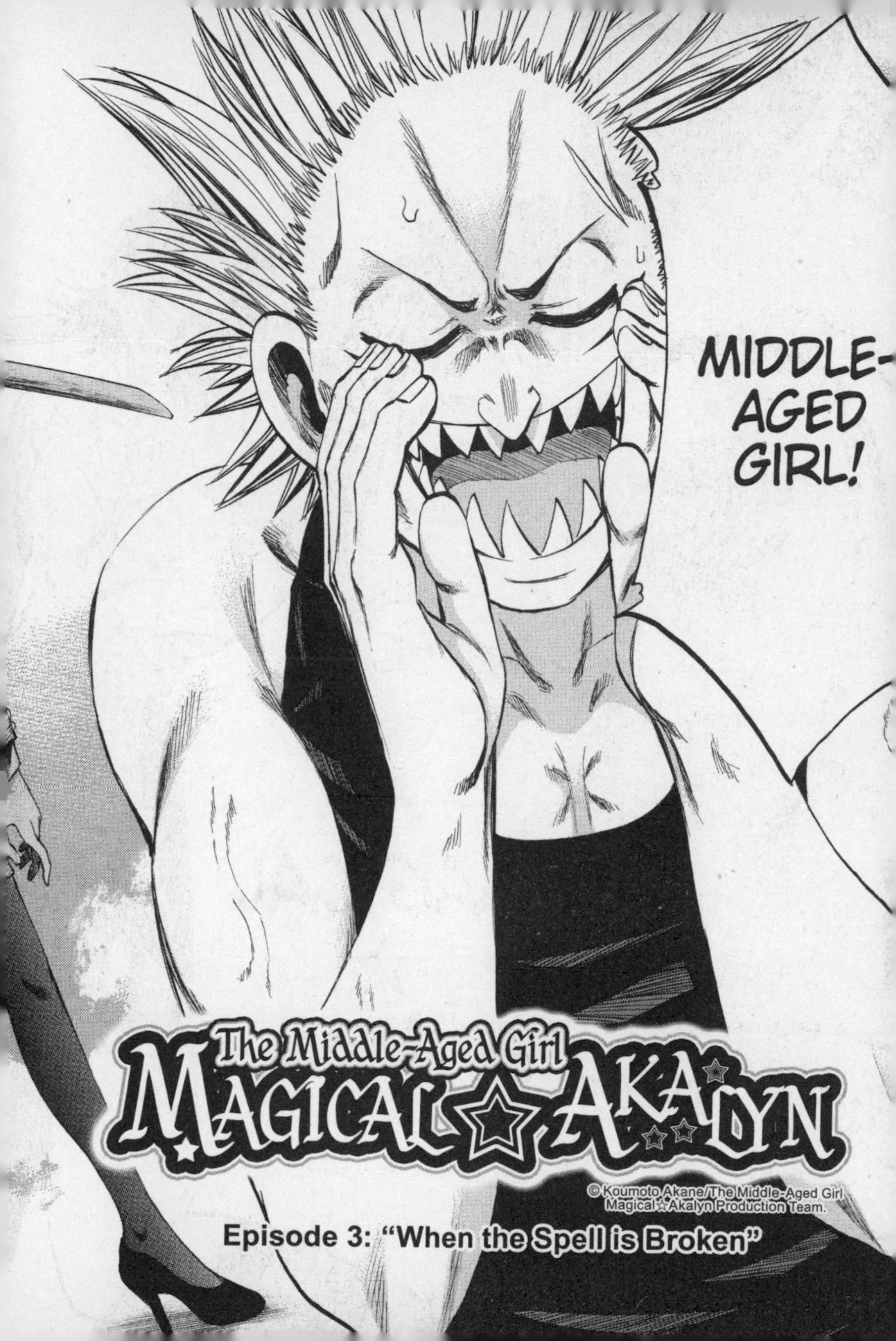
MIDDLE-AGED GIRL!
The Middle-Aged Girl
MAGICAL☆AKALYN
© Koumoto Akane/The Middle-Aged Girl Magical☆Akalyn Production Team.
Episode 3: "When the Spell is Broken"

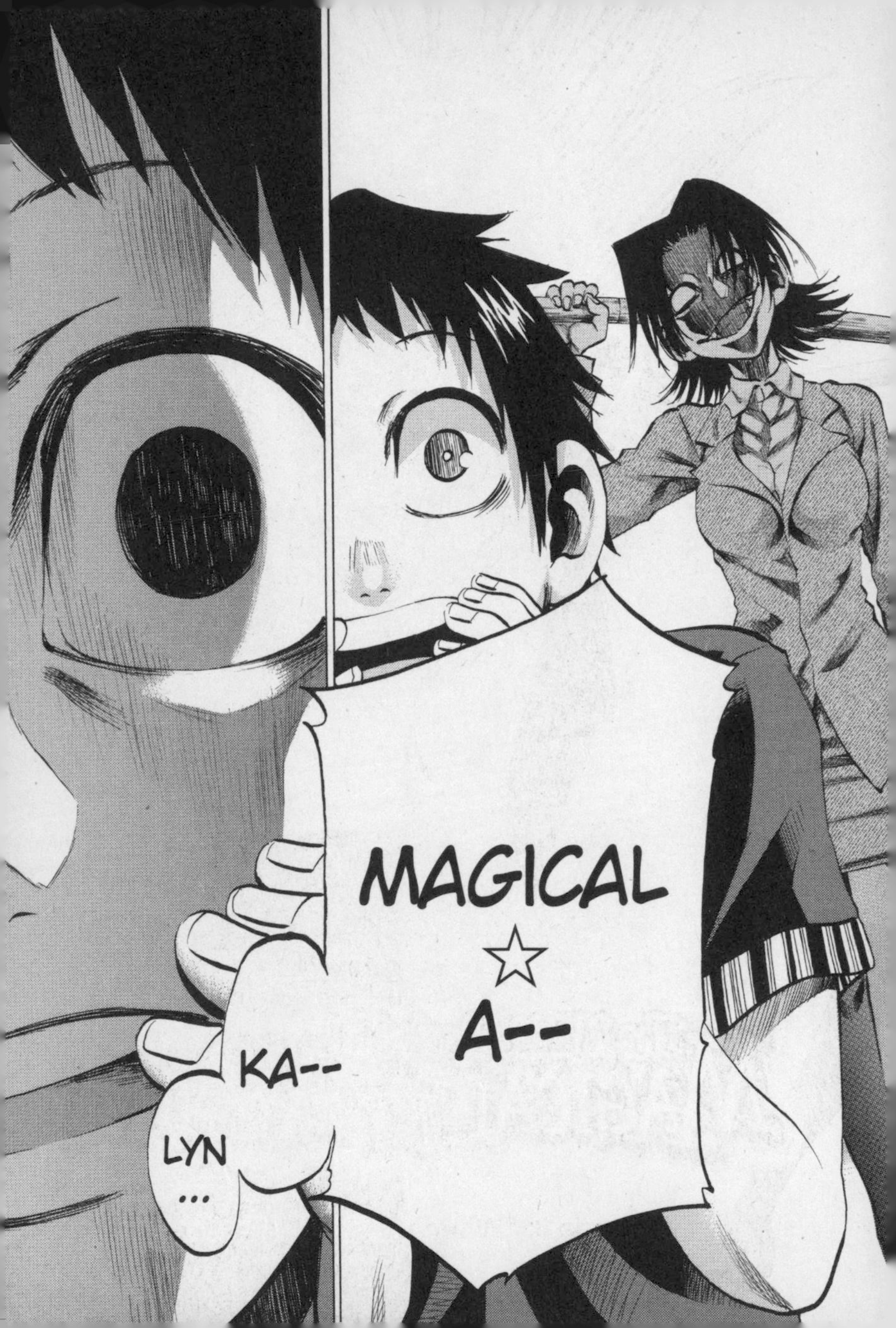
MAGICAL ☆ A--
KA--
LYN ...

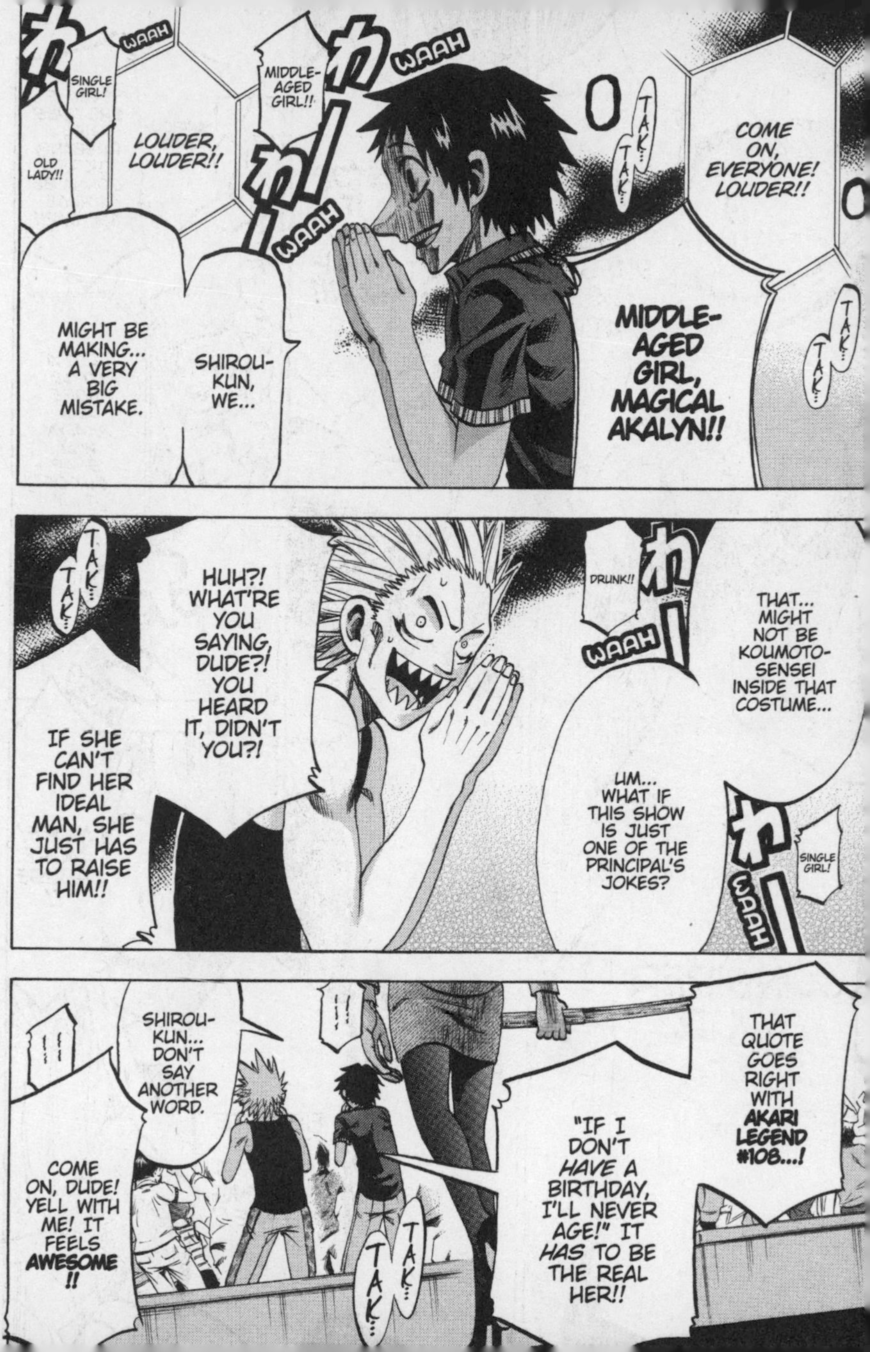
COME ON, EVERYONE! LOUDER!!
TAK... TAK...
MIDDLE-AGED GIRL, MAGICAL AKALYN!!
TAK... TAK...
WAAH
MIDDLE-AGED GIRL!!
WAAH
LOUDER, LOUDER!!
WAAH
SINGLE GIRL!
OLD LADY!!
SHIROU-KUN, WE...
MIGHT BE MAKING... A VERY BIG MISTAKE.
THAT... MIGHT NOT BE KOUMOTO-SENSEI INSIDE THAT COSTUME...
DRUNK!!
WAAH
SINGLE GIRL!
WAAH
UM... WHAT IF THIS SHOW IS JUST ONE OF THE PRINCIPAL'S JOKES?
HUH?! WHAT'RE YOU SAYING, DUDE?! YOU HEARD IT, DIDN'T YOU?!
TAK... TAK...
IF SHE CAN'T FIND HER IDEAL MAN, SHE JUST HAS TO RAISE HIM!!
THAT QUOTE GOES RIGHT WITH AKARI LEGEND #108...!
"IF I DON'T HAVE A BIRTHDAY, I'LL NEVER AGE!" IT HAS TO BE THE REAL HER!!
TAK... TAK...
!!
SHIROU-KUN... DON'T SAY ANOTHER WORD.
!!
COME ON, DUDE! YELL WITH ME! IT FEELS AWESOME!!

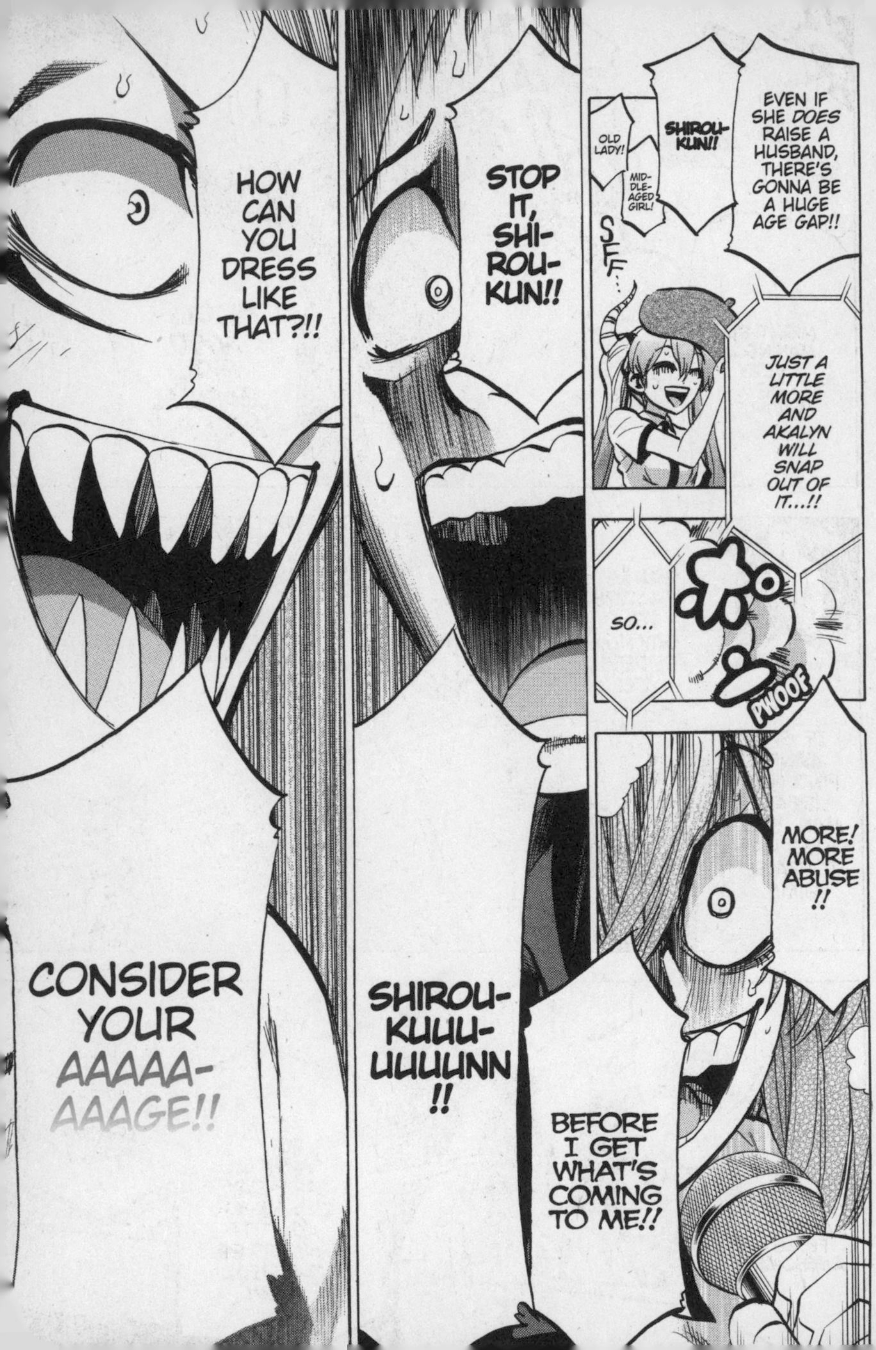

EVEN IF SHE DOES RAISE A HUSBAND, THERE'S GONNA BE A HUGE AGE GAP!!
SHIROU-KUN!!
OLD LADY!
MID-DLE-AGED GIRL!
SFF...
JUST A LITTLE MORE AND AKALYN WILL SNAP OUT OF IT...!!
SO...
PWOOF
MORE! MORE ABUSE!!
BEFORE I GET WHAT'S COMING TO ME!!
STOP IT, SHI-ROU-KUN!!
SHIROU-KUUU-UUUUNN!!
HOW CAN YOU DRESS LIKE THAT?!!
CONSIDER YOUR AAAAA-AAAGE!!

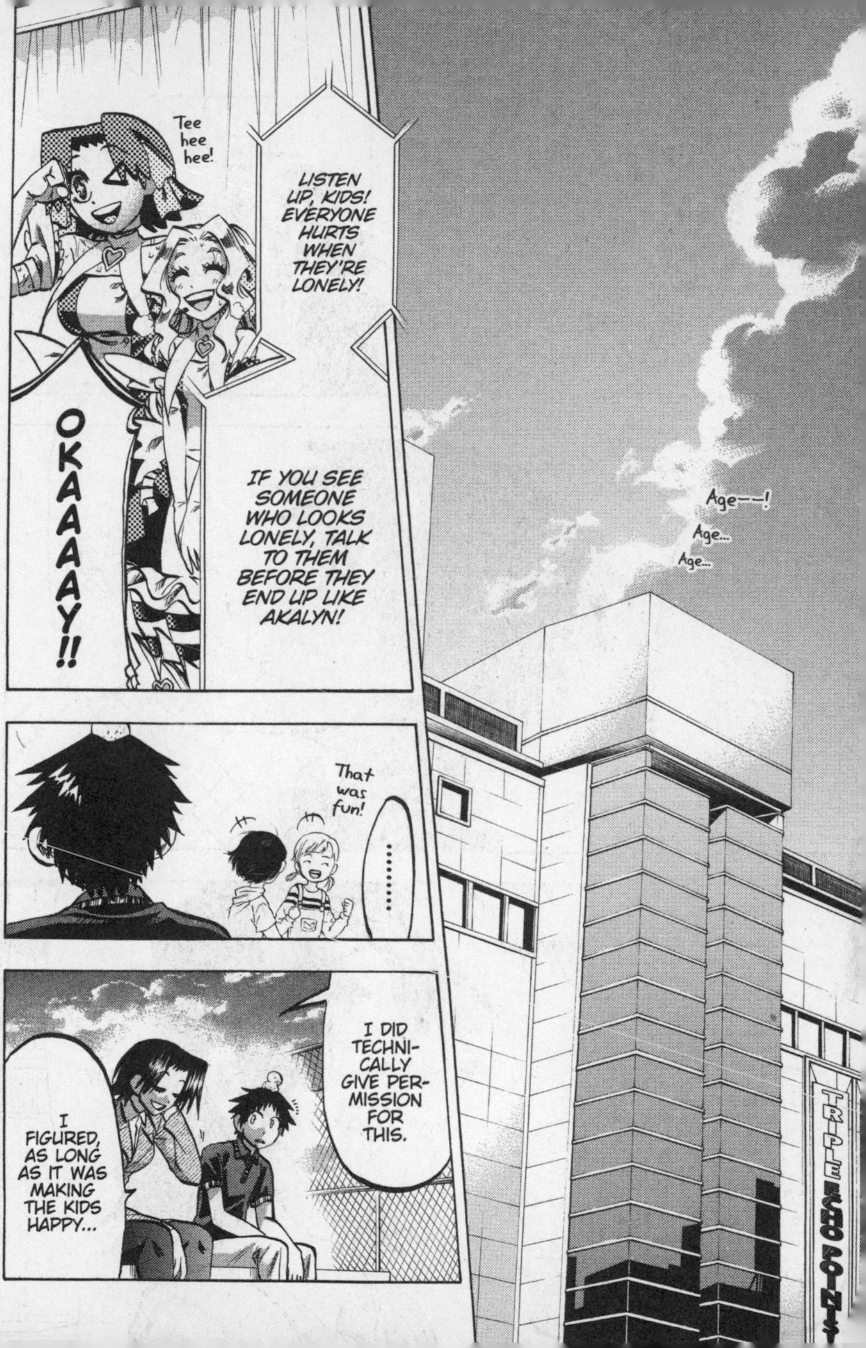

Age—!
Age...
Age...
TRIPLE ECHO POINT
LISTEN UP, KIDS! EVERYONE HURTS WHEN THEY'RE LONELY!
Tee hee hee!
IF YOU SEE SOMEONE WHO LOOKS LONELY, TALK TO THEM BEFORE THEY END UP LIKE AKALYN!
OKAAAAAY!!
....
That was fun!
I DID TECHNICALLY GIVE PERMISSION FOR THIS.
I FIGURED, AS LONG AS IT WAS MAKING THE KIDS HAPPY...

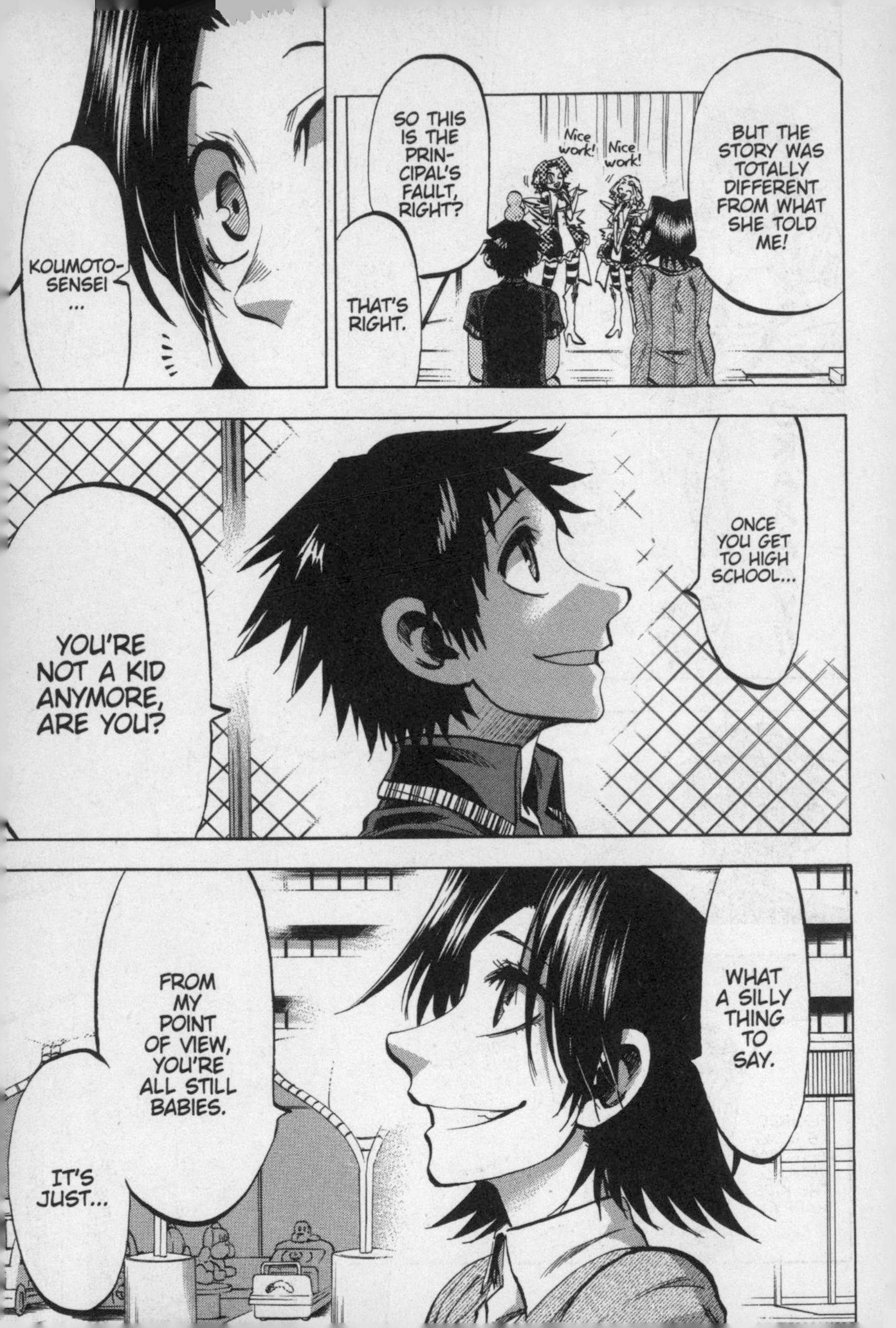
BUT THE STORY WAS TOTALLY DIFFERENT FROM WHAT SHE TOLD ME!
Nice work!
Nice work!
SO THIS IS THE PRIN-CIPAL'S FAULT, RIGHT?
THAT'S RIGHT.
KOUMOTO-SENSEI ...
ONCE YOU GET TO HIGH SCHOOL...
YOU'RE NOT A KID ANYMORE, ARE YOU?
WHAT A SILLY THING TO SAY.
FROM MY POINT OF VIEW, YOU'RE ALL STILL BABIES.
IT'S JUST...

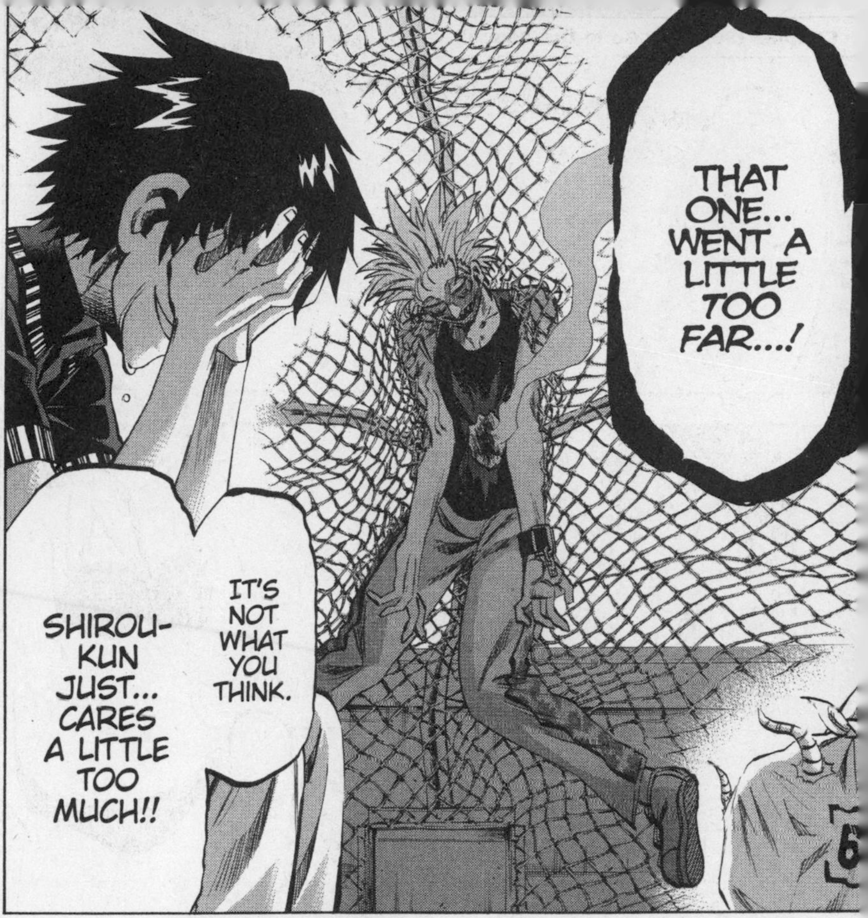
THAT ONE... WENT A LITTLE TOO FAR...!
IT'S NOT WHAT YOU THINK.
SHIROU-KUN JUST... CARES A LITTLE TOO MUCH!!
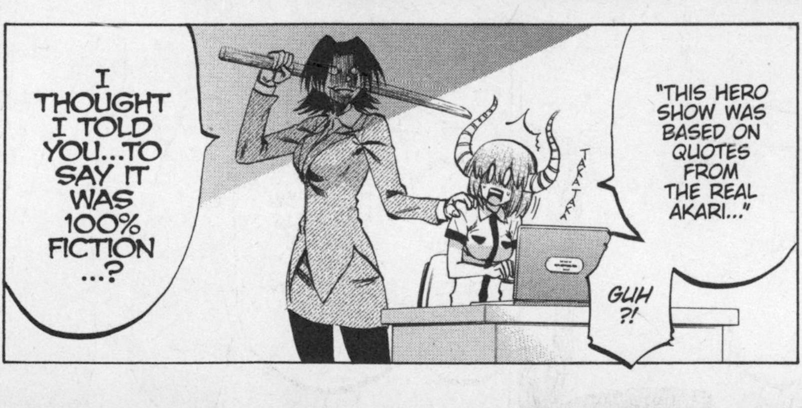
"THIS HERO SHOW WAS BASED ON QUOTES FROM THE REAL AKARI..."
TAKATAKA
GUH ?!
I THOUGHT I TOLD YOU...TO SAY IT WAS 100% FICTION ...?

Chapter 130: "Let's Go to the Beach!"

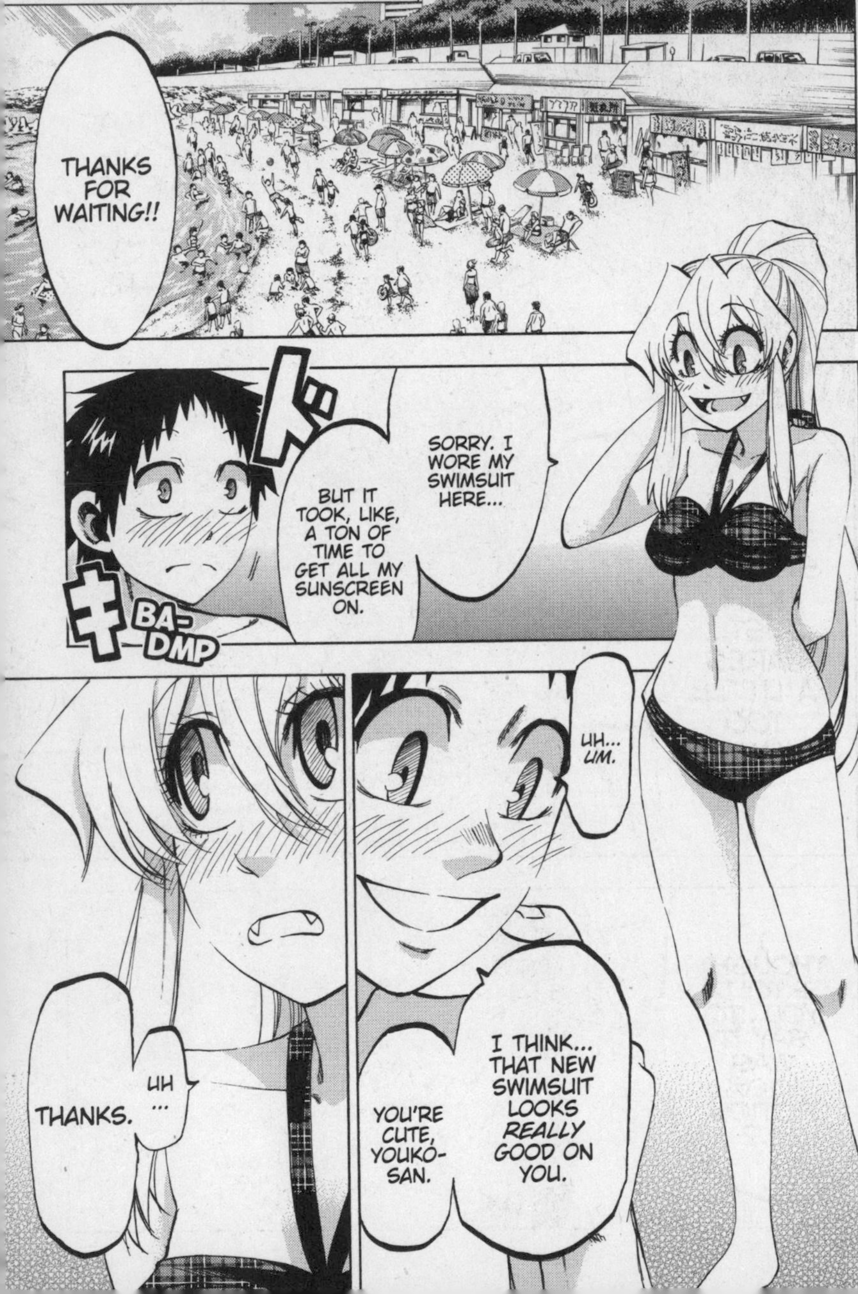
THANKS FOR WAITING!!
SORRY. I WORE MY SWIMSUIT HERE...
BUT IT TOOK, LIKE, A TON OF TIME TO GET ALL MY SUNSCREEN ON.
ドキ
BA-DMP
UH... UM.
I THINK... THAT NEW SWIMSUIT LOOKS *REALLY* GOOD ON YOU.
YOU'RE CUTE, YOUKO-SAN.
UH ...
THANKS.

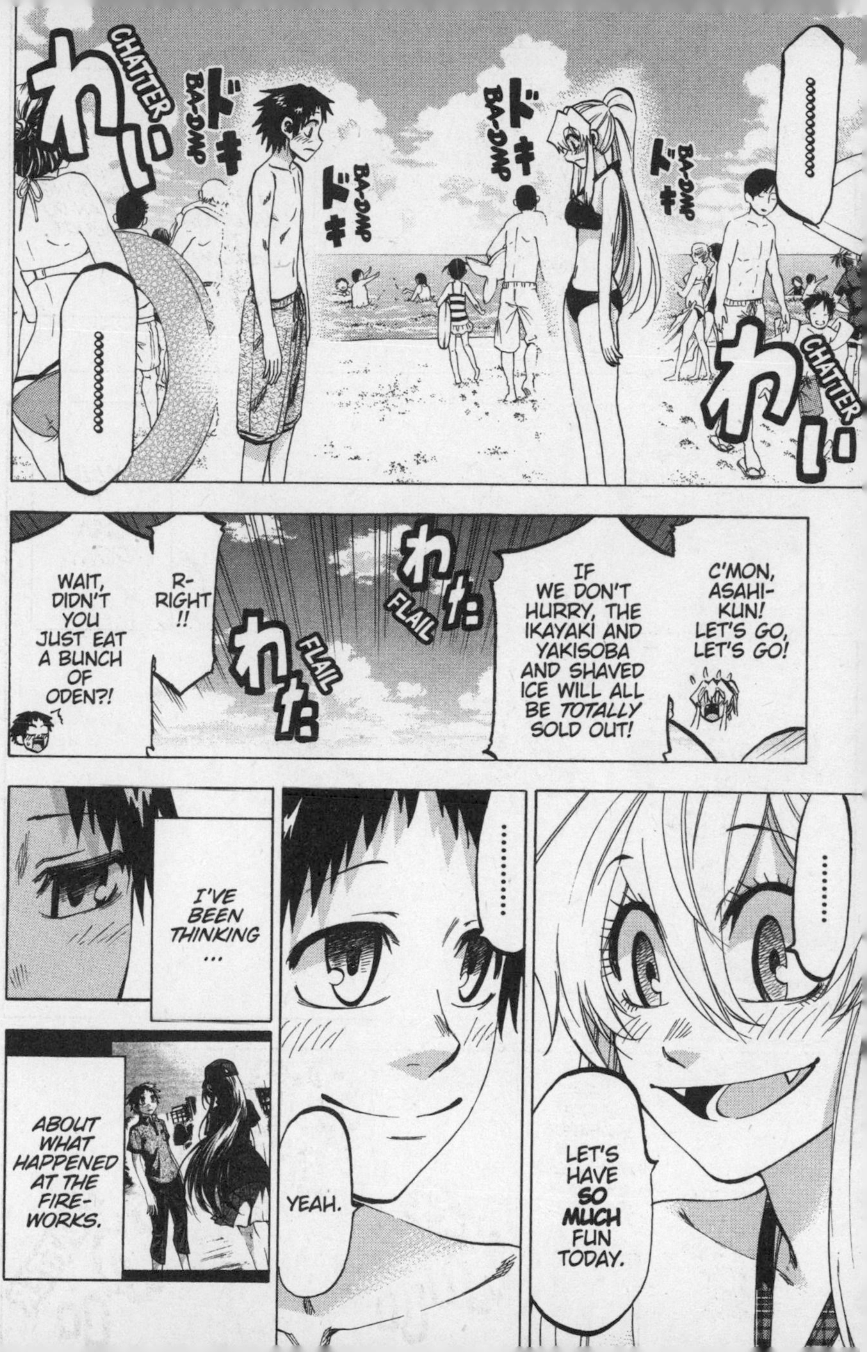

......
BA-DMP
ドキ
CHATTER
わい
BA-DMP
ドキ
BA-DMP
ドキ
BA-DMP
ドキ
......
CHATTER
わい
C'MON, ASAHI-KUN! LET'S GO, LET'S GO!
IF WE DON'T HURRY, THE IKAYAKI AND YAKISOBA AND SHAVED ICE WILL ALL BE *TOTALLY* SOLD OUT!
わた
FLAIL
わた
FLAIL
R-RIGHT!!
WAIT, DIDN'T YOU JUST EAT A BUNCH OF ODEN?!
......
LET'S HAVE **SO MUCH** FUN TODAY.
......
YEAH.
I'VE BEEN THINKING...
ABOUT WHAT HAPPENED AT THE FIRE-WORKS.

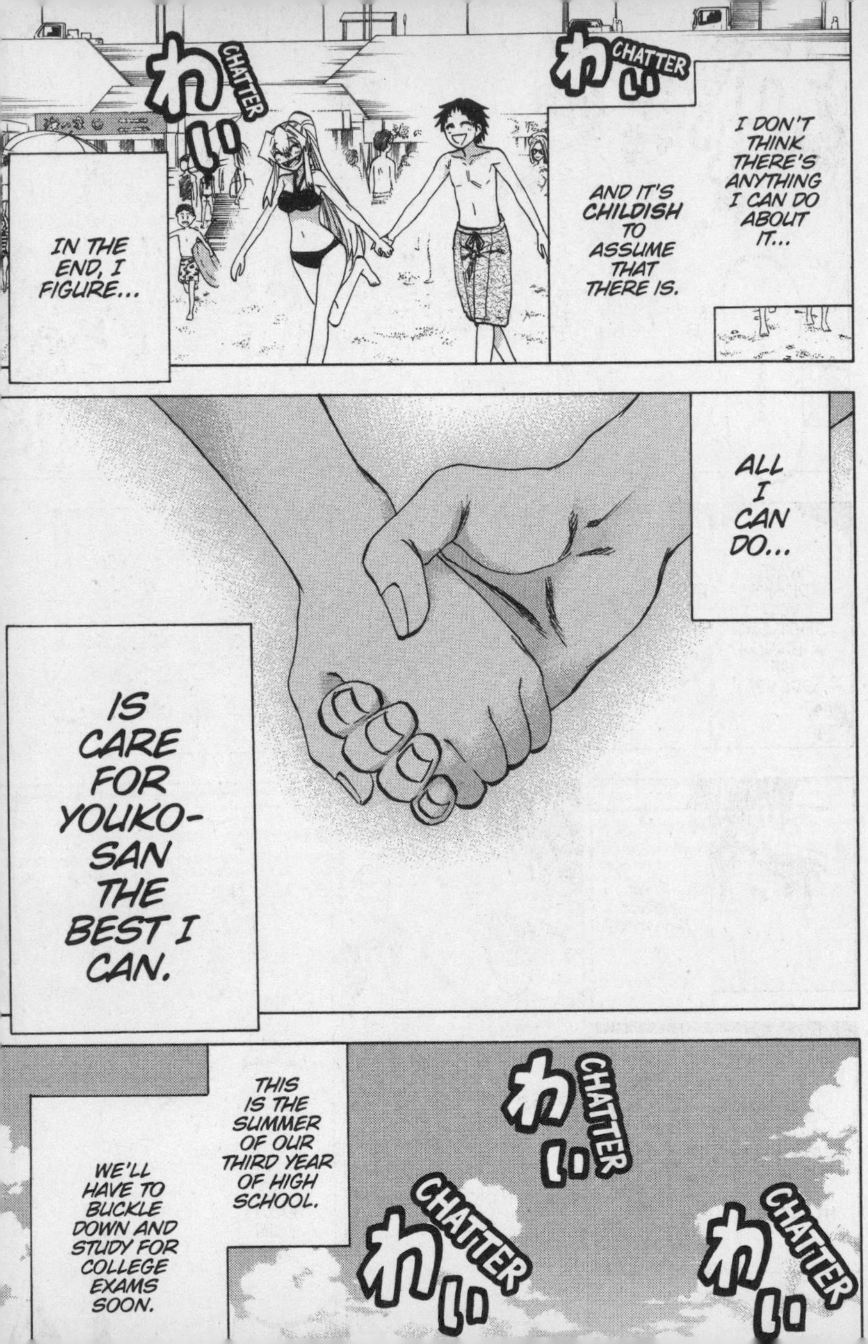

わい CHATTER
I DON'T THINK THERE'S ANYTHING I CAN DO ABOUT IT...
AND IT'S CHILDISH TO ASSUME THAT THERE IS.
わい CHATTER
IN THE END, I FIGURE...
ALL I CAN DO...
IS CARE FOR YOUKO-SAN THE BEST I CAN.
わい CHATTER
わい CHATTER
THIS IS THE SUMMER OF OUR THIRD YEAR OF HIGH SCHOOL.
わい CHATTER
WE'LL HAVE TO BUCKLE DOWN AND STUDY FOR COLLEGE EXAMS SOON.

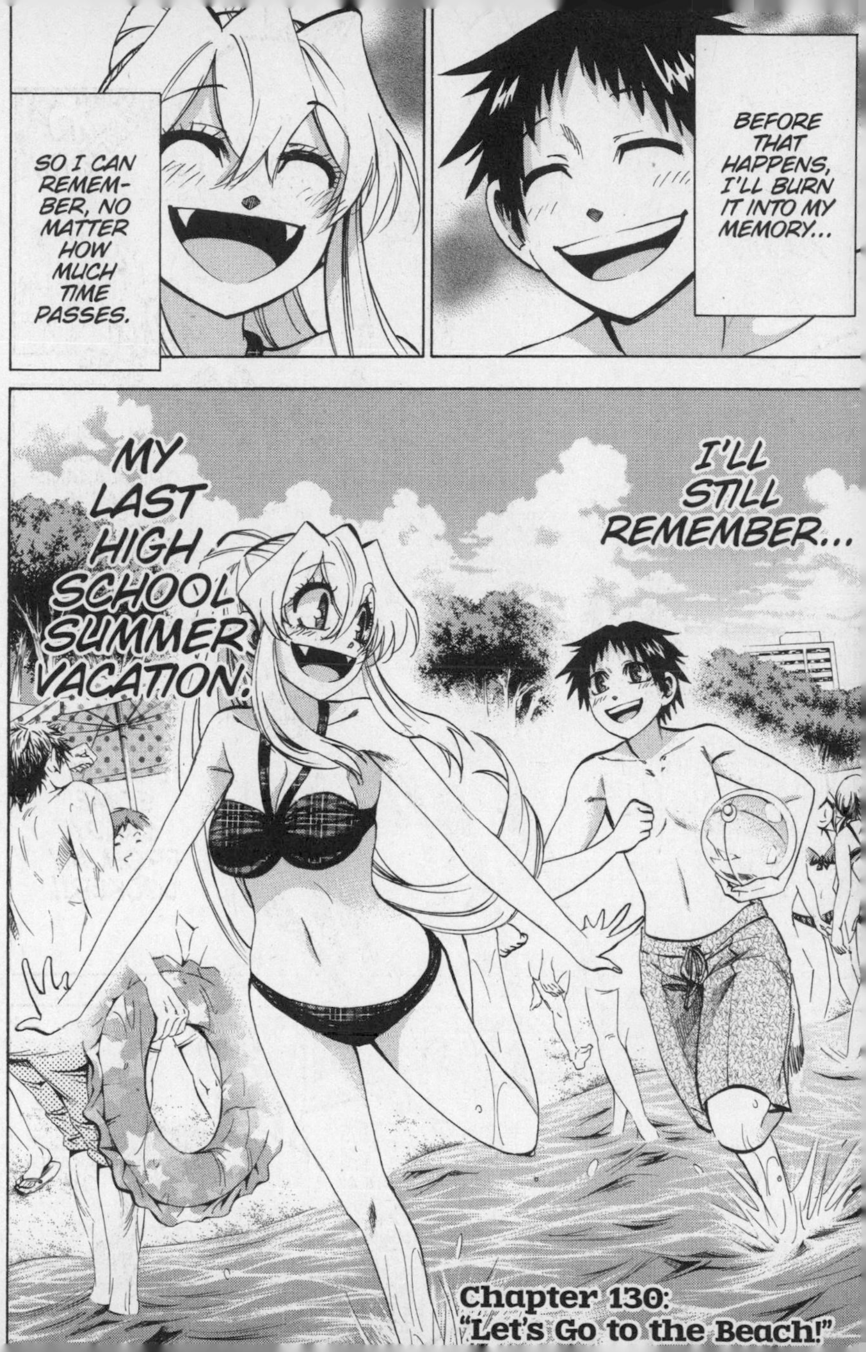
BEFORE THAT HAPPENS, I'LL BURN IT INTO MY MEMORY...
SO I CAN REMEMBER, NO MATTER HOW MUCH TIME PASSES.
I'LL STILL REMEMBER...
MY LAST HIGH SCHOOL SUMMER VACATION.
Chapter 130: "Let's Go to the Beach!"

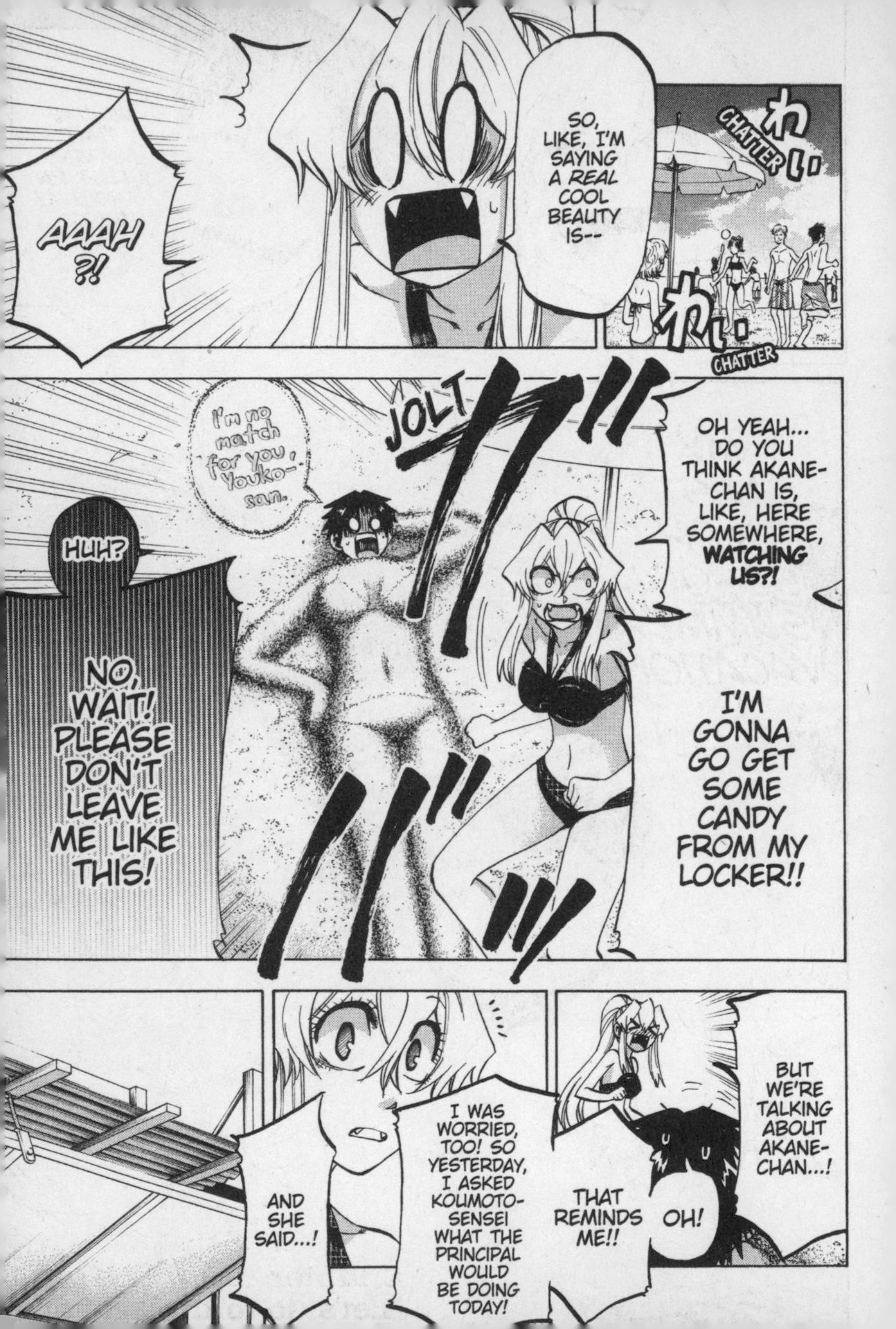

わい
CHATTER
わい
CHATTER
SO, LIKE, I'M SAYING A *REAL* COOL BEAUTY IS--
AAAH ?!
OH YEAH... DO YOU THINK AKANE-CHAN IS, LIKE, HERE SOMEWHERE, **WATCHING US?!**
JOLT
I'M GONNA GO GET SOME CANDY FROM MY LOCKER!!
I'm no match for you, Youko-san.
HUH?
NO, WAIT! PLEASE DON'T LEAVE ME LIKE THIS!
BUT WE'RE TALKING ABOUT AKANE-CHAN...!
OH!
THAT REMINDS ME!!
I WAS WORRIED, TOO! SO YESTERDAY, I ASKED KOUMOTO-SENSEI WHAT THE PRINCIPAL WOULD BE DOING TODAY!
AND SHE SAID...!

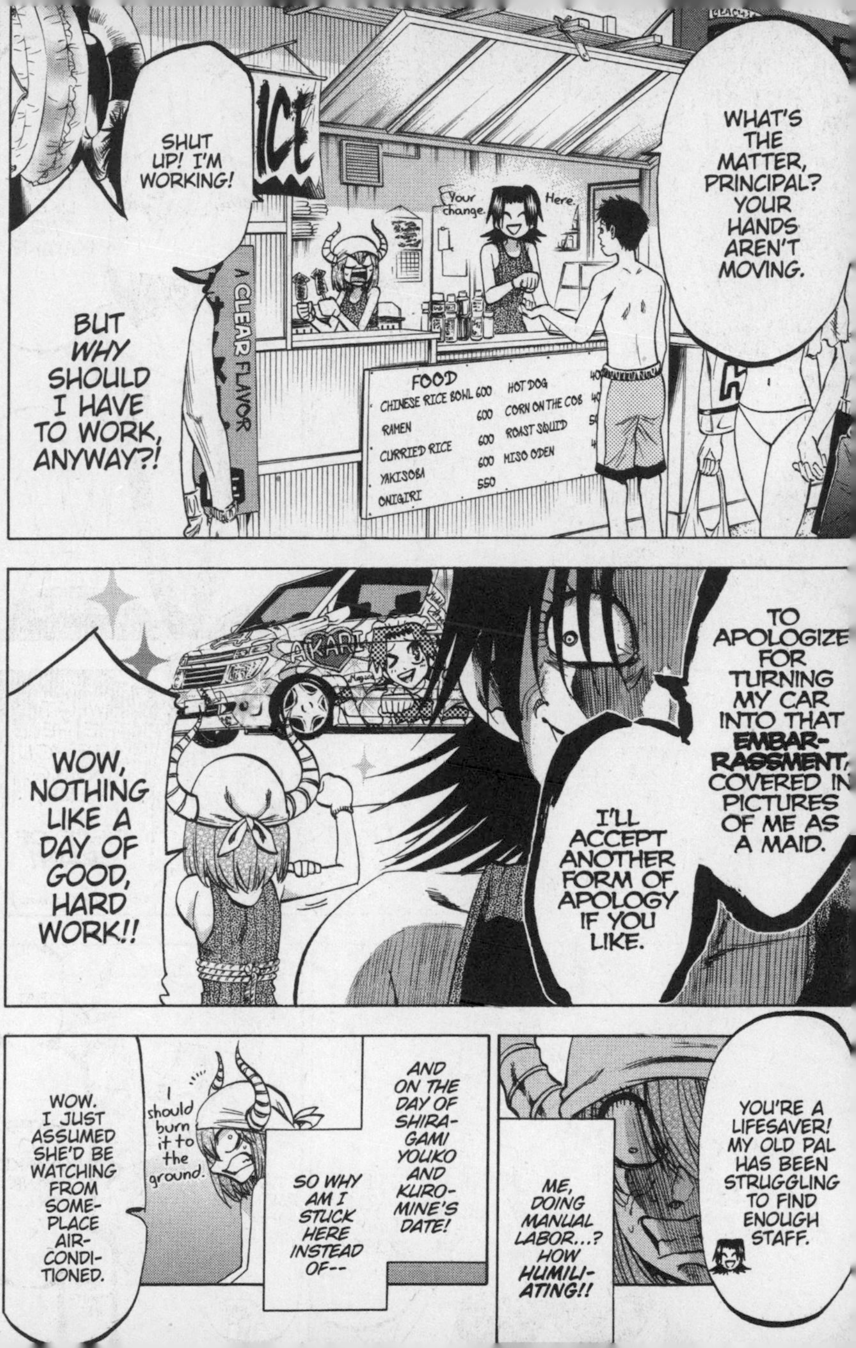
WHAT'S THE MATTER, PRINCIPAL? YOUR HANDS AREN'T MOVING.
Here.
Your change.
SHUT UP! I'M WORKING!
ICE
A CLEAR FLAVOR
FOOD
CHINESE RICE BOWL 600
RAMEN 600
CURRIED RICE 600
YAKISOBA 600
ONIGIRI 550
HOT DOG
CORN ON THE COB
ROAST SQUID
MISO ODEN
BUT *WHY* SHOULD I HAVE TO WORK, ANYWAY?!
TO APOLOGIZE FOR TURNING MY CAR INTO THAT **EMBARRASSMENT**, COVERED IN PICTURES OF ME AS A MAID.
I'LL ACCEPT ANOTHER FORM OF APOLOGY IF YOU LIKE.
AKARI
WOW, NOTHING LIKE A DAY OF GOOD, HARD WORK!!
YOU'RE A LIFESAVER! MY OLD PAL HAS BEEN STRUGGLING TO FIND ENOUGH STAFF.
ME, DOING MANUAL LABOR...? HOW **HUMILIATING!!**
AND ON THE DAY OF SHIRAGAMI YOUKO AND KUROMINE'S DATE!
SO WHY AM I STUCK HERE INSTEAD OF--
I should burn it to the ground.
WOW. I JUST ASSUMED SHE'D BE WATCHING FROM SOMEPLACE AIR-CONDITIONED.

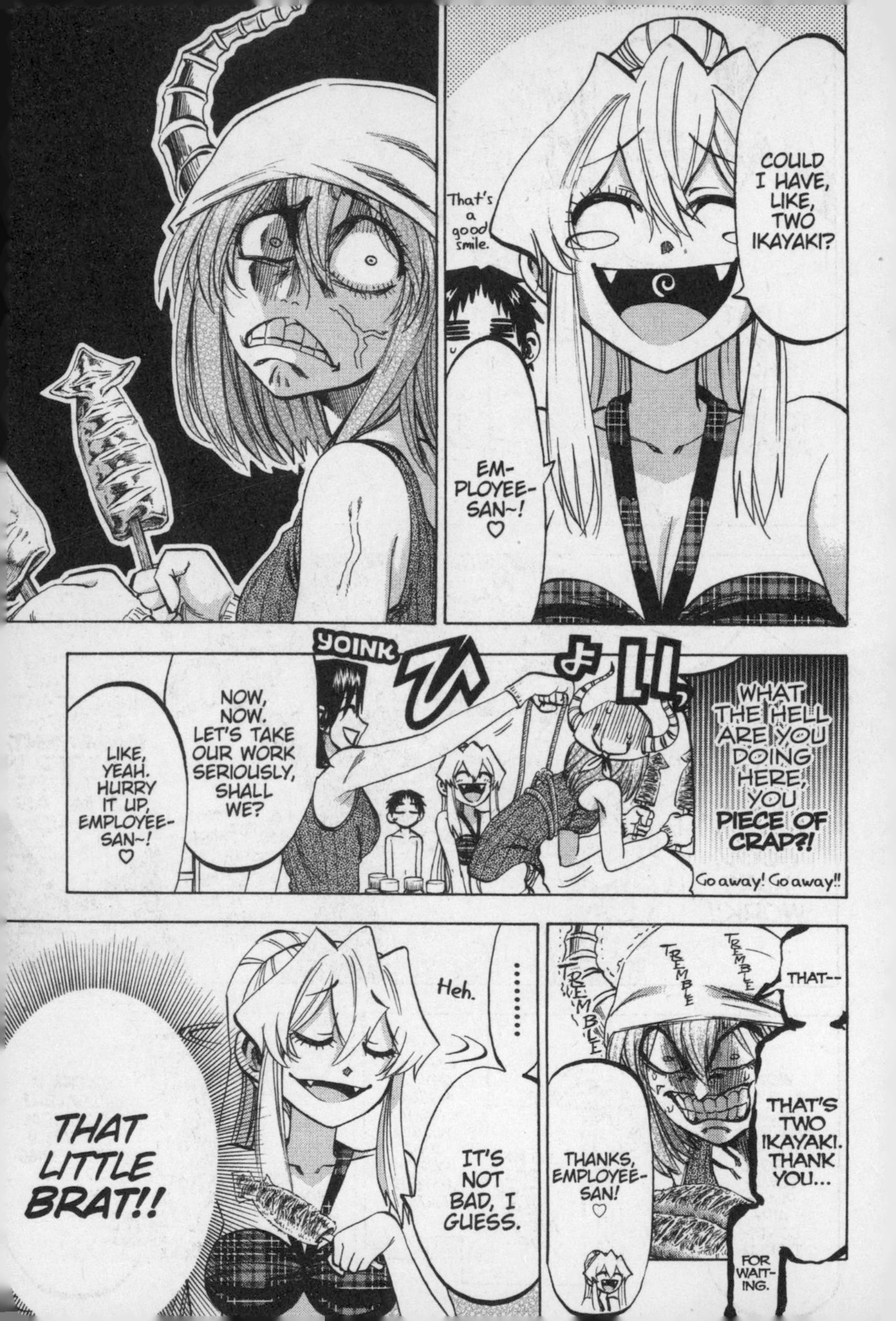
COULD I HAVE, LIKE, TWO IKAYAKI?
That's a good smile.
EMPLOYEE-SAN~! ♡
WHAT THE HELL ARE YOU DOING HERE, YOU PIECE OF CRAP?!
Go away! Go away!!
YOINK
NOW, NOW. LET'S TAKE OUR WORK SERIOUSLY, SHALL WE?
LIKE, YEAH. HURRY IT UP, EMPLOYEE-SAN~! ♡
TREMBLE
TREMBLE
TREMBLE
THAT--
THAT'S TWO IKAYAKI. THANK YOU...
FOR WAITING.
THANKS, EMPLOYEE-SAN! ♡
......
Heh.
IT'S NOT BAD, I GUESS.
THAT LITTLE BRAT!!

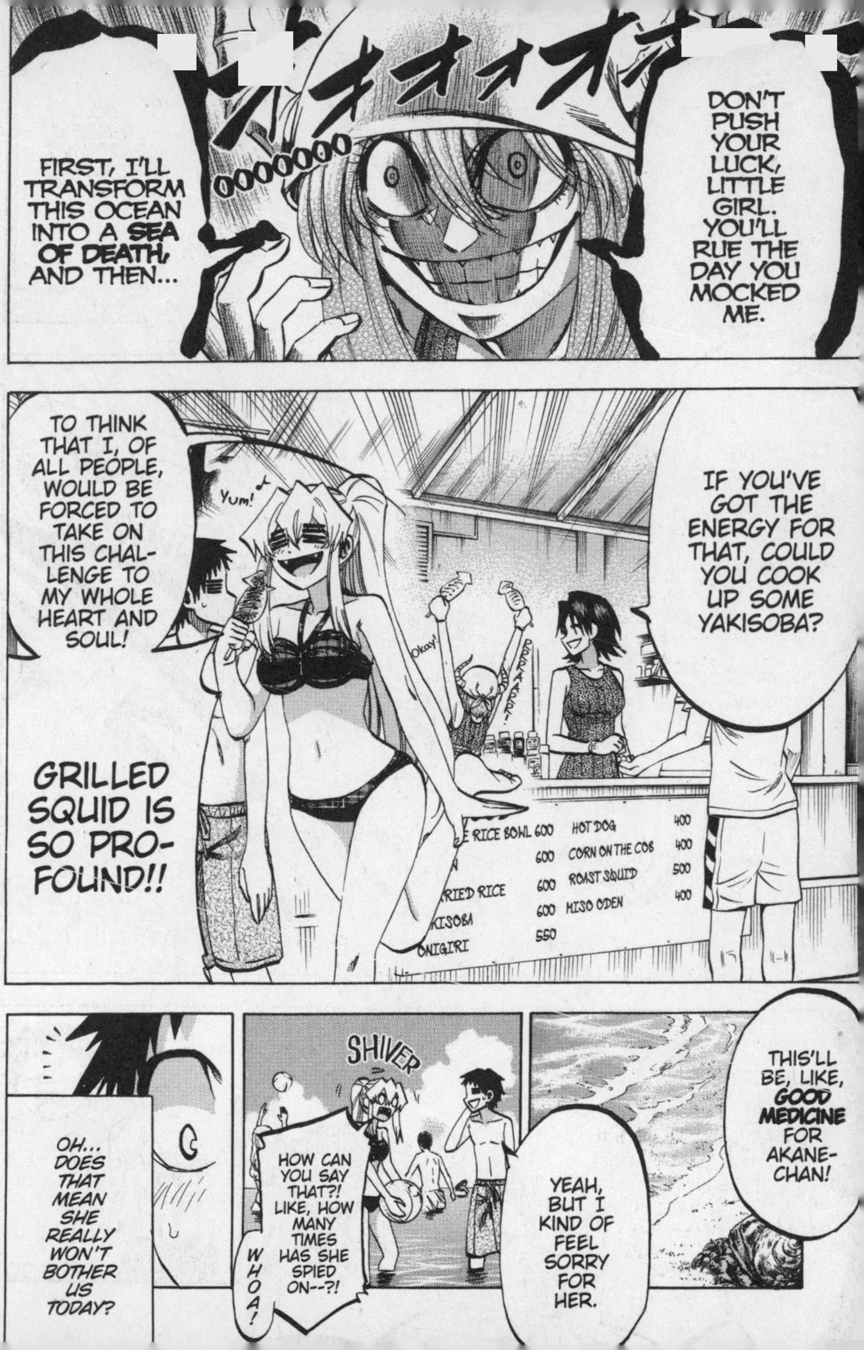
DON'T PUSH YOUR LUCK, LITTLE GIRL. YOU'LL RUE THE DAY YOU MOCKED ME.
OOOOOOO
FIRST, I'LL TRANSFORM THIS OCEAN INTO A SEA OF DEATH, AND THEN...
IF YOU'VE GOT THE ENERGY FOR THAT, COULD YOU COOK UP SOME YAKISOBA?
Okay!
RICE BOWL 600
600
RIED RICE 600
KISOBA 600
ONIGIRI 550
HOT DOG 400
CORN ON THE COB 400
ROAST SQUID 500
MISO ODEN 400
Yum!
TO THINK THAT I, OF ALL PEOPLE, WOULD BE FORCED TO TAKE ON THIS CHALLENGE TO MY WHOLE HEART AND SOUL!
GRILLED SQUID IS SO PROFOUND!!
THIS'LL BE, LIKE, GOOD MEDICINE FOR AKANE-CHAN!
YEAH, BUT I KIND OF FEEL SORRY FOR HER.
SHIVER
HOW CAN YOU SAY THAT?! LIKE, HOW MANY TIMES HAS SHE SPIED ON--?!
WHOA!
OH... DOES THAT MEAN SHE REALLY WON'T BOTHER US TODAY?

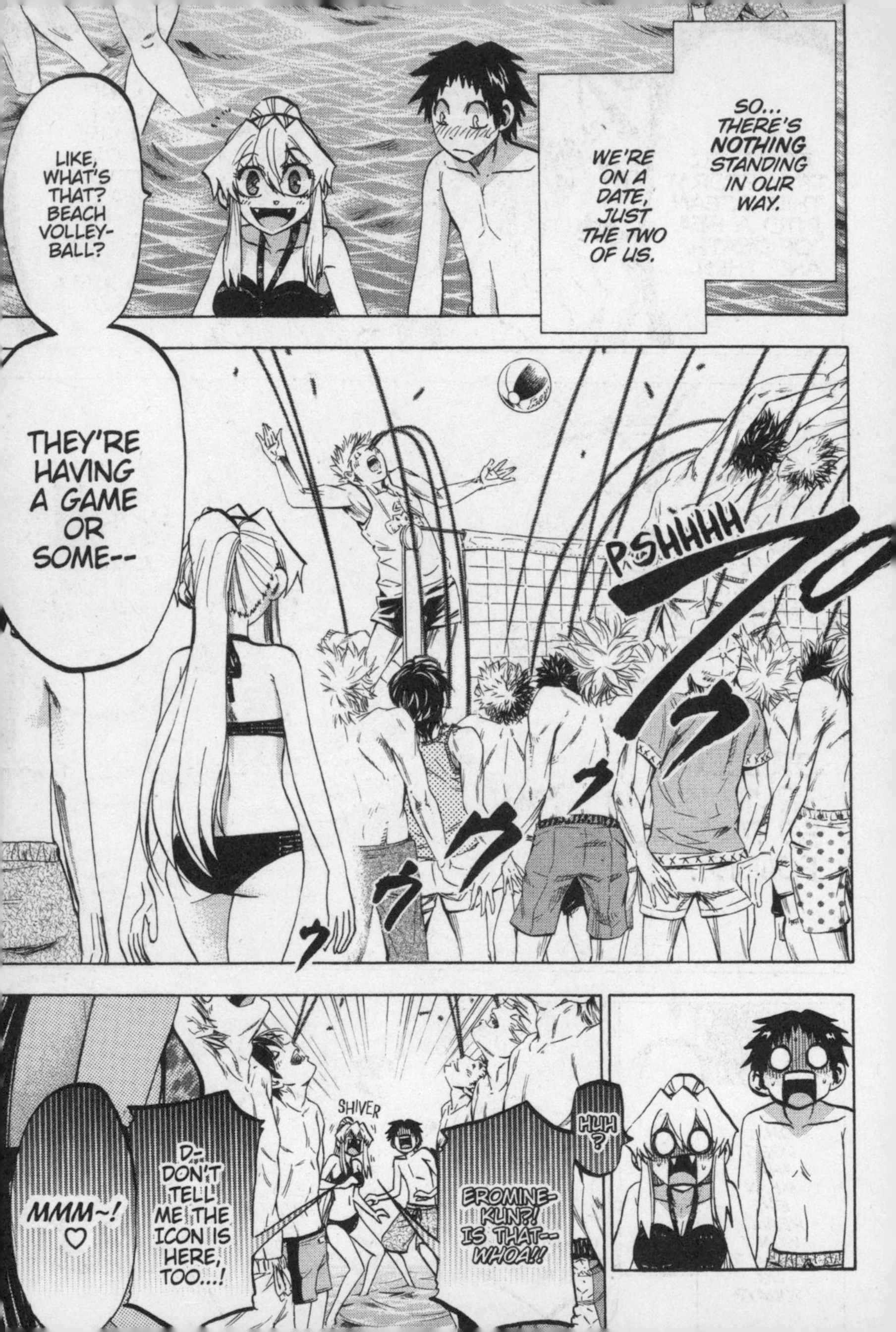
SO... THERE'S NOTHING STANDING IN OUR WAY.
WE'RE ON A DATE, JUST THE TWO OF US.
LIKE, WHAT'S THAT? BEACH VOLLEY-BALL?
THEY'RE HAVING A GAME OR SOME--
PSHHHH
HUH?
EROMINE-KUN?! IS THAT-- WHOA!!
SHIVER
D-DON'T TELL ME THE ICON IS HERE, TOO...!
MMM~! ♡

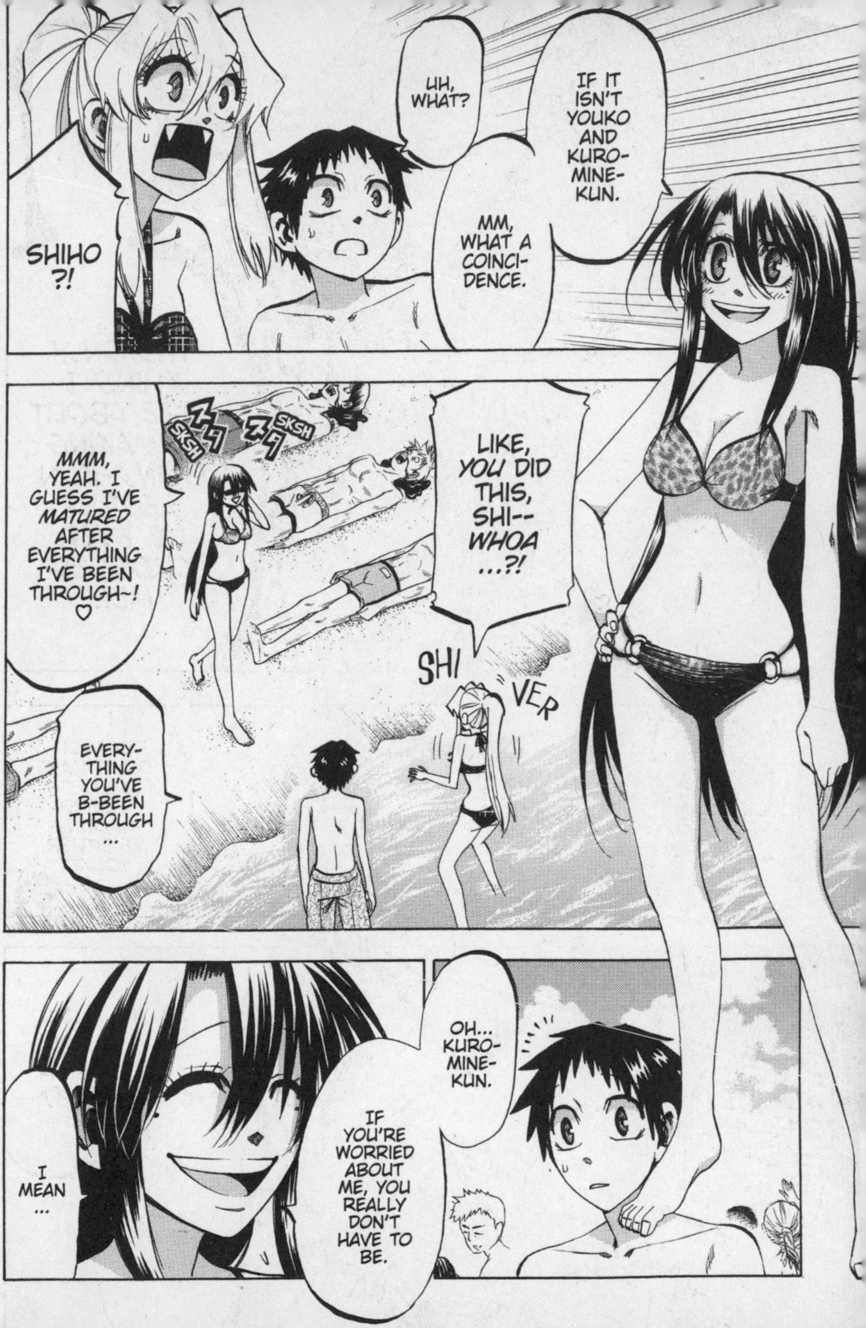
IF IT ISN'T YOUKO AND KURO-MINE-KUN.
MM, WHAT A COINCI-DENCE.
UH, WHAT?
SHIHO ?!
LIKE, YOU DID THIS, SHI-- WHOA ...?!
SHI VER
SKSH
SKSH
MMM, YEAH. I GUESS I'VE MATURED AFTER EVERYTHING I'VE BEEN THROUGH~! ♡
EVERY-THING YOU'VE B-BEEN THROUGH ...
OH... KURO-MINE-KUN.
IF YOU'RE WORRIED ABOUT ME, YOU REALLY DON'T HAVE TO BE.
I MEAN ...

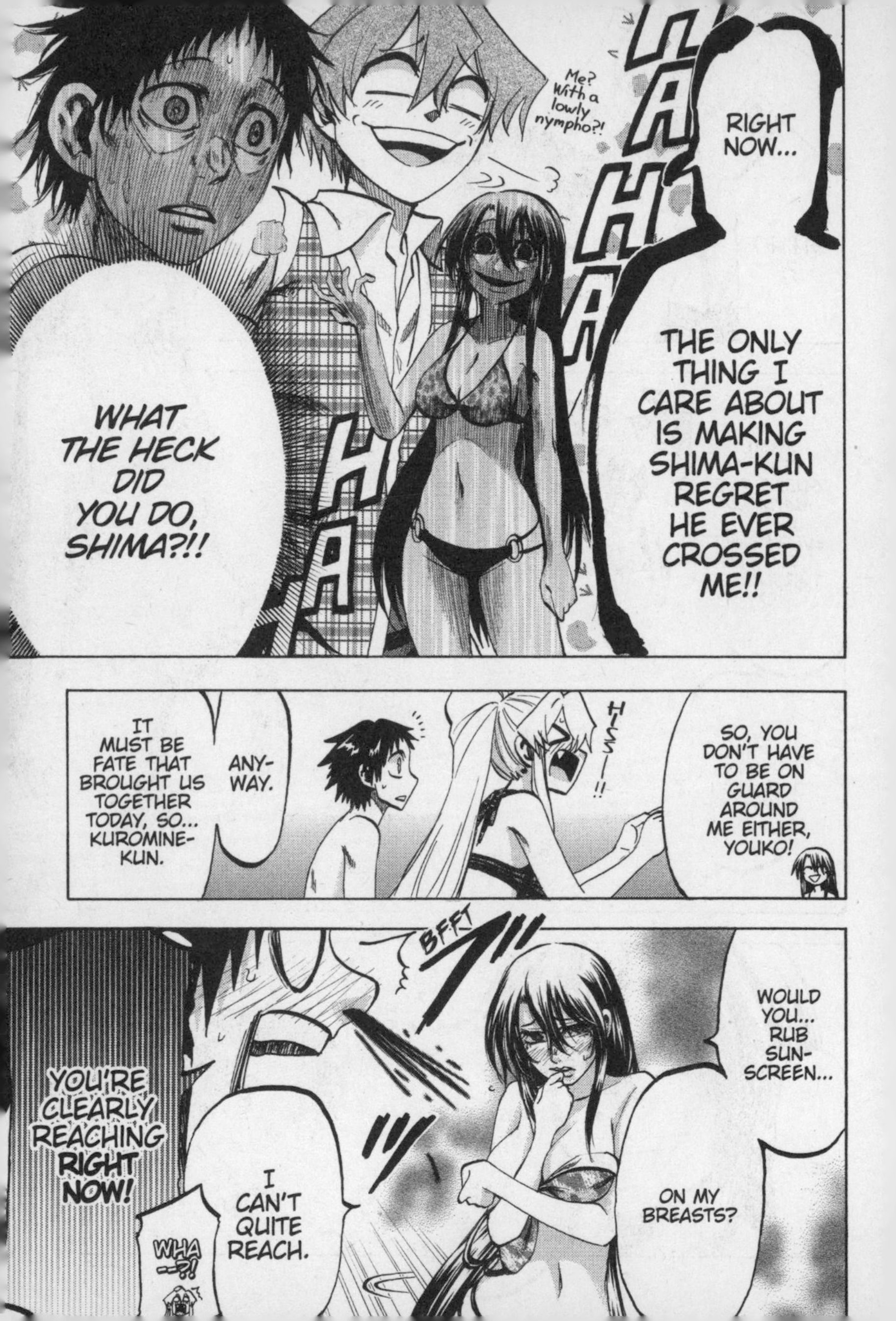
RIGHT NOW...
THE ONLY THING I CARE ABOUT IS MAKING SHIMA-KUN REGRET HE EVER CROSSED ME!!
HAHAHAHA
Me? With a lowly nympho?!
WHAT THE HECK DID YOU DO, SHIMA?!!
SO, YOU DON'T HAVE TO BE ON GUARD AROUND ME EITHER, YOUKO!
HISS—!!
ANY-WAY.
IT MUST BE FATE THAT BROUGHT US TOGETHER TODAY, SO... KUROMINE-KUN.
WOULD YOU... RUB SUN-SCREEN...
ON MY BREASTS?
BFFT
I CAN'T QUITE REACH.
YOU'RE CLEARLY REACHING RIGHT NOW!
WHA--?!

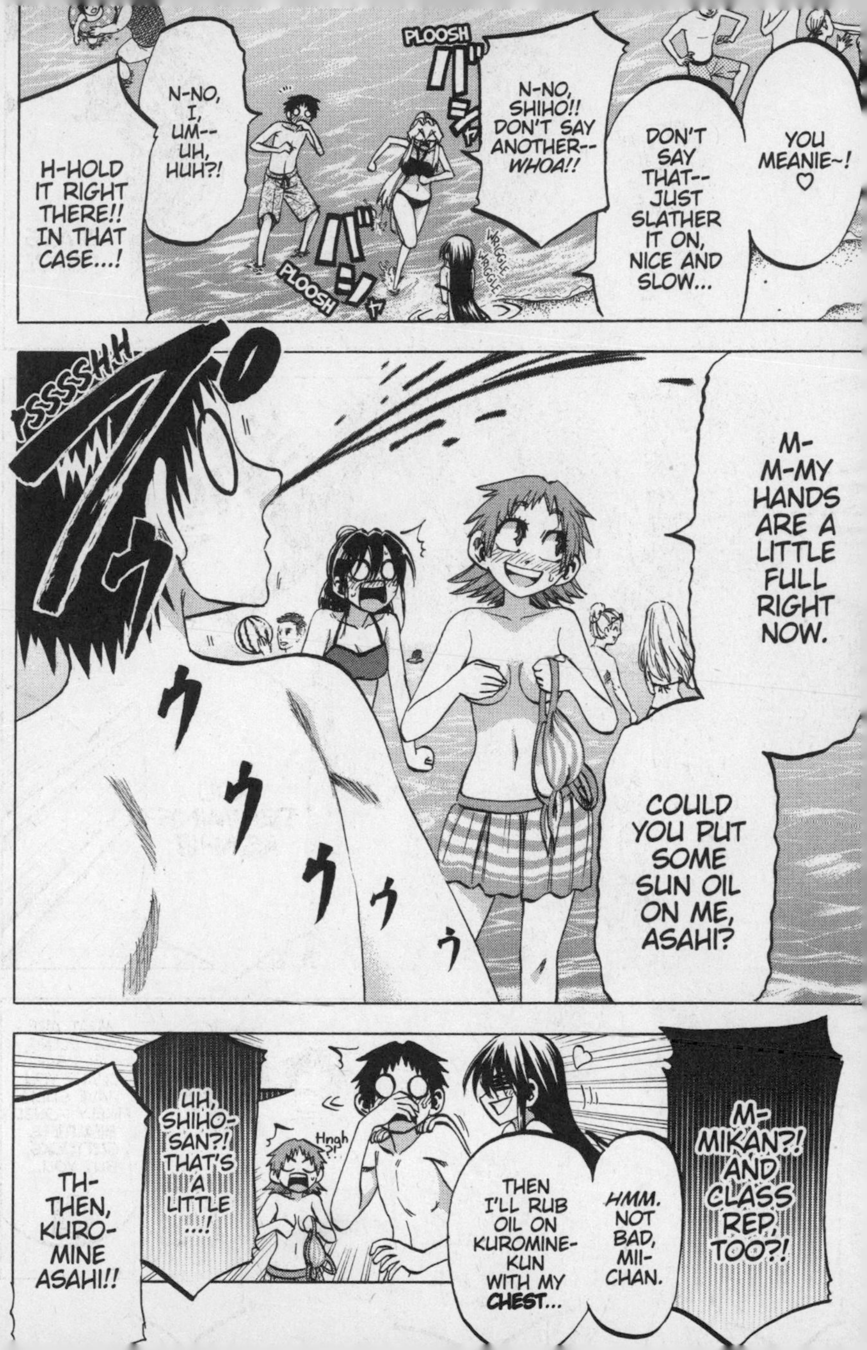
YOU MEANIE~! ♡
DON'T SAY THAT-- JUST SLATHER IT ON, NICE AND SLOW...
PLOOSH
N-NO, SHIHO!! DON'T SAY ANOTHER-- *WHOA!!*
N-NO, I, UM-- UH, HUH?!
H-HOLD IT RIGHT THERE!! IN THAT CASE...!
WRIGGLE WRIGGLE
PLOOSH
M-M-MY HANDS ARE A LITTLE FULL RIGHT NOW.
COULD YOU PUT SOME SUN OIL ON ME, ASAHI?
TSSSSSHH
M-MIKAN?! AND CLASS REP, TOO?!
HMM. NOT BAD, MII-CHAN.
THEN I'LL RUB OIL ON KUROMINE-KUN WITH MY **CHEST**...
Hngh ?!
UH, SHIHO-SAN?! THAT'S A LITTLE ...!
TH-THEN, KUROMINE ASAHI!!

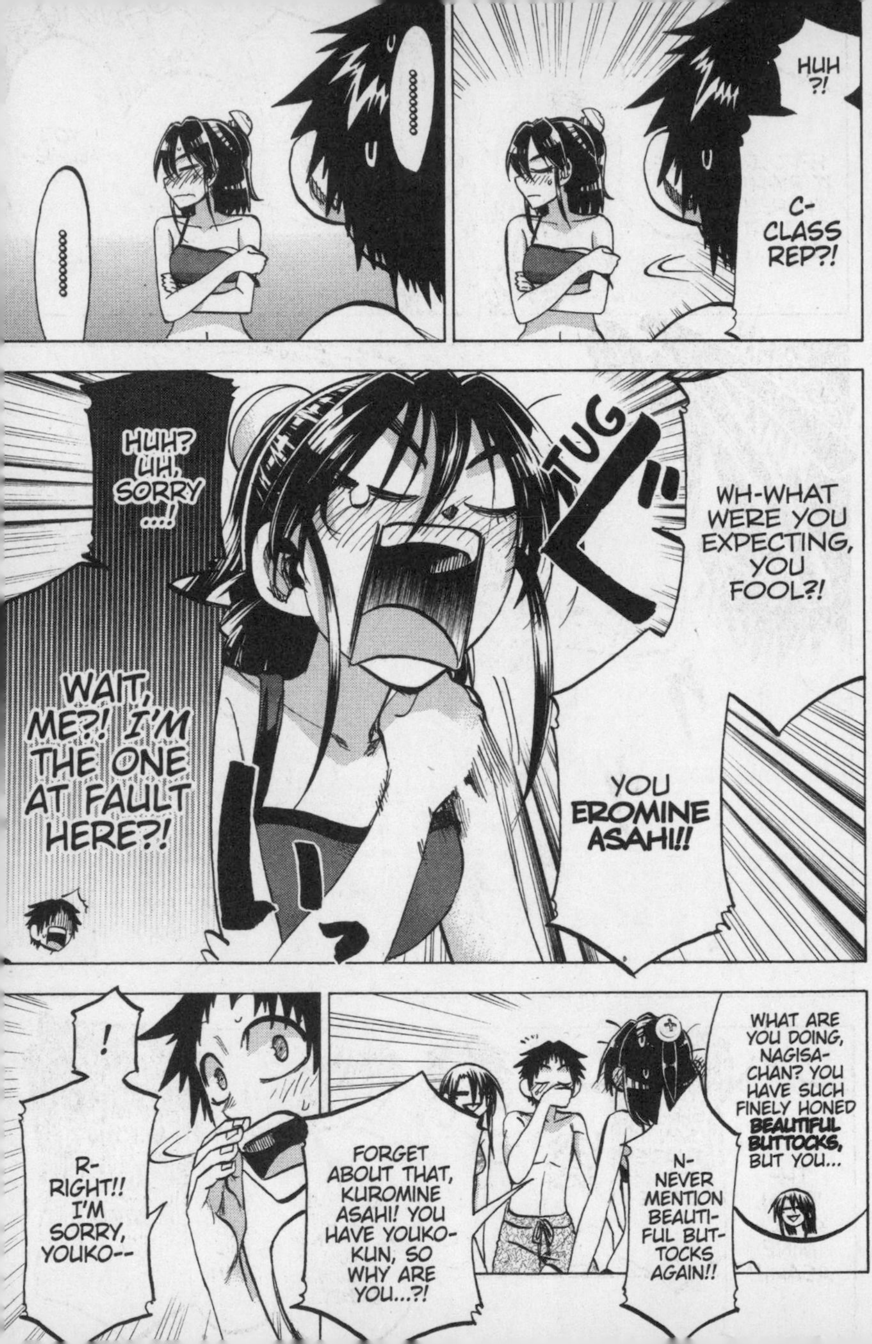
HUH ?!
C-CLASS REP?!
......
......
WH-WHAT WERE YOU EXPECTING, YOU FOOL?!
TUG
YOU EROMINE ASAHI!!
HUH? UH, SORRY ...!
WAIT, ME?! I'M THE ONE AT FAULT HERE?!
WHAT ARE YOU DOING, NAGISA-CHAN? YOU HAVE SUCH FINELY HONED **BEAUTIFUL BUTTOCKS,** BUT YOU...
N-NEVER MENTION BEAUTIFUL BUTTOCKS AGAIN!!
FORGET ABOUT THAT, KUROMINE ASAHI! YOU HAVE YOUKO-KUN, SO WHY ARE YOU...?!
!
R-RIGHT!! I'M SORRY, YOUKO--

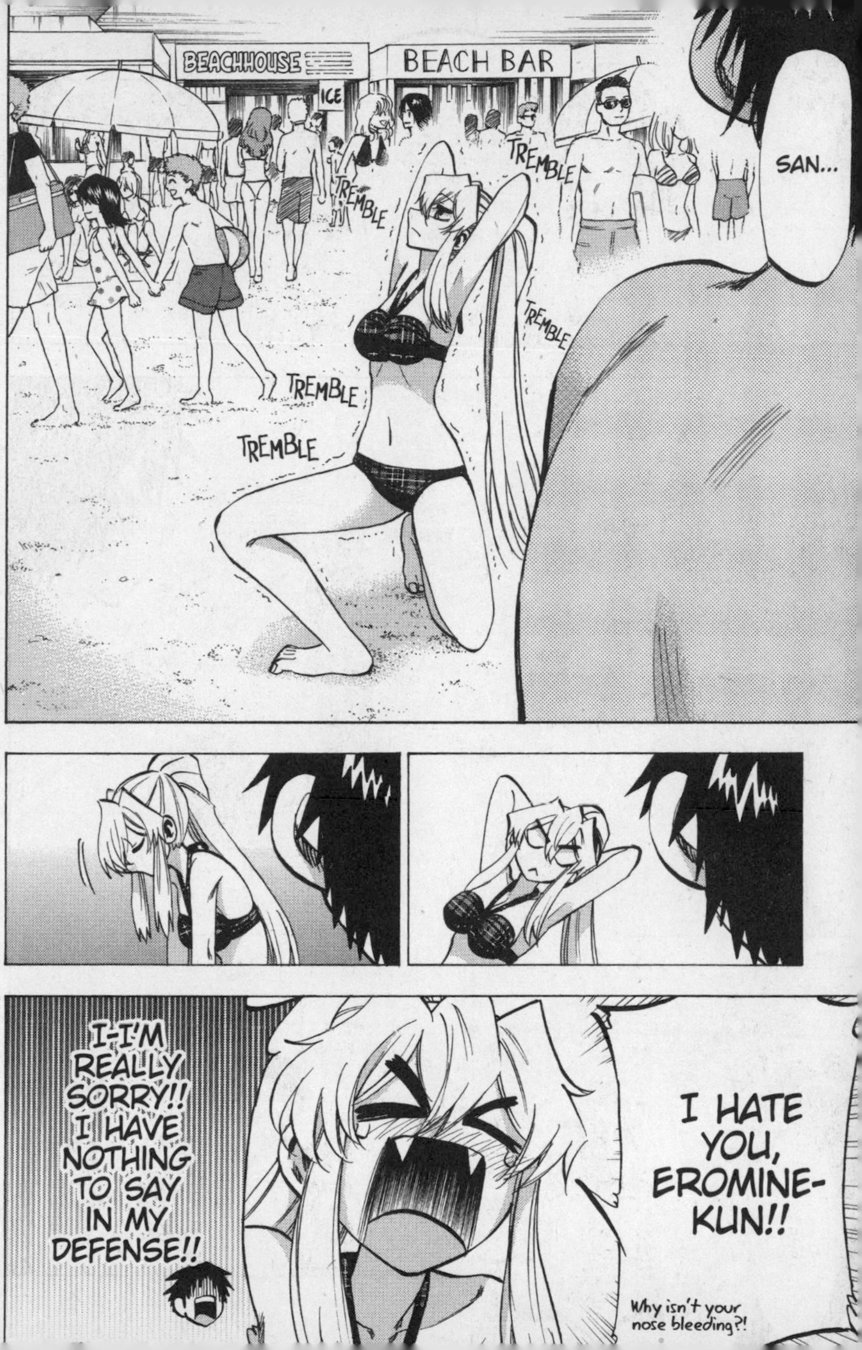

BEACHHOUSE
BEACH BAR
ICE
SAN...
TREMBLE
TREMBLE
TREMBLE
TREMBLE
TREMBLE
I HATE YOU, EROMINE-KUN!!
Why isn't your nose bleeding?!
I-I'M REALLY SORRY!! I HAVE NOTHING TO SAY IN MY DEFENSE!!

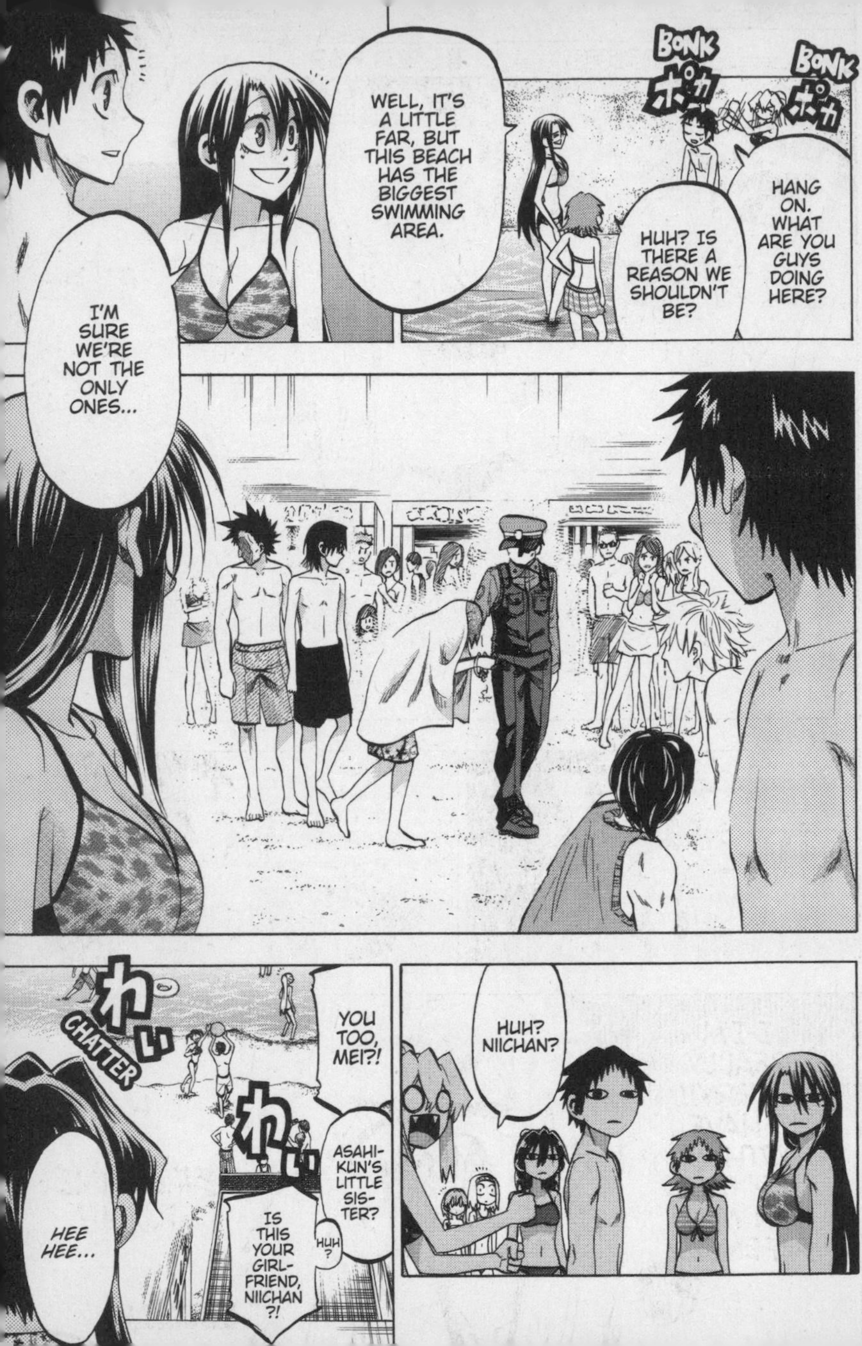
BONK ポカ
BONK ポカ
HANG ON. WHAT ARE YOU GUYS DOING HERE?
HUH? IS THERE A REASON WE SHOULDN'T BE?
WELL, IT'S A LITTLE FAR, BUT THIS BEACH HAS THE BIGGEST SWIMMING AREA.
I'M SURE WE'RE NOT THE ONLY ONES...
HUH? NIICHAN?
YOU TOO, MEI?!
ASAHI-KUN'S LITTLE SIS-TER?
HUH?
IS THIS YOUR GIRL-FRIEND, NIICHAN?!
わい CHATTER
わい
HEE HEE...

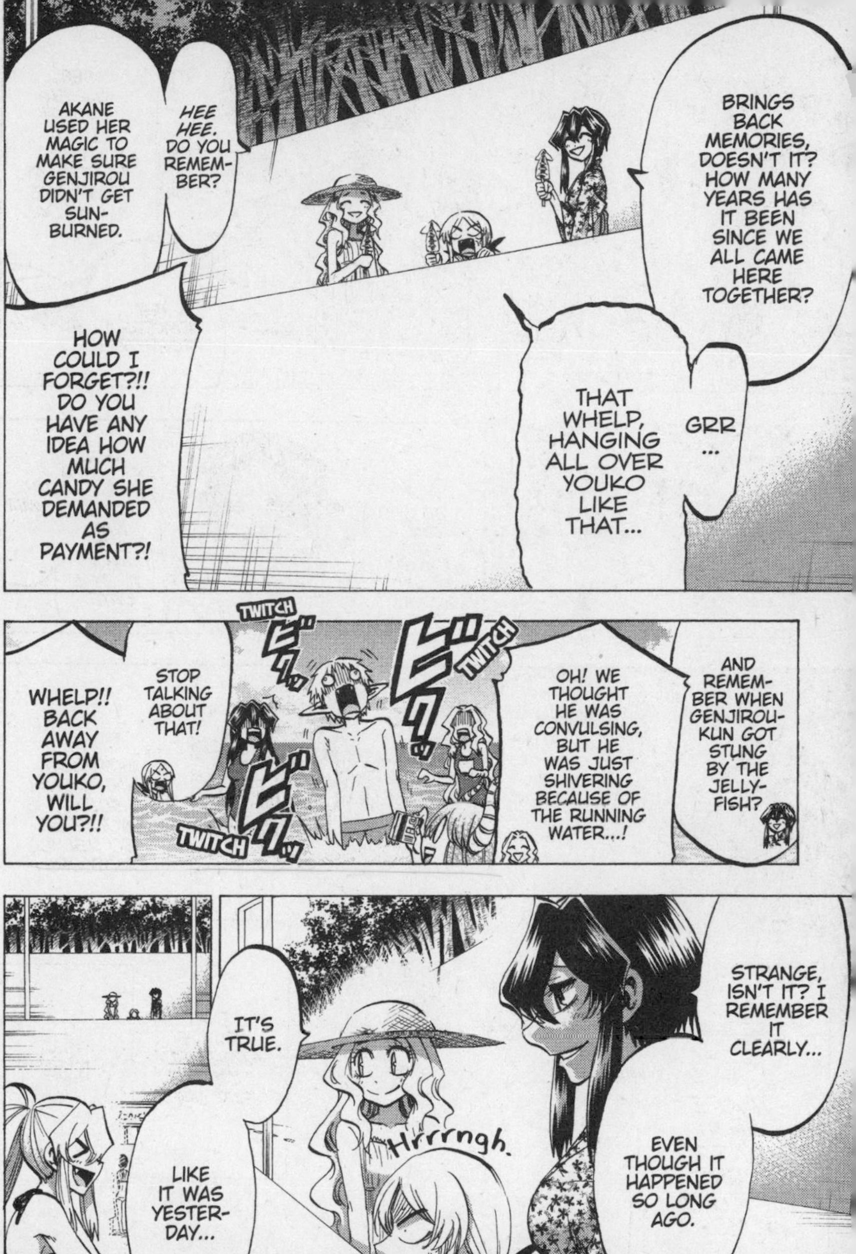

BRINGS BACK MEMORIES, DOESN'T IT? HOW MANY YEARS HAS IT BEEN SINCE WE ALL CAME HERE TOGETHER?
HEE HEE. DO YOU REMEMBER?
AKANE USED HER MAGIC TO MAKE SURE GENJIROU DIDN'T GET SUNBURNED.
GRR...
THAT WHELP, HANGING ALL OVER YOUKO LIKE THAT...
HOW COULD I FORGET?!! DO YOU HAVE ANY IDEA HOW MUCH CANDY SHE DEMANDED AS PAYMENT?!
AND REMEMBER WHEN GENJIROU-KUN GOT STUNG BY THE JELLYFISH?
OH! WE THOUGHT HE WAS CONVULSING, BUT HE WAS JUST SHIVERING BECAUSE OF THE RUNNING WATER...!
TWITCH
TWITCH
TWITCH
STOP TALKING ABOUT THAT!
WHELP!! BACK AWAY FROM YOUKO, WILL YOU?!!
STRANGE, ISN'T IT? I REMEMBER IT CLEARLY...
EVEN THOUGH IT HAPPENED SO LONG AGO.
IT'S TRUE.
Hrrrngh.
LIKE IT WAS YESTERDAY...

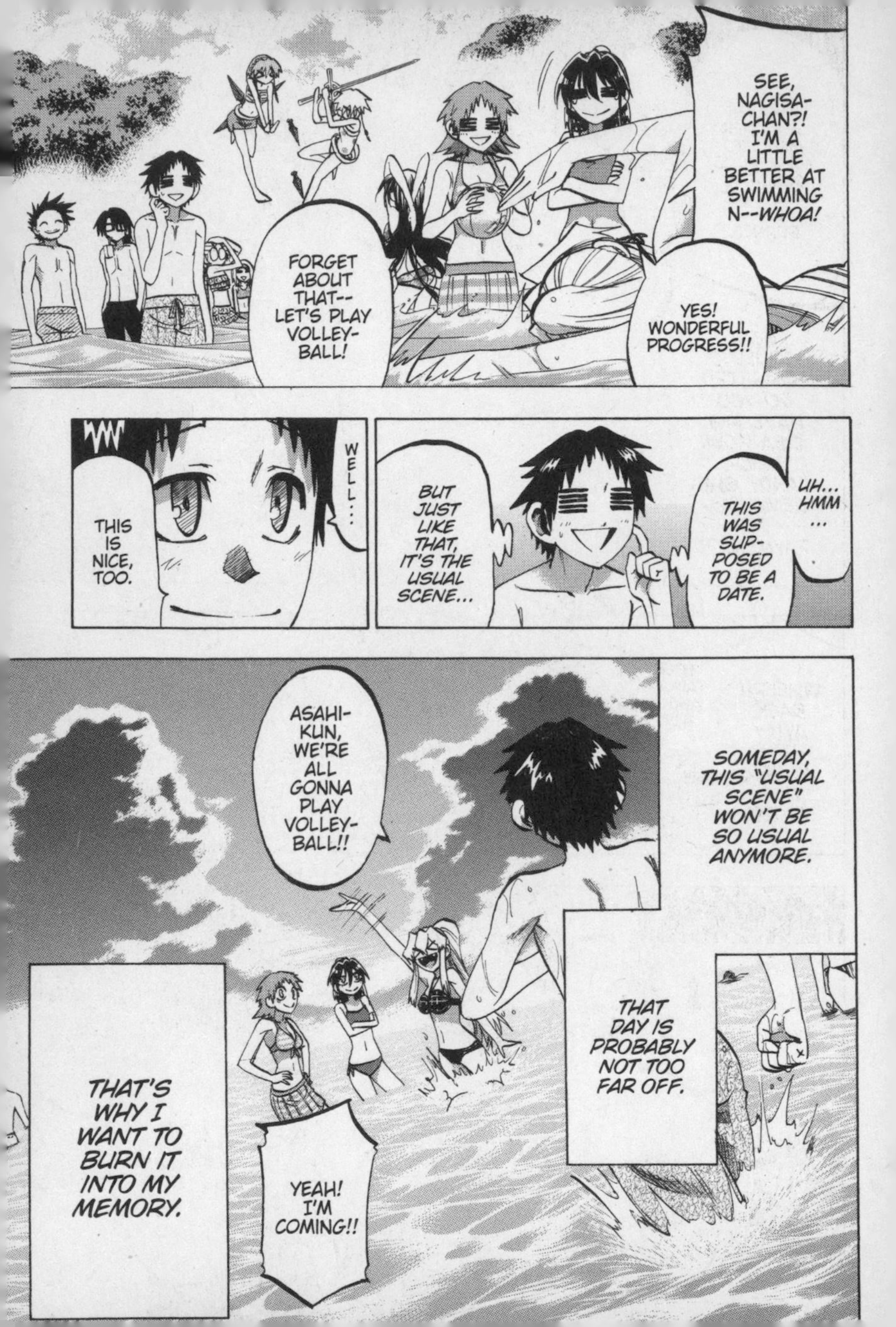
SEE, NAGISA-CHAN?! I'M A LITTLE BETTER AT SWIMMING N--WHOA!
YES! WONDERFUL PROGRESS!!
FORGET ABOUT THAT--LET'S PLAY VOLLEY-BALL!
UH... HMM...
THIS WAS SUP-POSED TO BE A DATE.
BUT JUST LIKE THAT, IT'S THE USUAL SCENE...
WELL...
THIS IS NICE, TOO.
SOMEDAY, THIS "USUAL SCENE" WON'T BE SO USUAL ANYMORE.
ASAHI-KUN, WE'RE ALL GONNA PLAY VOLLEY-BALL!!
THAT DAY IS PROBABLY NOT TOO FAR OFF.
YEAH! I'M COMING!!
THAT'S WHY I WANT TO BURN IT INTO MY MEMORY.

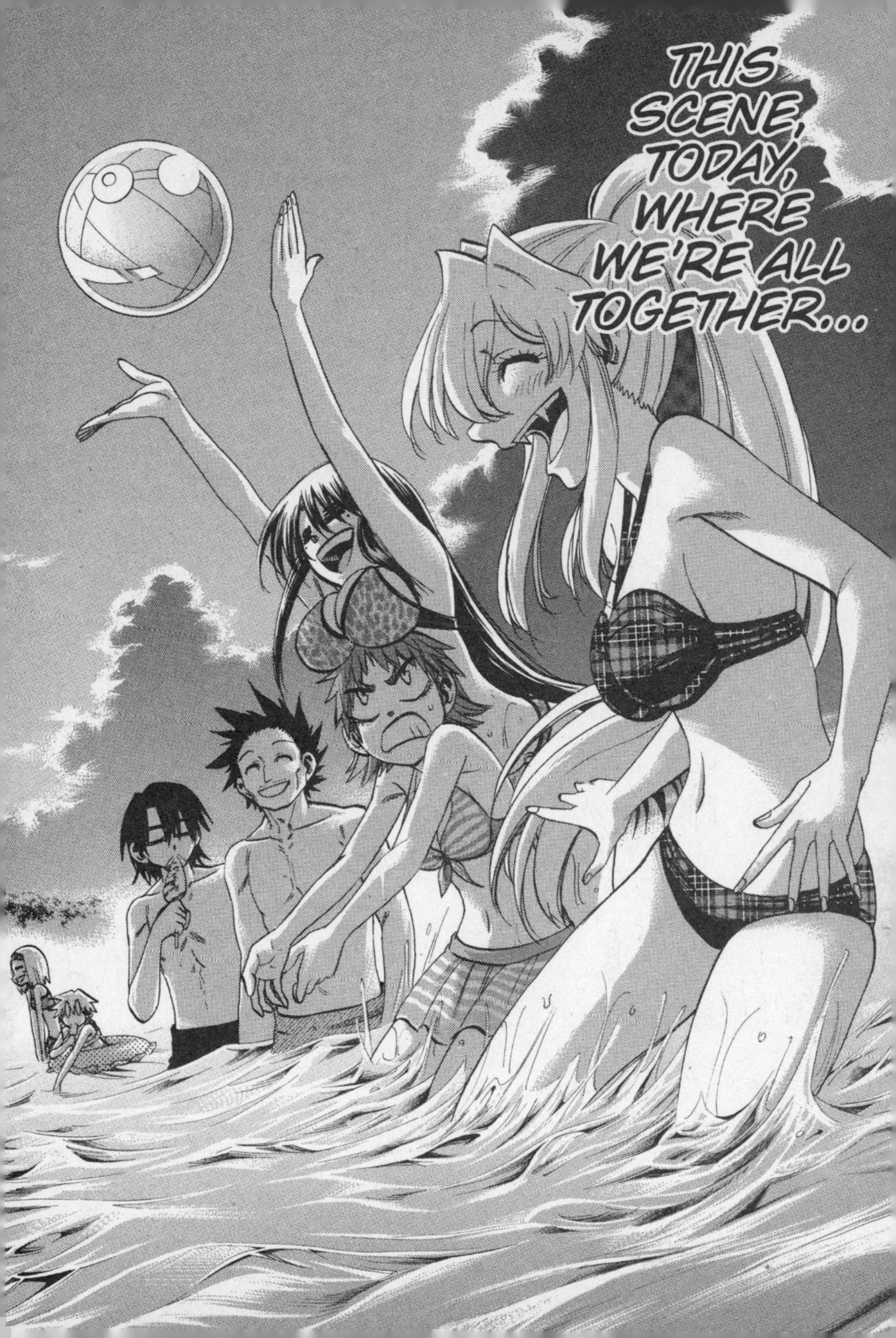
THIS SCENE, TODAY, WHERE WE'RE ALL TOGETHER...

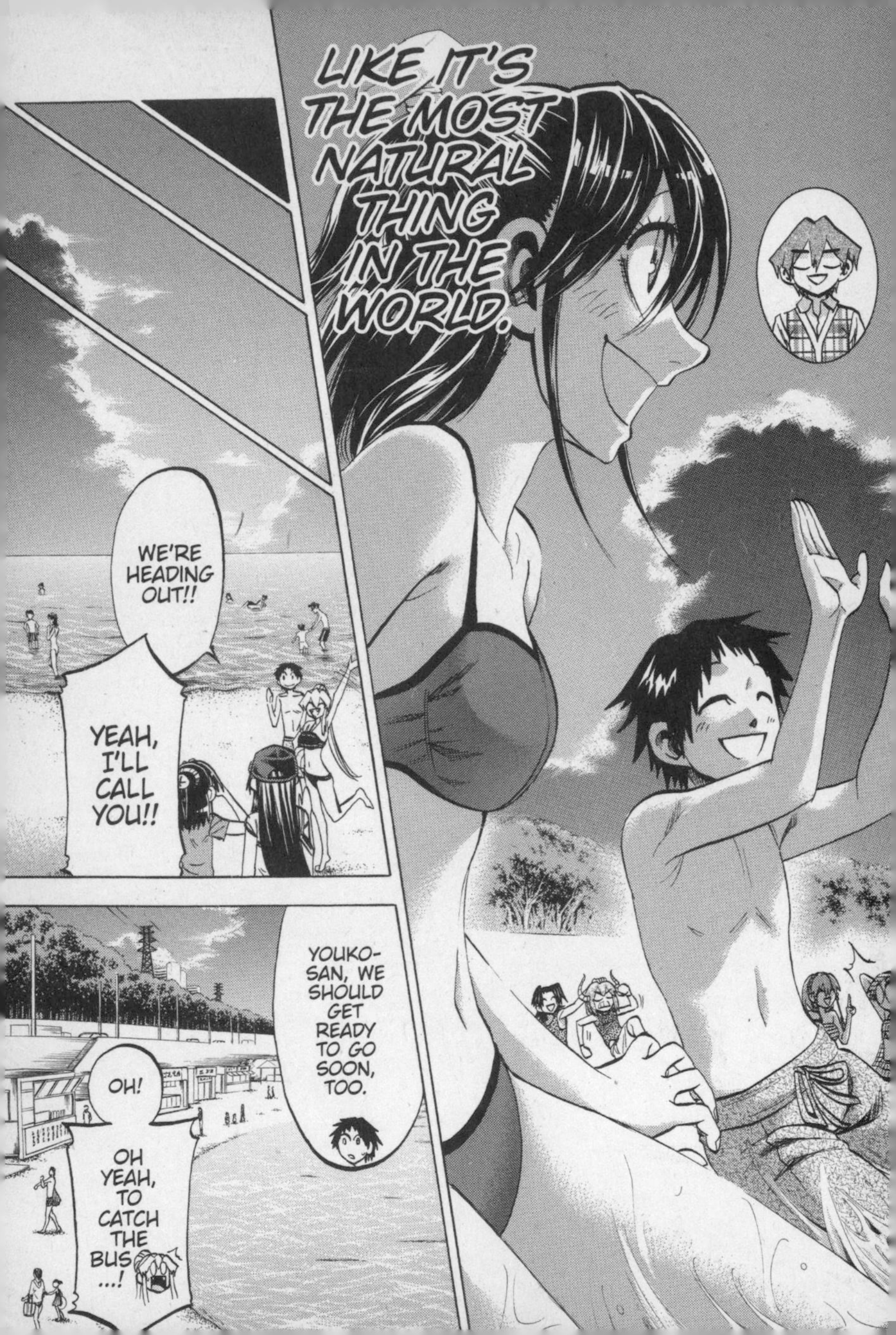
LIKE IT'S THE MOST NATURAL THING IN THE WORLD.
WE'RE HEADING OUT!!
YEAH, I'LL CALL YOU!!
YOUKO-SAN, WE SHOULD GET READY TO GO SOON, TOO.
OH!
OH YEAH, TO CATCH THE BUS ...!

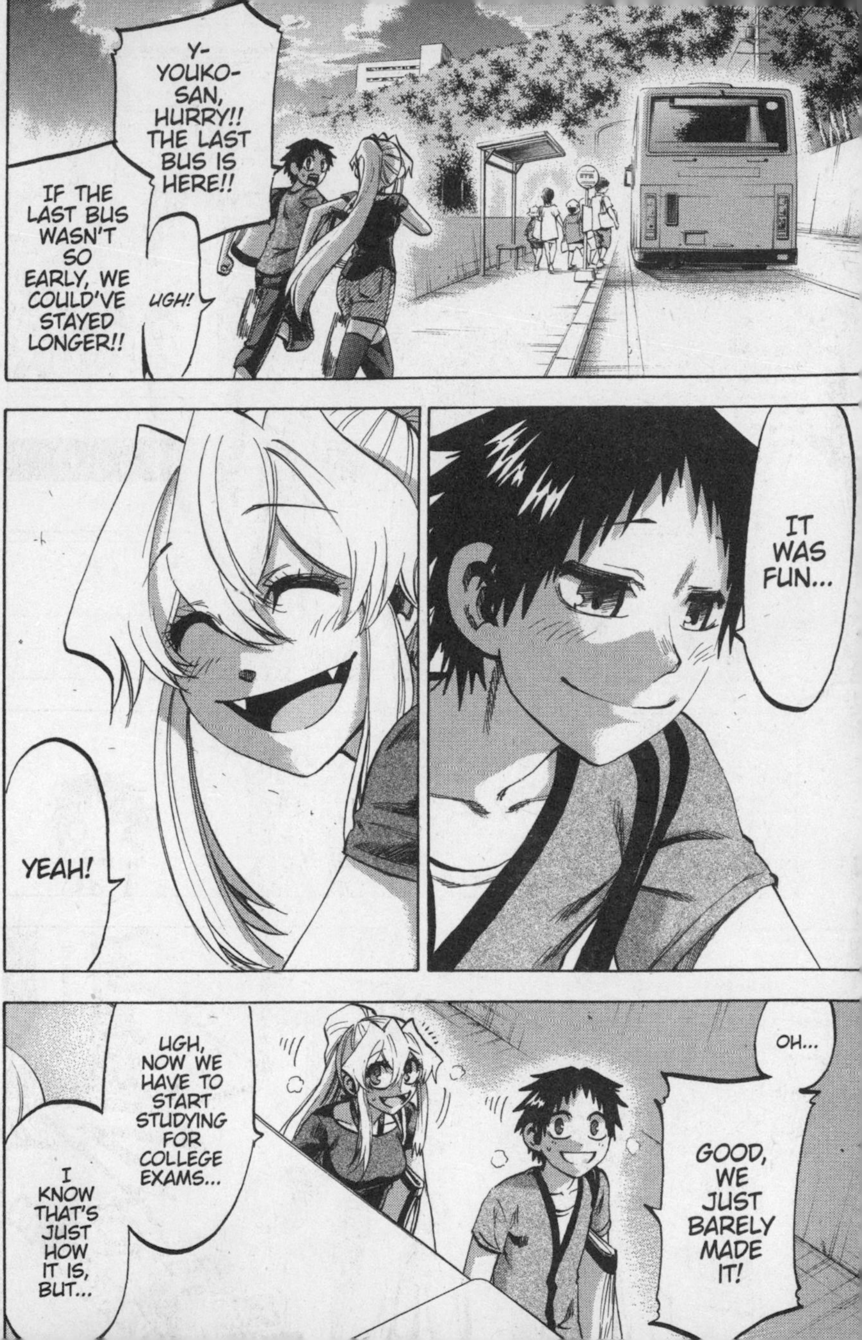
Y-YOUKO-SAN, HURRY!! THE LAST BUS IS HERE!!
UGH!
IF THE LAST BUS WASN'T SO EARLY, WE COULD'VE STAYED LONGER!!
IT WAS FUN...
YEAH!
OH...
GOOD, WE JUST BARELY MADE IT!
UGH, NOW WE HAVE TO START STUDYING FOR COLLEGE EXAMS...
I KNOW THAT'S JUST HOW IT IS, BUT...

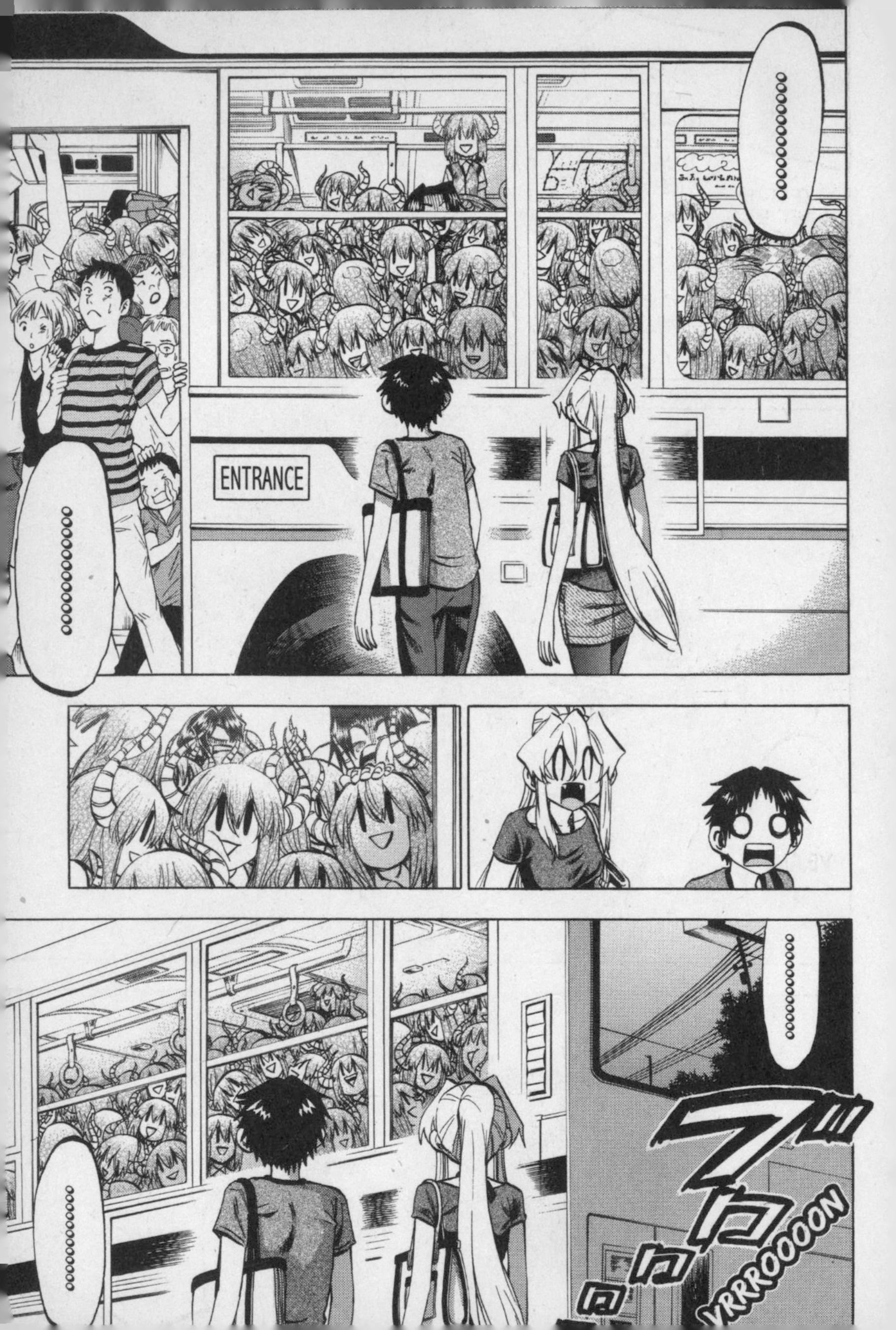
ENTRANCE
VRRROOOON

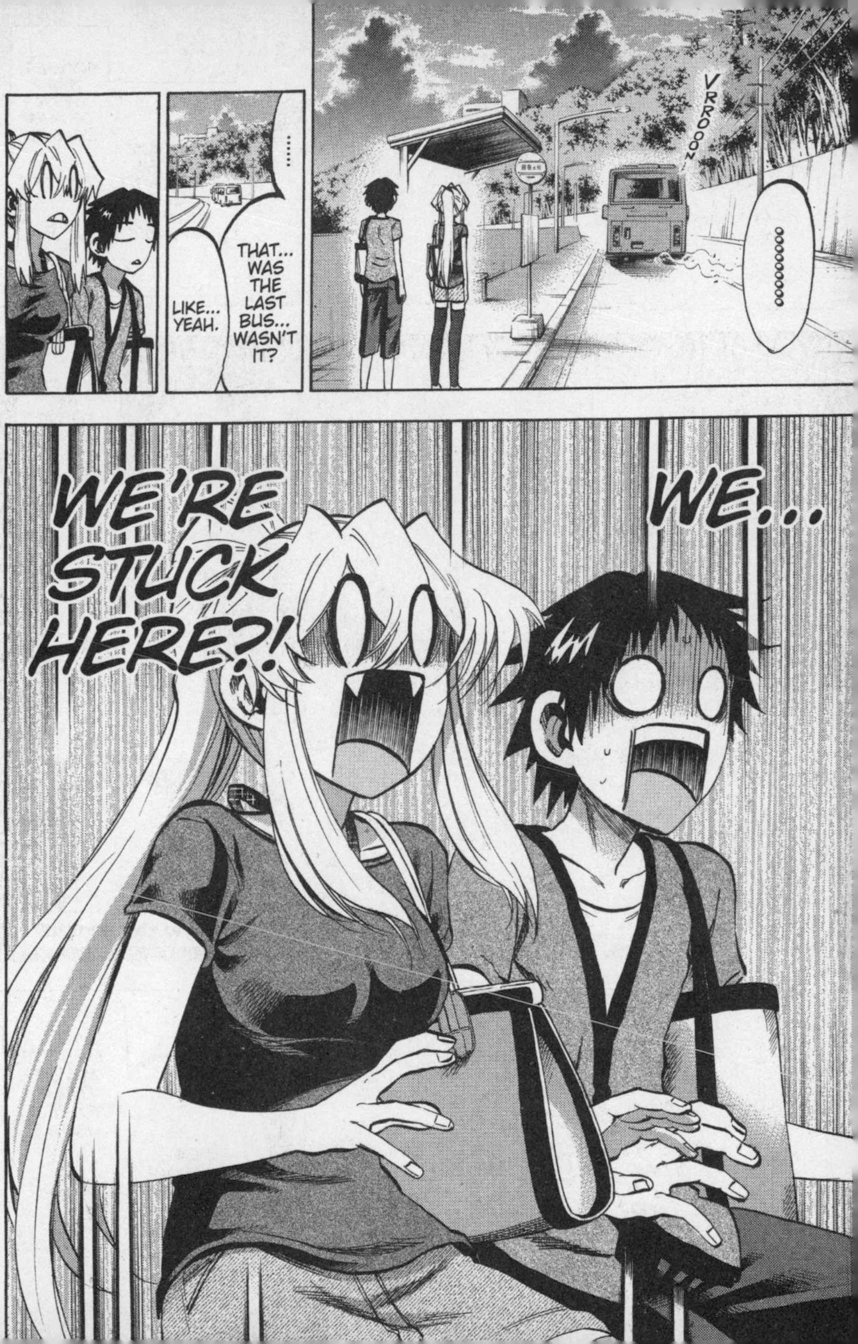

VRROOON!
OOOOOOOO...
......
THAT... WAS THE LAST BUS... WASN'T IT?
LIKE... YEAH.
WE...
WE'RE STUCK HERE?!

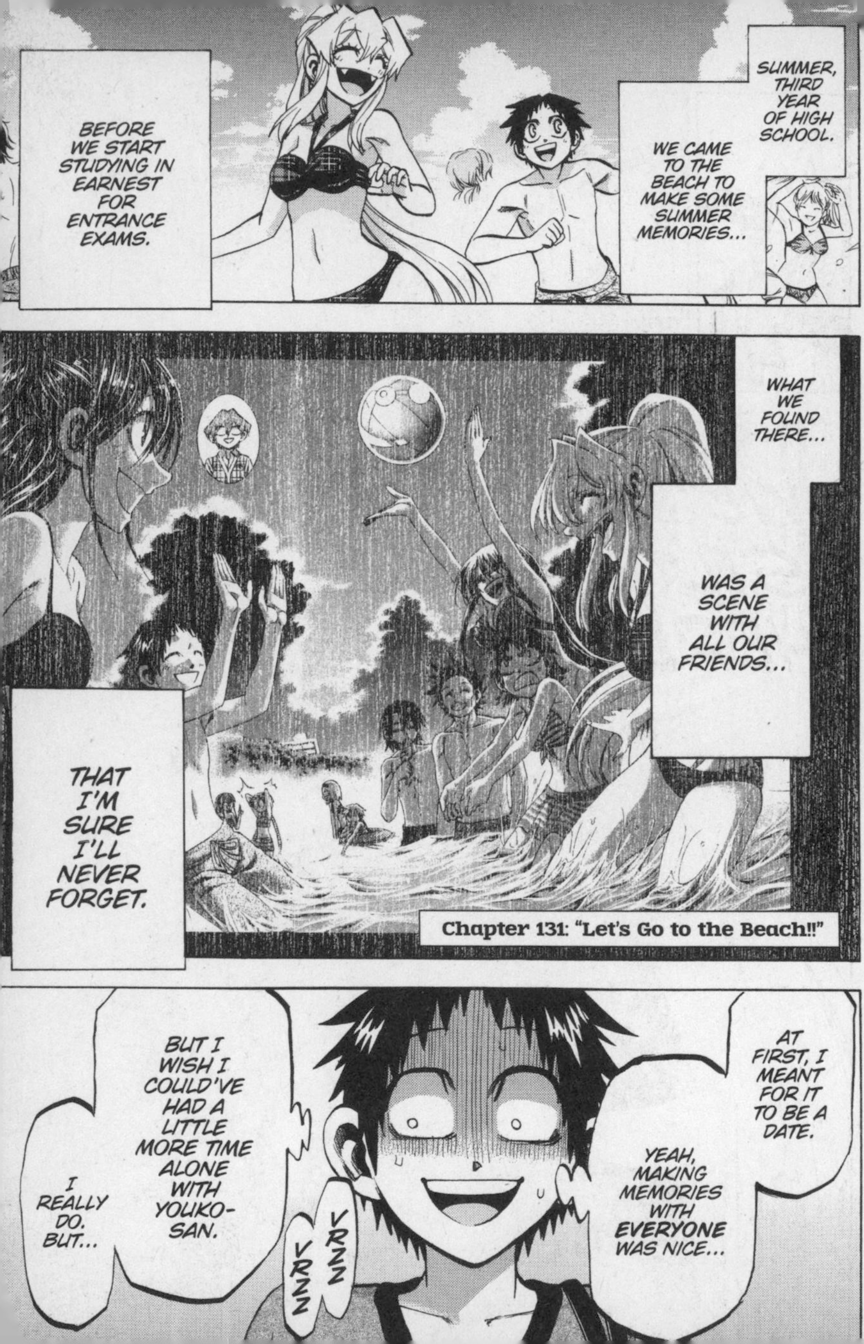
SUMMER, THIRD YEAR OF HIGH SCHOOL.
WE CAME TO THE BEACH TO MAKE SOME SUMMER MEMORIES…
BEFORE WE START STUDYING IN EARNEST FOR ENTRANCE EXAMS.
WHAT WE FOUND THERE…
WAS A SCENE WITH ALL OUR FRIENDS…
THAT I'M SURE I'LL NEVER FORGET.
Chapter 131: "Let's Go to the Beach!!"
AT FIRST, I MEANT FOR IT TO BE A DATE.
YEAH, MAKING MEMORIES WITH EVERYONE WAS NICE…
VRZZ
VRZZ
BUT I WISH I COULD'VE HAD A LITTLE MORE TIME ALONE WITH YOUKO-SAN.
I REALLY DO. BUT…

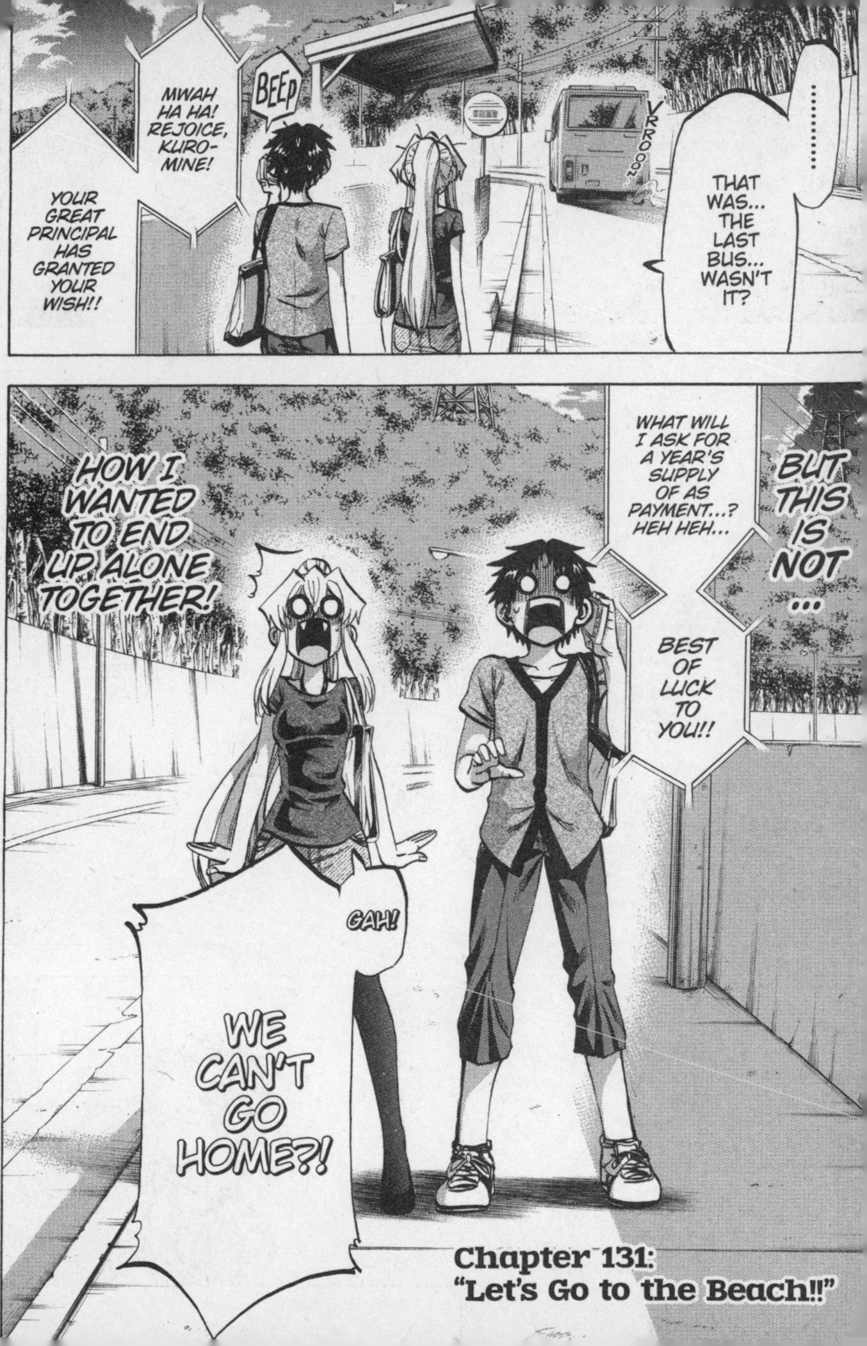
......
THAT WAS... THE LAST BUS... WASN'T IT?
VRROOON
BEEP
MWAH HA HA! REJOICE, KURO-MINE!
YOUR GREAT PRINCIPAL HAS GRANTED YOUR WISH!!
BUT THIS IS NOT...
WHAT WILL I ASK FOR A YEAR'S SUPPLY OF AS PAYMENT...? HEH HEH...
BEST OF LUCK TO YOU!!
HOW I WANTED TO END UP ALONE TOGETHER!
GAH!
WE CAN'T GO HOME?!
Chapter 131:
"Let's Go to the Beach!!"

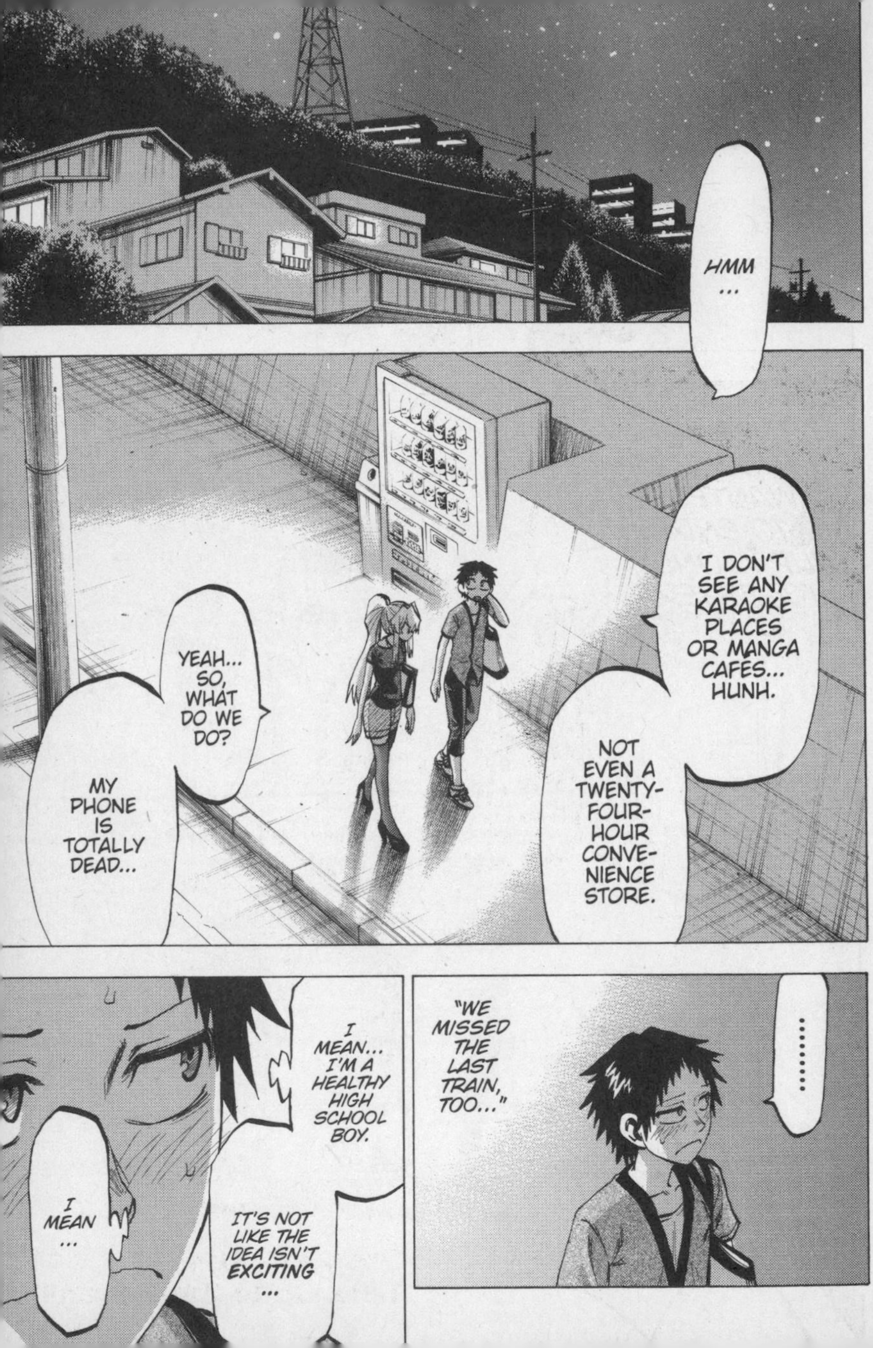
HMM ...
I DON'T SEE ANY KARAOKE PLACES OR MANGA CAFES... HUNH.
NOT EVEN A TWENTY-FOUR-HOUR CONVE-NIENCE STORE.
YEAH... SO, WHAT DO WE DO?
MY PHONE IS TOTALLY DEAD...
....
"WE MISSED THE LAST TRAIN, TOO..."
I MEAN... I'M A HEALTHY HIGH SCHOOL BOY.
IT'S NOT LIKE THE IDEA ISN'T EXCITING ...
I MEAN ...

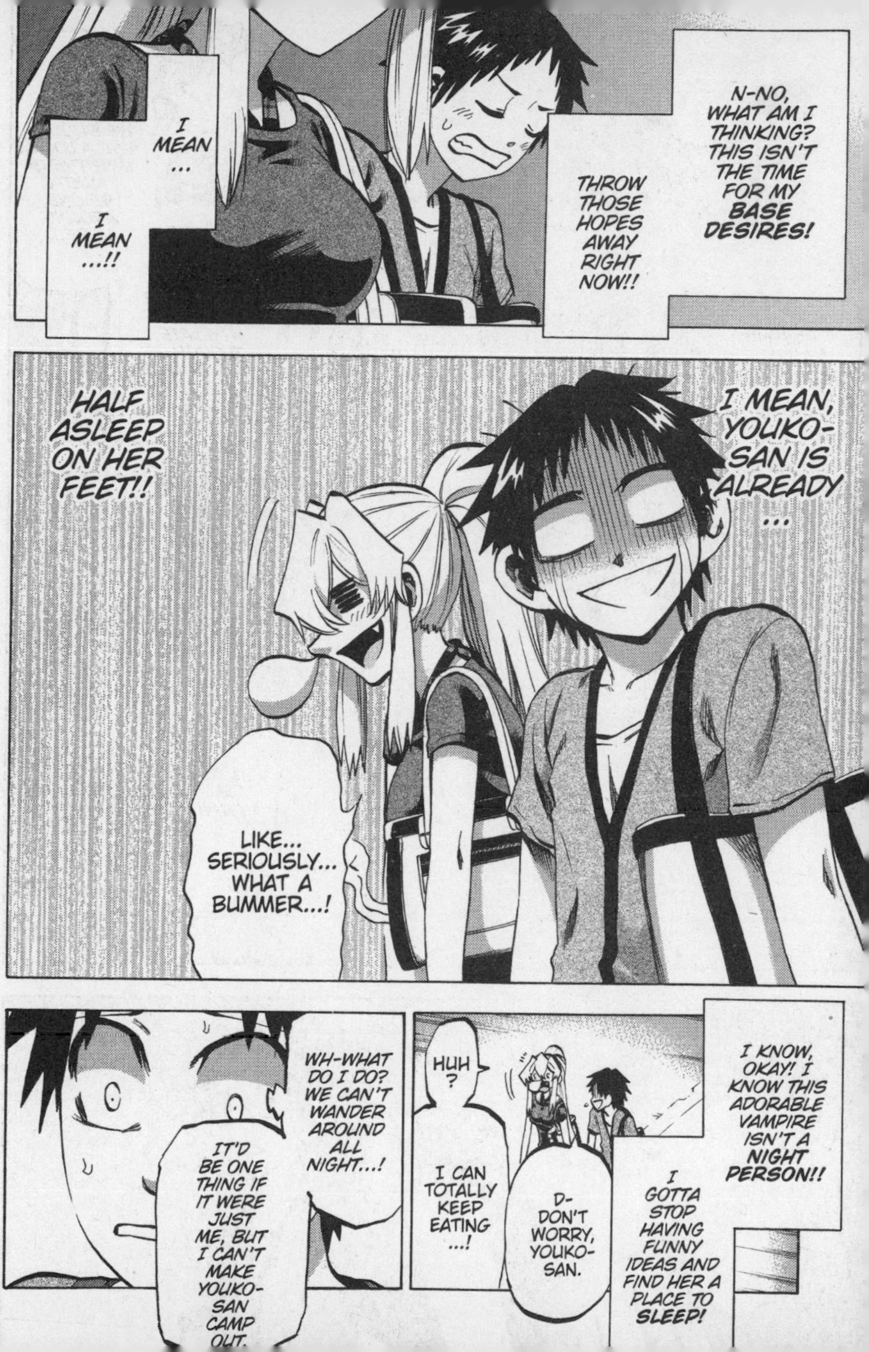
N-NO, WHAT AM I THINKING? THIS ISN'T THE TIME FOR MY BASE DESIRES!
THROW THOSE HOPES AWAY RIGHT NOW!!
I MEAN...
I MEAN...!!
I MEAN, YOUKO-SAN IS ALREADY...
HALF ASLEEP ON HER FEET!!
LIKE... SERIOUSLY... WHAT A BUMMER...!
I KNOW, OKAY! I KNOW THIS ADORABLE VAMPIRE ISN'T A NIGHT PERSON!!
I GOTTA STOP HAVING FUNNY IDEAS AND FIND HER A PLACE TO SLEEP!
HUH?
I CAN TOTALLY KEEP EATING...!
D-DON'T WORRY, YOUKO-SAN.
WH-WHAT DO I DO? WE CAN'T WANDER AROUND ALL NIGHT...!
IT'D BE ONE THING IF IT WERE JUST ME, BUT I CAN'T MAKE YOUKO-SAN CAMP OUT.

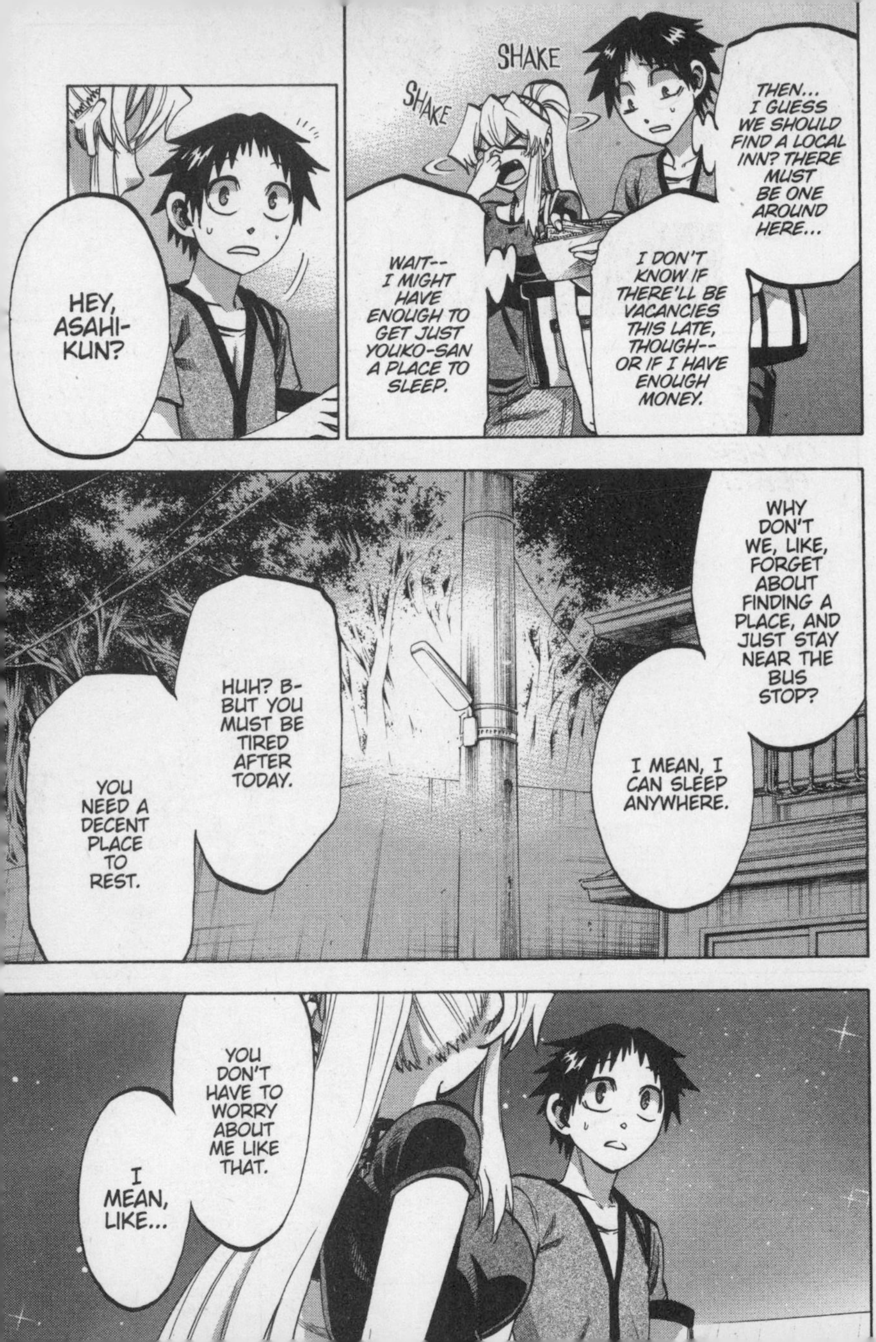
THEN... I GUESS WE SHOULD FIND A LOCAL INN? THERE MUST BE ONE AROUND HERE...
SHAKE
SHAKE
I DON'T KNOW IF THERE'LL BE VACANCIES THIS LATE, THOUGH-- OR IF I HAVE ENOUGH MONEY.
WAIT-- I MIGHT HAVE ENOUGH TO GET JUST YOUKO-SAN A PLACE TO SLEEP.
HEY, ASAHI-KUN?
WHY DON'T WE, LIKE, FORGET ABOUT FINDING A PLACE, AND JUST STAY NEAR THE BUS STOP?
I MEAN, I CAN SLEEP ANYWHERE.
HUH? B-BUT YOU MUST BE TIRED AFTER TODAY.
YOU NEED A DECENT PLACE TO REST.
YOU DON'T HAVE TO WORRY ABOUT ME LIKE THAT.
I MEAN, LIKE...

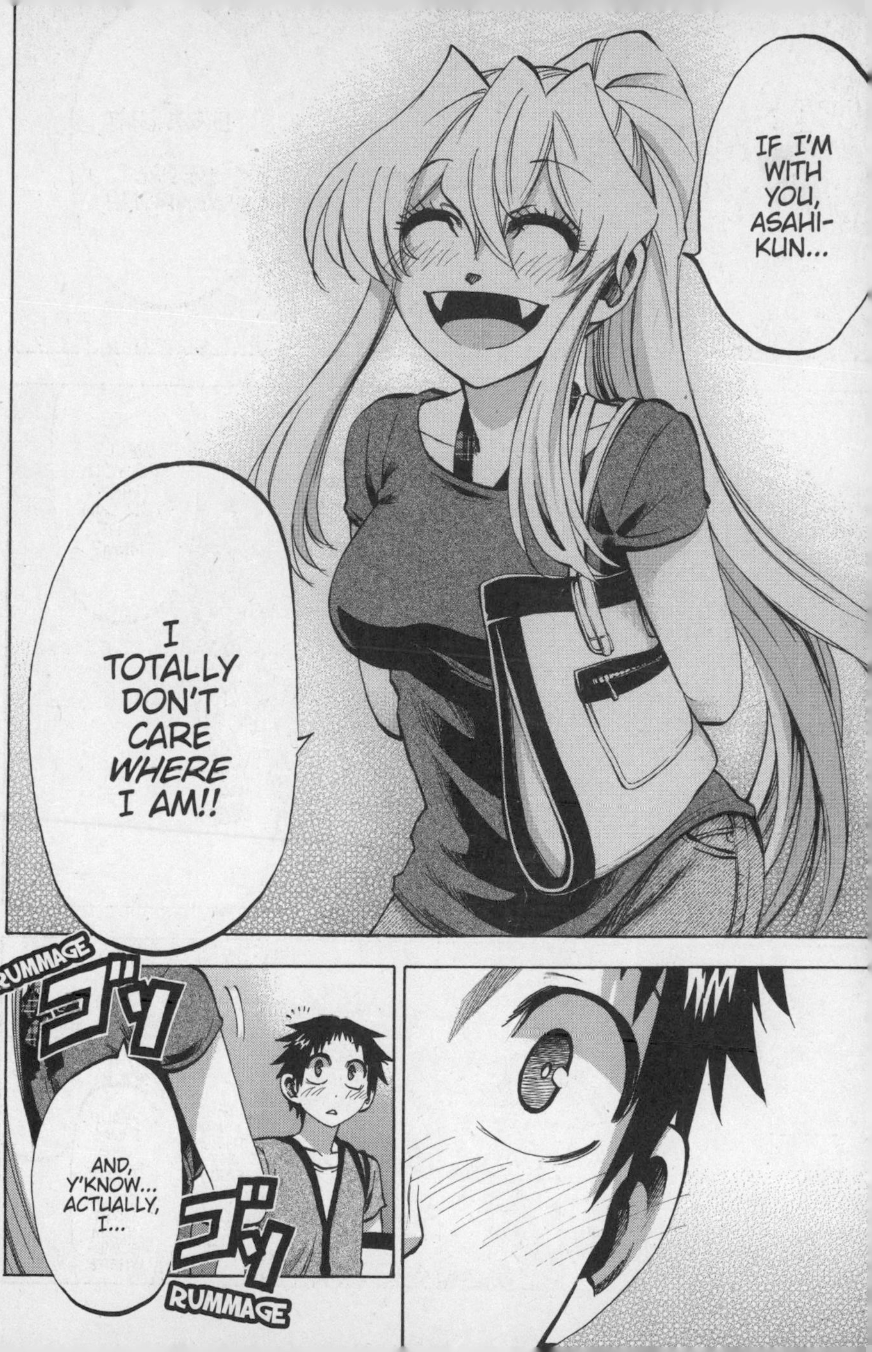

IF I'M WITH YOU, ASAHI-KUN...
I TOTALLY DON'T CARE *WHERE* I AM!!
RUMMAGE
AND, Y'KNOW... ACTUALLY, I...
RUMMAGE

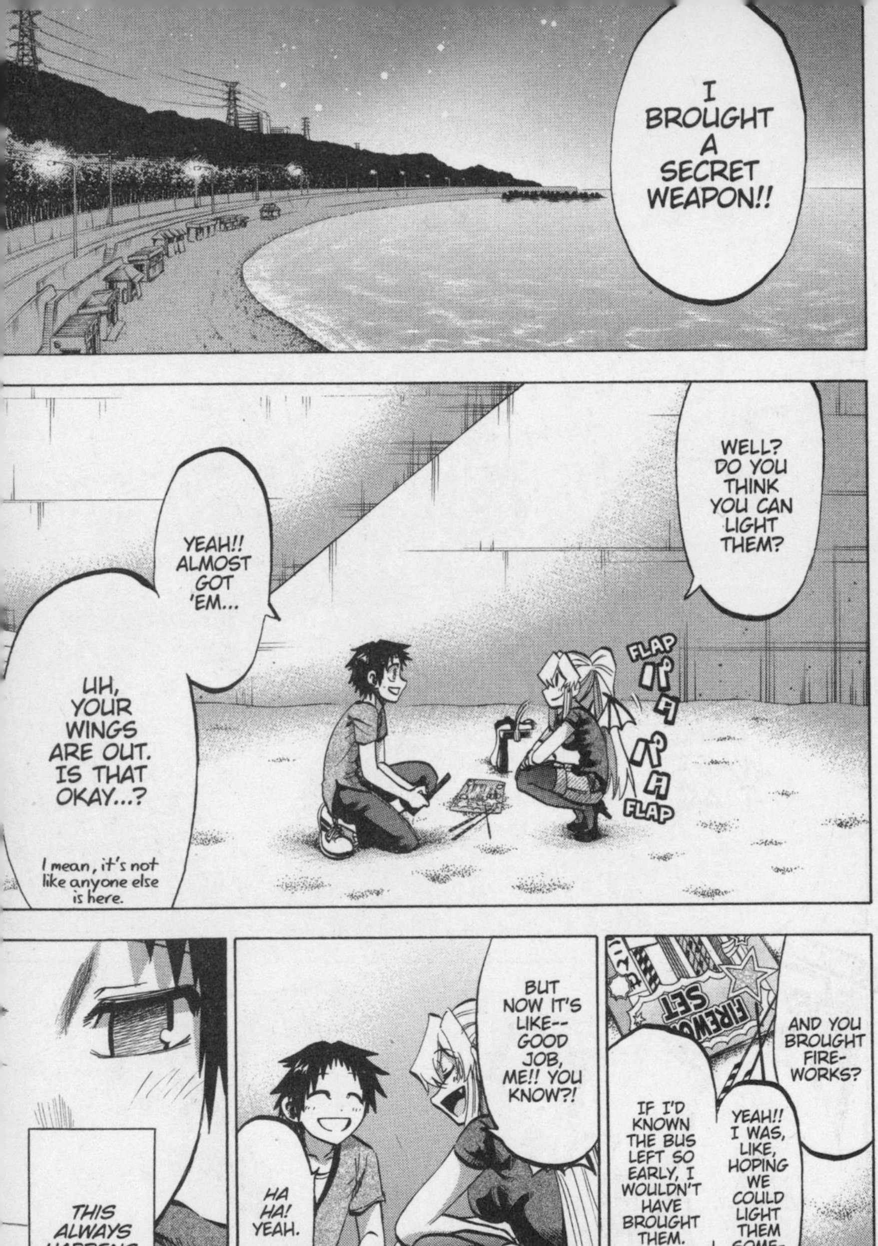
I BROUGHT A SECRET WEAPON!!
WELL? DO YOU THINK YOU CAN LIGHT THEM?
FLAP FLAP
YEAH!! ALMOST GOT 'EM...
UH, YOUR WINGS ARE OUT. IS THAT OKAY...?
I mean, it's not like anyone else is here.
AND YOU BROUGHT FIRE-WORKS?
YEAH!! I WAS, LIKE, HOPING WE COULD LIGHT THEM SOME-WHERE.
IF I'D KNOWN THE BUS LEFT SO EARLY, I WOULDN'T HAVE BROUGHT THEM.
BUT NOW IT'S LIKE-- GOOD JOB, ME!! YOU KNOW?!
HA HA! YEAH.
THIS ALWAYS HAPPENS.

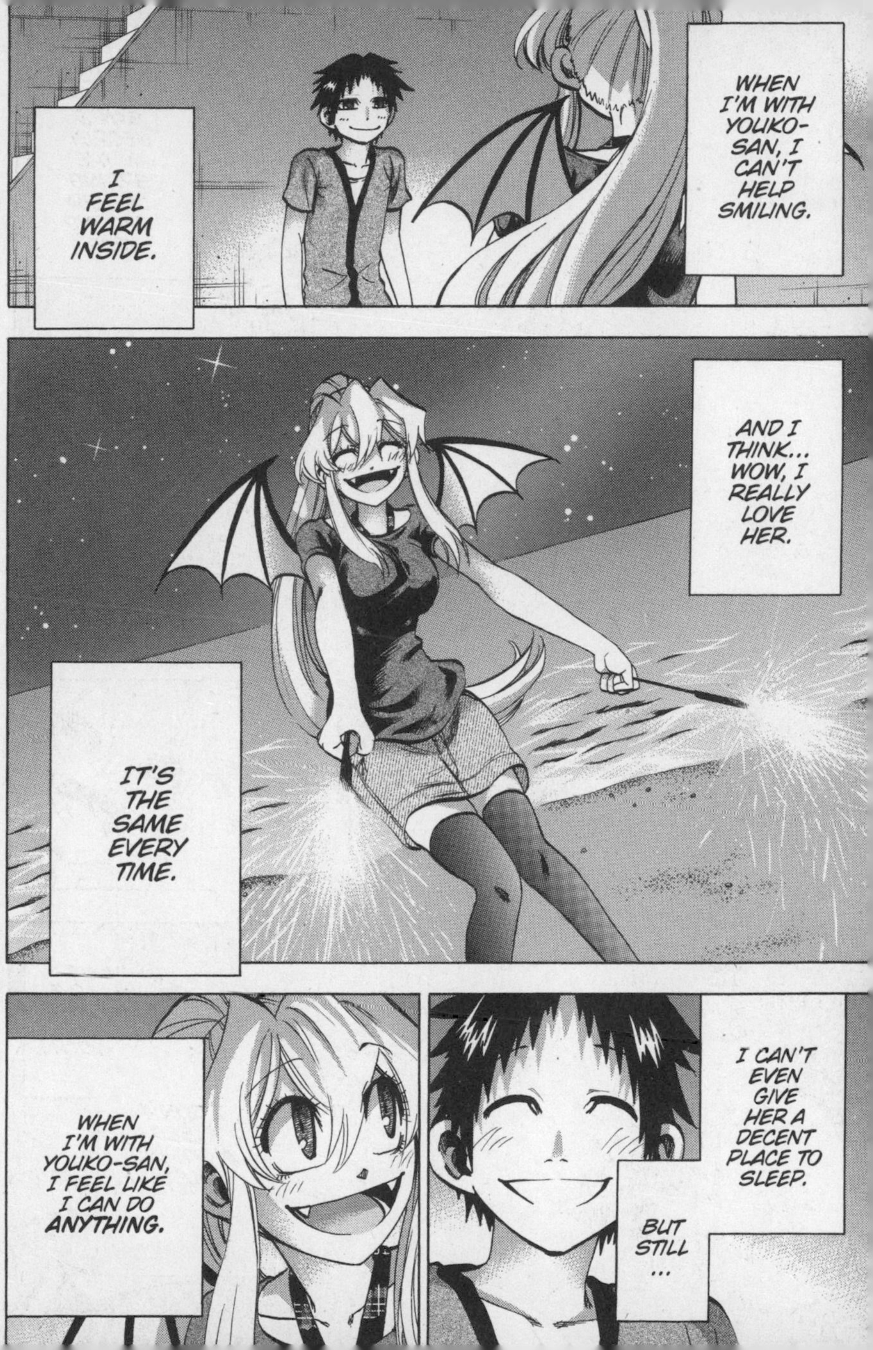
WHEN I'M WITH YOUKO-SAN, I CAN'T HELP SMILING.
I FEEL WARM INSIDE.
AND I THINK... WOW, I REALLY LOVE HER.
IT'S THE SAME EVERY TIME.
I CAN'T EVEN GIVE HER A DECENT PLACE TO SLEEP.
BUT STILL...
WHEN I'M WITH YOUKO-SAN, I FEEL LIKE I CAN DO ANYTHING.

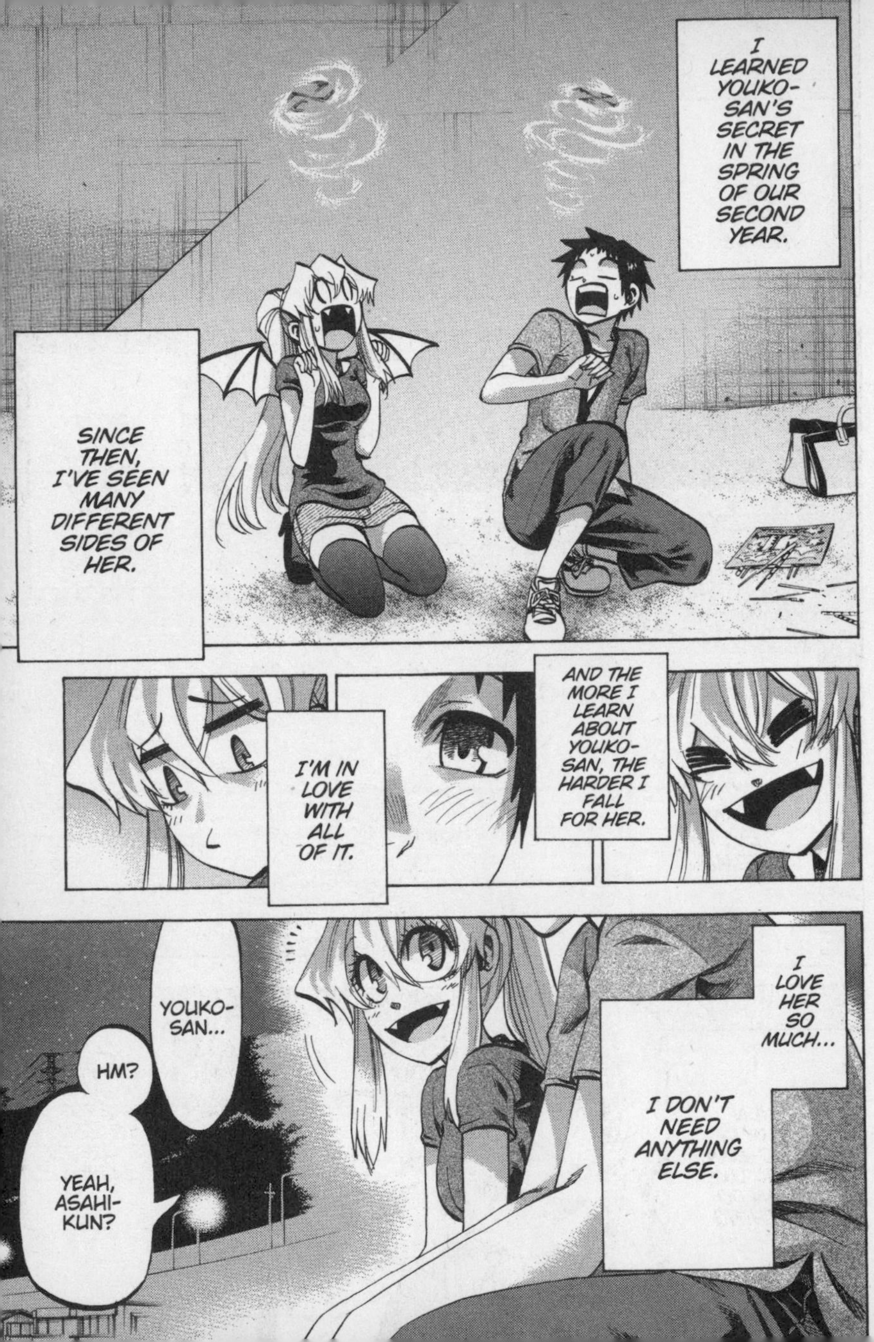
I LEARNED YOUKO-SAN'S SECRET IN THE SPRING OF OUR SECOND YEAR.
SINCE THEN, I'VE SEEN MANY DIFFERENT SIDES OF HER.
AND THE MORE I LEARN ABOUT YOUKO-SAN, THE HARDER I FALL FOR HER.
I'M IN LOVE WITH ALL OF IT.
I LOVE HER SO MUCH...
I DON'T NEED ANYTHING ELSE.
YOUKO-SAN...
HM?
YEAH, ASAHI-KUN?

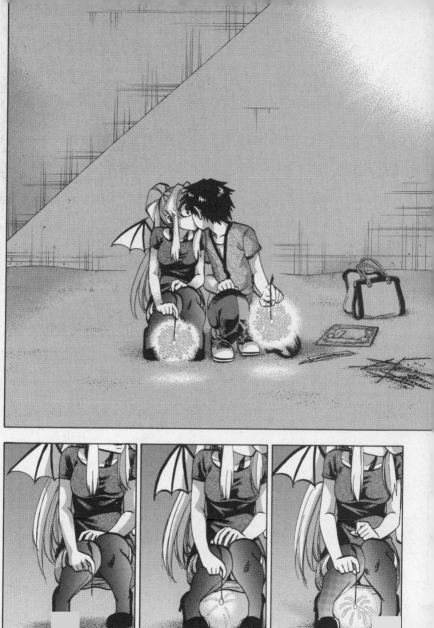

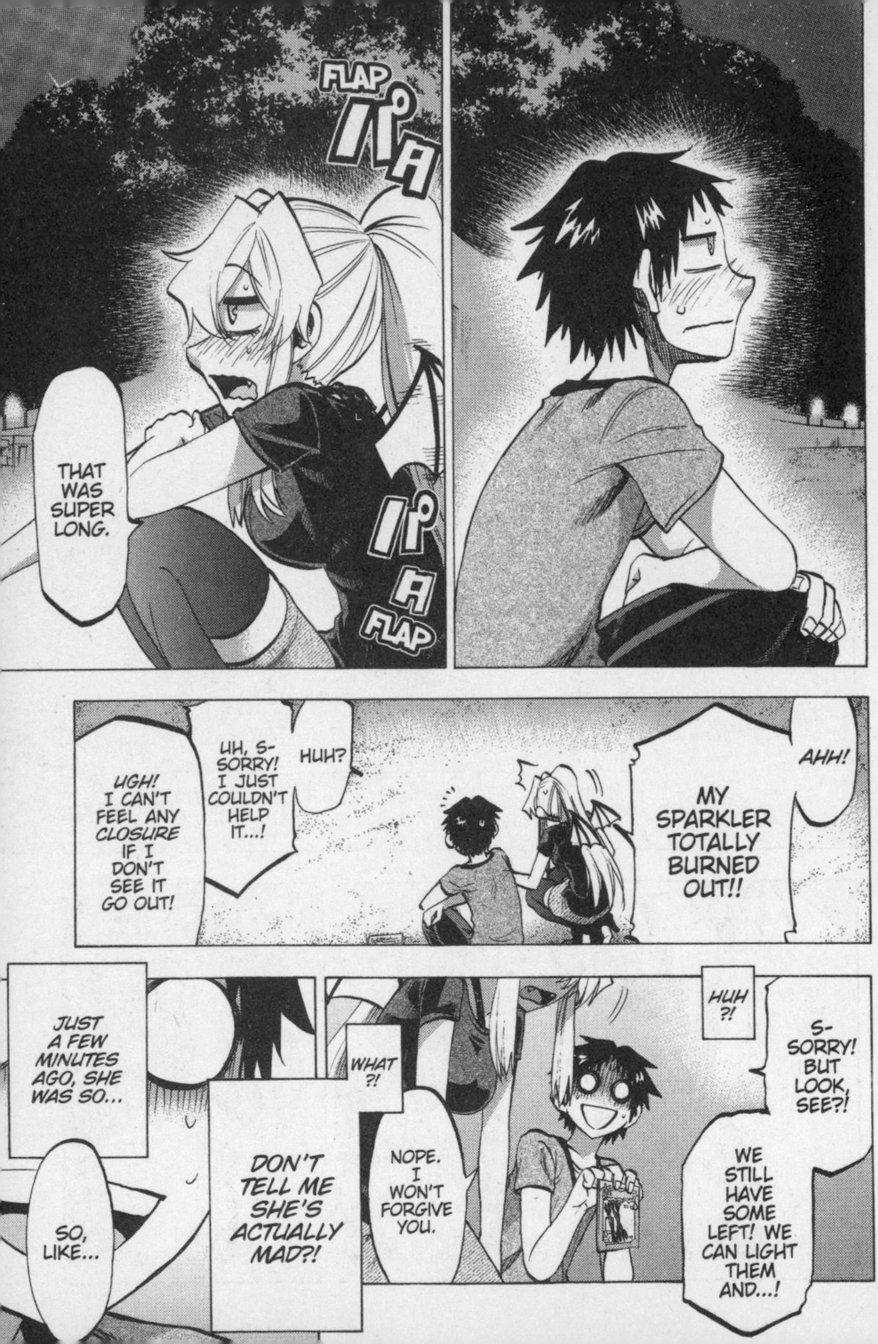
FLAP
パタ
THAT WAS SUPER LONG.
パタ
FLAP
AHH!
MY SPARKLER TOTALLY BURNED OUT!!
HUH?
UH, S-SORRY! I JUST COULDN'T HELP IT...!
UGH! I CAN'T FEEL ANY CLOSURE IF I DON'T SEE IT GO OUT!
HUH?!
S-SORRY! BUT LOOK, SEE?!
WE STILL HAVE SOME LEFT! WE CAN LIGHT THEM AND...!
WHAT?!
NOPE. I WON'T FORGIVE YOU.
DON'T TELL ME SHE'S ACTUALLY MAD?!
JUST A FEW MINUTES AGO, SHE WAS SO...
SO, LIKE...

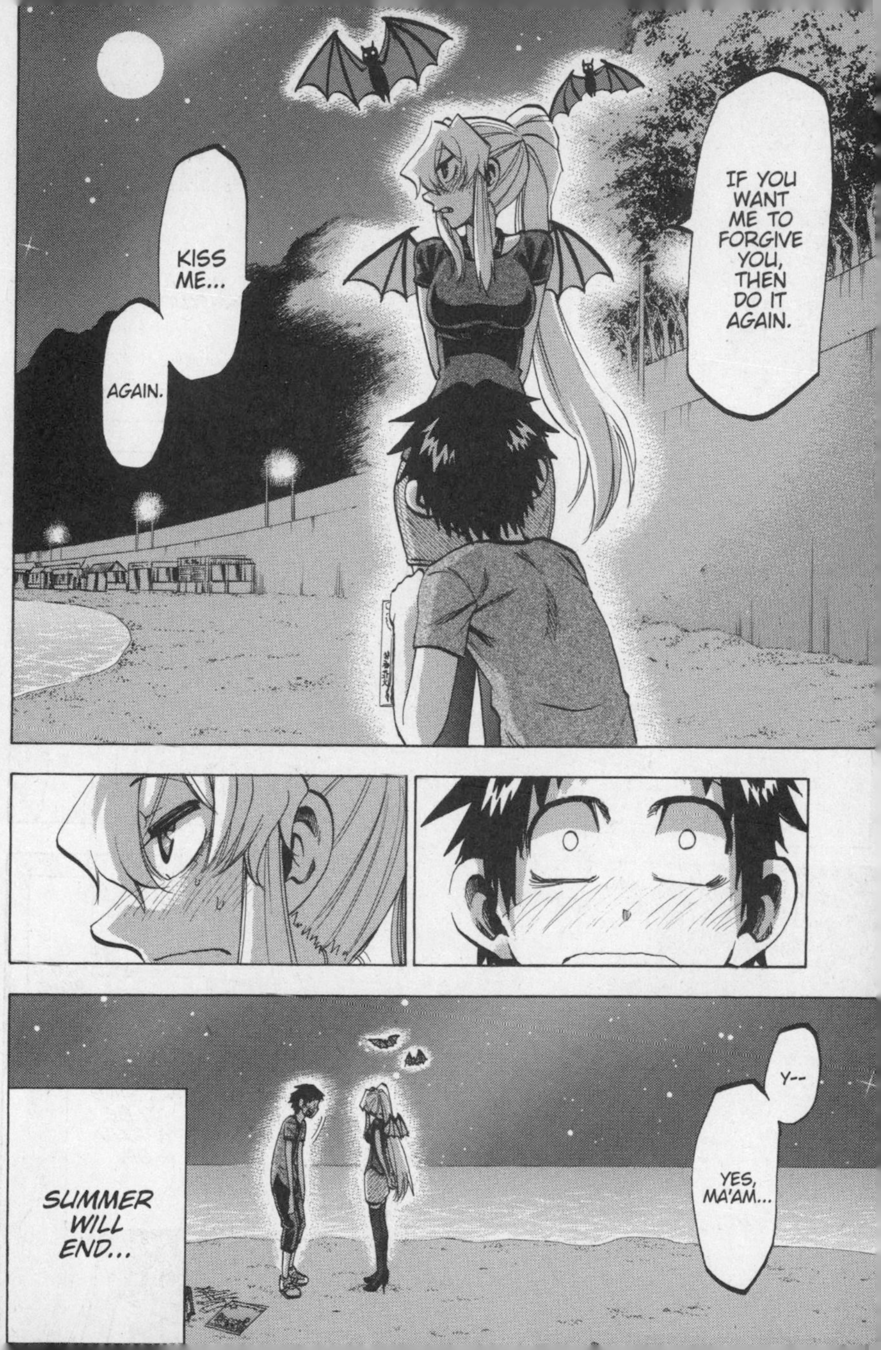
IF YOU WANT ME TO FORGIVE YOU, THEN DO IT AGAIN.
KISS ME...
AGAIN.
Y--
YES, MA'AM...
SUMMER WILL END...

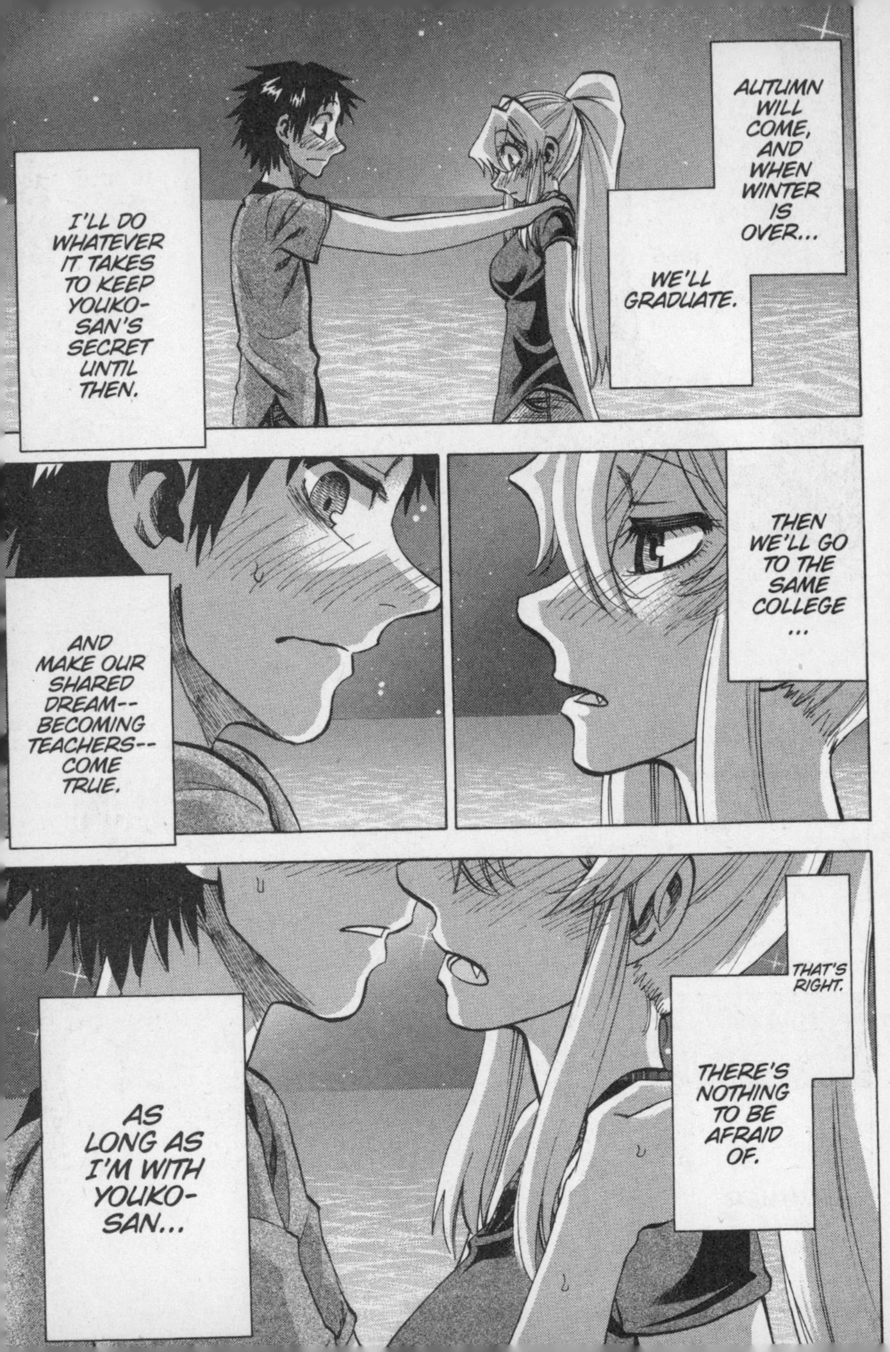
AUTUMN WILL COME, AND WHEN WINTER IS OVER...
WE'LL GRADUATE.
I'LL DO WHATEVER IT TAKES TO KEEP YOUKO-SAN'S SECRET UNTIL THEN.
THEN WE'LL GO TO THE SAME COLLEGE ...
AND MAKE OUR SHARED DREAM--BECOMING TEACHERS--COME TRUE.
THAT'S RIGHT.
THERE'S NOTHING TO BE AFRAID OF.
AS LONG AS I'M WITH YOUKO-SAN...

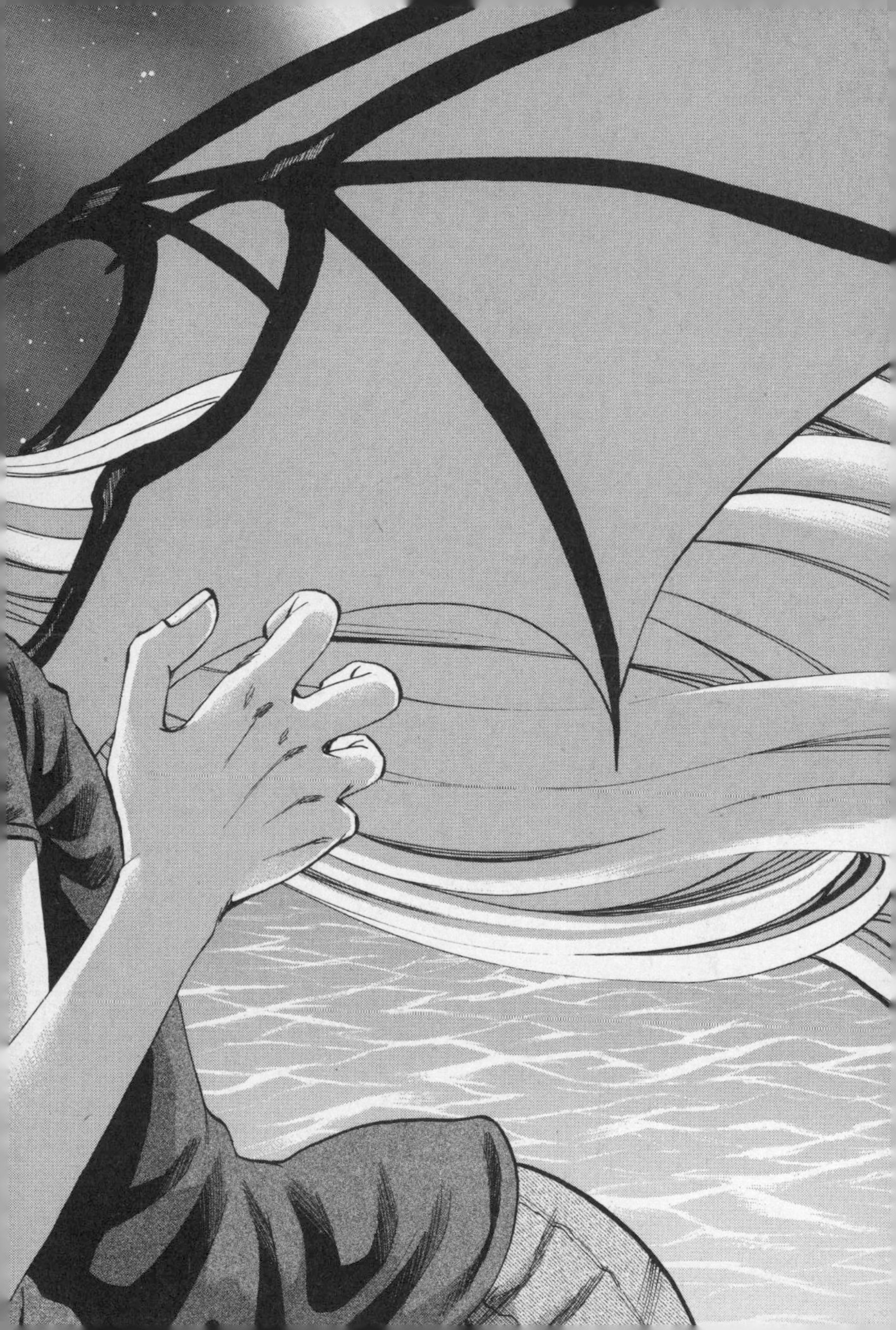

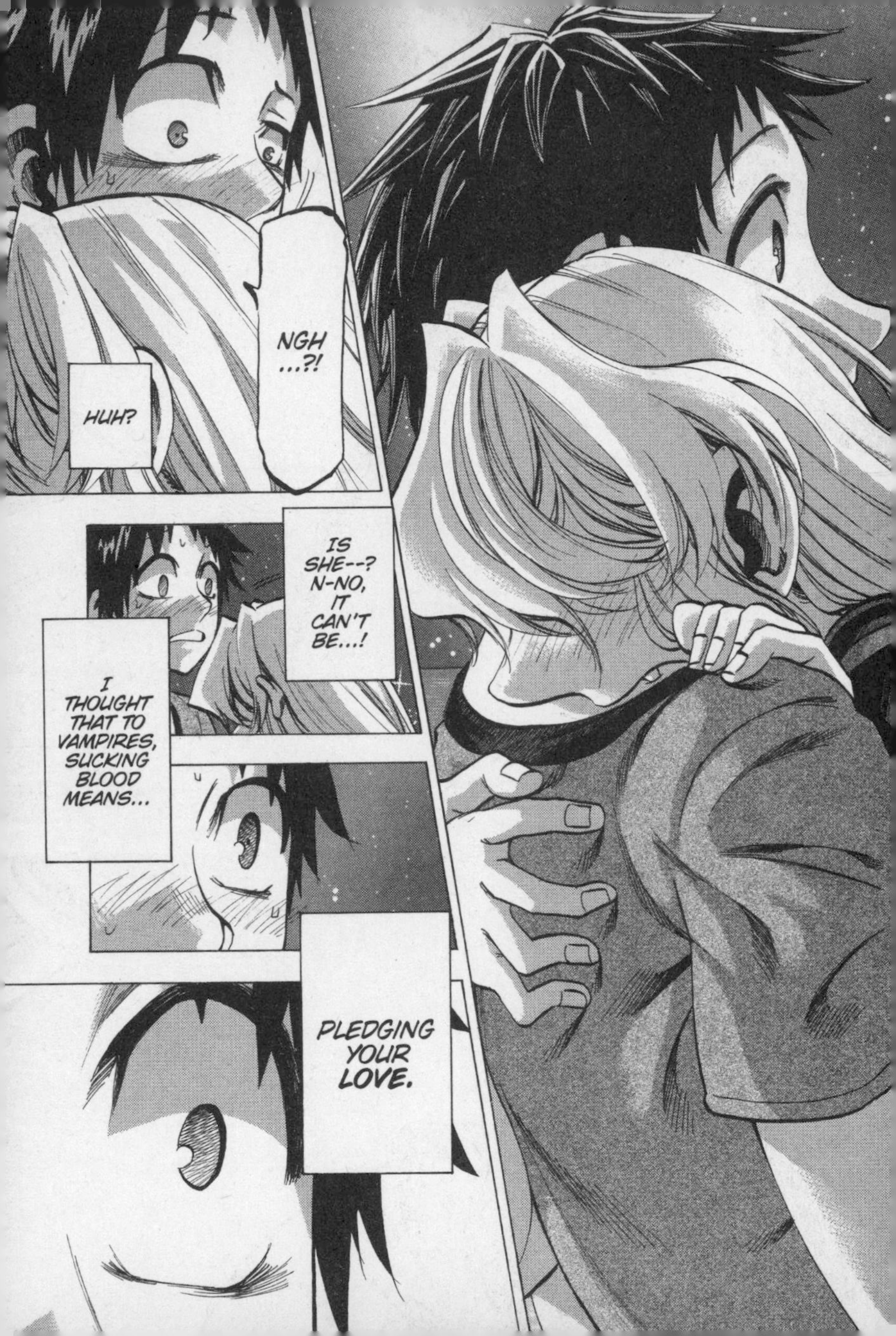
NGH ...?!
HUH?
IS SHE--? N-NO, IT CAN'T BE...!
I THOUGHT THAT TO VAMPIRES, SUCKING BLOOD MEANS...
PLEDGING YOUR LOVE.

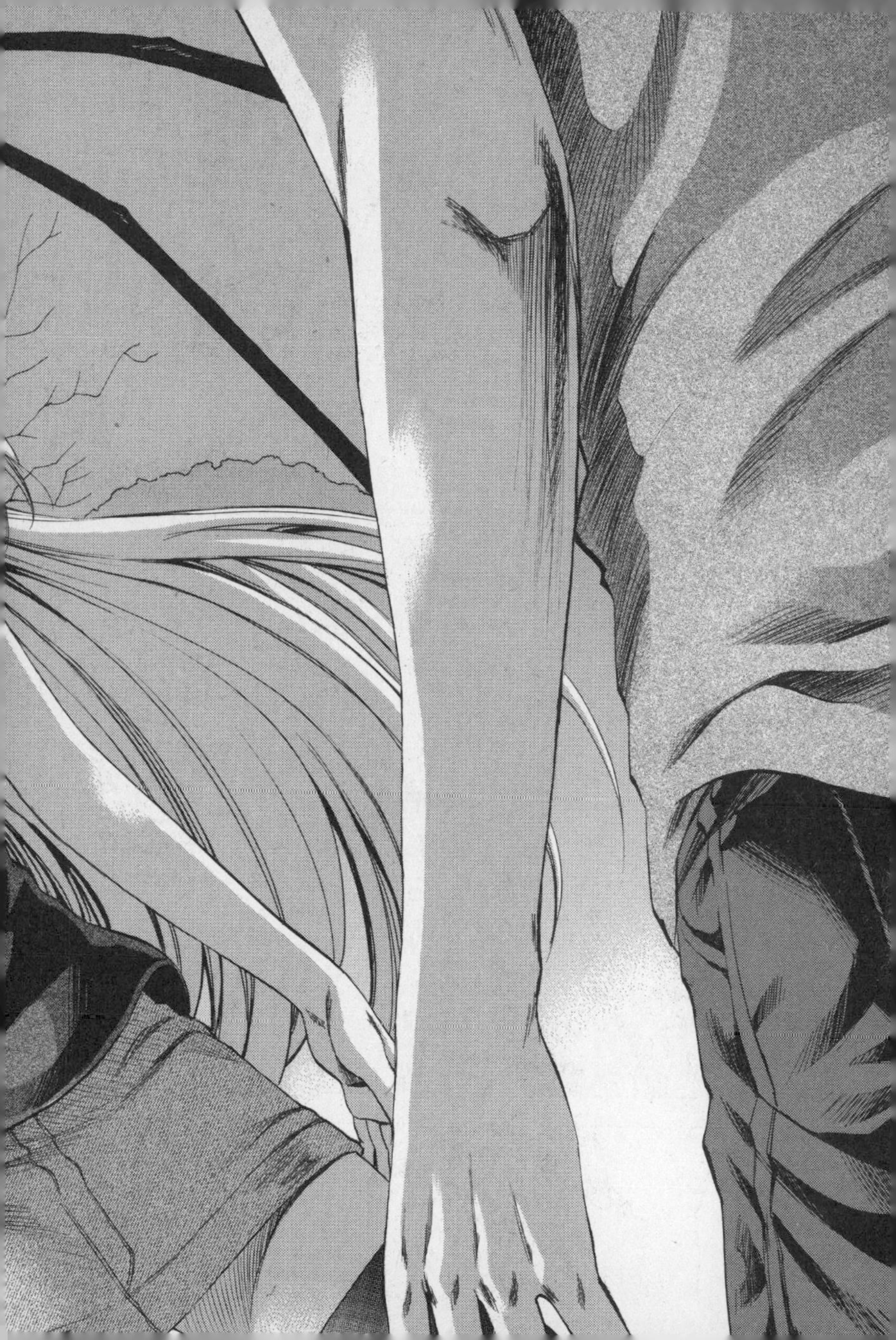

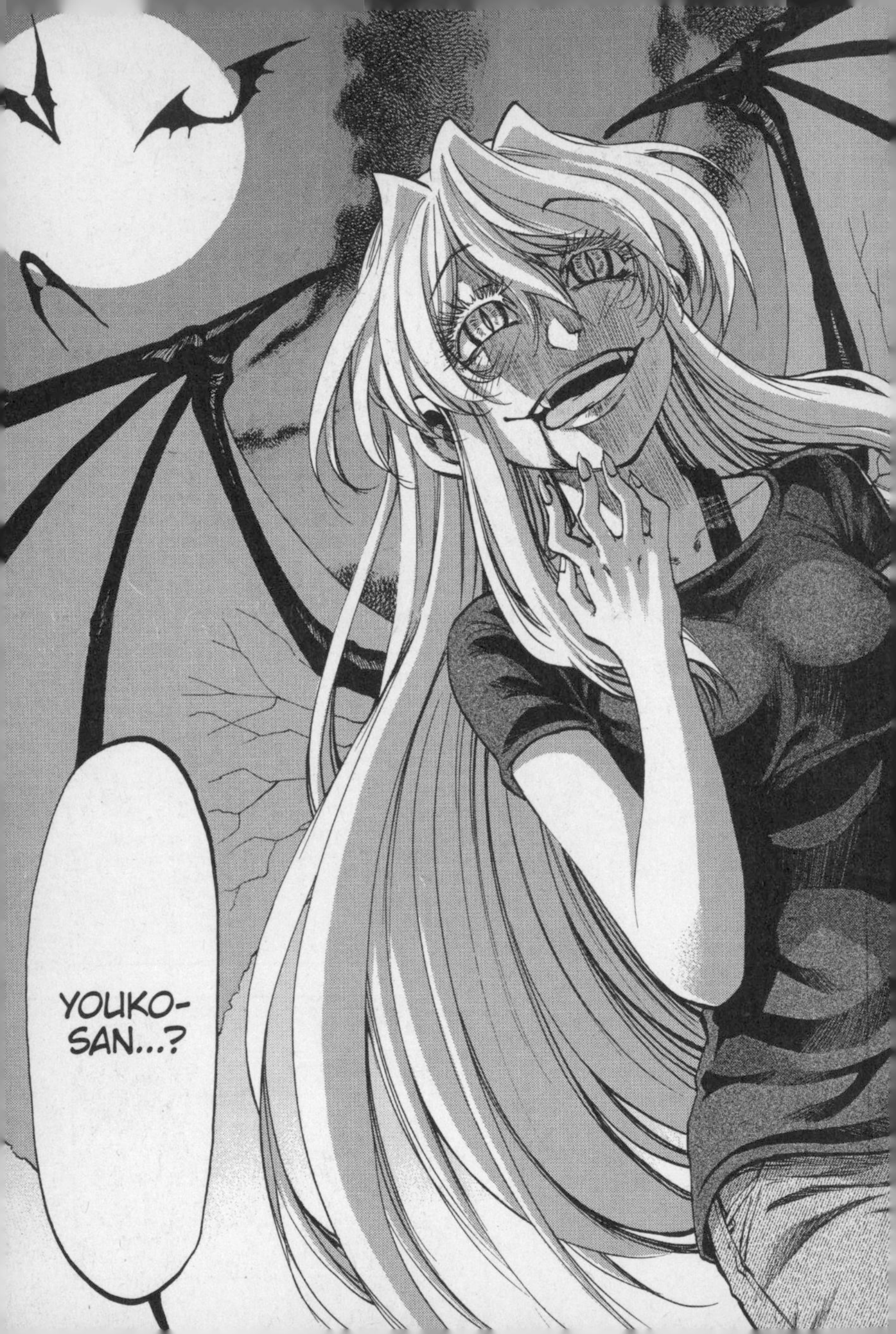
YOUKO-SAN...?

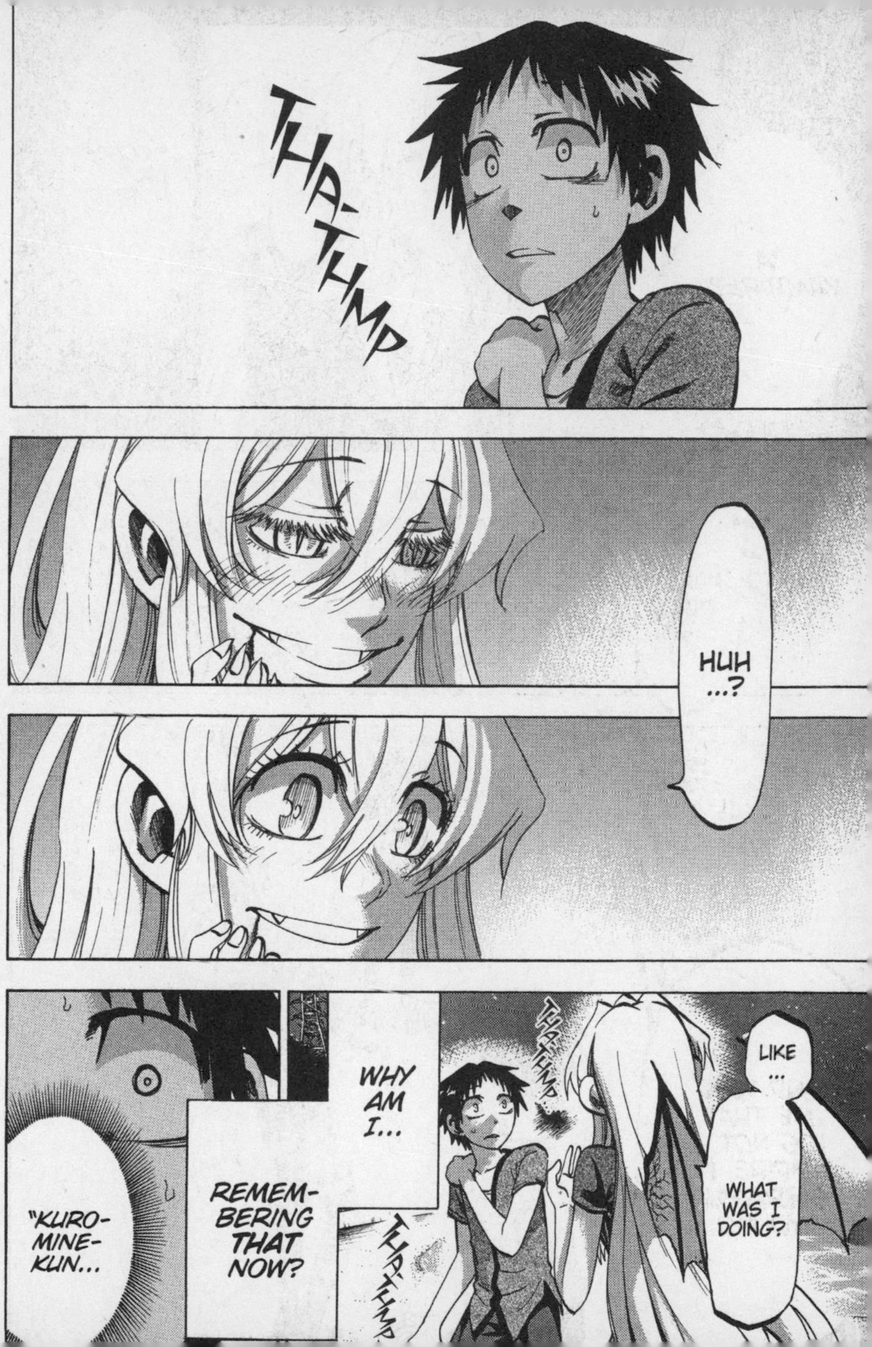
THA-THUMP
HUH...?
LIKE...
WHAT WAS I DOING?
THA-THUMP
WHY AM I...
REMEMBERING THAT NOW?
THA-THUMP
"KURO-MINE-KUN...

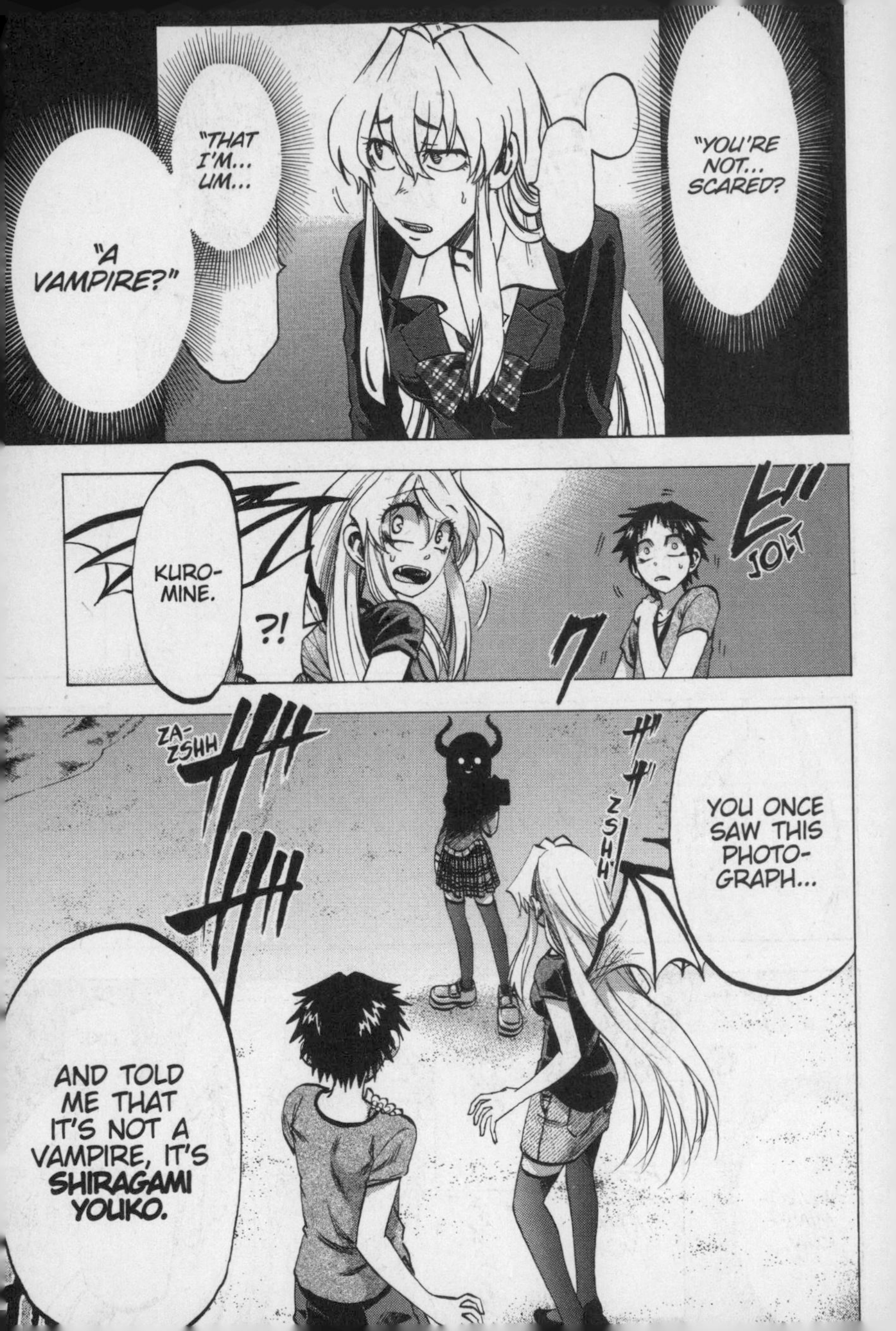
"YOU'RE NOT... SCARED?
"THAT I'M... UM...
"A VAMPIRE?"
JOLT
KURO-MINE.
?!
YOU ONCE SAW THIS PHOTOGRAPH...
ZSHH
ZA-ZSHH
AND TOLD ME THAT IT'S NOT A VAMPIRE, IT'S **SHIRAGAMI YOUKO.**

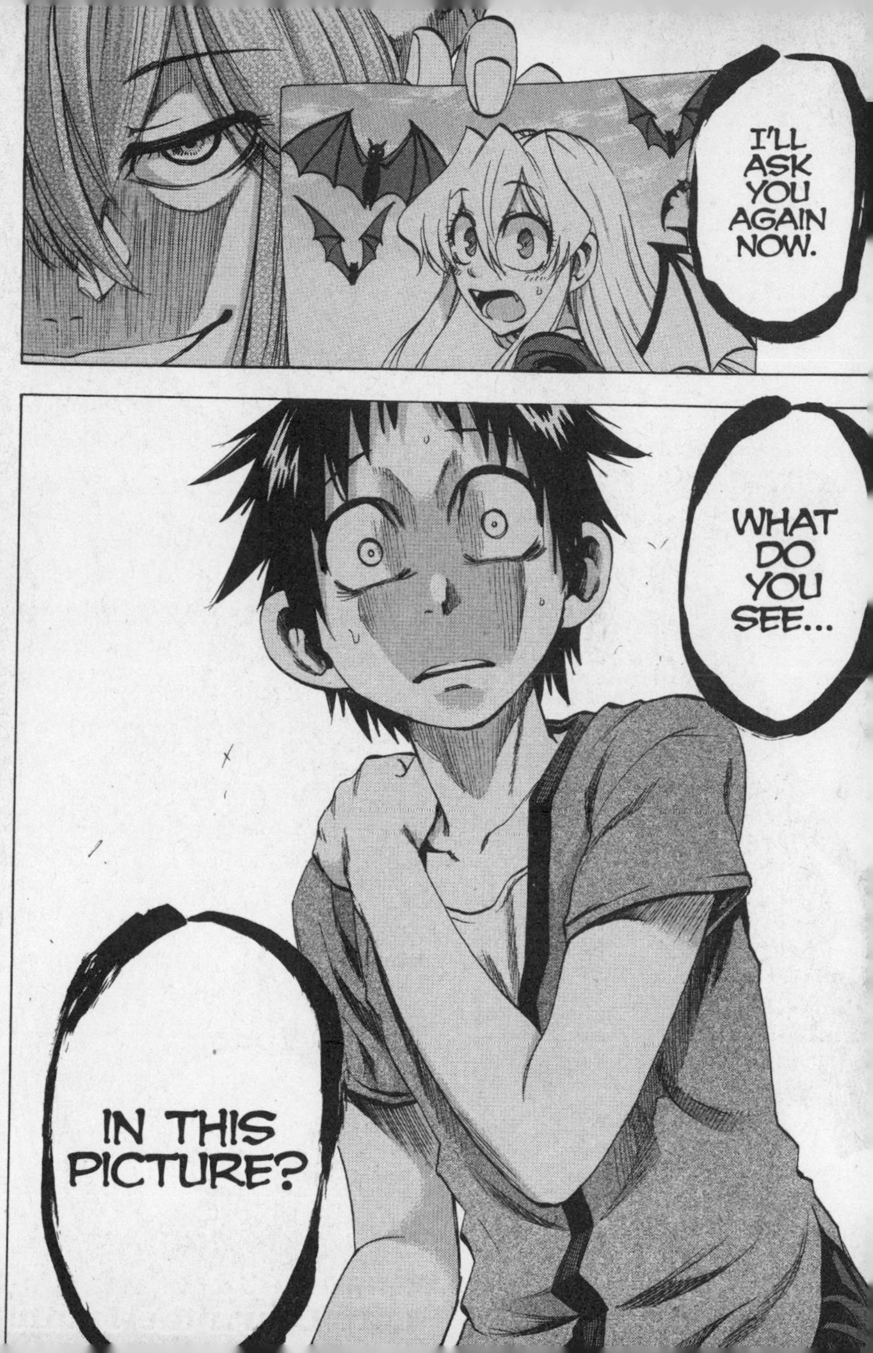
I'LL ASK YOU AGAIN NOW.
WHAT DO YOU SEE...
IN THIS PICTURE?

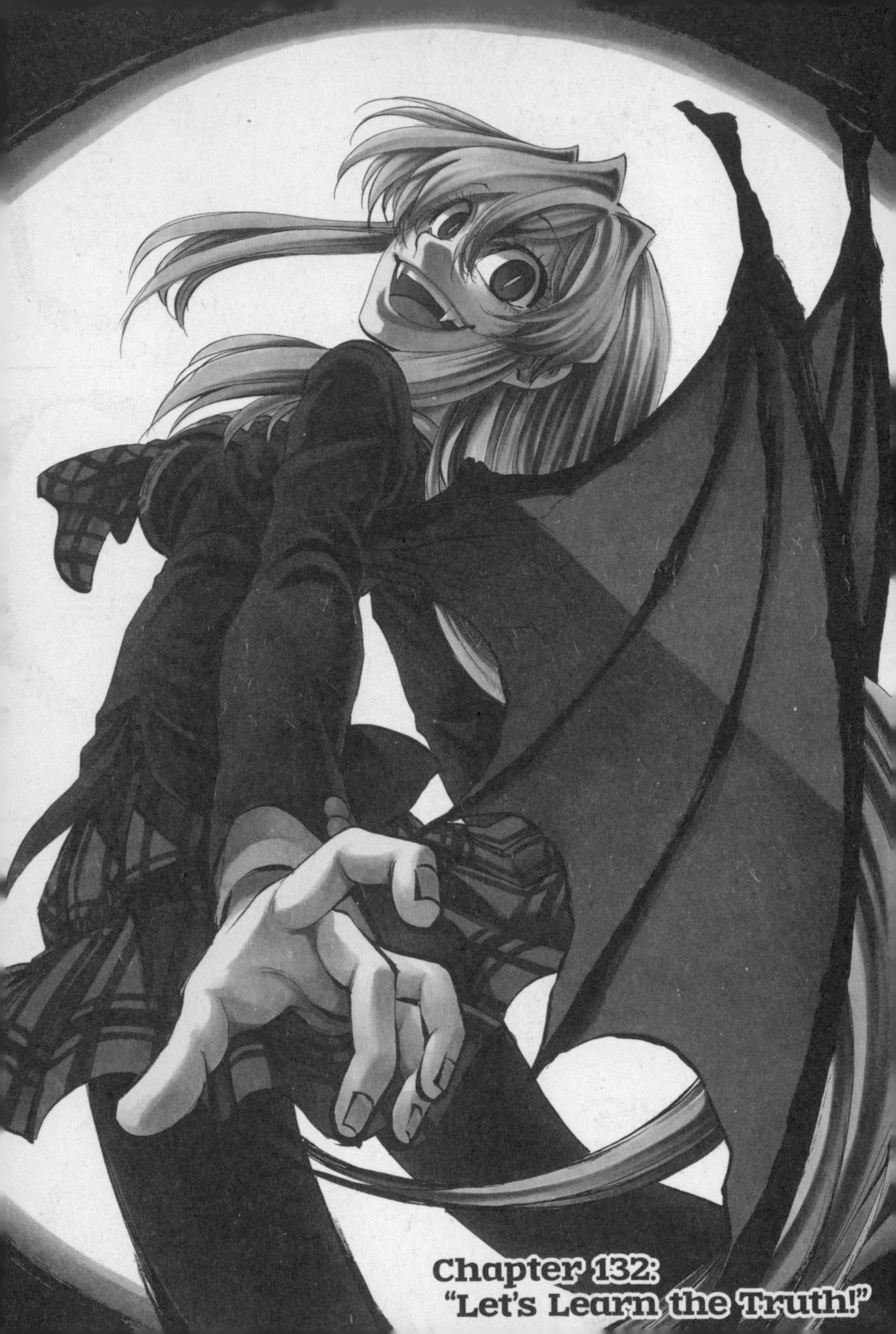

Chapter 132: "Let's Learn the Truth!"

TOP SECRET

My Monster Secret 15

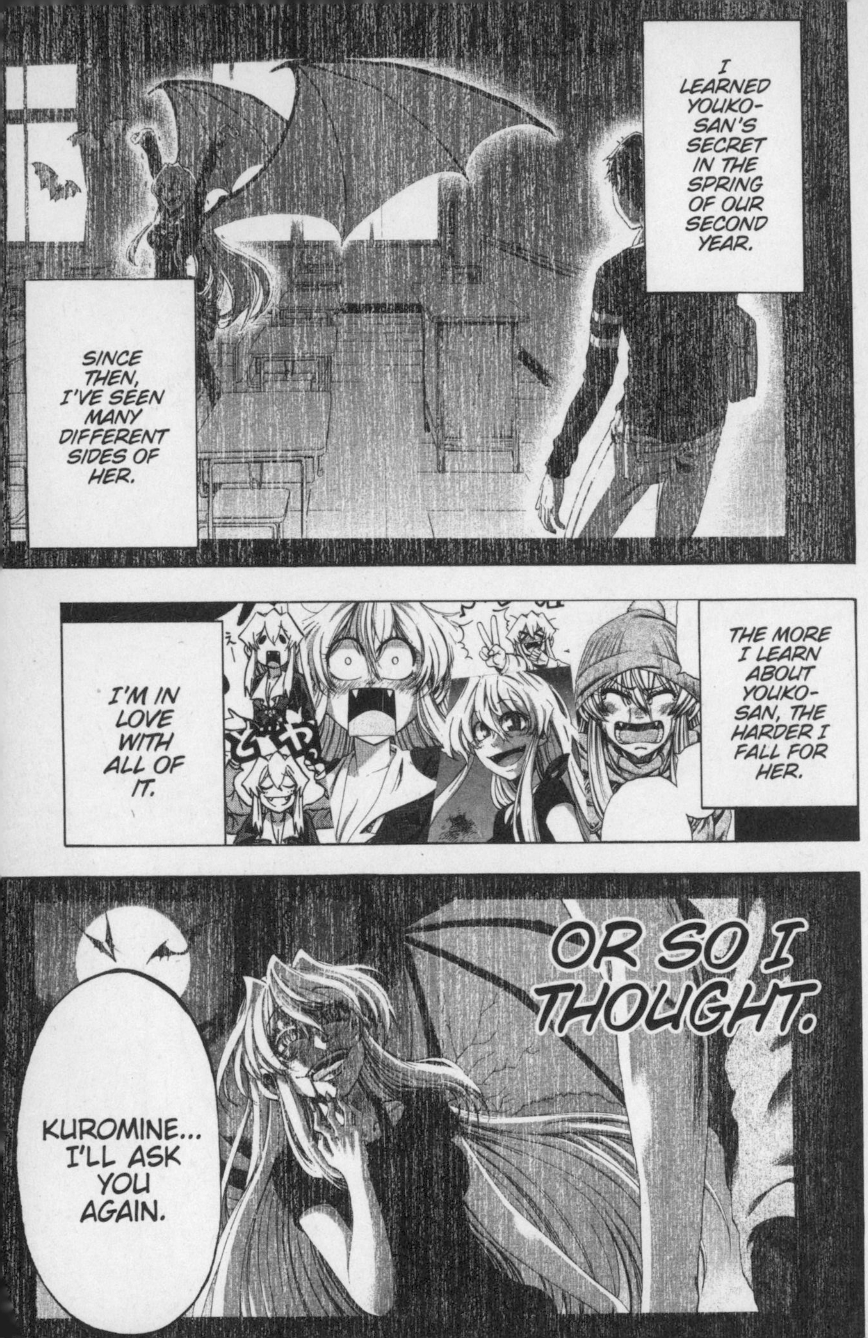
I LEARNED YOUKO-SAN'S SECRET IN THE SPRING OF OUR SECOND YEAR.
SINCE THEN, I'VE SEEN MANY DIFFERENT SIDES OF HER.
THE MORE I LEARN ABOUT YOUKO-SAN, THE HARDER I FALL FOR HER.
I'M IN LOVE WITH ALL OF IT.
OR SO I THOUGHT.
KUROMINE... I'LL ASK YOU AGAIN.

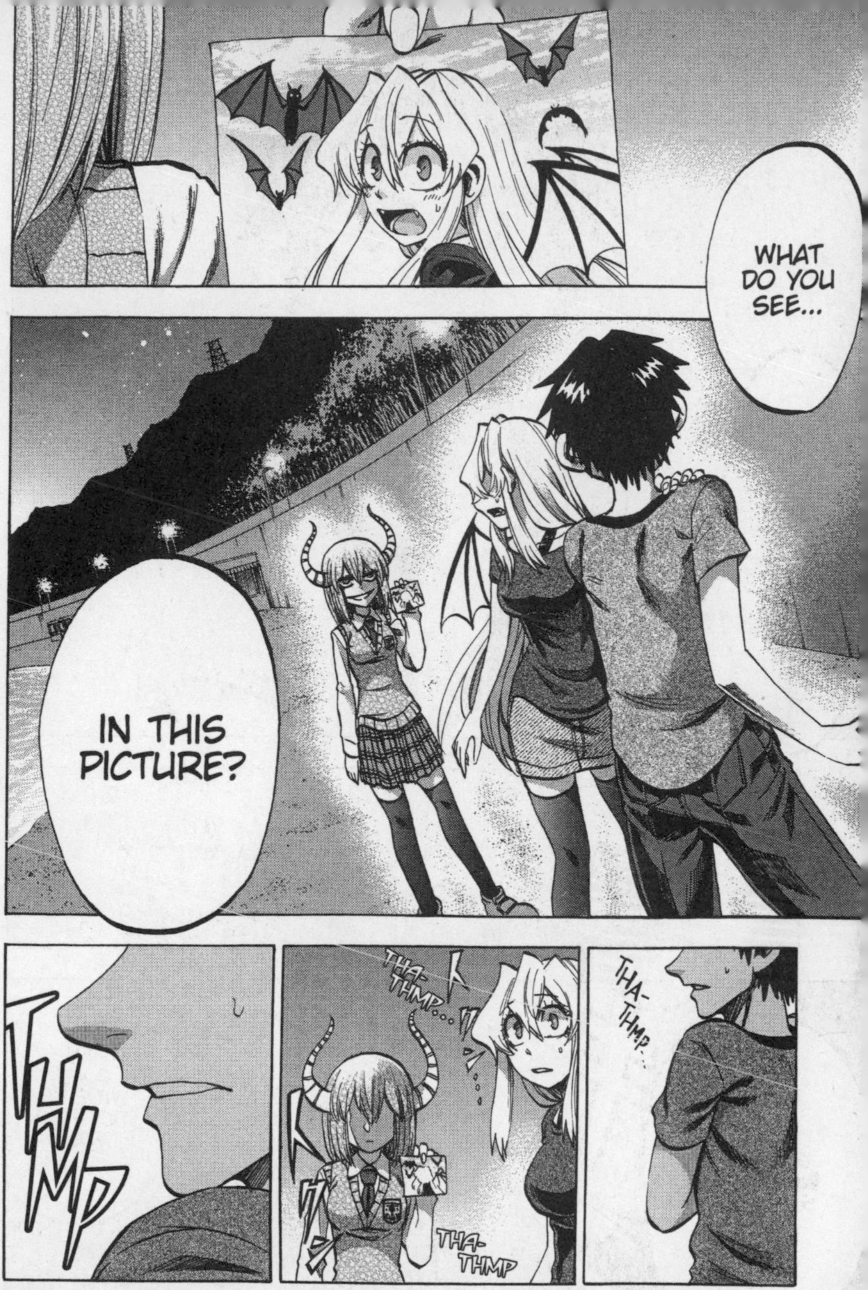
WHAT DO YOU SEE...
IN THIS PICTURE?
THA-THMP...
THA-THMP...
THA-THMP
THUMP

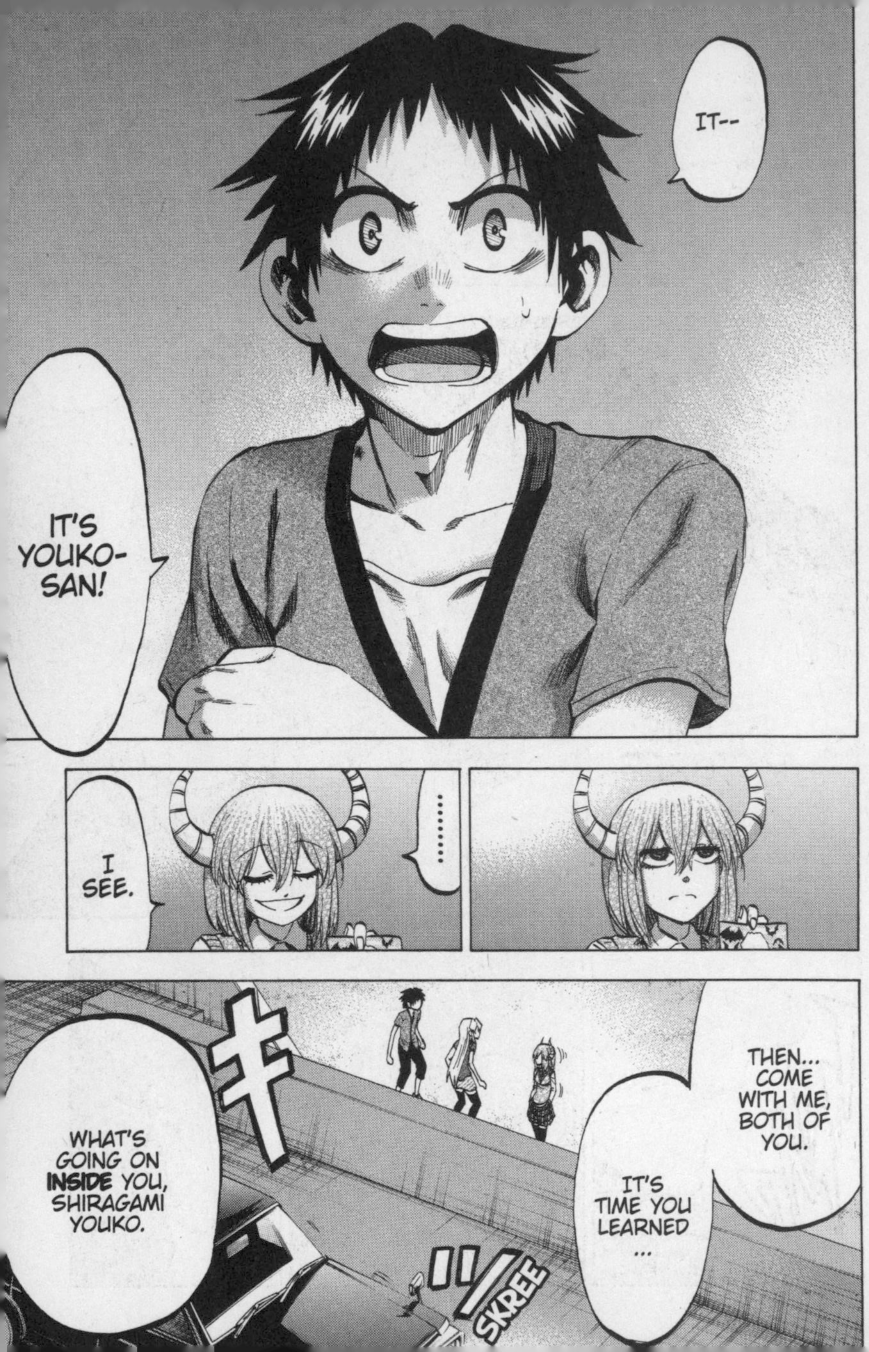
IT--
IT'S YOUKO-SAN!
......
I SEE.
THEN... COME WITH ME, BOTH OF YOU.
IT'S TIME YOU LEARNED ...
SKREE
WHAT'S GOING ON **INSIDE** YOU, SHIRAGAMI YOUKO.

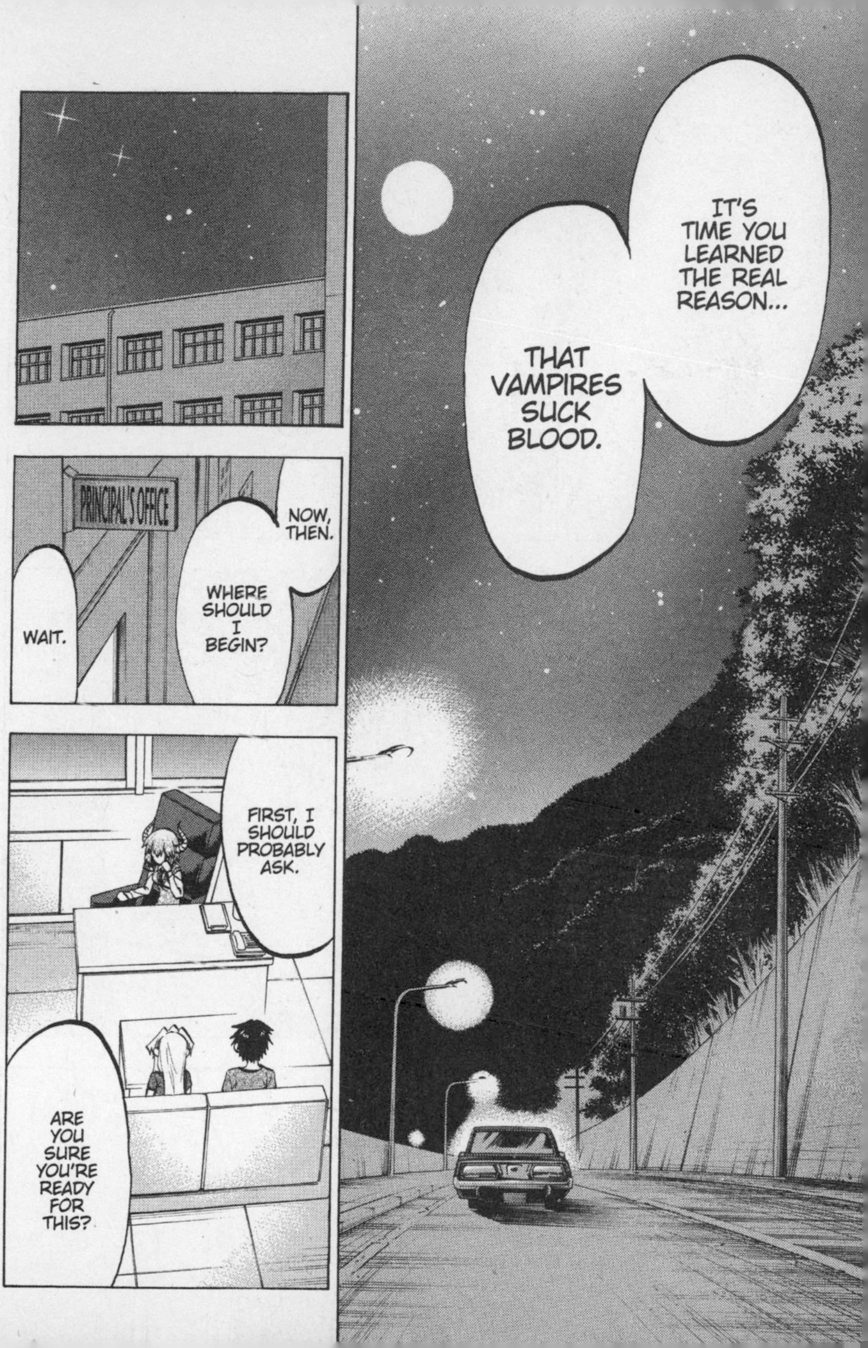
IT'S TIME YOU LEARNED THE REAL REASON...
THAT VAMPIRES SUCK BLOOD.
PRINCIPAL'S OFFICE
NOW, THEN.
WHERE SHOULD I BEGIN?
WAIT.
FIRST, I SHOULD PROBABLY ASK.
ARE YOU SURE YOU'RE READY FOR THIS?

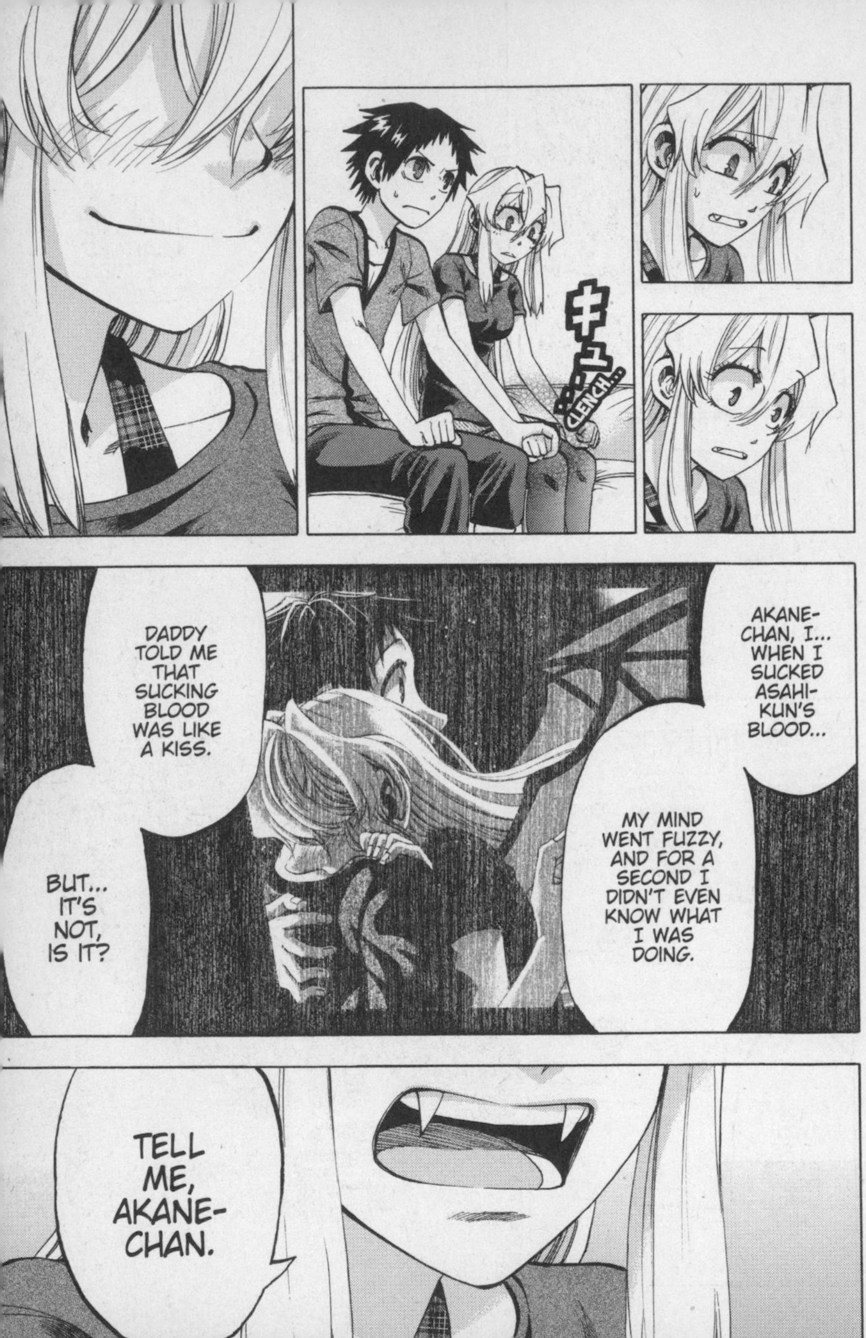
キュ...
CLENCH...
AKANE-CHAN, I... WHEN I SUCKED ASAHI-KUN'S BLOOD...
MY MIND WENT FUZZY, AND FOR A SECOND I DIDN'T EVEN KNOW WHAT I WAS DOING.
DADDY TOLD ME THAT SUCKING BLOOD WAS LIKE A KISS.
BUT... IT'S NOT, IS IT?
TELL ME, AKANE-CHAN.

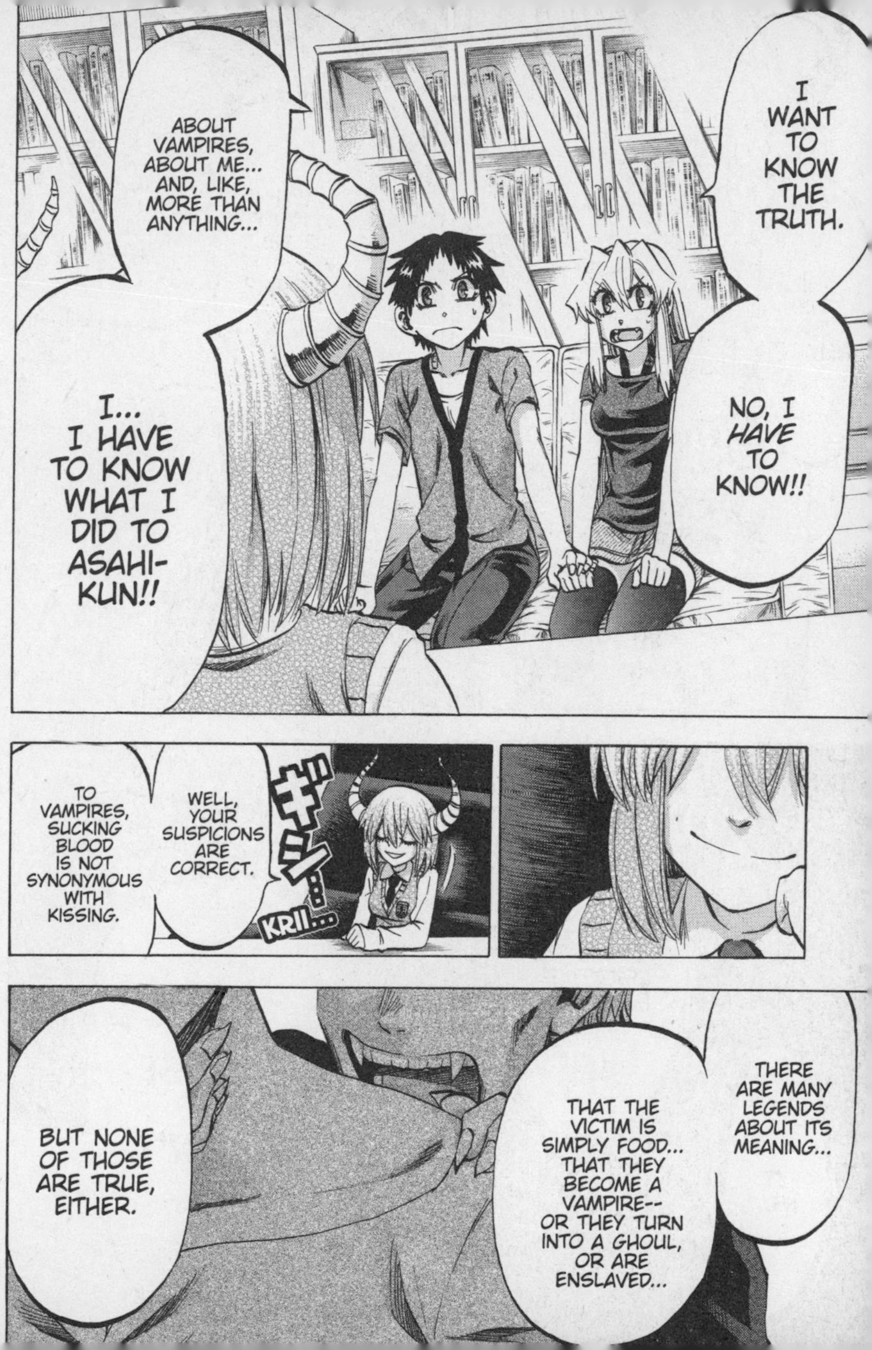
I WANT TO KNOW THE TRUTH.
NO, I *HAVE* TO KNOW!!
ABOUT VAMPIRES, ABOUT ME... AND, LIKE, MORE THAN ANYTHING...
I... I HAVE TO KNOW WHAT I DID TO ASAHI-KUN!!
WELL, YOUR SUSPICIONS ARE CORRECT.
KRII...
TO VAMPIRES, SUCKING BLOOD IS NOT SYNONYMOUS WITH KISSING.
THERE ARE MANY LEGENDS ABOUT ITS MEANING...
THAT THE VICTIM IS SIMPLY FOOD... THAT THEY BECOME A VAMPIRE-- OR THEY TURN INTO A GHOUL, OR ARE ENSLAVED...
BUT NONE OF THOSE ARE TRUE, EITHER.

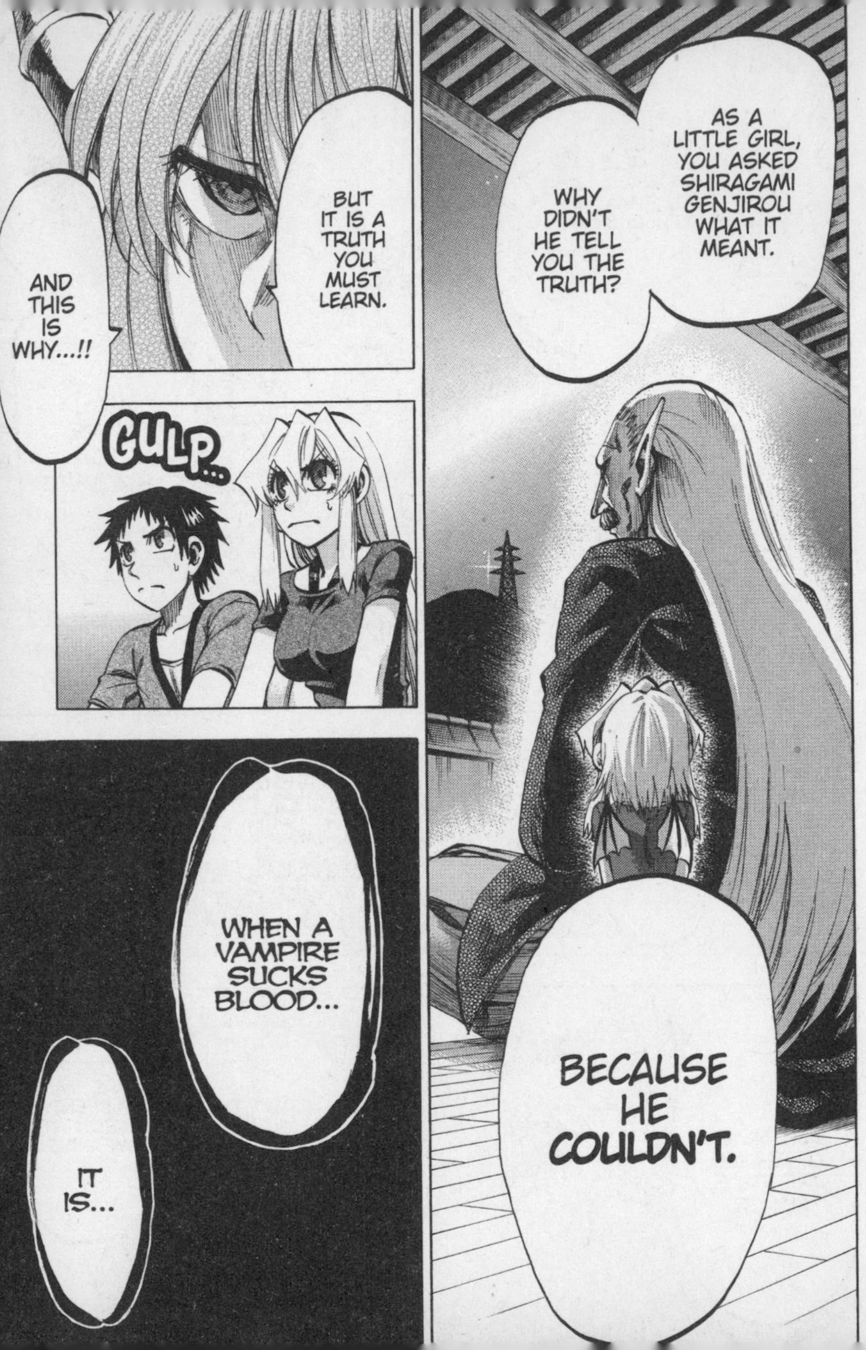
AS A LITTLE GIRL, YOU ASKED SHIRAGAMI GENJIROU WHAT IT MEANT.
WHY DIDN'T HE TELL YOU THE TRUTH?
BECAUSE HE COULDN'T.
BUT IT IS A TRUTH YOU MUST LEARN.
AND THIS IS WHY...!!
GULP...
WHEN A VAMPIRE SUCKS BLOOD...
IT IS...

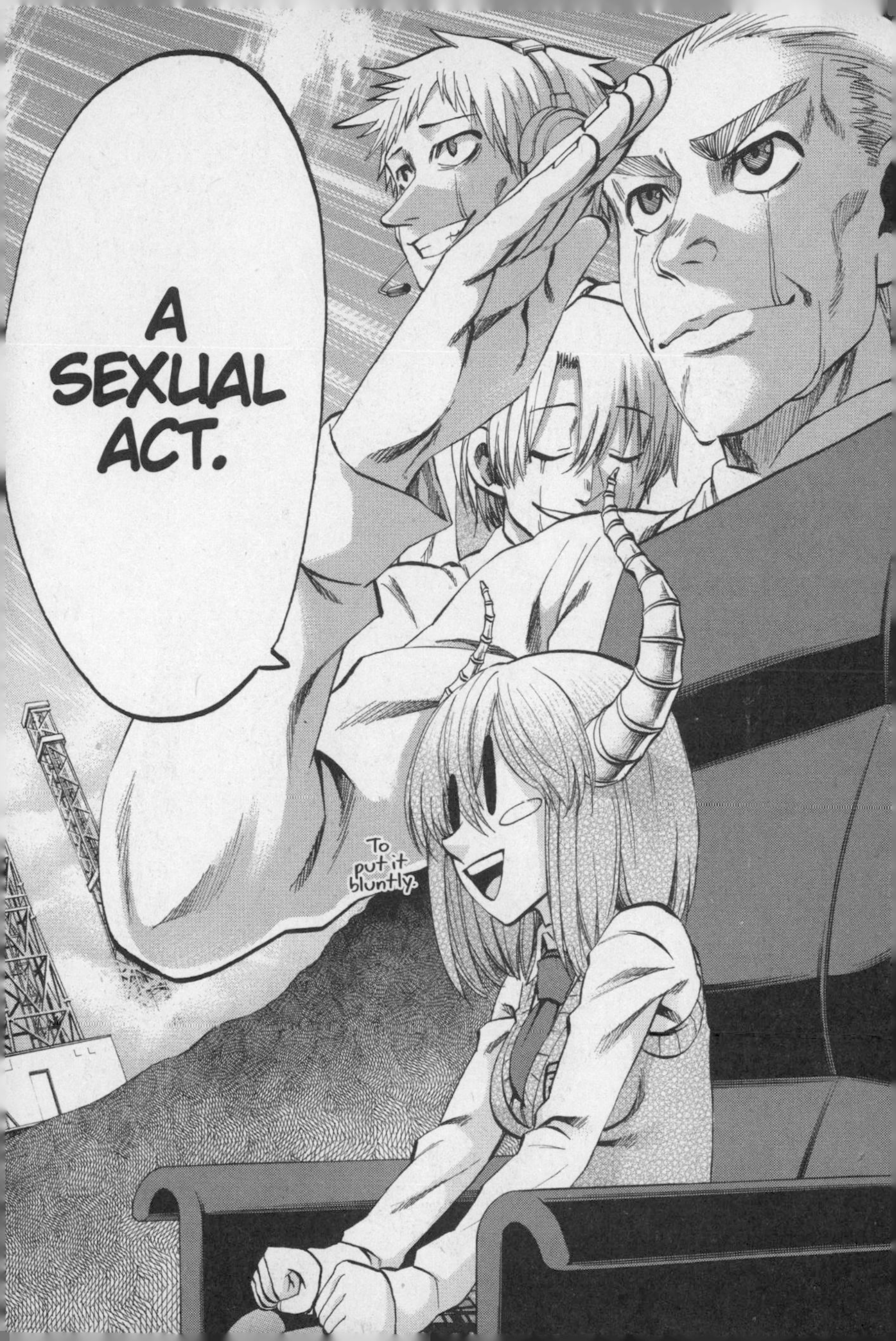
A SEXUAL ACT.
To put it bluntly.

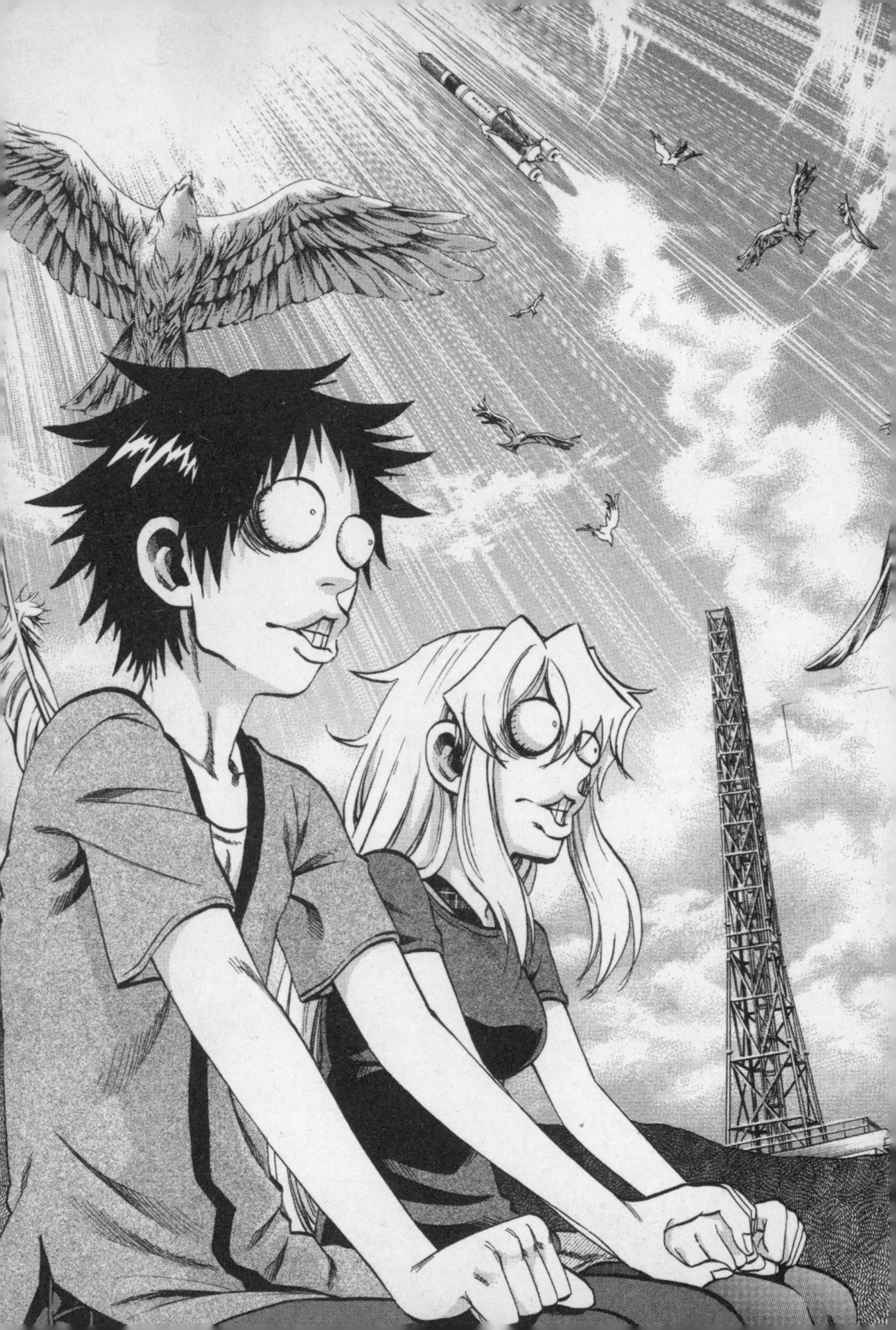

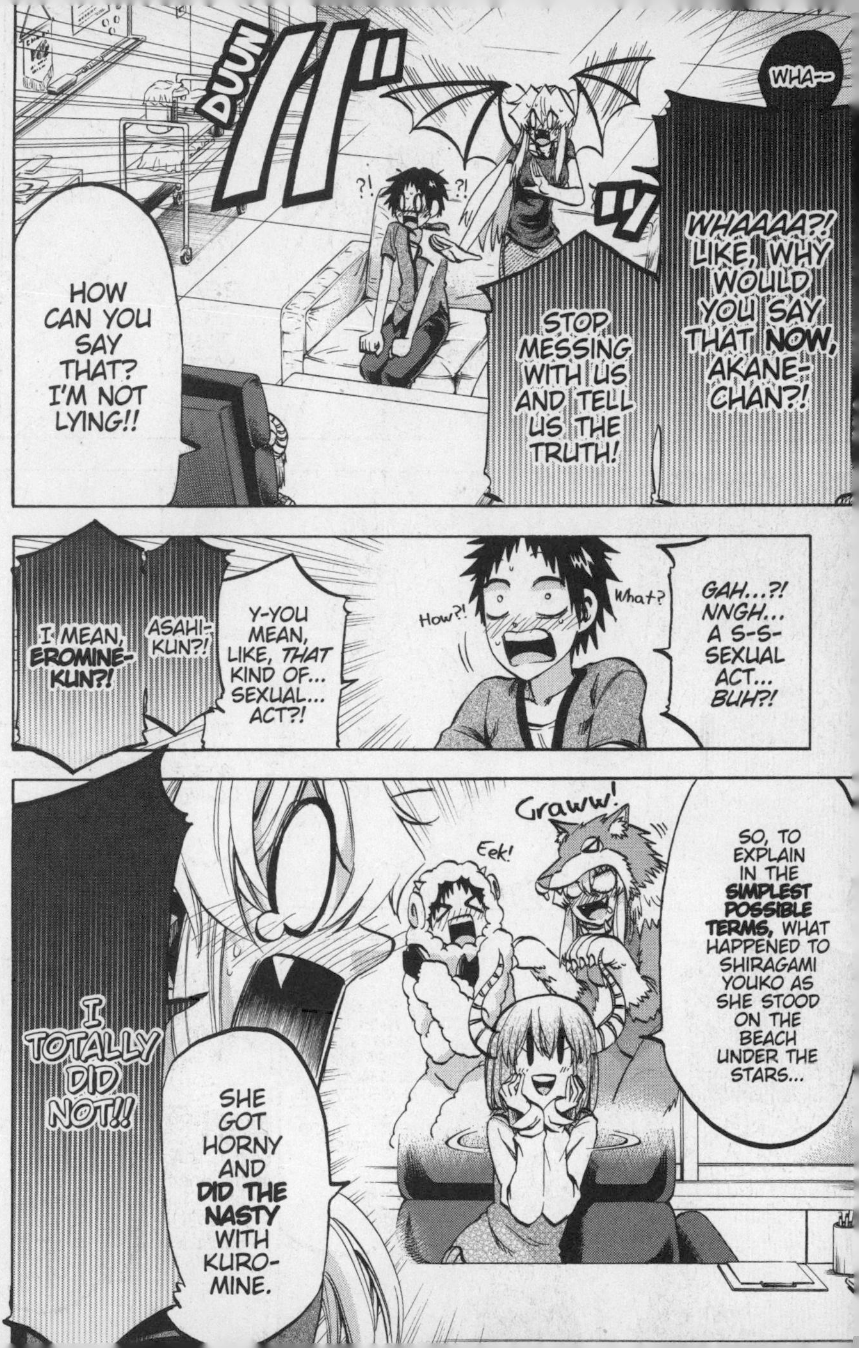
WHA--
WHAAAA?! LIKE, WHY WOULD YOU SAY THAT NOW, AKANE-CHAN?!
DUN
STOP MESSING WITH US AND TELL US THE TRUTH!
?!
?!
HOW CAN YOU SAY THAT? I'M NOT LYING!!
GAH...?! NNGH... A S-S-SEXUAL ACT... BUH?!
What?
How?!
Y-YOU MEAN, LIKE, THAT KIND OF... SEXUAL... ACT?!
ASAHI-KUN?!
I MEAN, EROMINE-KUN?!
SO, TO EXPLAIN IN THE SIMPLEST POSSIBLE TERMS, WHAT HAPPENED TO SHIRAGAMI YOUKO AS SHE STOOD ON THE BEACH UNDER THE STARS...
Graww!
Eek!
SHE GOT HORNY AND DID THE NASTY WITH KURO-MINE.
I TOTALLY DID NOT!!

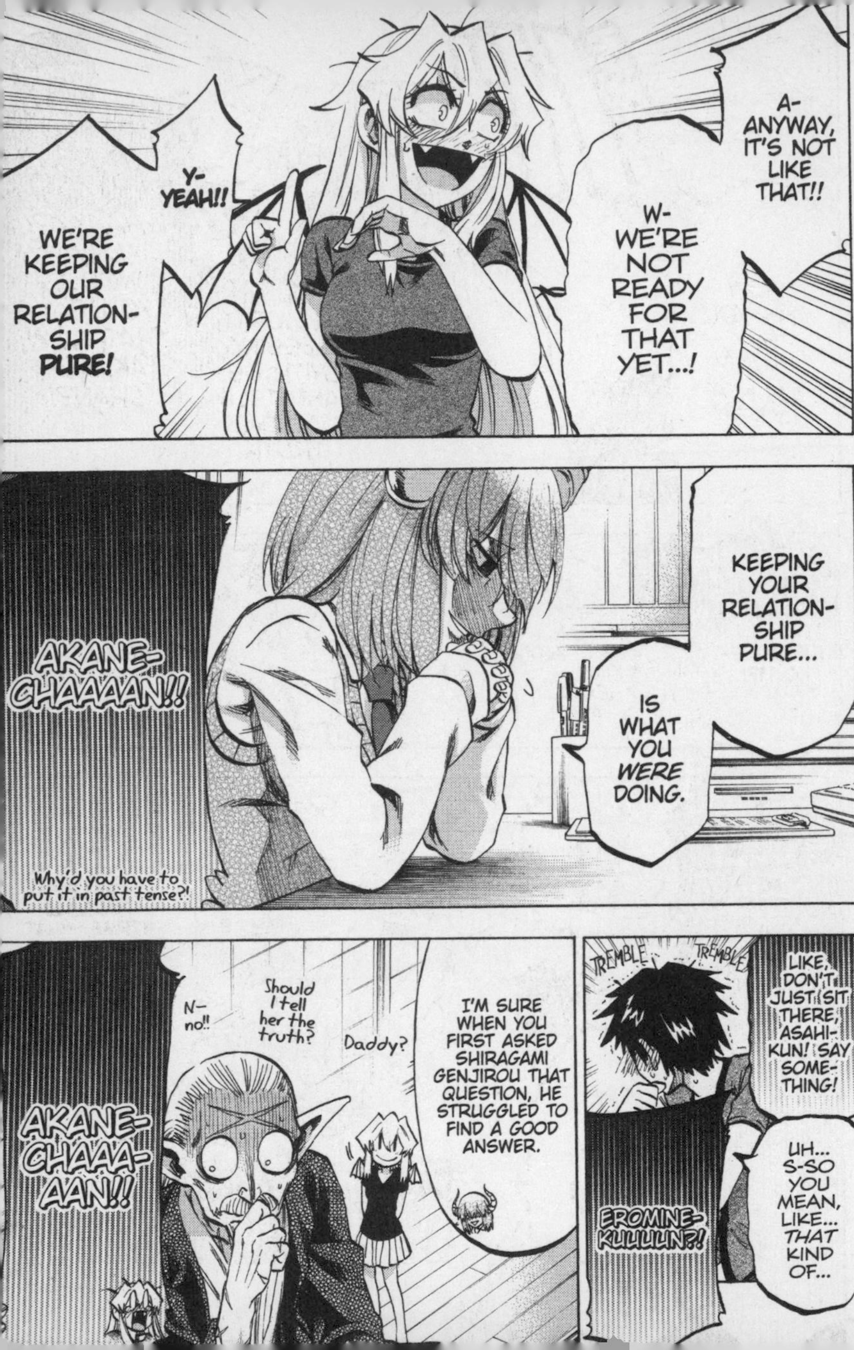
A- ANYWAY, IT'S NOT LIKE THAT!!
W- WE'RE NOT READY FOR THAT YET...!
Y- YEAH!!
WE'RE KEEPING OUR RELATION-SHIP PURE!
KEEPING YOUR RELATION-SHIP PURE...
IS WHAT YOU WERE DOING.
AKANE-CHAAAAAN!!
Why'd you have to put it in past tense?!
TREMBLE TREMBLE
LIKE, DON'T JUST SIT THERE, ASAHI-KUN! SAY SOME-THING!
UH... S-SO YOU MEAN, LIKE... THAT KIND OF...
EROMINE-KUUUUN?!
I'M SURE WHEN YOU FIRST ASKED SHIRAGAMI GENJIROU THAT QUESTION, HE STRUGGLED TO FIND A GOOD ANSWER.
Daddy?
Should I tell her the truth?
N- no!!
AKANE-CHAAAA-AAN!!

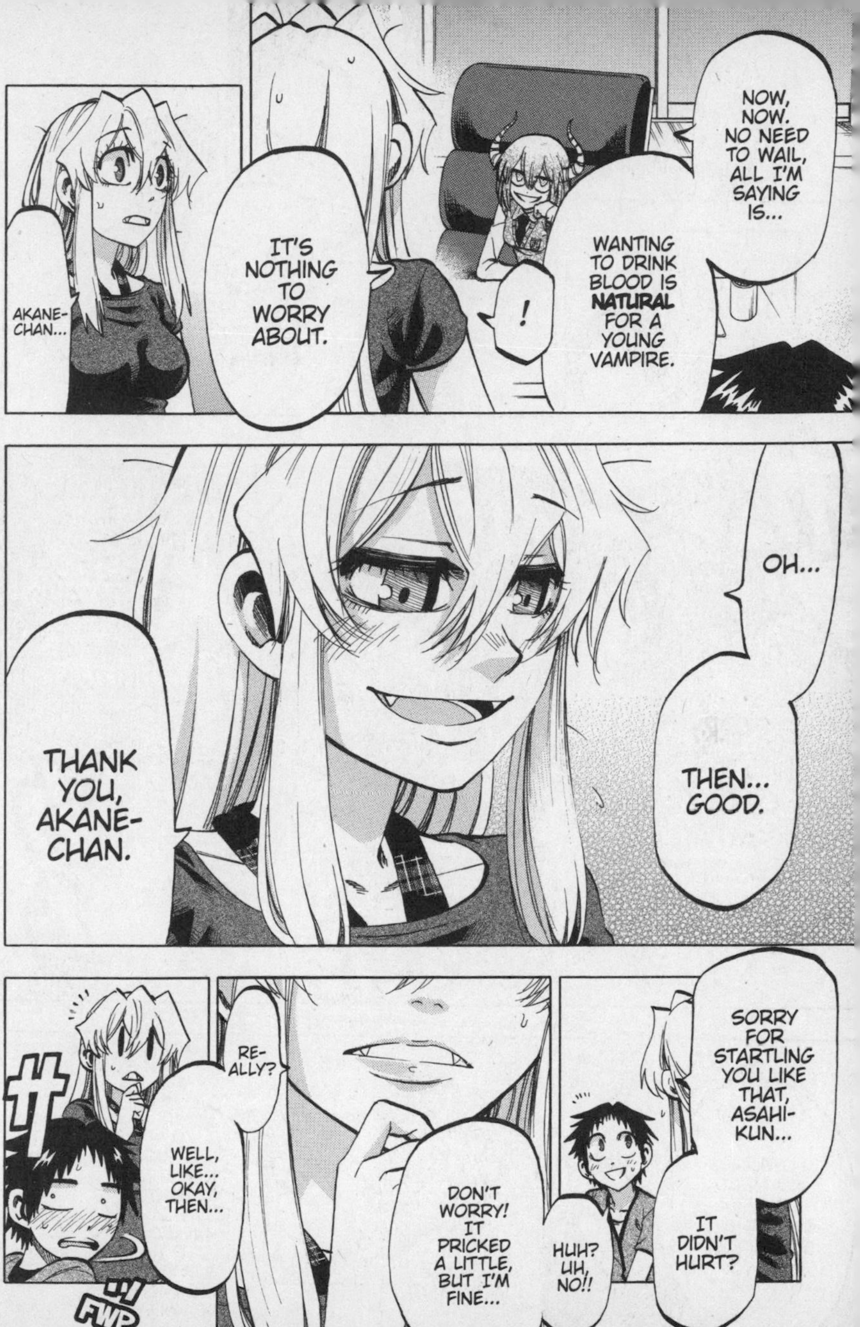
NOW, NOW. NO NEED TO WAIL, ALL I'M SAYING IS...
WANTING TO DRINK BLOOD IS **NATURAL** FOR A YOUNG VAMPIRE.
!
IT'S NOTHING TO WORRY ABOUT.
AKANE-CHAN...
OH...
THEN... GOOD.
THANK YOU, AKANE-CHAN.
SORRY FOR STARTLING YOU LIKE THAT, ASAHI-KUN...
IT DIDN'T HURT?
HUH? UH, NO!!
DON'T WORRY! IT PRICKED A LITTLE, BUT I'M FINE...
RE-ALLY?
WELL, LIKE... OKAY, THEN...
FWP

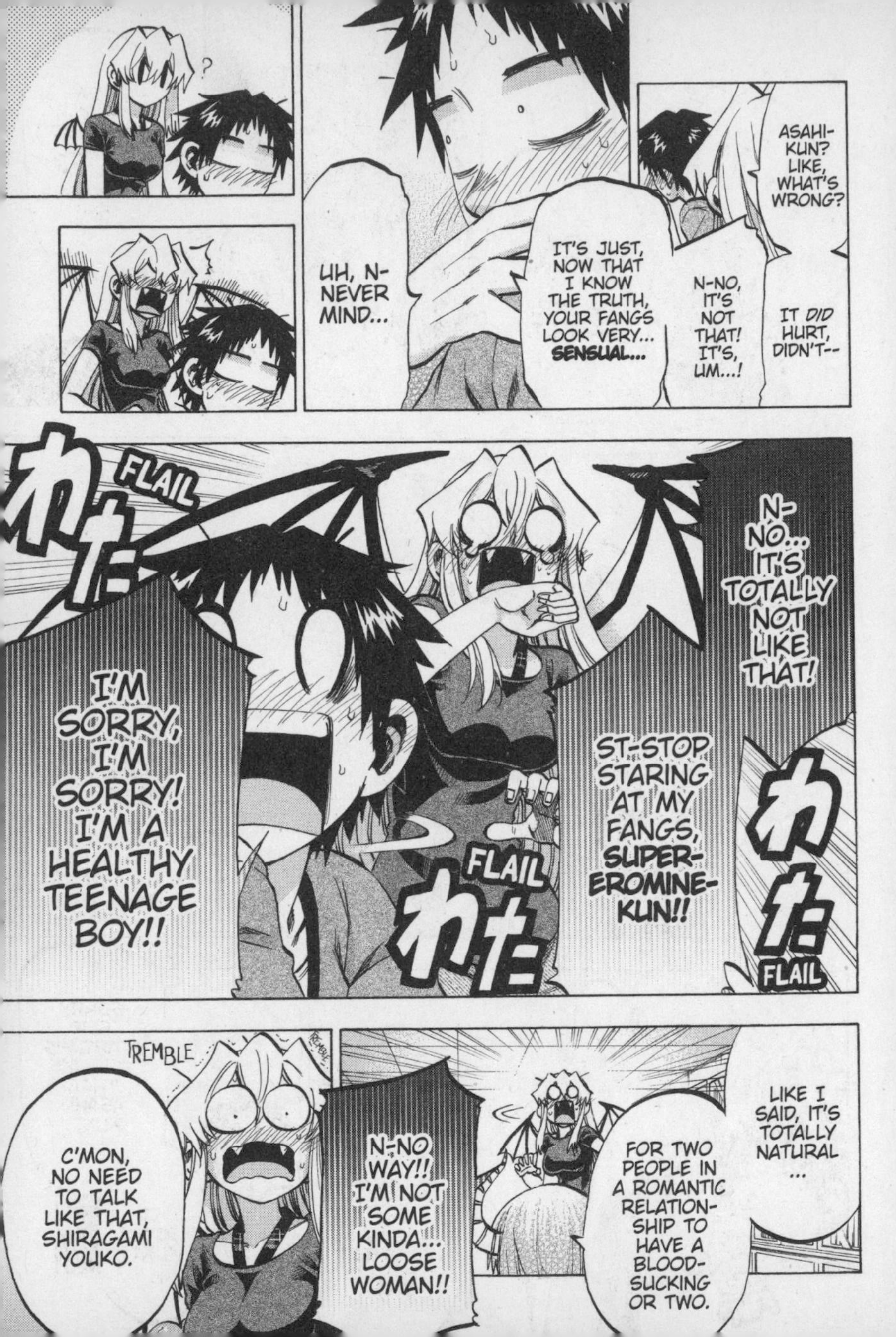
ASAHI-KUN? LIKE, WHAT'S WRONG?
IT *DID* HURT, DIDN'T--
N-NO, IT'S NOT THAT! IT'S, UM...!
IT'S JUST, NOW THAT I KNOW THE TRUTH, YOUR FANGS LOOK VERY... **SENSUAL...**
UH, N-NEVER MIND...
?
N-NO... IT'S TOTALLY NOT LIKE THAT!
わた
FLAIL
ST-STOP STARING AT MY FANGS, **SUPER-EROMINE-KUN!!**
FLAIL
わた
I'M SORRY, I'M SORRY! I'M A HEALTHY TEENAGE BOY!!
わた
FLAIL
LIKE I SAID, IT'S TOTALLY NATURAL ...
FOR TWO PEOPLE IN A ROMANTIC RELATIONSHIP TO HAVE A BLOOD-SUCKING OR TWO.
TREMBLE
TREMBLE
N-NO WAY!! I'M NOT SOME KINDA... LOOSE WOMAN!!
C'MON, NO NEED TO TALK LIKE THAT, SHIRAGAMI YOUKO.

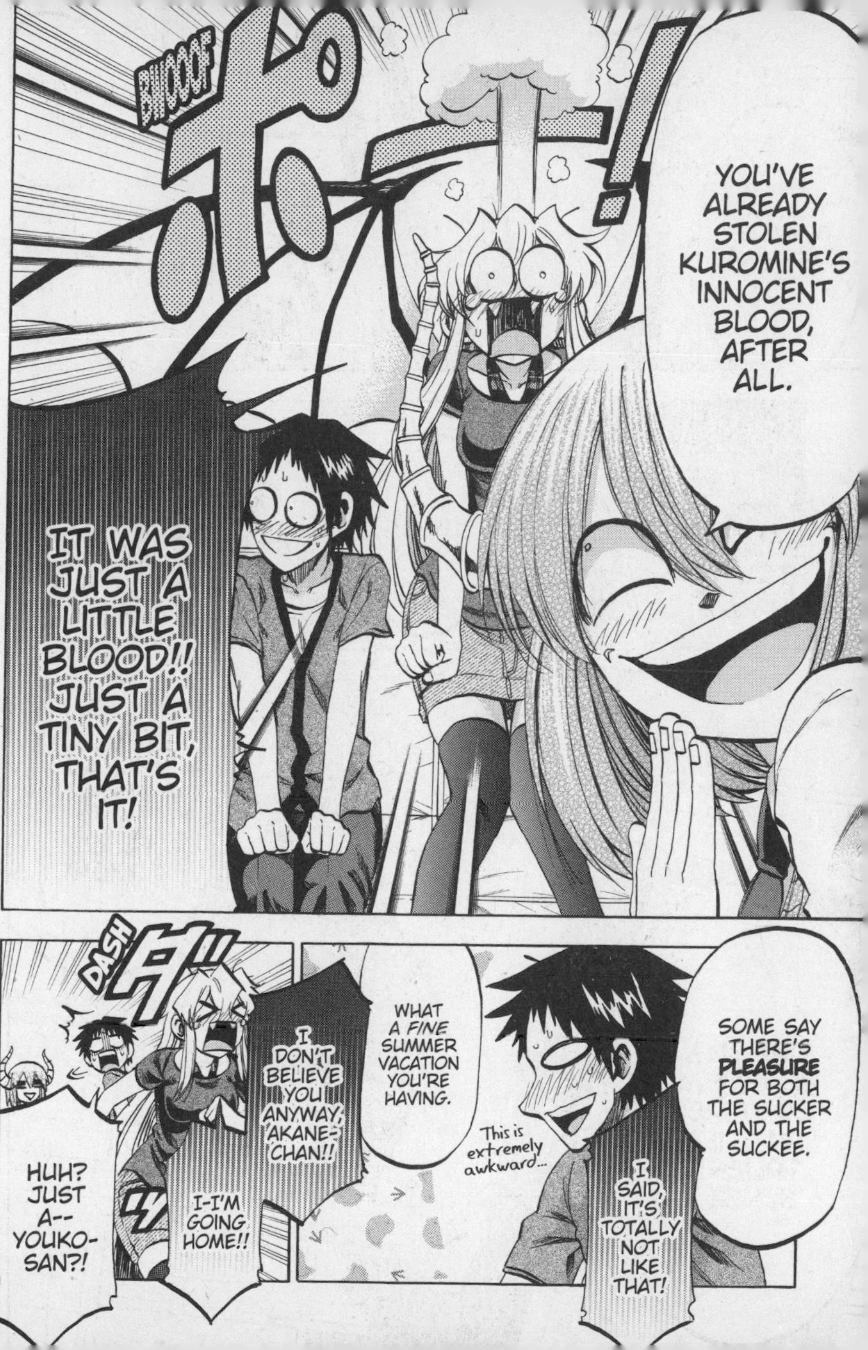
BWOOOF
YOU'VE ALREADY STOLEN KUROMINE'S INNOCENT BLOOD, AFTER ALL.
IT WAS JUST A LITTLE BLOOD!! JUST A TINY BIT, THAT'S IT!
SOME SAY THERE'S **PLEASURE** FOR BOTH THE SUCKER AND THE SUCKEE.
WHAT A *FINE* SUMMER VACATION YOU'RE HAVING.
This is extremely awkward...
I SAID, IT'S TOTALLY NOT LIKE THAT!
I DON'T BELIEVE YOU ANYWAY, AKANE-CHAN!!
I-I'M GOING HOME!!
DASH
HUH? JUST A-- YOUKO-SAN?!

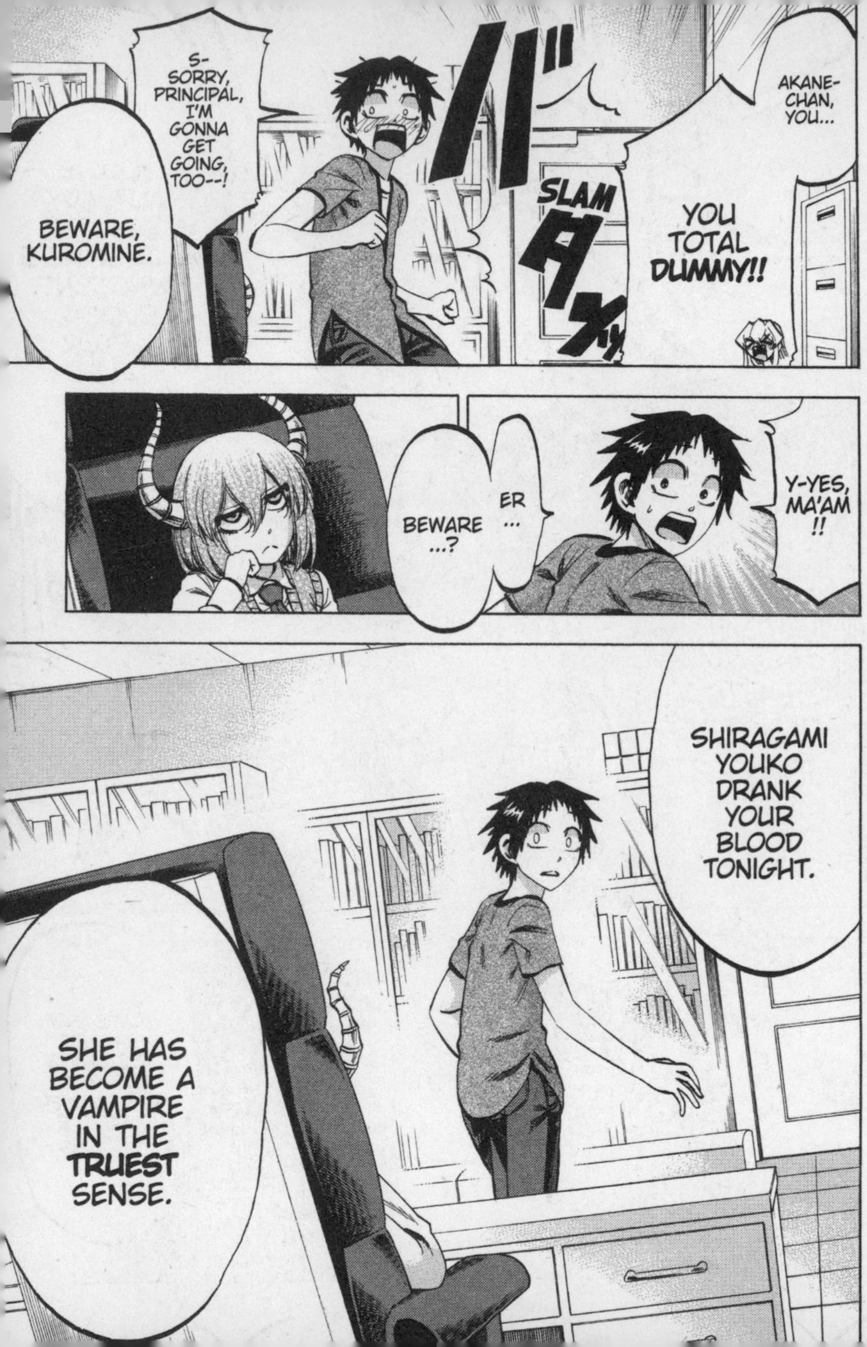
AKANE-CHAN, YOU...
YOU TOTAL DUMMY!!
SLAM
S-SORRY, PRINCIPAL, I'M GONNA GET GOING, TOO--!
BEWARE, KUROMINE.
Y-YES, MA'AM!!
ER ...
BEWARE ...?
SHIRAGAMI YOUKO DRANK YOUR BLOOD TONIGHT.
SHE HAS BECOME A VAMPIRE IN THE TRUEST SENSE.

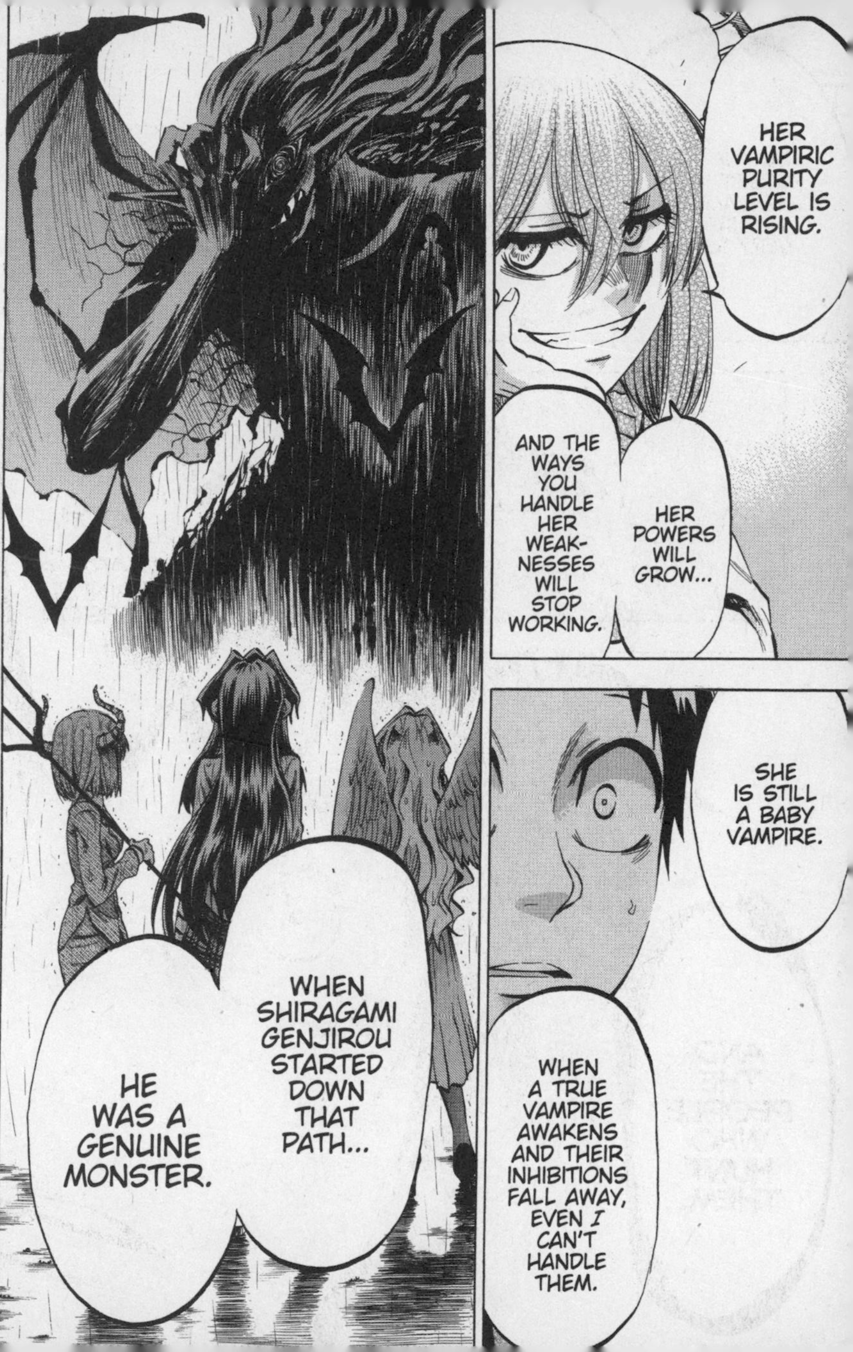
HER VAMPIRIC PURITY LEVEL IS RISING.
HER POWERS WILL GROW...
AND THE WAYS YOU HANDLE HER WEAKNESSES WILL STOP WORKING.
SHE IS STILL A BABY VAMPIRE.
WHEN A TRUE VAMPIRE AWAKENS AND THEIR INHIBITIONS FALL AWAY, EVEN I CAN'T HANDLE THEM.
WHEN SHIRAGAMI GENJIROU STARTED DOWN THAT PATH...
HE WAS A GENUINE MONSTER.

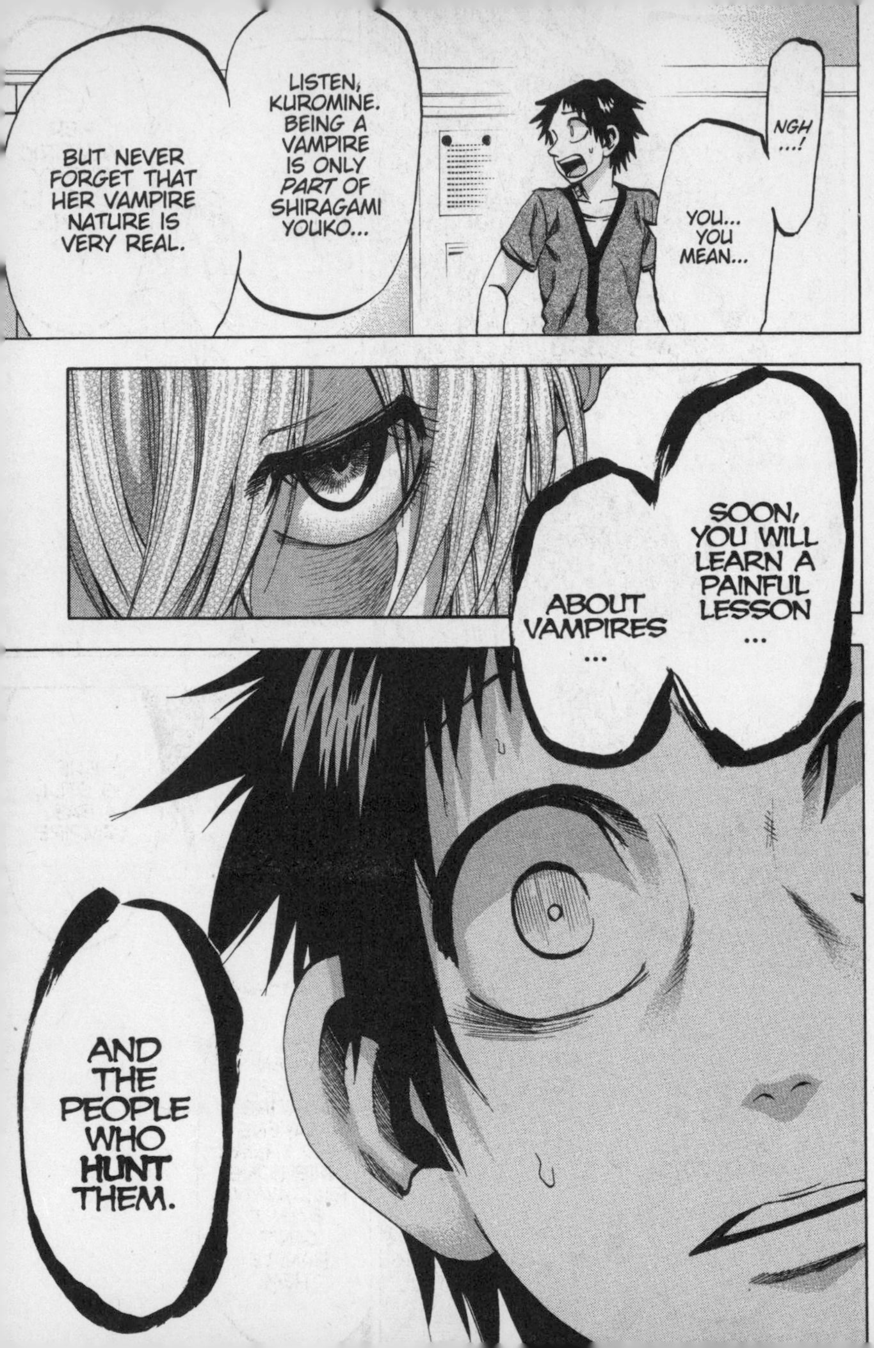
NGH ...!
YOU... YOU MEAN...
LISTEN, KUROMINE. BEING A VAMPIRE IS ONLY *PART* OF SHIRAGAMI YOUKO...
BUT NEVER FORGET THAT HER VAMPIRE NATURE IS VERY REAL.
SOON, YOU WILL LEARN A PAINFUL LESSON ...
ABOUT VAMPIRES ...
AND THE PEOPLE WHO **HUNT** THEM.

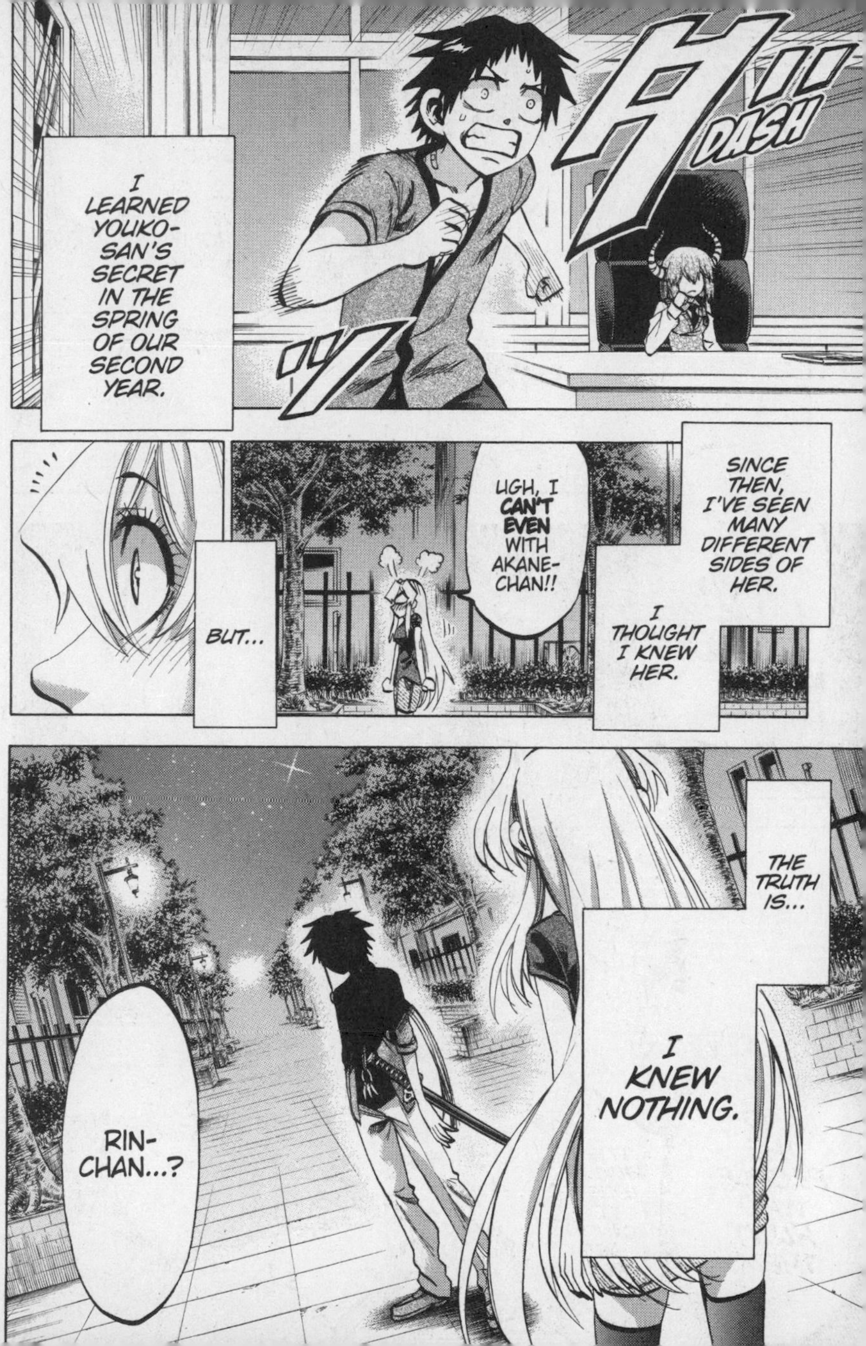
DASH
I LEARNED YOUKO-SAN'S SECRET IN THE SPRING OF OUR SECOND YEAR.
SINCE THEN, I'VE SEEN MANY DIFFERENT SIDES OF HER.
I THOUGHT I KNEW HER.
UGH, I CAN'T EVEN WITH AKANE-CHAN!!
BUT...
THE TRUTH IS...
I KNEW NOTHING.
RIN-CHAN...?

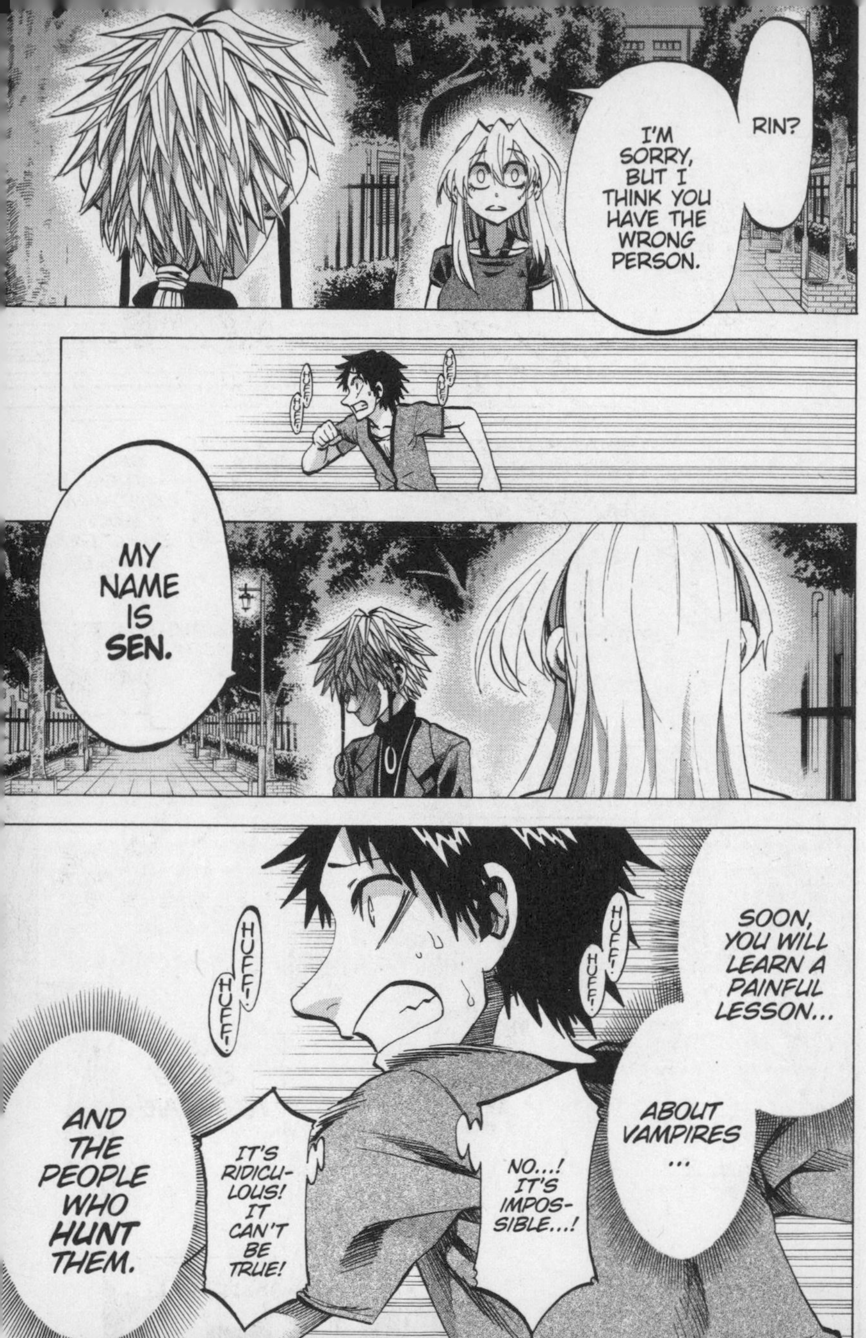
RIN?
I'M SORRY, BUT I THINK YOU HAVE THE WRONG PERSON.
HUFF HUFF
HUFF HUFF
MY NAME IS SEN.
SOON, YOU WILL LEARN A PAINFUL LESSON...
HUFF! HUFF!
HUFF! HUFF!
ABOUT VAMPIRES...
NO...! IT'S IMPOSSIBLE...!
IT'S RIDICULOUS! IT CAN'T BE TRUE!
AND THE PEOPLE WHO HUNT THEM.

Chapter 133: "Let's Propose!"

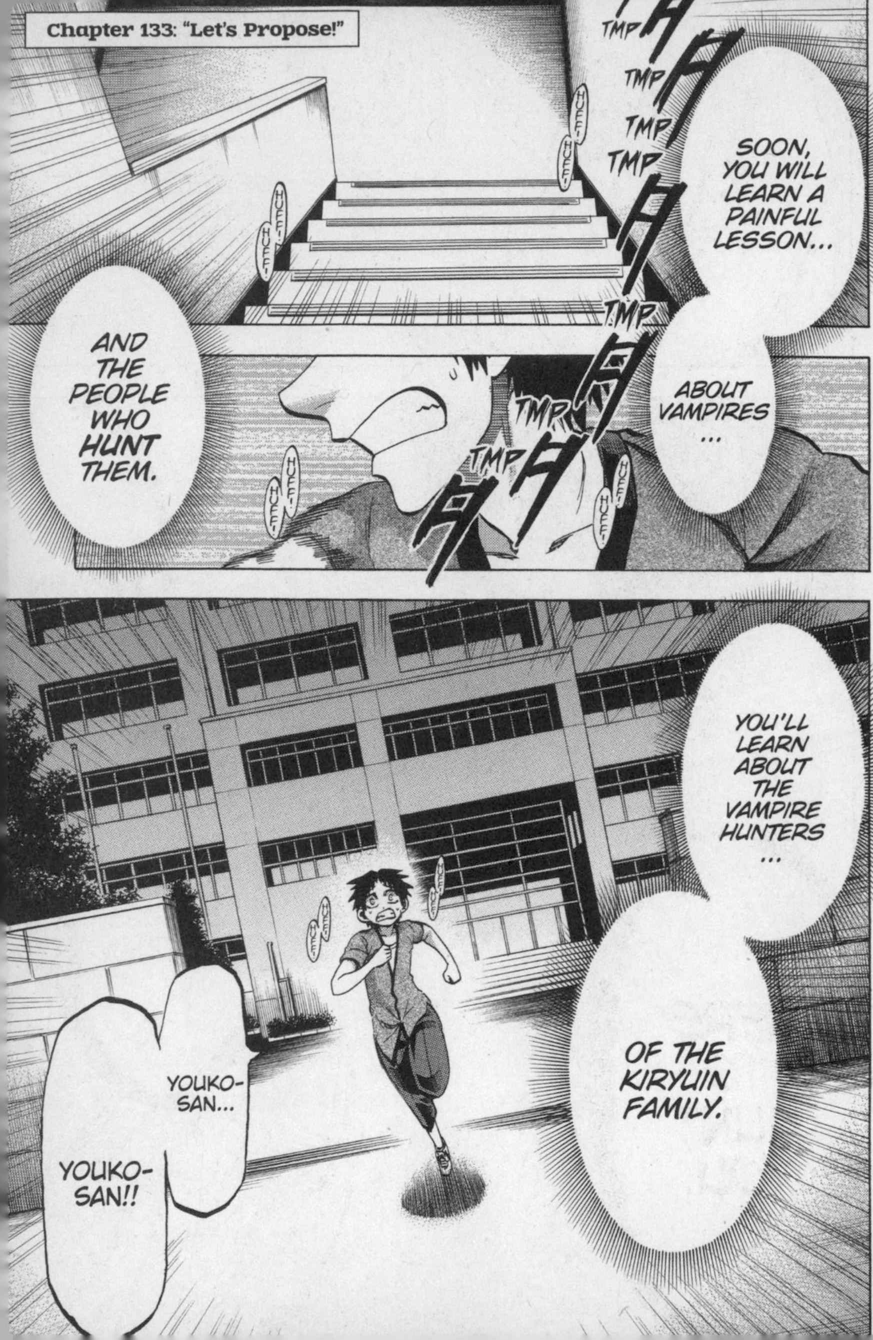
TMP TMP TMP TMP
SOON, YOU WILL LEARN A PAINFUL LESSON...
HUFF! HUFF!
HUFF! HUFF!
TMP TMP TMP
ABOUT VAMPIRES...
HUFF! HUFF!
AND THE PEOPLE WHO HUNT THEM.
HUFF! HUFF!
YOU'LL LEARN ABOUT THE VAMPIRE HUNTERS...
OF THE KIRYUIN FAMILY.
HUFF! HUFF!
HUFF! HUFF!
YOUKO-SAN...
YOUKO-SAN!!

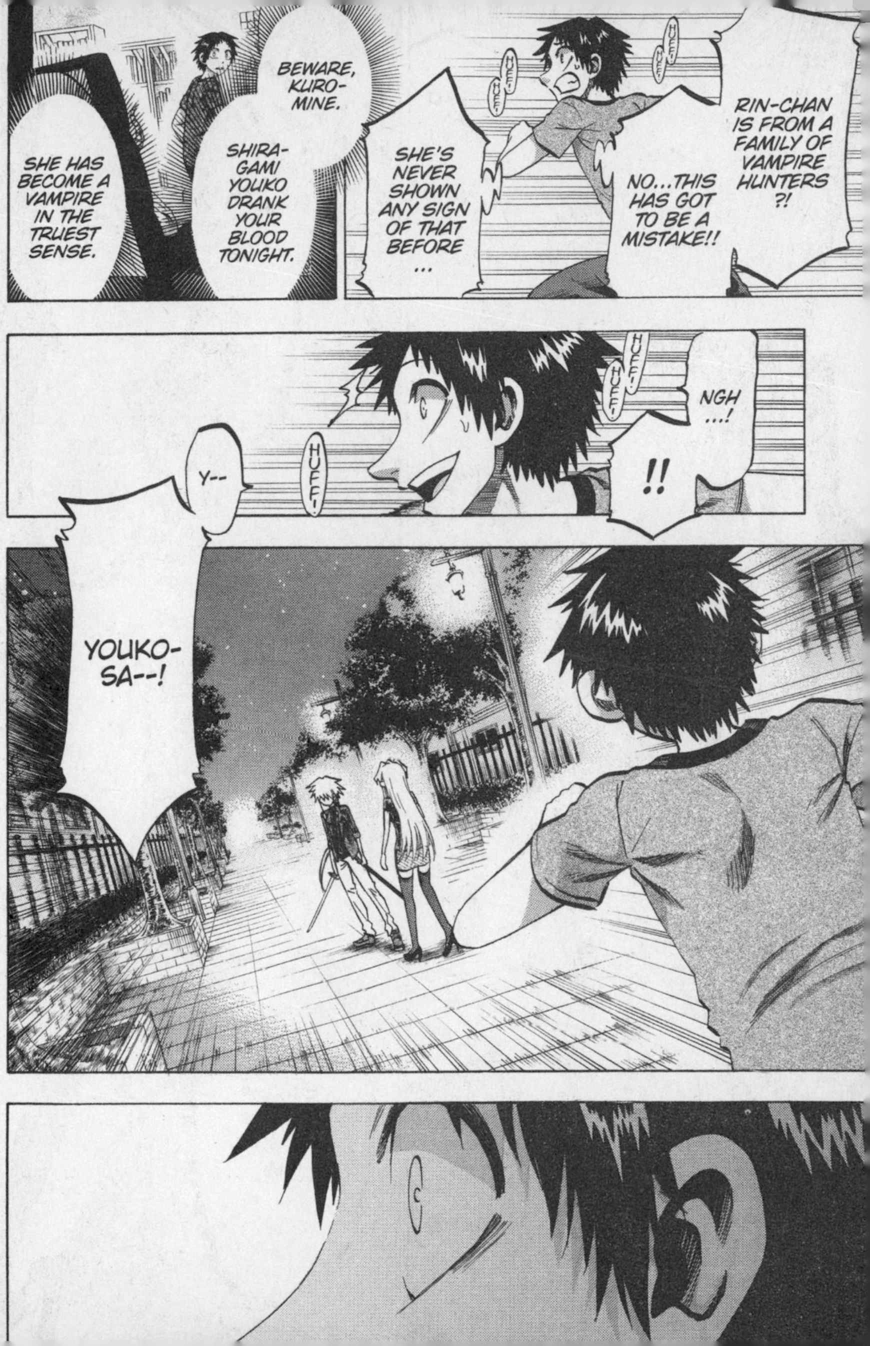
RIN-CHAN IS FROM A FAMILY OF VAMPIRE HUNTERS ?!
NO...THIS HAS GOT TO BE A MISTAKE!!
HUFF! HUFF!
HUFF! HUFF!
SHE'S NEVER SHOWN ANY SIGN OF THAT BEFORE ...
BEWARE, KURO-MINE.
SHIRA-GAMI YOUKO DRANK YOUR BLOOD TONIGHT.
SHE HAS BECOME A VAMPIRE IN THE TRUEST SENSE.
NGH ...!
HUFF! HUFF!
!!
HUFF!
Y--
YOUKO-SA--!

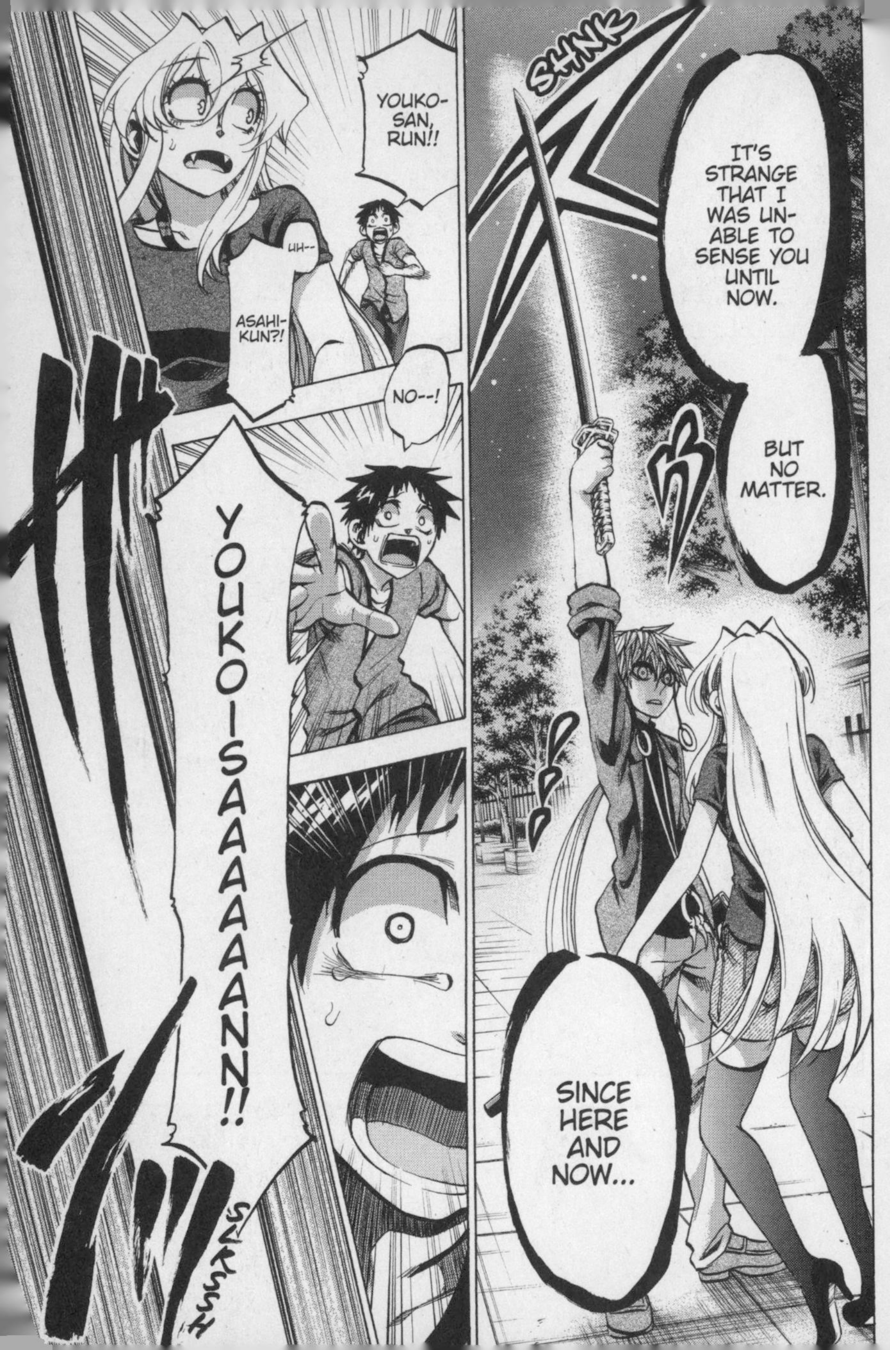
SHINK
IT'S STRANGE THAT I WAS UN-ABLE TO SENSE YOU UNTIL NOW.
BUT NO MATTER.
SINCE HERE AND NOW...
YOUKO-SAN, RUN!!
UH--
ASAHI-KUN?!
NO--!
YOUKO-SAAAAAAAANN!!
SLKSSH

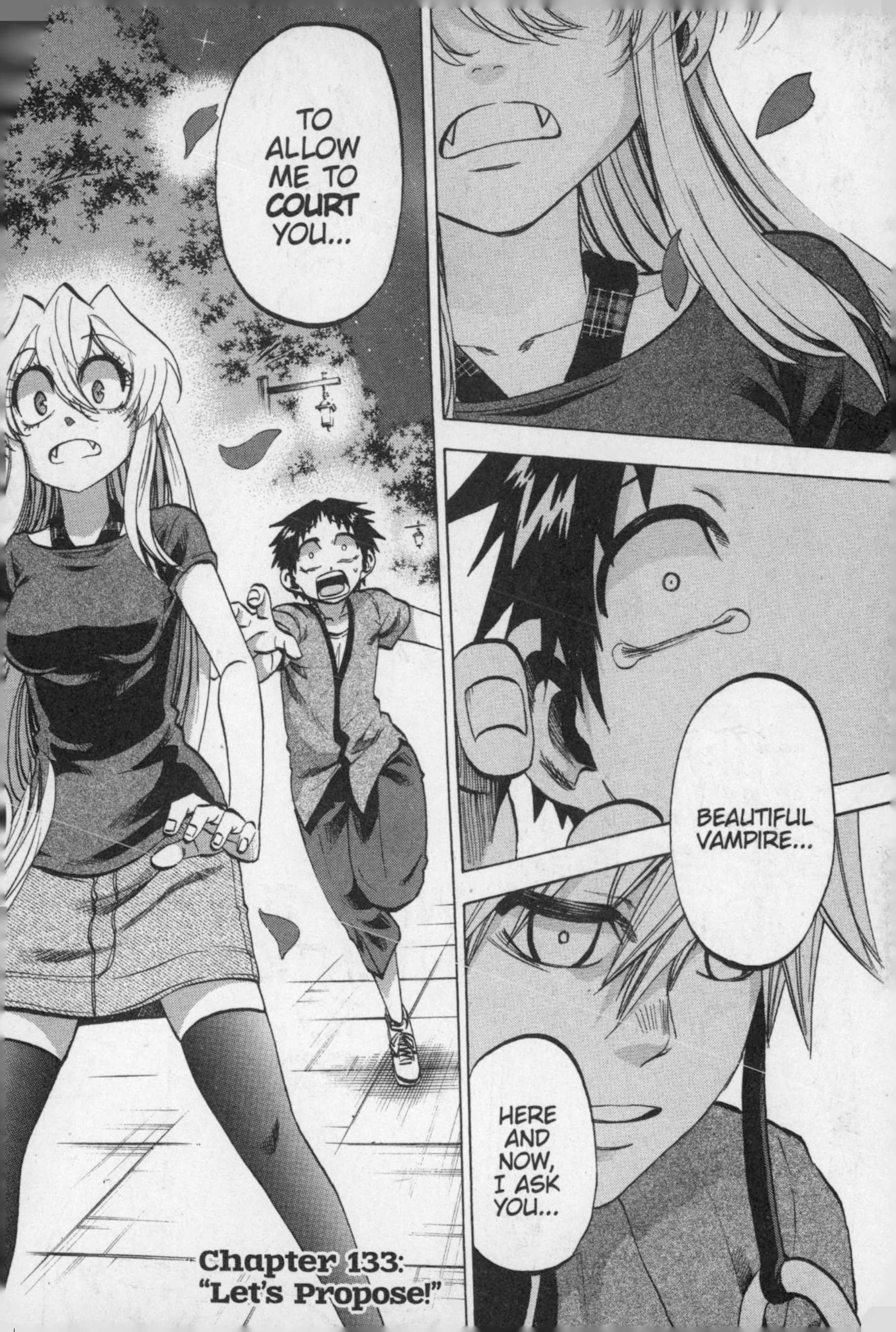
BEAUTIFUL VAMPIRE...
HERE AND NOW, I ASK YOU...
TO ALLOW ME TO COURT YOU...
Chapter 133: "Let's Propose!"

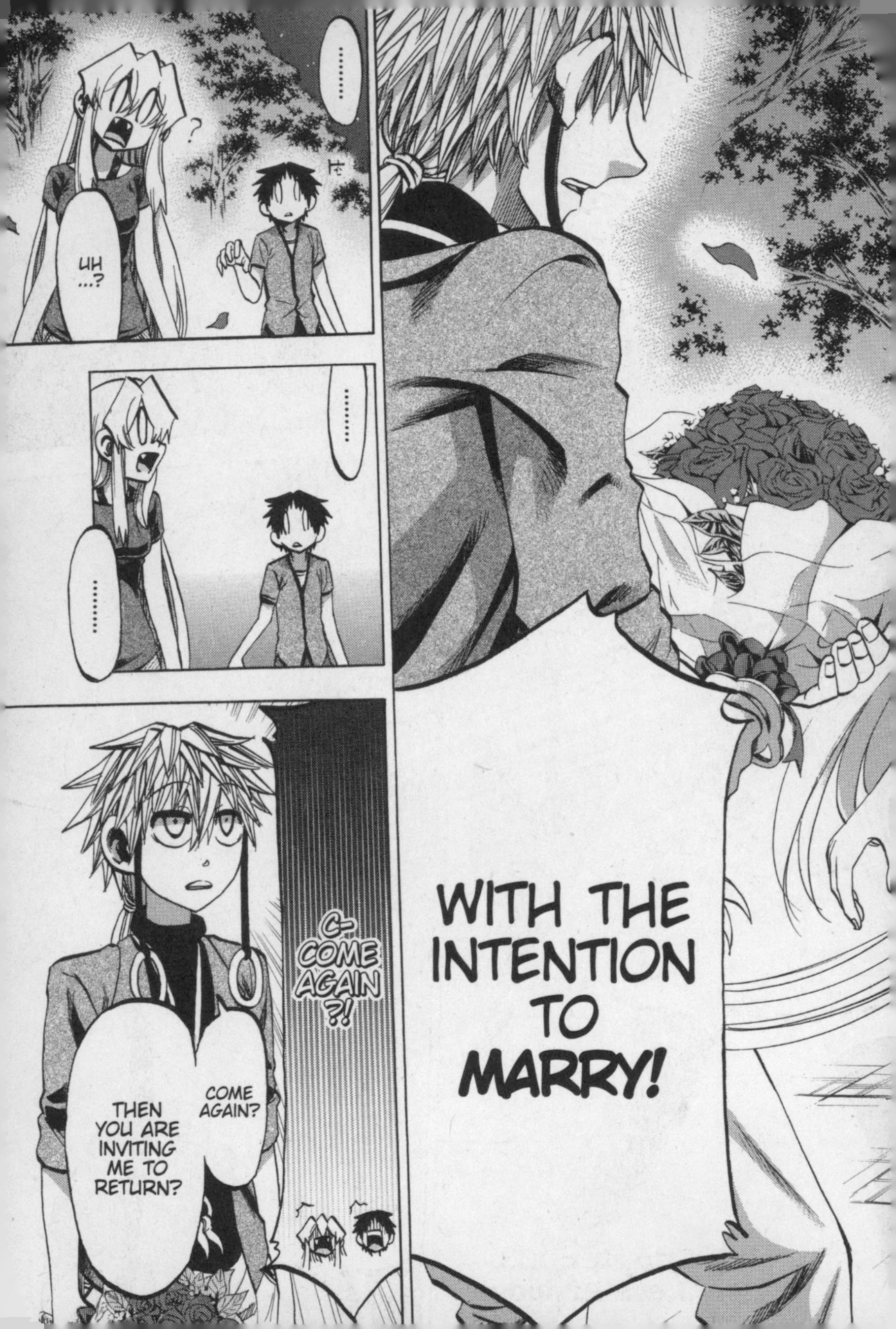
WITH THE INTENTION TO MARRY!
......
?
UH ...?
......
......
C-COME AGAIN?!
COME AGAIN?
THEN YOU ARE INVITING ME TO RETURN?

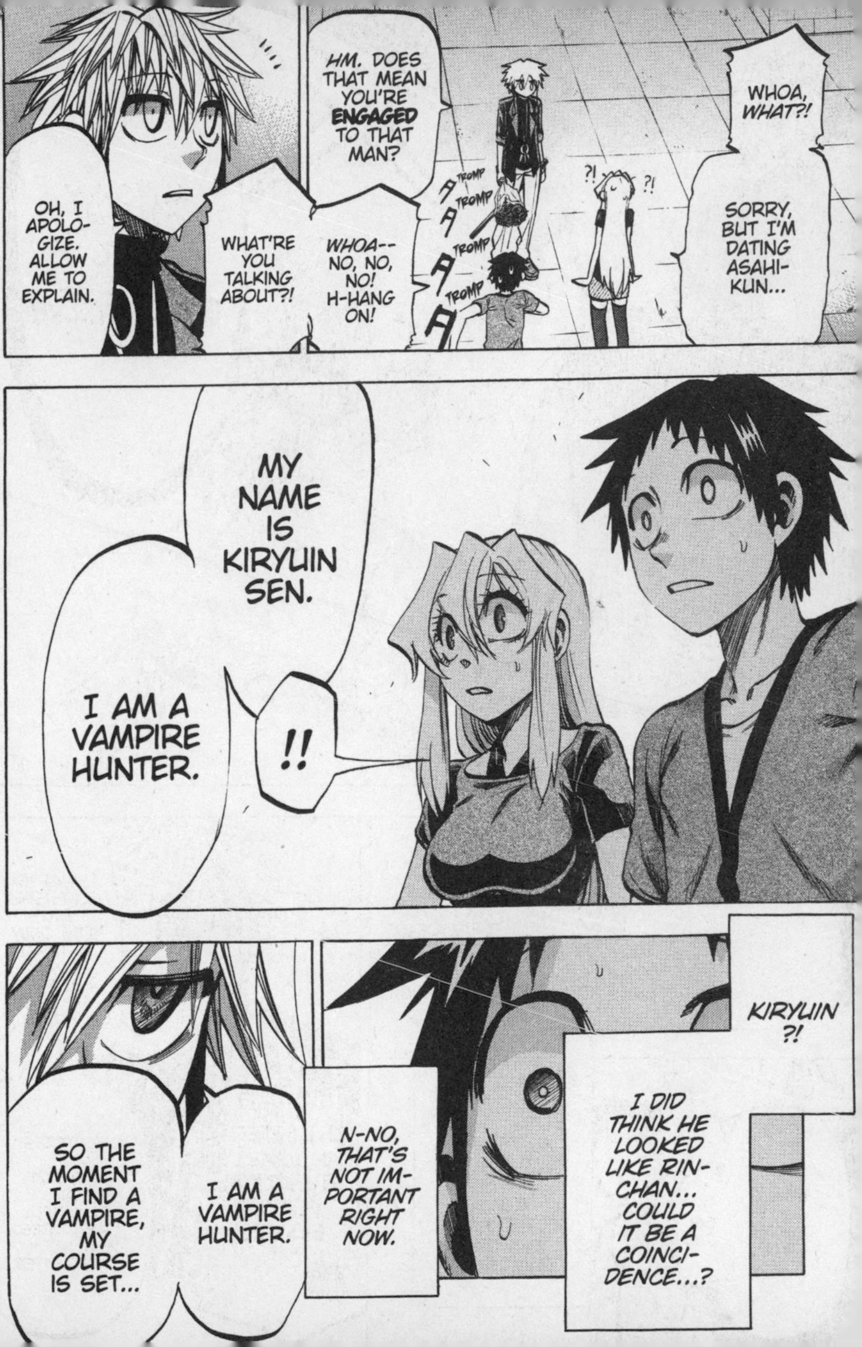
WHOA, WHAT?!
HM. DOES THAT MEAN YOU'RE **ENGAGED** TO THAT MAN?
?!
?!
SORRY, BUT I'M DATING ASAHI-KUN...
TROMP TROMP TROMP TROMP
WHOA-- NO, NO, NO! H-HANG ON!
WHAT'RE YOU TALKING ABOUT?!
OH, I APOLOGIZE. ALLOW ME TO EXPLAIN.
MY NAME IS KIRYUIN SEN.
!!
I AM A VAMPIRE HUNTER.
KIRYUIN ?!
I DID THINK HE LOOKED LIKE RIN-CHAN... COULD IT BE A COINCIDENCE...?
N-NO, THAT'S NOT IMPORTANT RIGHT NOW.
I AM A VAMPIRE HUNTER.
SO THE MOMENT I FIND A VAMPIRE, MY COURSE IS SET...

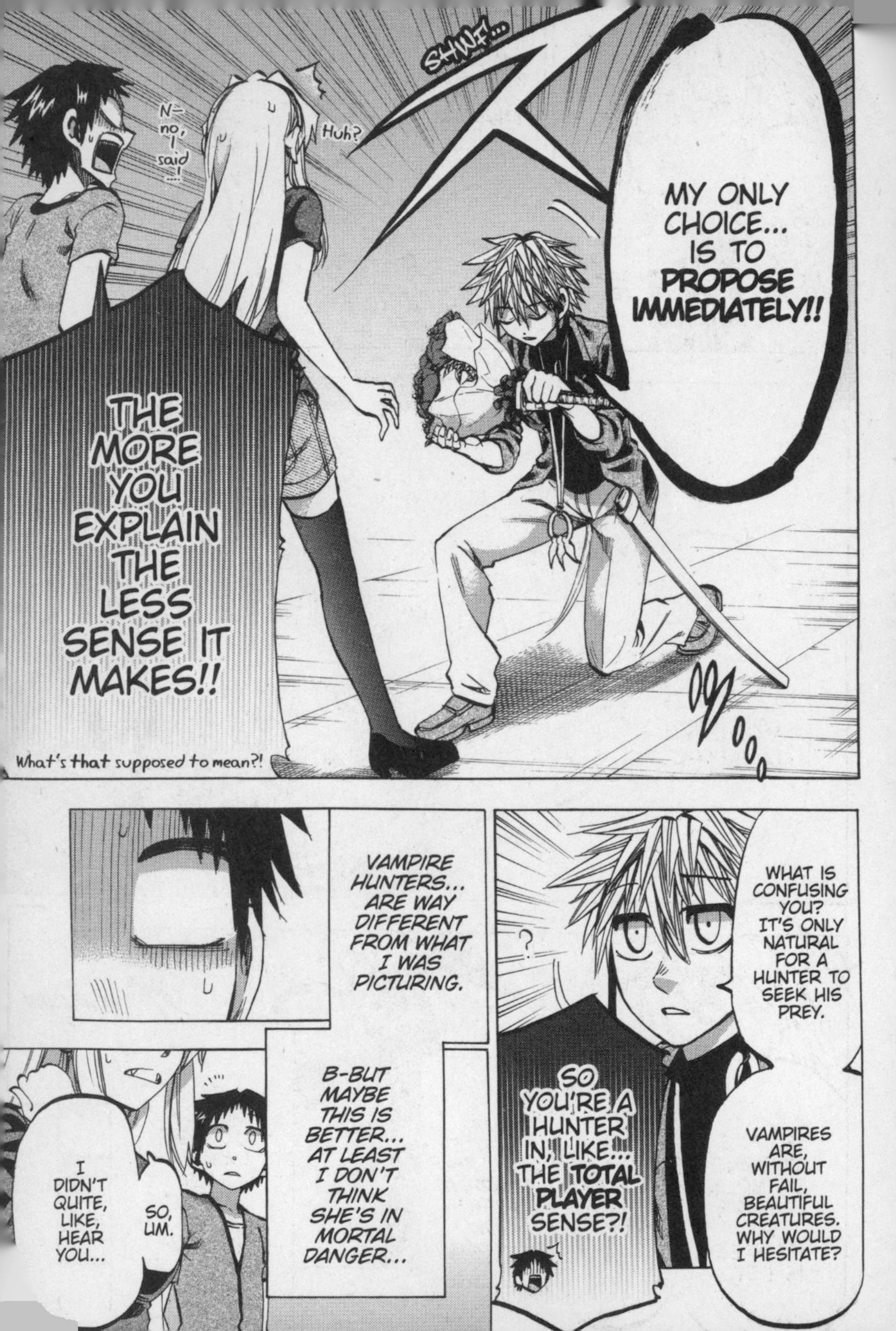
SHWF...
MY ONLY CHOICE... IS TO PROPOSE IMMEDIATELY!!
Huh?
N— no, I said—!...
THE MORE YOU EXPLAIN THE LESS SENSE IT MAKES!!
What's that supposed to mean?!
WHAT IS CONFUSING YOU? IT'S ONLY NATURAL FOR A HUNTER TO SEEK HIS PREY.
VAMPIRES ARE, WITHOUT FAIL, BEAUTIFUL CREATURES. WHY WOULD I HESITATE?
SO YOU'RE A HUNTER IN, LIKE... THE TOTAL PLAYER SENSE?!
VAMPIRE HUNTERS... ARE WAY DIFFERENT FROM WHAT I WAS PICTURING.
B-BUT MAYBE THIS IS BETTER... AT LEAST I DON'T THINK SHE'S IN MORTAL DANGER...
SO, UM.
I DIDN'T QUITE, LIKE, HEAR YOU...

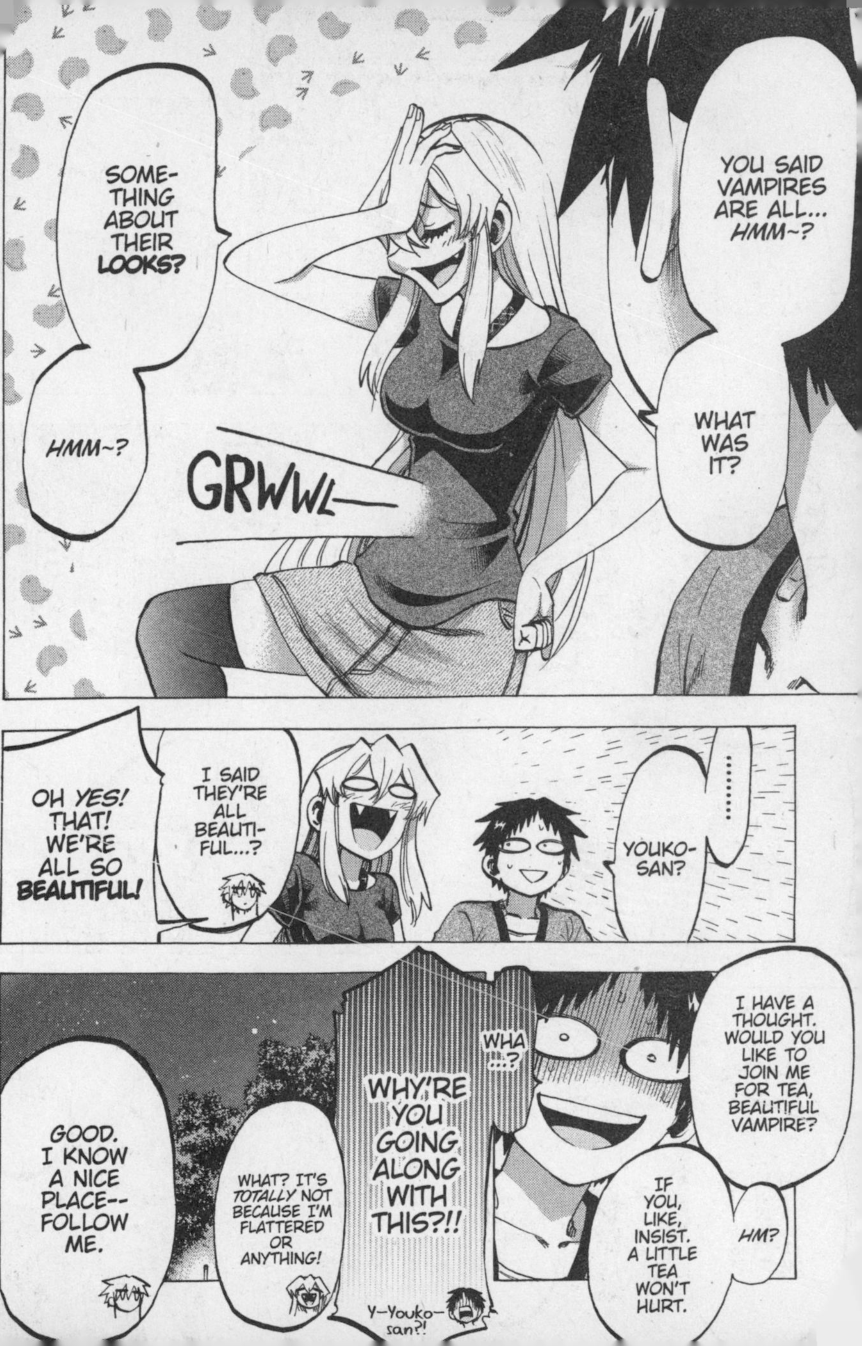
YOU SAID VAMPIRES ARE ALL... HMM~?
WHAT WAS IT?
SOME-THING ABOUT THEIR LOOKS?
HMM~?
GRWWL
......
YOUKO-SAN?
I SAID THEY'RE ALL BEAUTI-FUL...?
OH YES! THAT! WE'RE ALL SO BEAUTIFUL!
I HAVE A THOUGHT. WOULD YOU LIKE TO JOIN ME FOR TEA, BEAUTIFUL VAMPIRE?
HM?
IF YOU, LIKE, INSIST. A LITTLE TEA WON'T HURT.
WHA...?
WHY'RE YOU GOING ALONG WITH THIS?!!
Y-Youko-san?!
WHAT? IT'S TOTALLY NOT BECAUSE I'M FLATTERED OR ANYTHING!
GOOD. I KNOW A NICE PLACE--FOLLOW ME.

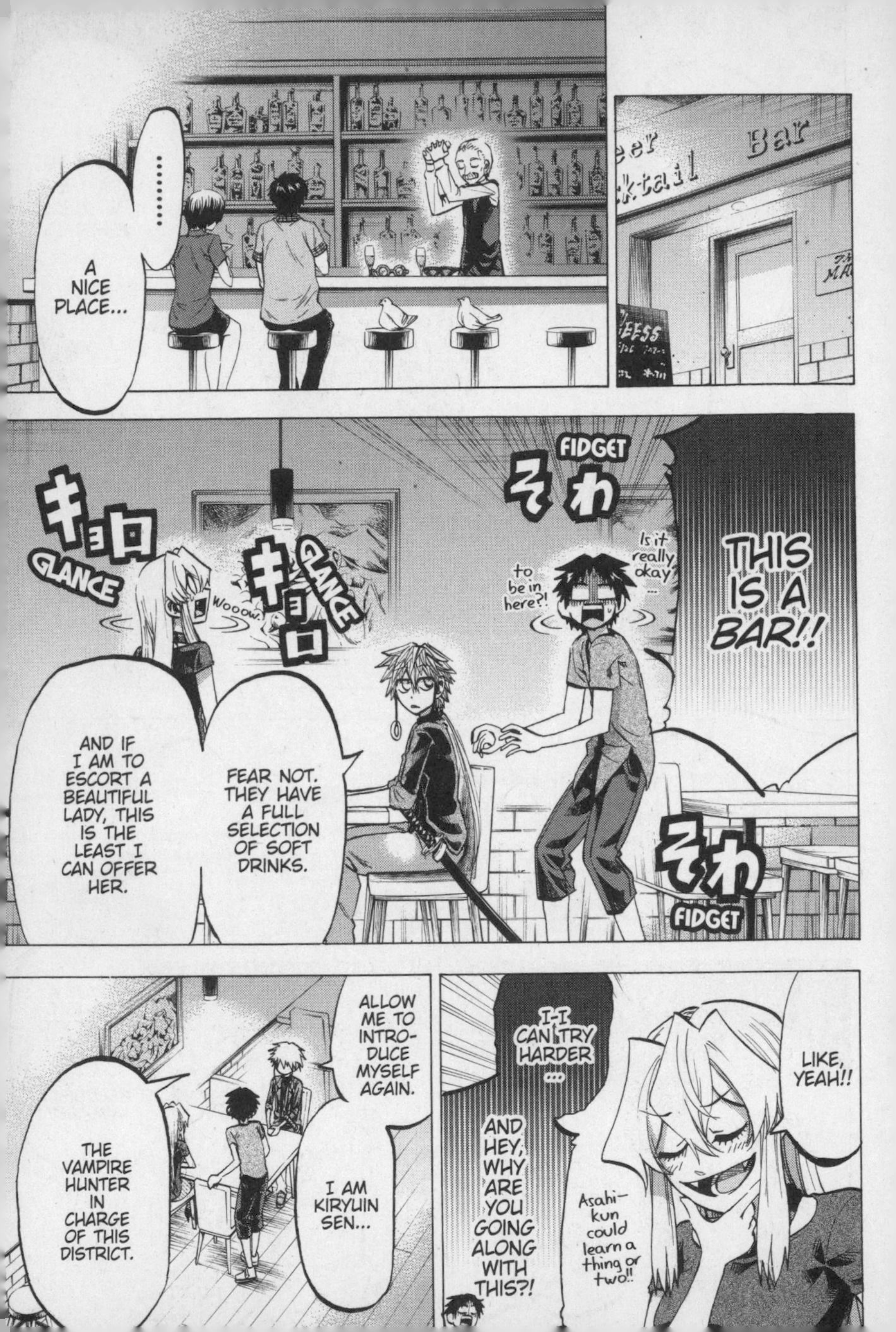
……
A NICE PLACE…
THIS IS A BAR!!
FIDGET
そわ
Is it really okay… to be in here?!
キョロ
GLANCE
キョロ
GLANCE
Wooow!
FEAR NOT. THEY HAVE A FULL SELECTION OF SOFT DRINKS.
AND IF I AM TO ESCORT A BEAUTIFUL LADY, THIS IS THE LEAST I CAN OFFER HER.
そわ
FIDGET
LIKE, YEAH!!
Asahi-kun could learn a thing or two!!
I-I CAN TRY HARDER…
AND HEY, WHY ARE YOU GOING ALONG WITH THIS?!
ALLOW ME TO INTRO-DUCE MYSELF AGAIN.
I AM KIRYUIN SEN…
THE VAMPIRE HUNTER IN CHARGE OF THIS DISTRICT.

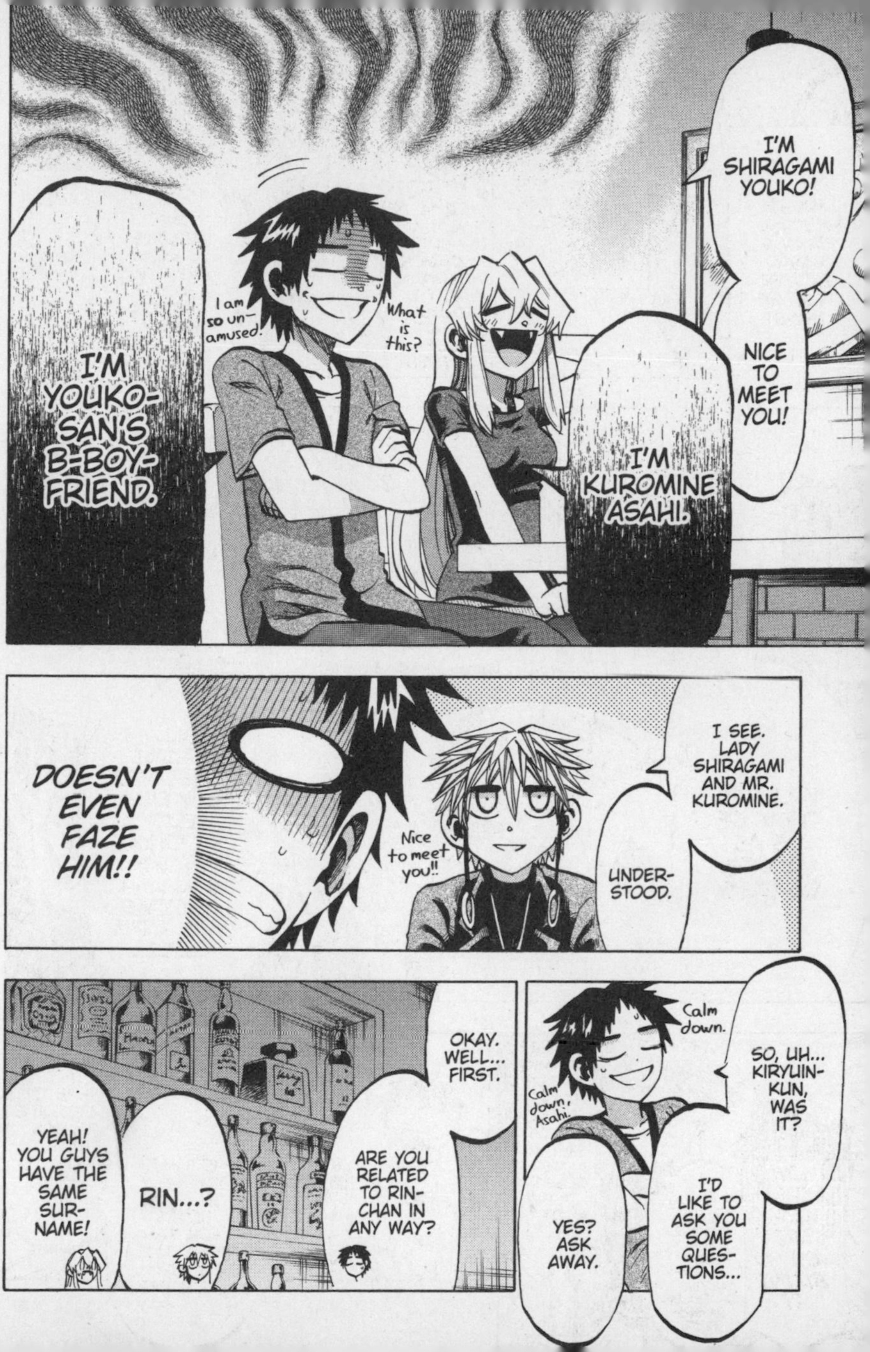
I'M SHIRAGAMI YOUKO!
NICE TO MEET YOU!
I'M KUROMINE ASAHI.
What is this?
I am so un-amused!
I'M YOUKO-SAN'S B-BOY-FRIEND.
I SEE. LADY SHIRAGAMI AND MR. KUROMINE.
UNDER-STOOD.
Nice to meet you!!
DOESN'T EVEN FAZE HIM!!
Calm down.
SO, UH... KIRYUIN-KUN, WAS IT?
I'D LIKE TO ASK YOU SOME QUES-TIONS...
Calm down, Asahi.
YES? ASK AWAY.
OKAY. WELL... FIRST.
ARE YOU RELATED TO RIN-CHAN IN ANY WAY?
RIN...?
YEAH! YOU GUYS HAVE THE SAME SUR-NAME!

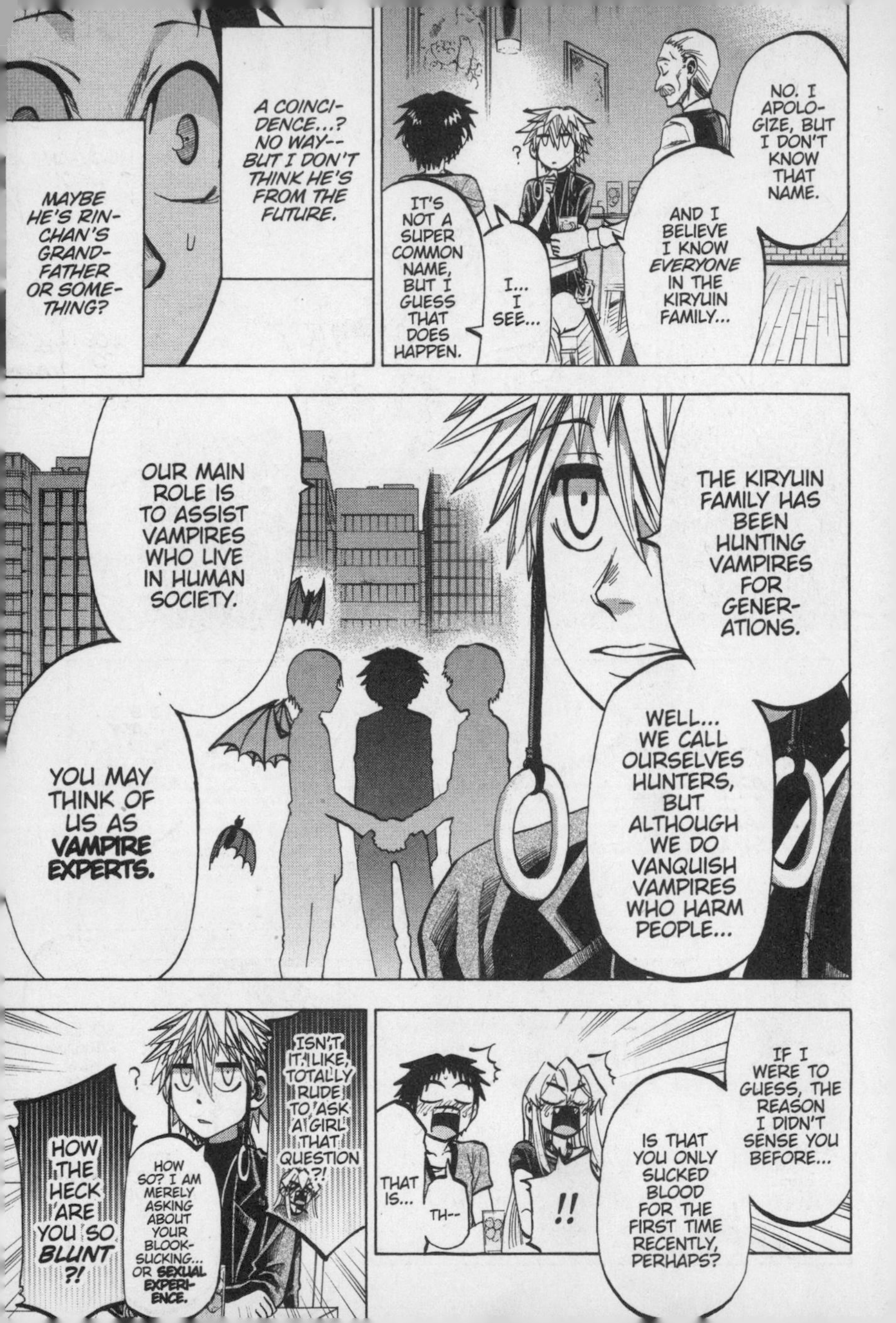

NO. I APOLOGIZE, BUT I DON'T KNOW THAT NAME.
AND I BELIEVE I KNOW EVERYONE IN THE KIRYUIN FAMILY...
?
I... I SEE...
IT'S NOT A SUPER COMMON NAME, BUT I GUESS THAT DOES HAPPEN.
A COINCIDENCE...? NO WAY-- BUT I DON'T THINK HE'S FROM THE FUTURE.
MAYBE HE'S RIN-CHAN'S GRANDFATHER OR SOMETHING?
THE KIRYUIN FAMILY HAS BEEN HUNTING VAMPIRES FOR GENERATIONS.
WELL... WE CALL OURSELVES HUNTERS, BUT ALTHOUGH WE DO VANQUISH VAMPIRES WHO HARM PEOPLE...
OUR MAIN ROLE IS TO ASSIST VAMPIRES WHO LIVE IN HUMAN SOCIETY.
YOU MAY THINK OF US AS VAMPIRE EXPERTS.
IF I WERE TO GUESS, THE REASON I DIDN'T SENSE YOU BEFORE...
IS THAT YOU ONLY SUCKED BLOOD FOR THE FIRST TIME RECENTLY, PERHAPS?
!!
THAT IS...
TH--
ISN'T IT, LIKE, TOTALLY RUDE TO ASK A GIRL THAT QUESTION?!
?
HOW SO? I AM MERELY ASKING ABOUT YOUR BLOOK-SUCKING... OR SEXUAL EXPERIENCE.
HOW THE HECK ARE YOU SO BLUNT?!

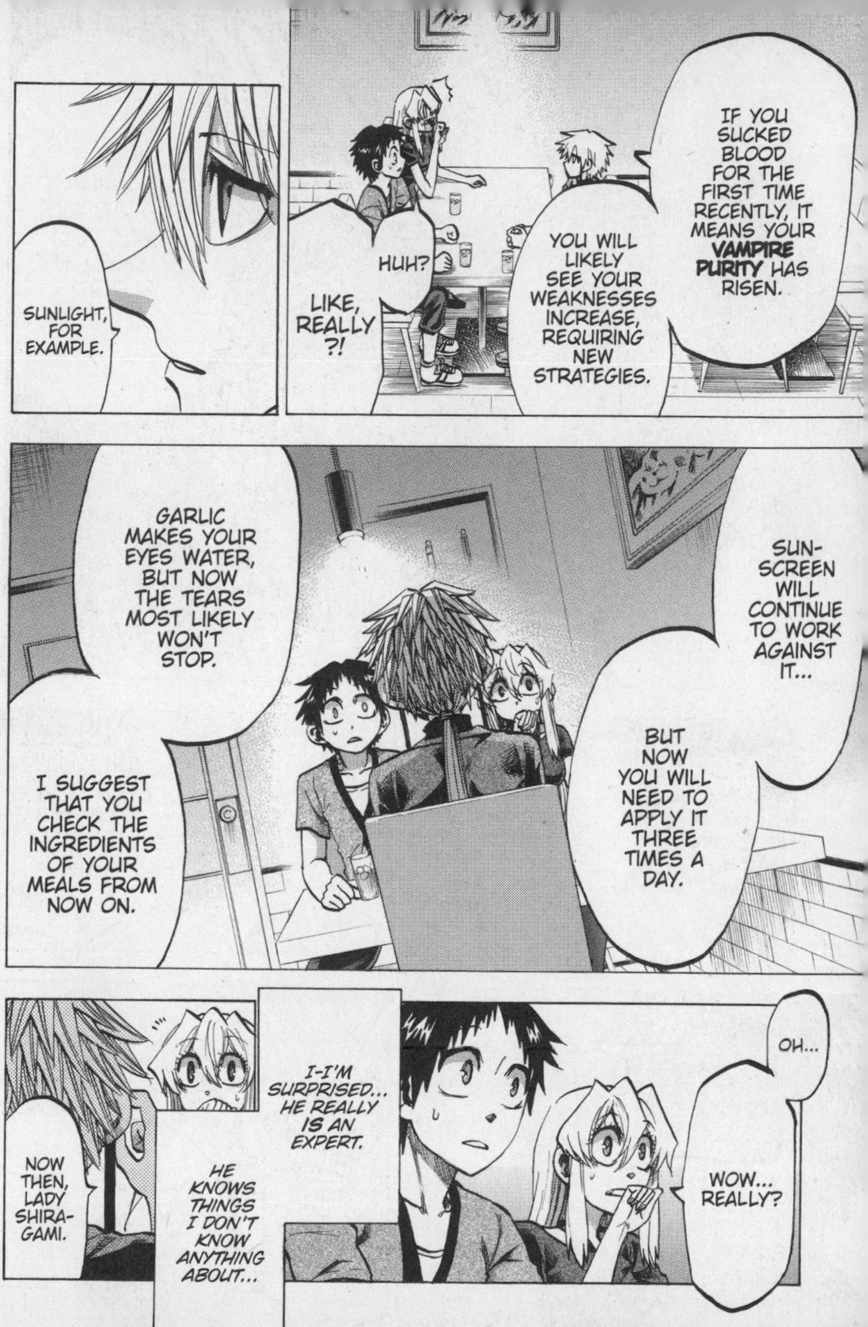
IF YOU SUCKED BLOOD FOR THE FIRST TIME RECENTLY, IT MEANS YOUR **VAMPIRE PURITY** HAS RISEN.
YOU WILL LIKELY SEE YOUR WEAKNESSES INCREASE, REQUIRING NEW STRATEGIES.
HUH?
LIKE, REALLY ?!
SUNLIGHT, FOR EXAMPLE.
SUN-SCREEN WILL CONTINUE TO WORK AGAINST IT...
BUT NOW YOU WILL NEED TO APPLY IT THREE TIMES A DAY.
GARLIC MAKES YOUR EYES WATER, BUT NOW THE TEARS MOST LIKELY WON'T STOP.
I SUGGEST THAT YOU CHECK THE INGREDIENTS OF YOUR MEALS FROM NOW ON.
OH...
WOW... REALLY?
I-I'M SURPRISED... HE REALLY IS AN EXPERT.
HE KNOWS THINGS I DON'T KNOW ANYTHING ABOUT...
NOW THEN, LADY SHIRA-GAMI.

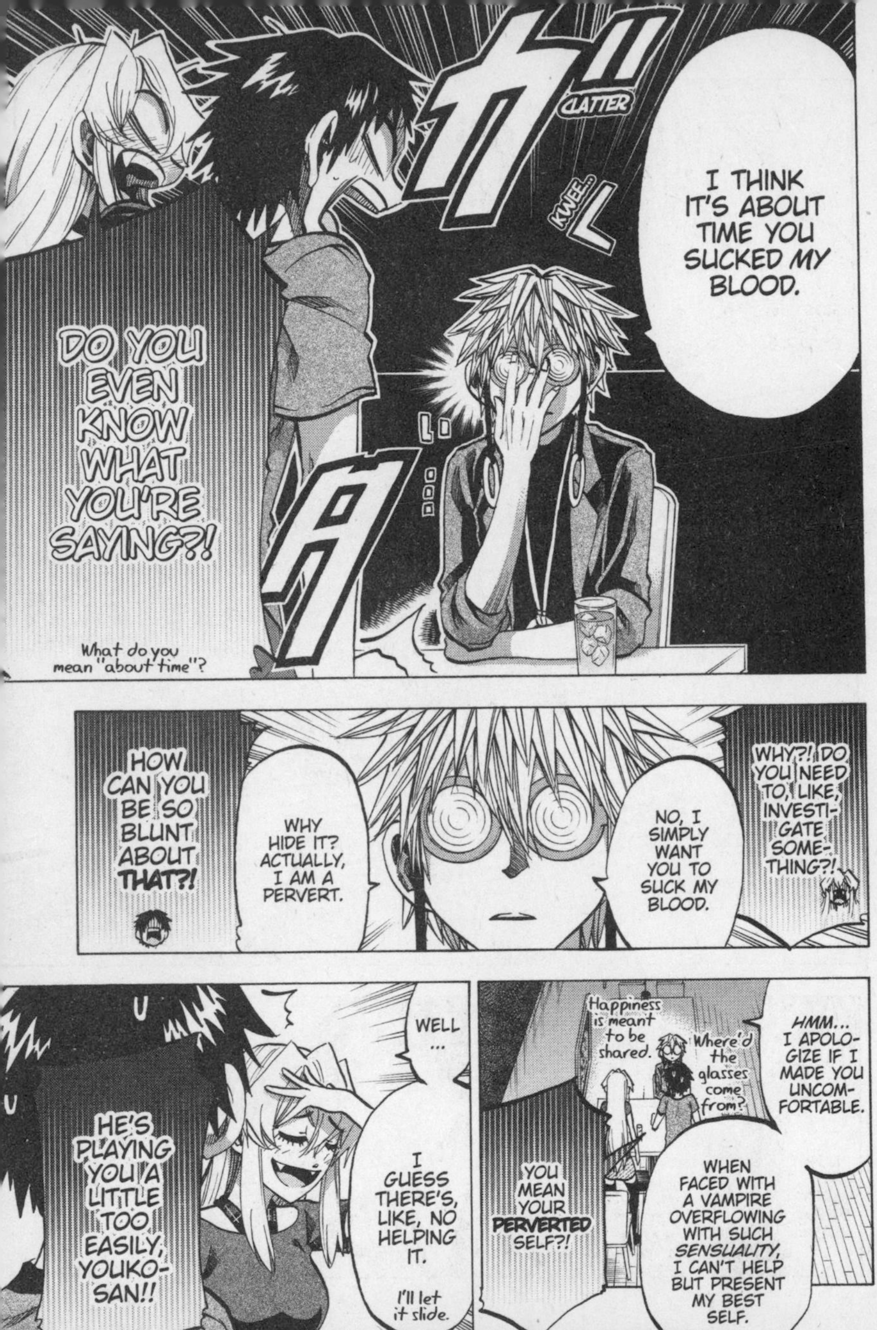
I THINK IT'S ABOUT TIME YOU SUCKED MY BLOOD.
CLATTER
KWEE...
DO YOU EVEN KNOW WHAT YOU'RE SAYING?!
What do you mean "about time"?
WHY?! DO YOU NEED TO, LIKE, INVESTIGATE SOMETHING?!
NO, I SIMPLY WANT YOU TO SUCK MY BLOOD.
WHY HIDE IT? ACTUALLY, I AM A PERVERT.
HOW CAN YOU BE SO BLUNT ABOUT THAT?!
HMM... I APOLOGIZE IF I MADE YOU UNCOMFORTABLE.
Happiness is meant to be shared.
Where'd the glasses come from?
WHEN FACED WITH A VAMPIRE OVERFLOWING WITH SUCH SENSUALITY, I CAN'T HELP BUT PRESENT MY BEST SELF.
YOU MEAN YOUR PERVERTED SELF?!
WELL ...
I GUESS THERE'S, LIKE, NO HELPING IT.
I'll let it slide.
HE'S PLAYING YOU A LITTLE TOO EASILY, YOUKO-SAN!!

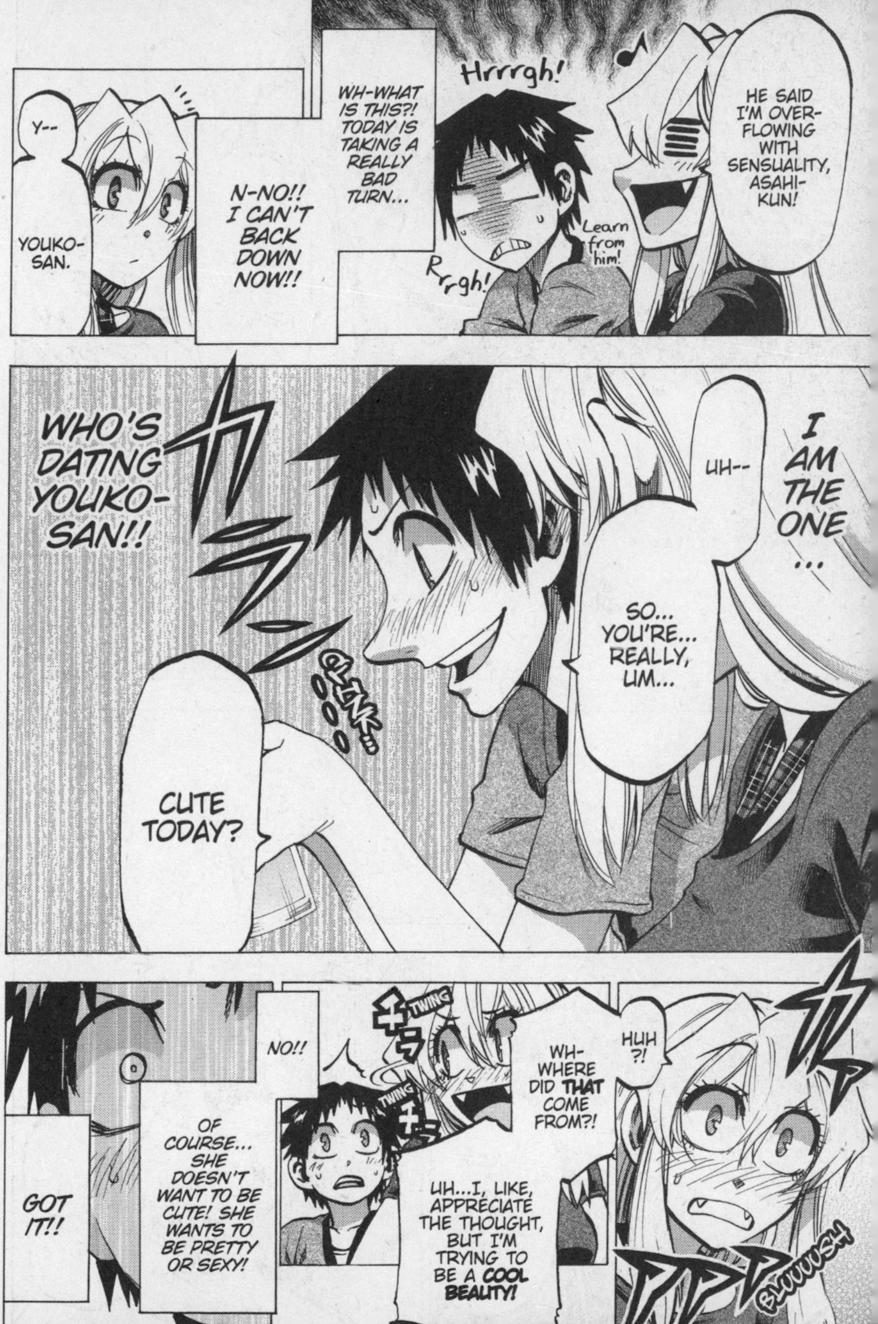
HE SAID I'M OVER-FLOWING WITH SENSUALITY, ASAHI-KUN!
Learn from him!
Hrrrgh!
Rrrgh!
WH-WHAT IS THIS?! TODAY IS TAKING A REALLY BAD TURN...
N-NO!! I CAN'T BACK DOWN NOW!!
Y--
YOUKO-SAN.
I AM THE ONE...
UH--
WHO'S DATING YOUKO-SAN!!
SO... YOU'RE... REALLY, UM...
CLINK...
CUTE TODAY?
HUH?!
WH-WHERE DID THAT COME FROM?!
UH...I, LIKE, APPRECIATE THE THOUGHT, BUT I'M TRYING TO BE A COOL BEAUTY!
BLUUUUSH
TWING
TWING
NO!!
OF COURSE... SHE DOESN'T WANT TO BE CUTE! SHE WANTS TO BE PRETTY OR SEXY!
GOT IT!!

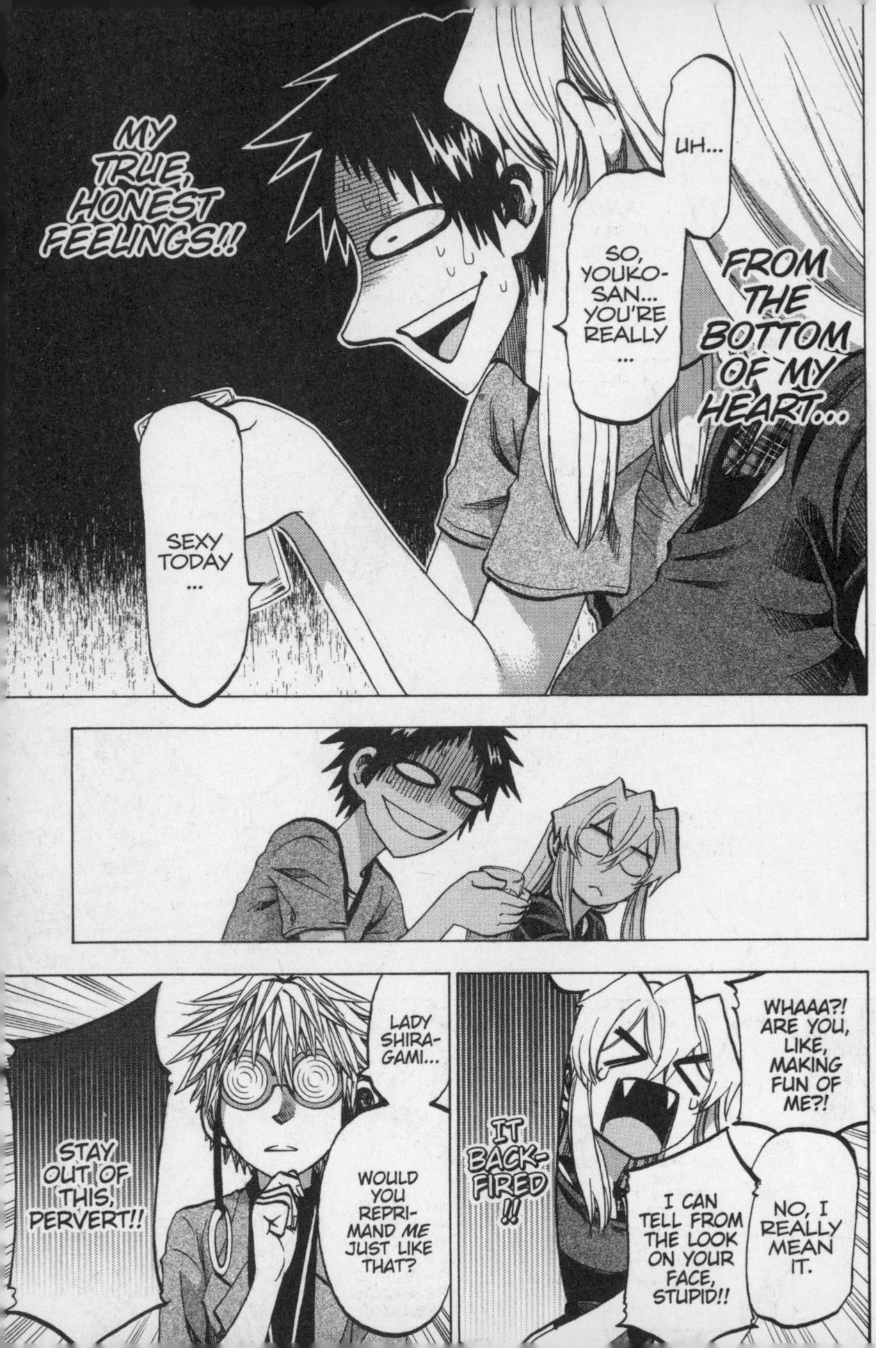
UH...
FROM THE BOTTOM OF MY HEART...
SO, YOUKO-SAN... YOU'RE REALLY ...
MY TRUE, HONEST FEELINGS!!
SEXY TODAY ...
WHAAA?! ARE YOU, LIKE, MAKING FUN OF ME?!
NO, I REALLY MEAN IT.
I CAN TELL FROM THE LOOK ON YOUR FACE, STUPID!!
IT BACK-FIRED!!
LADY SHIRA-GAMI...
WOULD YOU REPRI-MAND *ME* JUST LIKE THAT?
STAY OUT OF THIS, PERVERT!!

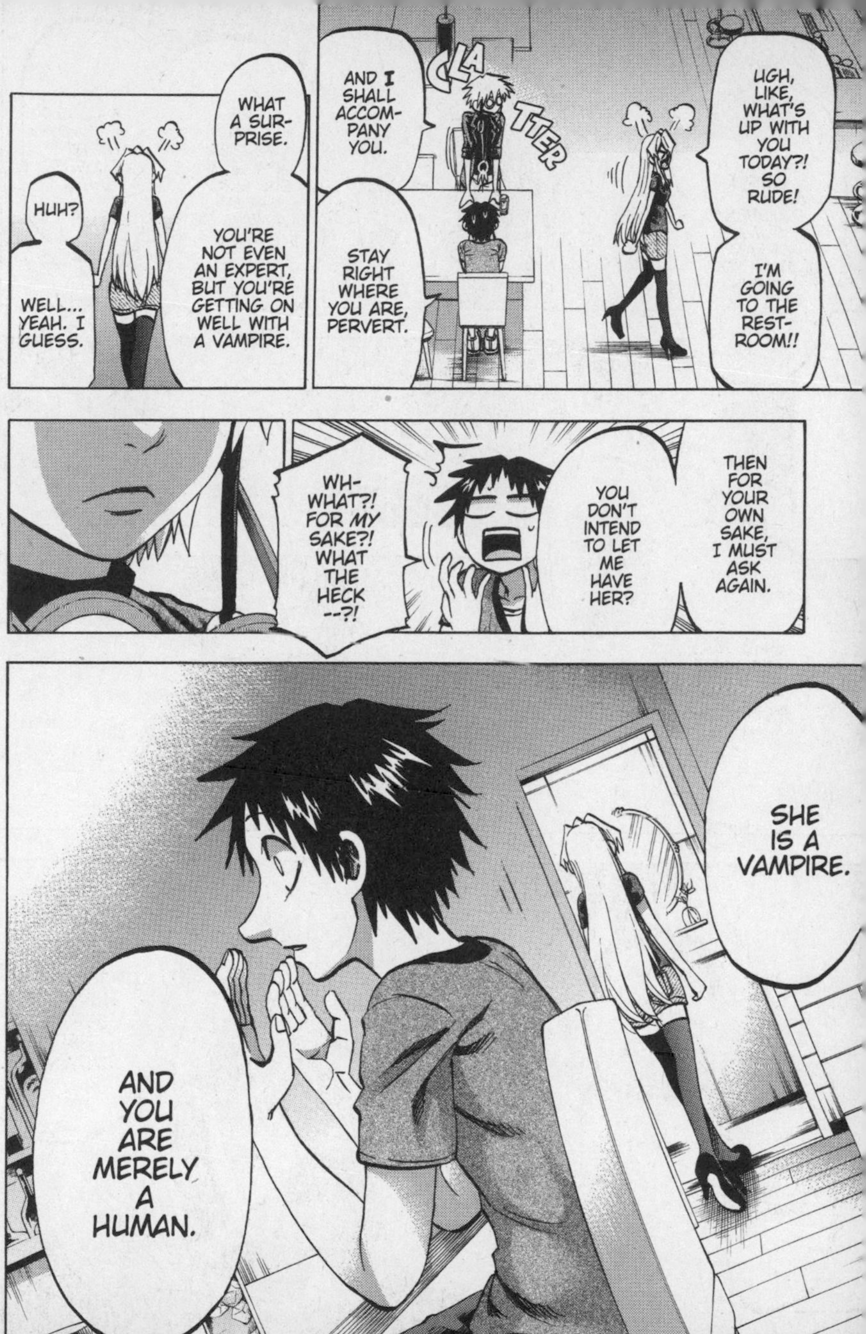
UGH, LIKE, WHAT'S UP WITH YOU TODAY?! SO RUDE!
I'M GOING TO THE REST-ROOM!!
CLATTER
AND I SHALL ACCOMPANY YOU.
STAY RIGHT WHERE YOU ARE, PERVERT.
WHAT A SUR-PRISE.
YOU'RE NOT EVEN AN EXPERT, BUT YOU'RE GETTING ON WELL WITH A VAMPIRE.
HUH?
WELL... YEAH. I GUESS.
THEN FOR YOUR OWN SAKE, I MUST ASK AGAIN.
YOU DON'T INTEND TO LET ME HAVE HER?
WH-WHAT?! FOR MY SAKE?! WHAT THE HECK--?!
SHE IS A VAMPIRE.
AND YOU ARE MERELY A HUMAN.

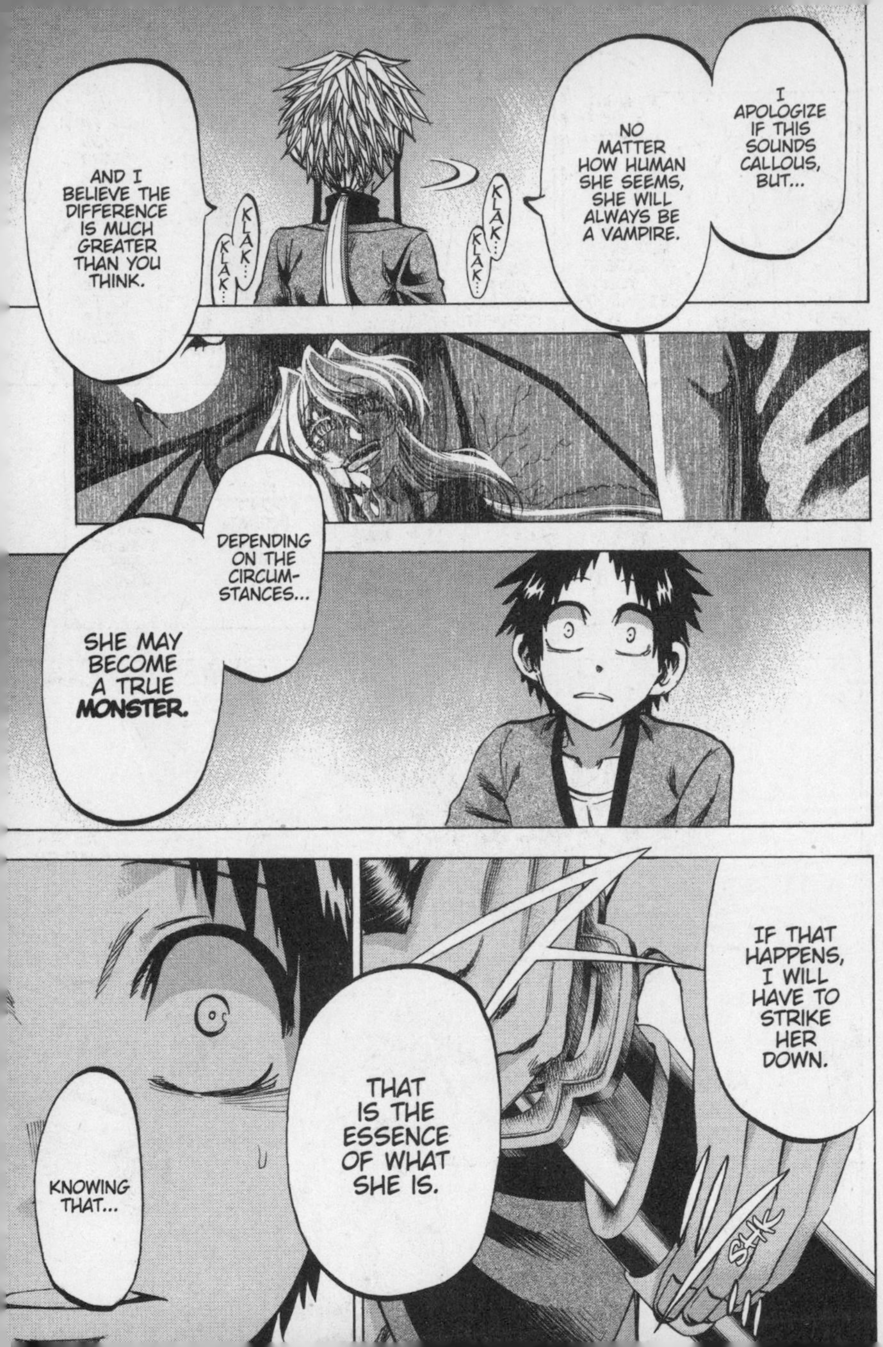
I APOLOGIZE IF THIS SOUNDS CALLOUS, BUT...
NO MATTER HOW HUMAN SHE SEEMS, SHE WILL ALWAYS BE A VAMPIRE.
KLAK... KLAK...
KLAK... KLAK...
AND I BELIEVE THE DIFFERENCE IS MUCH GREATER THAN YOU THINK.
DEPENDING ON THE CIRCUM-STANCES...
SHE MAY BECOME A TRUE **MONSTER.**
IF THAT HAPPENS, I WILL HAVE TO STRIKE HER DOWN.
SLIK
THAT IS THE ESSENCE OF WHAT SHE IS.
KNOWING THAT...

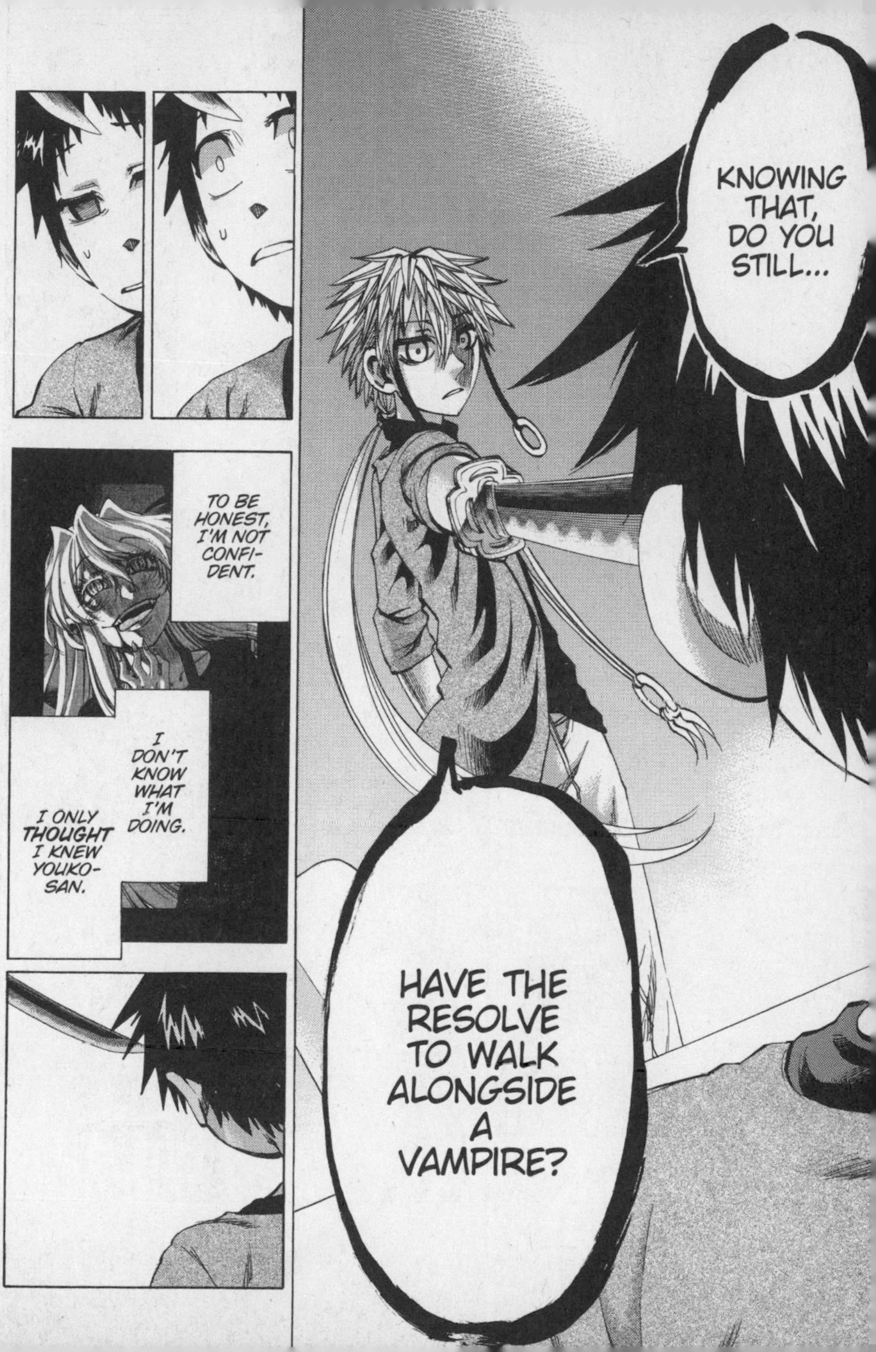
KNOWING THAT, DO YOU STILL...
HAVE THE RESOLVE TO WALK ALONGSIDE A VAMPIRE?
TO BE HONEST, I'M NOT CONFIDENT.
I DON'T KNOW WHAT I'M DOING.
I ONLY THOUGHT I KNEW YOUKO-SAN.

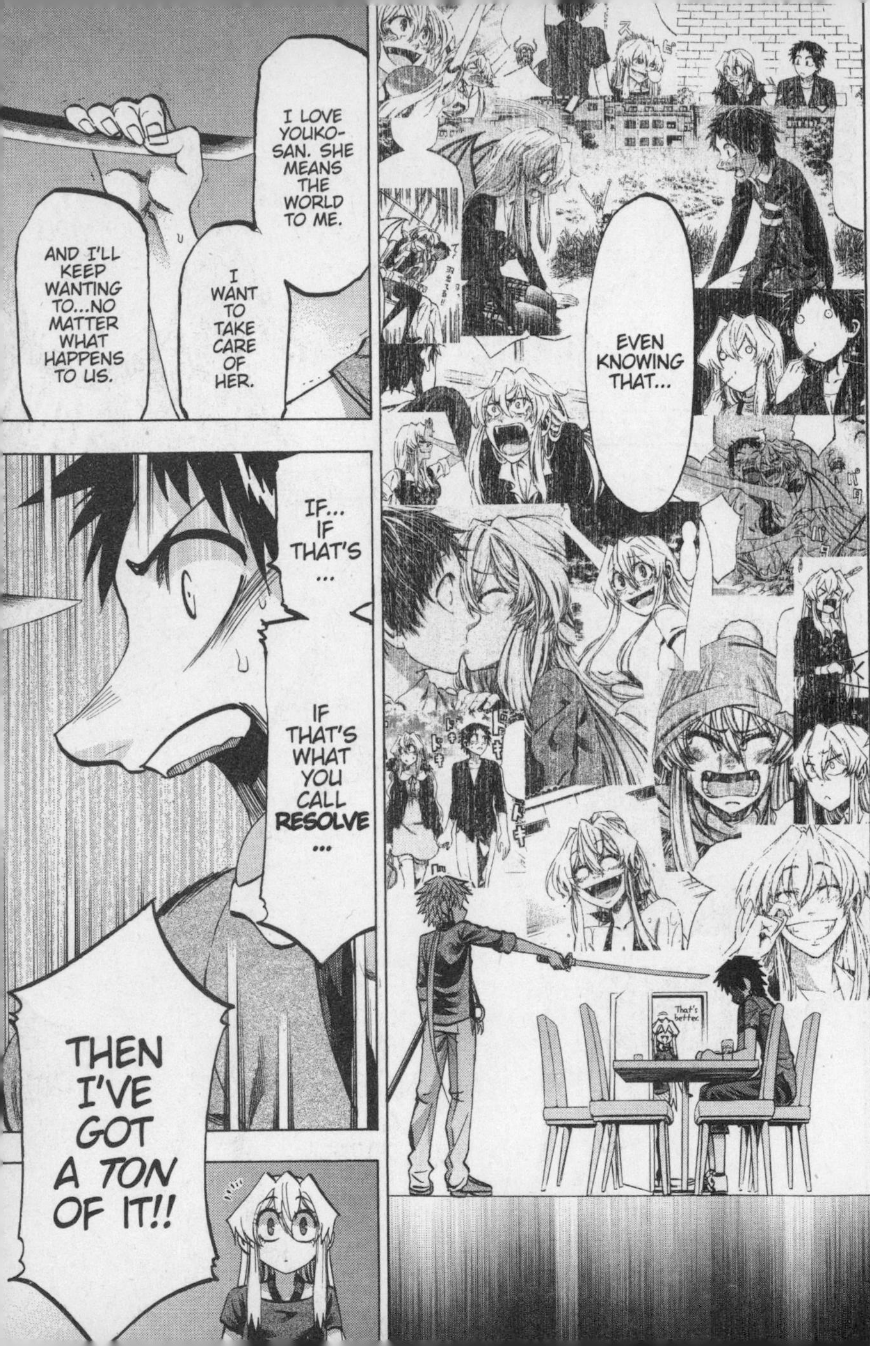
EVEN KNOWING THAT...
That's better.
I LOVE YOUKO-SAN. SHE MEANS THE WORLD TO ME.
I WANT TO TAKE CARE OF HER.
AND I'LL KEEP WANTING TO...NO MATTER WHAT HAPPENS TO US.
IF... IF THAT'S ...
IF THAT'S WHAT YOU CALL **RESOLVE** ...
THEN I'VE GOT A *TON* OF IT!!

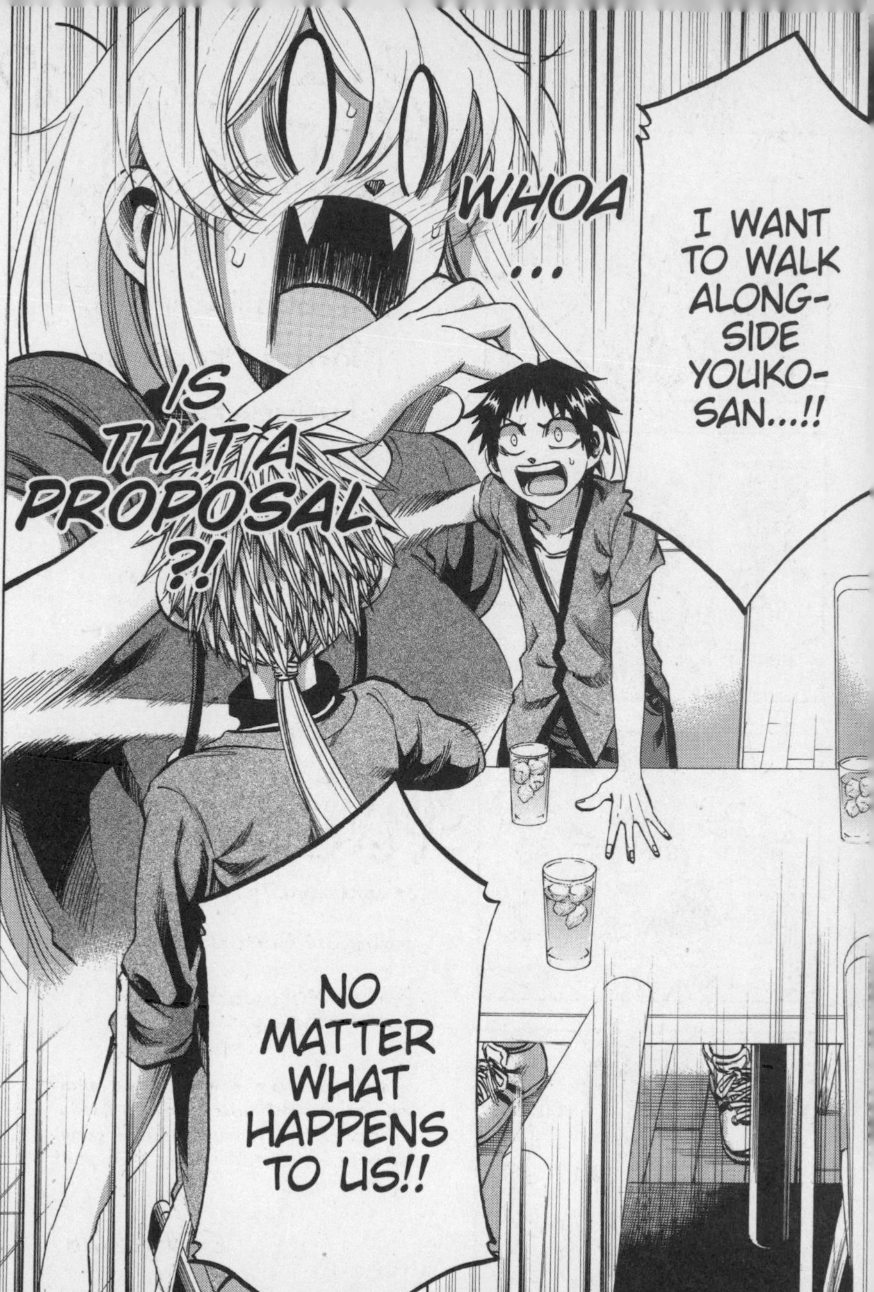
I WANT TO WALK ALONG-SIDE YOUKO-SAN...!!
WHOA ...
IS THAT A PROPOSAL ?!
NO MATTER WHAT HAPPENS TO US!!

My Monster Secret Volume 15 / end

STAFF!

- Katou Shinichi-san
- Garage Okada-san
- Shuumeigiku-san
- Seijun Suzuki-san
- Nakamura Yuji-san
- Hayashi Rie-san
- Mana Haruki-san
- Hiroki Minemura-san
- Mori Keiko-san (in syllabary order)

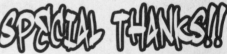

SPECIAL THANKS!!

- Sakuraya Tatsushi-san
- Tamura Hanzou-san

Editor: Mukawa-san,
Otsuka-san

Thank you to everyone who's holding this book right now, everyone who watched the anime, and everyone who let me and this work be a part of their lives.

Eiji Masuda

After Hero Show

I WAS SURE IT WAS REALLY KOU-MOTO-SENSEI.
HMPH.
IT WOULDN'T BE MUCH OF A JOKE IF I MADE AKARI DO IT HERSELF.
YEAH, BUT SHE'S THE SAME HEIGHT AND EVERYTHING... WHERE DID YOU FIND HER?
I DON'T KNOW WHO SHE IS, BUT SHE RECREATED AKARI'S SINGLE WOMAN POWERS BRILLIANTLY.
HUH?
YOU DON'T KNOW WHO'S IN THAT COS-TUME--
I LET TESAKI HANDLE ALL THAT...
IS SHE... GETTING CLOSER ?!
WHAT THE HELL?! STAY AWAY FROM US, SINGLE GIRL!!
IT'S REALLY NOT KOUMOTO-SENSEI, RIGHT?!
HRR-I HRR-I
STOP IT!! DON'T GET ANY CLOS--!
GAA AAA AAR RRR GH!!
HRR-I HRR-I

Is it really possible to change the future?!

The curtain rises on the Shishido Shiho arc!

Shiho learns that in the future she will be married to Shima! And a shadow falls over Asahi and Shiragami-san's apparently happy relationship?! The shocking love comedy featuring a ditzy heroine continues!!

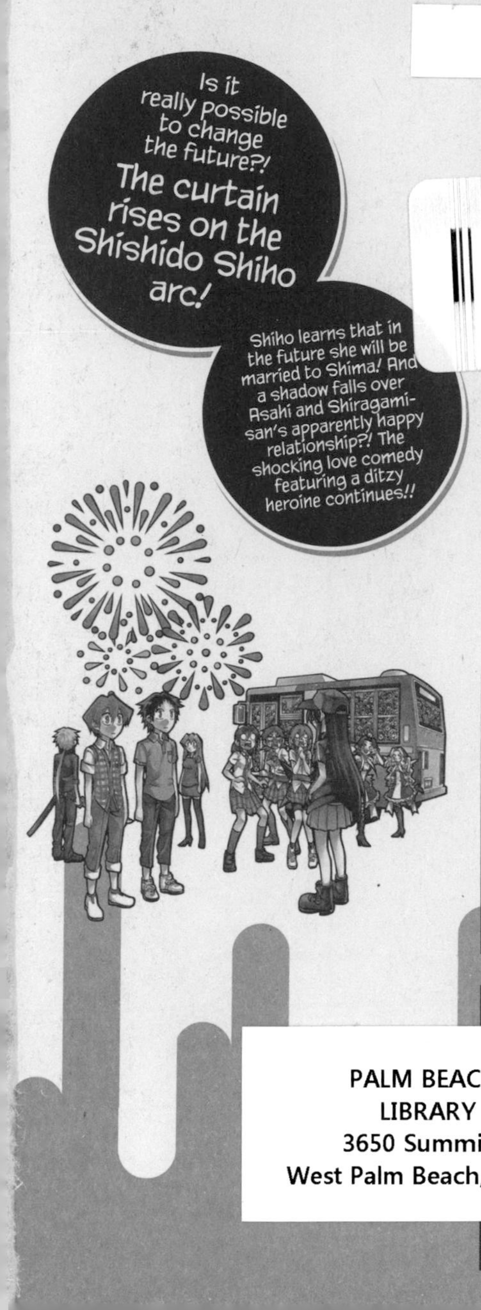

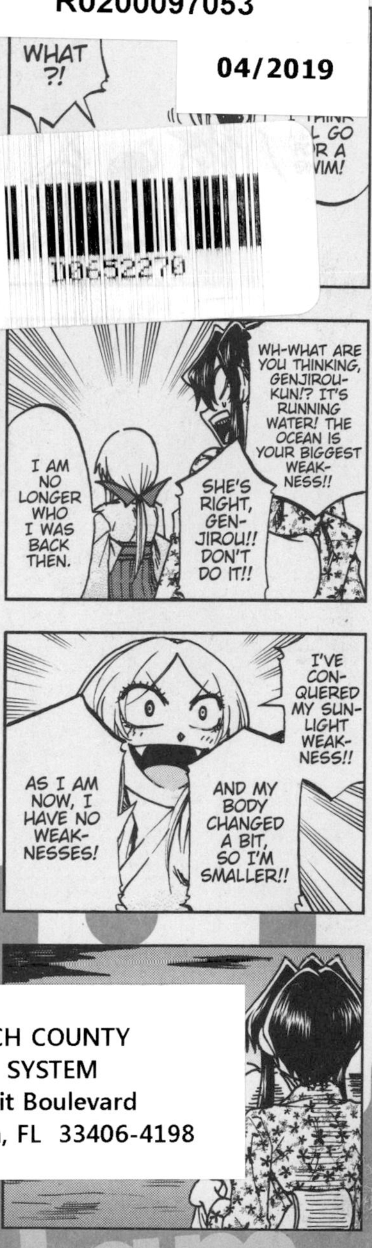
WHAT ?!
WH-WHAT ARE YOU THINKING, GENJIROU-KUN!? IT'S RUNNING WATER! THE OCEAN IS YOUR BIGGEST WEAK-NESS!!
SHE'S RIGHT, GEN-JIROU!! DON'T DO IT!!
I AM NO LONGER WHO I WAS BACK THEN.
I'VE CON-QUERED MY SUN-LIGHT WEAK-NESS!!
AND MY BODY CHANGED A BIT, SO I'M SMALLER!!
AS I AM NOW, I HAVE NO WEAK-NESSES!